BUSINESS AND HUMAN RIGHTS

This book analyses the accountability of European home States for their failure to secure the human rights of victims from host States against transnational enterprises. It argues for a reconfiguration of the relationship between multinational enterprises and individuals, both of which have been profoundly changed by globalisation. Enterprises are now supranational entities with numerous affiliates all over the world. Likewise, individuals are increasingly part of a global community. Despite this, the relationship between the two is deregulated. Addressing this gap, this study proposes an innovative business and human rights litigation strategy. Human rights advocates could file a test case against a European home State, at the European Court of Human Rights, for its failure to secure the rights of victims vis-à-vis European multinational enterprises. The book illustrates why such a strategy is needed, and points to the lack of effective legal remedies against European multinationals. The goal is to empower victims from developing countries against European States which are failing to hold multinational enterprises accountable for human rights abuses.

Business and Human Rights

The Obligations of the European Home States

Dalia Palombo

•HART•
OXFORD • LONDON • NEW YORK • NEW DELHI • SYDNEY

HART PUBLISHING
Bloomsbury Publishing Plc
Kemp House, Chawley Park, Cumnor Hill, Oxford, OX2 9PH, UK
1385 Broadway, New York, NY 10018, USA

HART PUBLISHING, the Hart/Stag logo, BLOOMSBURY and the Diana logo are trademarks of Bloomsbury Publishing Plc

First published in Great Britain 2019

A catalogue record for this book is available from the British Library.

Library of Congress Cataloging-in-Publication data

Names: Palombo, Dalia, author.

Title: Business and human rights : the obligations of the European home states / Dalia Palombo.

Description: Chicago : Hart Publishing, an imprint of Bloomsbury Publishing, 2019. | Includes bibliographical references and index.

Identifiers: LCCN 2019029240 (print) | LCCN 2019029241 (ebook) | ISBN 9781509928033 (hardback) | ISBN 9781509928040 (Epub)

Subjects: LCSH: Human rights—European Union countries. | International business enterprises—Law and legislation—European Union countries. | Social responsibility of business. | International business enterprises—Moral and ethical aspects.

Classification: LCC KJE5132 .P35 2019 (print) | LCC KJE5132 (ebook) | DDC 342.408—dc23

LC record available at https://lccn.loc.gov/2019029240

LC ebook record available at https://lccn.loc.gov/2019029241

ISBN: HB: 978-1-50992-803-3
ePDF: 978-1-50992-805-7
ePub: 978-1-50992-804-0

Typeset by Compuscript Ltd, Shannon
Printed and bound in Great Britain by CPI Group (UK) Ltd, Croydon CR0 4YY

FSC www.fsc.org MIX Paper from responsible sources FSC® C013604

To my husband Alex

Acknowledgements

IF I HAVE learned anything during these years, it is that it is impossible to write a book without the invaluable help of people who support you in the good and bad days of this process. I would like to take this opportunity to thank all of those who helped me in my research and writing.

First, I would like to warmly thank a number of academics and practitioners who have helped me enormously during these years of research. A profound thanks goes to my PhD supervisors, Fons Coomans and Bruno De Witte, for having both contributed enormously with their different expertise to bring the best out of my thesis. I would also like to thank all of my examiners: Jan Eijsbouts, Menno Kamminga, David Kershaw and Yuval Shany. A special thank goes to David Kershaw for teaching me how to teach and for inspiring me beyond words to pursue an academic career. A warm thanks goes also to Yuval Shany for encouraging me to publish my thesis as a book and for supporting me throughout this process. Thanks to Andrea Bianchi, who was the first person who ever inspired me to open a book of international law. Thanks to Tyler Giannini and Susan Farbstein who have introduced me to the issue of business and human rights at the Harvard Law School International Human Rights Clinic. A warm thanks to Susan Marks and Conor Gearty for their invaluable help and support in the transformation of my thesis into a book and for all they have taught and are continuing to teach me everyday. Thanks also to all of those academics and institutions who funded my PhD research: Hélène Ruiz Fabri from the Max Planck Institute Luxembourg for Procedural Law, Eyal Benvenisti from Tel Aviv University and Armin von Bogdandy and Anne Peters from the Max Planck Institute for Comparative Public Law and International Law in Heidelberg. I am also extremely grateful to the Department of Law at the London School of Economics for funding my post-doc which allowed me to transform my PhD thesis into this book. Thanks so much to Daniel Leader, from the law firm Leigh Day, for the time he took to discuss with me the business and human rights cases that he had litigated. Also, a warm thanks to Sinead Moloney, Tom Adams, Sasha Jawed and Richard Cox for their invaluable help during the review and editorial process, and to the anonymous reviewers who have supported the publication of my book.

Second, my heartfelt thanks to my family and friends. I dedicate this manuscript to Alex, my husband. Thanks to his encouragement, I started a PhD when I was unsure as to the next steps I would have taken in my life. I thank him for always being there to support me and for having read over and over different versions of my work. Thanks to my parents, Viviano and Danila, and my brother, David, for their constant support in life. Grazie mamma, papa e David per avermi sempre aiutata a realizzare i miei sogni. Thanks to my aunt Carla who spent countless hours teaching me how to write in English and who has inspired me beyond belief to study law. A big thanks to my friends Tleuzhan, Parvathi, Alain and Edoardo, who have all shared with me the joys and difficulties of being a PhD student; thanks also to my good friends Cristiana and Gemma for their constant support throughout this process. Last but not least, thanks to my dog Erin, for always being there to cheer me up in the never-ending days of writing.

Contents

List of Abbreviations

AfrChHPR	African Charter on Human and Peoples' Rights
AfrCoHPR	African Commission on Human and Peoples' Rights
AfrCtHPR	African Court on Human and Peoples' Rights
ADHR	American Declaration on Human Rights
ACHR	American Convention on Human Rights
IACoHR	Inter-American Commission on Human Rights
IACtHR	Inter-American Court of Human Rights
ATS	Alien Tort Statute
BIT	Bilateral investment treaty
Brussels I	European Union Regulation Brussels I
CEDAW	Committee on the Elimination of Discrimination against Women of the United Nations
CERD	Committee on the Elimination of Racial Discrimination of the United Nations
CESCR	Committee on Economic Social and Cultural Rights
CRC	Committee on the Rights of the Child of the United Nations
CSR	corporate social responsibility
ECHR	European Convention on Human Rights
ECtHR	European Court of Human Rights
FTA	Free Trade Agreement
Guiding Principles	Guiding Principles on Business and Human Rights
HRC	Human Rights Committee of the United Nations
ICC	International Criminal Court
ICCPR	International Covenant on Civil and Political Rights

ICESCR	International Covenant on Economic, Social and Cultural Rights
ICJ	International Court of Justice
ICTR	International Criminal Tribunal for Rwanda
ICTY	International Criminal Tribunal for Yugoslavia
ILO	International Labour Organization
ILO Declarations	ILO Work Declaration and ILO Tripartite Declaration
ILO Tripartite Declaration	Tripartite Declaration of Principles concerning Multinational Enterprises and Social Policies
ILO Work Declaration	ILO Declaration on Fundamental Principles and Rights at Work
ISCID	International Centre for Settlement of Investment Disputes
Maastricht Principles	Maastricht Principles on Extraterritorial Obligations of States in the Area of Economic, Social and Cultural Rights
NAP	National Action Plan
NCP	National Contact Point of the OECD
NGO	non-governmental organisation
Norms	UN Norms on the Responsibility of Transnational Corporations and other Business Enterprises with Regard to Human Rights
OECD	Organisation on Economic Co-operation and Development
OECD Declaration	OECD Declaration on International Investments and Multinational Enterprises
OECD Guidelines	OECD Guidelines for Multinational Enterprises
Recommendation	Recommendation of the Committee of the Ministers to Member States on Human Rights and Business
Rome I	Regulation (EC) No 593/2008 of the European Parliament and the Council of 17 June 2008 on the law applicable to contractual obligations (Rome I)
Rome II	Regulation (EC) No 864/2007 of the European Parliament and of the Council of 11 July 2007 on the law applicable to non-contractual obligations (Rome II)

Table of Cases

1

The Case for Legal Reform

THE RELATIONSHIP BETWEEN enterprises and individuals has changed radically over the last hundred years. Enterprises are no longer simple associations of people who get together to conduct business; rather, they are supranational entities leading the global economy.[1] At the same time, in an ever more globalised world, individuals are connected not only to their national dimension, but are increasingly becoming part of a global community.[2] However, these changes have not been adequately reflected in the law.[3] The laws regulating the relationship between enterprises and individuals do not address the responsibility of multinational companies abusing the fundamental rights of people.[4] Human rights advocates have attempted to blame and shame companies for their adverse impact on the lives of people and the environment and to sue them in domestic courts. However, these attempts are often unsuccessful, because international and domestic laws fail to recognise the responsibility of multinational enterprises for human rights abuses.[5]

[1] See John Braithwaite, 'Neoliberalism or Regulatory Capitalism', in *Regulatory Capitalism: How It Works, Ideas for Making It Work Better* (Edward Elgar, 2008).

[2] See Harold Hongju Koh, 'Trasnational Legal Process' (1996) 75 *Nebraska Law Review* 181; Harold Hongju Koh, 'Why Transnational Law Matters' (2006) 24 *Penn State International Law Review* 745.

[3] See Dan Danielsen, 'Corporate Power and Global Order' in *International Law and its Others* (Cambridge University Press, 2006); Peter Muchlinski, *Multinational Enterprises and the Law*, 2nd edn (Oxford University Press, 2007).

[4] See Surya Deva, 'Human Rights Violations by Multinational Corporations and International Law: Where from Here?' (2003) 19 *Connecticut Journal of International Law* 1; Surya Deva, 'Human Rights Standards and Multinational Corporations: Dilemma between "Home" and "Rome"' (2003) 7 *Mediterranean Journal of Human Rights* 69; Niels Beisinghoff, *Corporations and Human Rights: An Analysis of ATCA Litigation against Corporations* (Peter Lang, 2009); Menno T Kamminga, 'Holding Multinational Corporations Accountable for Human Rights Abuses: A Challenge for the EC', in *The EU and Human Rights* (Oxford University Press, 1999); Detlev F Vagts, 'The Multinational Enterprise: A New Challenge for Transnational Law' (1970) 83 *Harvard Law Review* 739.

[5] See eg Richard Meeran, 'Tort Litigation against Multinational Corporations for Violation of Human Rights: An Overview of the Position Outside the United States' (2011) 3 *City University of Hong Kong Law Review* 1; Philipp Wesche and Miriam Saage-Maaß, 'Holding Companies Liable for Human Rights Abuses Related to Foreign Subsidiaries and Suppliers before German Civil Courts: Lessons from *Jabir and Others v KiK*' (2016) 16 *Human Rights Law Review* 370; Menno T Kamminga, 'Transnational Human Rights Litigation against Multinational Corporations Post-Kiobel', *What's Wrong with International Law?: Liber Amicorum AHA Soons* (Brill-Nijhoff, 2015); Sarah Joseph, *Corporations and Transnational Human Rights Litigation* (Hart Publishing,

This book reacts to these unsuccessful cases filed against companies in domestic courts. It proposes to file suits against the European home states of multinational enterprises for their failure to regulate corporate groups incorporated within their jurisdiction and that abuse human rights extraterritorially. It advocates for the use of international courts as a tool for legal change.

In Europe, human rights advocates could implement this litigation strategy by filing a test case against a European state at the European Court of Human Rights (ECtHR). Under the European Convention on Human Rights (ECHR), states have a positive obligation to secure that private persons respect human rights. Human rights advocates should argue that such an obligation includes the duty to protect individuals against extraterritorial abuses committed by multinational companies and the duty to fulfil corporate socially responsible policies.[6]

The goal of human rights advocates should be to obtain an ECtHR's decision detailing the positive obligation of states to secure that European corporate groups respect human rights while operating extraterritorially. In the affirmative, European states would have to provide human rights victims with effective remedies against multinational companies in domestic courts. This would open the door to extensive litigation before domestic courts against European multinational enterprises abusing human rights in developing countries.

I. FROM STATES TO NON-STATE ACTORS

Numerous legal and non-legal scholars have analysed the shift in global governance from a state-centric to a multi-actor model. This section outlines the

2004); Michael Byers, 'English Courts and Serious Human Rights Violations Abroad: A Preliminary Assessment' in *Liability of Multinational Corporations under International Law* (Kluwer Law International, 2000); Nicola Jägers and Marie-Jose van der Heijden, 'Corporate Human Rights Violations: The Feasibility of Civil Recourse in the Netherlands' (2008) 33 *Brooklyn Journal of International Law* 833; *Jesner v Arab Bank, PLC* [2018] US Supreme Court 584; *Kiobel v Royal Dutch Petroleum Co* [2013] US Supreme Court 133 SCt 1659; *Kiobel v Royal Dutch Petroleum Co* [2010] US Court of Appeals 2d Cir F3d 621, 111; *Akpan v Royal Dutch Shell Plc* [2013] DC Hague C/09/337050/HA ZA 09-1580; *Akpan v Royal Dutch Shell Plc* [2015] Court of Appeal at the Hague (Den Haag); Liesbeth Enneking, 'The Future of Foreign Direct Liability? Exploring the International Relevance of the Dutch Shell Nigeria Case' (2014) 10 *Utrecht Law Review* 44; Judith Schrempf-Stirling and Florian Wettstein, 'Beyond Guilty Verdicts: Human Rights Litigation and Its Impact on Corporations' Human Rights Policies' [2015] *Journal of Business Ethics* 1.

[6] See eg Sarah Joseph and Melissa Castan, *The International Covenant on Civil and Political Rights: Cases, Materials, and Commentary*, 3rd edn (Oxford University Press, 2013) 9–120; Manfred Nowak, *UN Covenant on Civil and Political Rights: CCPR Commentary*, 2nd edn (Engel, 2005) 27–75; Dimitris Xenos, *The Positive Obligations of the State under the European Convention of Human Rights* (Routledge, 2011); Colombine Madelaine, *La technique des obligations positives en droit de la convention européenne des droits de l'homme* (Dalloz, 2014); Elisabet Fura-Sandstrom, 'Business and Human Rights: Who Cares?', in *Liber Amicorum Luzius Wildhaber: Human Rights – Strasbourg Views /Droits de l'homme – Regards de Strasbourg* (Engel, 2007); Rolf H. Weber and Rawer Baisch, 'Liability of Parent Companies for Human Rights Violations of Subsidiaries' [2016] *European business Law Review* 669.

debate, as it is the framework within which this book argues that states should be accountable for their failure to regulate the human rights abuses of non-state actors.

Traditionally, non-state actors did not have a clear voice in shaping the content of international law and determining global governance. Non-state actors, including individuals, non-governmental organisations (NGOs) and communities, were only considered to be objects of international law. States were the only representatives of non-state actors in the international arena. Therefore, the only way for non-state actors to express their views on global and foreign policies was through national elections. By selecting a particular candidate, a citizen could contribute to advancing and supporting a certain global policy.[7]

However, with globalisation, non-state actors have become increasingly able to take direct action in the development of international law and global governance through what Harold Koh defined as the transnational legal process.[8] This process allows non-state actors to judge and intervene in global political decisions. According to Koh, the transnational legal process is, first, non-traditional as opposed to the traditional process which views states as the subjects and people as the objects of international law; second, it is non-statist as it encourages direct action by non-state actors in the international arena; third, it is dynamic as it encourages action by private instead of public actors; and, fourth, it is normative as the process creates new binding rules. Nowadays non-state actors communicate through networks that allow everyone to have an active voice in the transnational legal process. Different actors, including '[t]he Security Council, the GATT, Exxon, Greenpeace, the Paris Club, Amnesty International, and the Lowenstein International Human Rights Clinic at Yale Law School',[9] interact in the transnational legal process with the objective and the expectation to change and influence global law and governance. Such an interactive and dynamic process is both legal and political, as private actors may act at both levels in order to shape global governance. The process is normative, as it enforces and creates international norms through the interaction of private non-state actors and public state actors.[10]

The question is whether this development from a state-centric to a multi-actor model is positive or negative. Different schools of thoughts are divided on this point. Some, especially those coming from the global constitutional law scholarship, describe globalisation in positive terms. They argue for a complete

[7] See generally on the evolution of international law, Samuel Moyn, *The Last Utopia: Human Rights in History* (Belknap Press of Harvard University Press, 2012) 11–43; Andrea Bianchi, *International Law Theories: An Inquiry into Different Ways of Thinking* (Oxford University Press, 2017) 21–43; Lori Damrosch et al, *International Law, Cases and Materials*, 6th edn (West, 2014).

[8] See Koh, 'Trasnational Legal Process' (n 2) 191; Koh, 'Why Transnational Law Matters' (n 2).

[9] Koh, 'Trasnational Legal Process' (n 2) 194.

[10] Rosalyn Higgins, *Problems and Process: International Law and How We Use It* (Clarendon Press, 1995) 39–55; Jennifer A Zerk, *Multinationals and Corporate Social Responsibility: Limitations and Opportunities in International Law* (Cambridge University Press, 2006) 60–103.

change of paradigm that would see a departure from a state-centric model to embrace a cosmopolitan reality based on global constitutional principles.[11] This would result in a network of private and public entities, such as international organisations, corporations and NGOs, becoming the main architects of global governance.[12] In most of these models, individuals are gaining an increasingly significant role in global governance while restraining states' authority.[13]

However, when states lose power and non-state actors gain it, new problems arise concerning the interaction between different private actors. States are in fact the only entities that have to respond to their own people and have therefore political responsibility and legal obligations towards them.[14] But this is not the case for private actors, which do not have political responsibility towards a particular community and are free to act in their own self-interest. The question is, therefore, what happens if global governance abandons state hegemony? Who will be the next powerful actor(s) in these portrayed utopias? According to some scholars, the interaction between different private actors has been and will be detrimental to individuals for the benefit of the most powerful non-state actors, such as multinational corporations, which have their own agenda that does not necessarily take into consideration the will of people. Some argue that cosmopolitanism is in fact an imperialistic project.[15] This debate, which started with the no-globalisation movements a few decades ago, is particularly current nowadays with the rise of populism as a backlash against cosmopolitanism and internationalism.[16] The demands for nationalistic policies and a reappropriation of the state's central role in global governance are increasingly popular.

Multinational corporations are only a part of this complex debate on the role of state and non-state actors in global governance. However, they are a fundamental piece in any possible global architecture, given their power, which

[11] See eg Armin von Bogdandy and Ingo Venzke, *In Whose Name?: A Public Law Theory of International Adjudication* (Oxford University Press, 2014); Anthony F Lang Jr and Antje Wiener, *Handbook on Global Constitutionalism* (Edward Elgar, 2017); Jeffrey L Dunoff and Joel P Trachtman, *Ruling the World? Constitutionalism, International Law, and Global Governance* (Cambridge University Press, 2009).

[12] Benedict Kingsbury, Nico Krisch and Richard B Stewart, 'The Emergence of Global Administrative Law' (2005) 68 *Law and Contemporary Problems* 15.

[13] Susan Marks, 'Naming Global Administrative Law' (2005) 37 *New York University Journal of International Law and Politics* 995.

[14] Hélène Ruiz Fabri, 'Human Rights and State Sovereignty: Have the Boundaries Been Significantly Redrawn?' in, *Human Rights, Intervention, and the Use of Force* (Oxford University Press, 2008).

[15] Balakrishnan Rajagopal, *International Law from below: Development, Social Movements, and Third World Resistance* (Cambridge University Press, 2003) 165–232; Antony Anghie, *Imperialism, Sovereignty, and the Making of International Law* (Cambridge University Press 2005) 245–72; Danielsen (n 3).

[16] Florian Hoffmann, 'Human Rights, the Self and the Other: Reflections on a Pragmatic Theory of Human Rights' in *International Law and its Others* (Cambridge University Press, 2009).

is now comparable to that of a number of states. If in the 1970s the mainstream view was that such powerful actors should be welcomed in developing countries and they should take power from the states in order to enable development and liberalisation, the rhetoric has shifted since it became clear that most transnational corporations would use that power to their benefit and to the detriment of the people.[17] For instance, according to John Braithwaite,[18] the shift of power from state to non-state actors has already happened. While analysing the interaction between multinational enterprises and the state, he wrote: '[I]t is not best to conceive of the era in which we live as one of the regulatory state, but of regulatory capitalism ... 1984 did arrive.'[19]

Essentially, the governments of most countries are no longer able to control global governance, because private actors impose their views and standards on both national and international policies. Companies are the current leaders, as they are the most powerful private actors in the global economy[20] Braithwaite analyses the history of governance in several passages. At the final stage, huge enterprises control the twenty-century state. The state is no longer able to determine its policies without relying on companies.[21]

Therefore, the traditional global order, based on state sovereignty and non-participation of private actors in the international arena, is gone. A new global order based on the interaction between private actors has arrived. The remaining question is how non-state actors interact with each other, when some parties, such as multinational companies, are more powerful than others, such as individuals.

II. THE LEGAL FRAMEWORK FOR MULTINATIONAL ENTERPRISES

Before analysing the law applicable to multinational enterprises, it is necessary to define the terms *enterprise* and *multinational* as they will be used in this book. A multinational enterprise is a non-legal term of art indicating a transnational business constituted of multiple entities. Such entities are typically companies incorporated in different jurisdictions (or other corporate or non-incorporated forms of organising commercial activities). Detlev Vagts borrows the following definition of multinational enterprises from the business literature: '[A] cluster of corporations of diverse nationality joined together by ties of common

[17] See generally David Kairys (ed), *The Politics Of Law: A Progressive Critique*, 3rd edn (Basic Books, 1998); George Taylor, 'Deconstructing the Law: The Politics of Law' (1982) 1 *Yale Law & Policy Review* 158; Milton Friedman, 'The Social Responsibility of Business Is to Increase its Profits' in *Corporate Ethics and Corporate Governance* (Springer, 2007).

[18] Braithwaite (n 1).

[19] ibid 1–4.

[20] ibid.

[21] Braithwaite (n 1); Joel Bakan, *The Corporation: The Pathological Pursuit of Profit and Power* (Free Press, 2004); Vagts (n 4).

ownership and responsive to a common management strategy.'[22] These multiple companies are affiliated by way of a diverse set of corporate arrangements.

First, they may be in a parent and subsidiary relationship, meaning that the parent is a shareholder (or any other holder of equity interest, however they are called under the laws of the relevant jurisdiction) of the subsidiary(ies). The International Accounting Standards provide the following definitions of corporate groups, parent and subsidiary companies: '[a corporate] group is a parent and all its subsidiaries',[23] '[a] parent [company] is an entity that has one or more subsidiaries',[24] '[a] subsidiary is an entity, including an unincorporated entity such as a partnership, that is controlled by another entity (known as the parent)'.[25]

Second, their relationship may be contract based when, for example, two or more companies agree to conduct a business activity jointly under the terms of a contract. Such a relationship may take many different forms, starting from a straightforward supply agreement and ending up with complex joint-venture agreements.

Whatever the exact form of such a business organisation, however, these companies, which are, as a matter of law, separate entities, would act as a single business in economic terms. This book uses the terms *multinational enterprise*, *multinational company* and *multinational group* interchangeably to address a single economic unit conducting transnational activities through multiple, legally separate, companies incorporated in different jurisdictions.[26]

The purpose of this section is to analyse the rules applicable to multinational enterprises and to argue that there is a glaring discrepancy between the obligations that corporations owe and the limited remedies available to victims to enforce such obligations in practice.

A. Primary and Secondary Rules

This section outlines the theoretical framework of primary and secondary rules,[27] which is well known among international lawyers,[28] but may be unfamiliar to private law scholars. The distinction between primary and secondary rules is fundamental to understand the accountability gap in respect of multinational enterprises. HLA Hart was the first to distinguish between primary

[22] Raymond Vernon, 'Economic Sovereignty at Bay' [1968] *Foreign Affairs* 110, 114; Vagts (n 4) 740; Christopher A Bartlett et al, *Transnational Management: Text and Cases*, 4th edn (McGraw-Hill/Irwin, 2003) 65.

[23] 'International Accounting Standard 27 Consolidated and Separate Financial Statements' 4.

[24] ibid.

[25] ibid.

[26] Michael Sharpston, 'International Sub-Contracting' (1975) 27 *Oxford Economic Papers* 94.

[27] HLA Hart, *The Concept of Law*, 3rd edn (Oxford University Press, 2012).

[28] See ibid; Ronald M Dworkin, 'The Model of Rules' (1967) 35 *University of Chicago Law Review* 14.

and secondary norms. Primary rules are the obligations of every member of a community; secondary rules are the procedural devices (remedies, causes of action, liability standards, rules of procedure, etc) that the members of such a community may use in case of a breach of an obligation set out in a primary rule.[29] In Hart's words:

> [Secondary rules] may all be said to be on a different level from the primary rules, for they are all about such rules; in the sense that while primary rules are concerned with the actions that individuals must or must not do, these secondary rules are all concerned with the primary rules themselves. They specify the ways in which the primary rules may be conclusively ascertained, introduced, eliminated, varied, and the fact of their violation conclusively determined.[30]

Secondary rules are emerging from and are based on the primary rules. In principle, if no one would ever breach primary rules, society would not need secondary rules. However, when someone breaches a primary rule, there is a need to establish a secondary rule to address such a breach. By ascertaining when a primary rule is violated, secondary rules identify the legal norms that regulate conduct. Therefore, there seems to be no apparent divergence between primary or secondary rules, because primary (substantive) rules weigh as much and in so far as they are buttressed by secondary (enforcement/procedural) rules.[31]

Good examples of primary rules are the Ten Commandments, as they describe which conduct a particular person should or should not adopt. For example, 'you shall not murder'[32] is a legal rule forbidding people from killing their peers. However, such a commandment says nothing concerning the liability of the people who violate the rule. For example, it says nothing about what the sanction would be, if any, for those who kill and how and when in the concrete case the sanction should apply. The secondary rule associated with this primary rule would be the cause of action establishing what elements are necessary to hold a person responsible for the violation of a particular rule. New York law provides an example of a secondary rule connected to the primary rule 'you shall not murder'.[33]

> 5-4.1 Action by personal representative for wrongful act, neglect or default causing death of decedent
>
> 1. The personal representative, duly appointed in this state or any other jurisdiction, of a decedent who is survived by distributees may maintain an action to recover damages for a wrongful act, neglect or default which caused the decedent's death against a person who would have been liable to the decedent by reason of such wrongful conduct if death had not ensued.[34]

[29] Hart (n 27).
[30] ibid 94.
[31] ibid.
[32] Bible, Exodus 20:1–17, Commandement VI.
[33] ibid.
[34] NY Est Pow & Trusts 2015 (L § 5-41).

Secondary rules are based on primary rules in order to determine the elements required to effectively hold a person liable in court.[35] Hart's distinction triggered some philosophical and intellectual debates as to the meaning of rules and laws.[36] Primary and secondary norms became part of international legal terminology, especially as it pertains to the issue of state responsibility. In fact, although States have a number of international legal obligations, there are just a few legal mechanisms to hold them responsible in international courts.[37] In essence, there are primary rules establishing the obligations of states and secondary rules detailing the responsibility of states for breaching primary rules.[38] As explained in the International Law Commission Draft Articles on Responsibility of States for Internationally Wrongful Acts:

> These articles seek to formulate, by way of codification and progressive development, the basic rules of international law concerning the responsibility of States for their internationally wrongful acts. The emphasis is on the secondary rules of State responsibility: that is to say, the general conditions under international law for the State to be considered responsible for wrongful actions or omissions, and the legal consequences which flow therefrom. The articles do not attempt to define the content of the international obligations, the breach of which gives rise to responsibility. This is the function of the primary rules, whose codification would involve restating most of substantive customary and conventional international law.[39]

Although international scholars have analysed the issue of primary and secondary rules and the lack of effective secondary rules as it pertains to a state's responsibility, they have hardly analysed the relationship between primary and secondary rules in the context of the liability of multinational companies.[40]

[35] See Hart (n 27); Jeremy Lever, 'Why Procedure Is More Important than Substantive Law' (1999) 48 *ICLQ* 285.

[36] Dworkin (n 28).

[37] Roberto Ago, 'Second Report on State Responsibility, by Roberto Ago, Special Rapporteur – The Origin of International Responsibility' (1970) II *Yearbook of the International Law Commission*; Martti Koskenniemi, 'Solidarity Measures: State Responsibility as a New International Order?' (2002) 72 *British Yearbook of International Law* 337; International Law Commission, 'Draft Articles on Responsibility of States for Internationally Wrongful Acts' (2001) II *Yearbook of the International Law Commission.*

[38] Ago (n 37); Koskenniemi (n 37); International Law Commission (n 37).

[39] International Law Commission (n 37) 31.

[40] See eg on state's responsibility Gerald G Fitzmaurice, 'The Foundations of the Authority of International Law and the Problem of Enforcement' (1956) 19 *MLR* 1; on corporate liability see Carlos Manuel Vazquez, 'Direct vs Indirect Obligations of Corporations under International Law' (2005) 43 *Columbia Journal of Transnational Law* 927. Carlos Manuel Vazquez is one of the few scholars who has rightly connected the primary and secondary norms applicable to states and the agency problems applicable to companies.

> A full discussion of whether the violation of such primary rules by corporate actors gives rise to the responsibility of corporations under current international law is beyond the scope of this Essay. It does seem to me, however, that recognizing such responsibility involves no significantly greater conceptual departure from the classic model. First, corporations bear a stronger resemblance than individuals to the classic addressees of international law (states); like states, corporations are artificial "persons" comprising groups of natural persons. Second, and perhaps more important, corporations act through individuals and are owned by individuals. For purposes of liability, the corporation's owners (the shareholders) *are* the corporation.

B. The Standards of Conduct and Review

Company law scholars have analysed primary and secondary rules as these pertain to the accountability of corporate officers, but not in relation to the liability of companies. They discovered that primary and secondary rules applicable to corporate officers often diverge, and have dedicated considerable intellectual effort to exploring and explaining this divergence.[41] They used different terminology, defining primary rules as *standards of conduct* and secondary rules as *standards of review*. In the words of Melvin Aron Eisenberg, the leading US corporate scholar on this matter:

> [A] standard of conduct states how an actor should conduct a given activity or play a given role. A standard of review states the test a court should apply when it reviews an actor's conduct to determine whether to impose liability or grant injunctive relief. In many or most areas of law, these two kinds of standards tend to be conflated. … [T]he conflation of standards of conduct and standards of review is so common that it is easy to overlook the fact that whether the two kinds of standards are or should be identical in any given area is a matter of prudential judgment. Perhaps standards of conduct and standards of review in corporate law would always be identical in a world in which information was perfect, the risk of liability for assuming a given corporate role was always commensurate with the incentives for assuming the role, and institutional considerations never required deference to a corporate organ. In the real world, however, these conditions seldom hold, and the standards of review in corporate law pervasively diverge from the standard of conduct. … [T]he distinction between standards of conduct and standards of review in corporate law is an instance of a more general distinction in the law between conduct rules, which are rules addressed to the general public, and decision rules, which are rules addressed to officials. The kinds of rules that I call standards of conduct are conduct rules, addressed to director and officers. The kinds of rules that call standards of review are decision rules, addressed to judges.[42]

> The question of corporate responsibility under international law thus boils down to the question of whether the individuals who own the corporation can be held responsible for violations of international norms by those acting on the corporation's behalf. An affirmative response requires only a straightforward application of agency principles. Indeed, a principal point of the corporate form is to enable the principals (the shareholders) to limit their liability for the actions of the directors of the corporation (the agents). The law recognizes the corporation as a separate legal person, answerable to the law as such, as the price for limiting the liability of shareholders. To unravel this bargain now by insisting that corporations are not persons for purposes of liability under international law norms that concededly apply to natural persons would appear detrimental to the interests of the individuals who own the corporation and would be subject to individual liability on an agency theory if the veil were pierced. In any event, because recognizing corporate liability is equivalent to recognizing shareholder liability, it would represent no greater conceptual departure from the classic model than the recognition of individual responsibility under international law. (ibid 944).

Another author who addressed the issue of primary and secondary norms as it pertains to multinational companies is Steven Ratner; see Steven R Ratner, 'Corporations and Human Rights: A Theory of Legal Responsibility' (2001) 111 *The Yale Law Journal* 443, 489–496.

[41] See Melvin Aron Eisenberg, 'The Divergence of Standards of Conduct and Standards of Review in Corporate Law' (1993) 62 *Fordham Law Review* 437; James Cox and Melvin Eisenberg, *Business Organizations Cases and Materials*, 12th edn (Foundation Press, 2019).

[42] See Eisenberg (n 41) 437, 437–38, 462.

In order to understand the conflict exposed by Eisenberg, it is necessary to take a step back and briefly describe the role that these standards play within the corporate governance agency theory. The agency theory applies when a person or entity (called an *agent*) is in a position of superior knowledge and power in managing a particular asset, but that person or entity has no ownership rights in respect of that asset, while a second person or entity (called a *principal*) is the owner of the asset but is lacking the information and knowledge required to manage it. The agency arises, as a matter of business reality, in the relationship of a powerful agent managing the assets (making decisions) for a powerless principal.[43] Corporate governance scholars identified three broad scenarios when agency problems arise. The first agency problem arises between corporate officers (managers, directors) and shareholders. The second agency problem arises between a majority (controlling) shareholder and minority shareholders. The third agency problem arises between companies and society as a whole.[44]

The first agency problem, called the managerial agency problem, defines the managers of a company as agents and the shareholders as principals. In corporations, the shareholders need professional managers to take sophisticated and potentially risky but profitable decisions that they do not have the ability and expertise to take on their own. On the one hand, this requires that managers have considerable discretion and independence from the shareholders. On the other hand, managers could potentially abuse their power to the company's detriment. Therefore, shareholders need a mechanism to ensure that managers work in the corporation's best interest. Such a mechanism could be, for instance, a liability framework for shareholders to hold managers accountable if they violate their duties towards the company. For this reason, corporate law sets out two main duties that the managers have towards the company: the duty of loyalty and the duty of care. These duties are supposed to serve as an essential instrument in protecting the shareholders against any acts of the managers that are not undertaken in the company's interests. However, the managers will not be willing to take risky but profitable decisions for the shareholders if they do not receive direct benefits when such decisions are successful, but they may be held personally accountable when such decisions result in losses.[45]

Various solutions have been proposed to balance the interests of shareholders and managers. In the United States, the solution is to maintain a divergence between the standard of conduct (normative rules as to how the managers shall

[43] See David Kershaw, *Company Law in Context: Text and Materials*, 2nd edn (Oxford University Press. 2012) 171–88; Reinier Kraakman et al, *The Anatomy of Corporate Law: A Comparative and Functional Approach*, 2nd edn (Oxford University Press, 2009) 35–53.

[44] See Kershaw (n 43) 171–88; Kraakman et al (n 43) 35–53.

[45] See Kershaw (n 43) 171–88; Kraakman et al (n 43) 35–53.

act) and the standard of review (the rules of enforcement applied by courts with respect to the managers' duties).[46]

The American Law Institute Principles of Corporate Governance state as follows:

> A director or officer has a duty to the corporation to perform the director's or officer's function in good faith, in a manner that he or she reasonably believes to be in the best interests of the corporation, and with the care that an ordinarily prudent person would reasonably be expected to exercise in a like position and under similar circumstances.[47]

The American Law Institute applies the generally accepted rule of negligence (aka the duty of care) to the directors of a corporation. The rule is rather straightforward: like any driver should drive 'with the care that an ordinarily prudent [driver] would reasonably be expected to exercise',[48] any corporate officer should act 'with the care that an ordinarily prudent [corporate officer] would reasonably be expected to exercise'.[49] Eisenberg defines this as a standard of conduct.[50] A number of courts embraced this standard in the nineteenth and early twentieth centuries in the United States and they applied it as an ordinary care standard, ie a director should act as a reasonable, prudent businessman would.[51] In these cases, the standard of conduct and the standard of review conflated because courts applied the ordinary care standard in practice and therefore, in Hart's terminology, courts transformed, through their legal analysis, the standard from a general primary rule to a secondary norm detailing the liability of corporate directors.

This standard is still widely recognised across the United States as a substantive yardstick which should be used to measure whether the directors' conduct is consistent with the law[52] (ie primary norm). However, with time, the jurisprudence evolved[53] and courts applied a secondary norm that was significantly lower than 'the care that an ordinarily prudent [corporate officer] would reasonably be expected to exercise'.[54] Nowadays, the standard of review that the courts apply to decide whether managers comply with their duty of care would typically be gross negligence.[55] Accordingly, provided that the manager is

[46] Eisenberg (n 41).

[47] American Law Institute, *Principles of Corporate Governance: Analysis and Recommendations* (American Law Institute, 2008) s 4.01.

[48] ibid s 4.01; Eisenberg (n 41) 440.

[49] American Law Institute (n 47) s 4.01.

[50] Eisenberg (n 41).

[51] See eg *Scott v Depeyster* [1832] NY Edw Ch 1 513; *Hun v Cary* [1880] NY CA 82 65; *Hanna v Lyon* [1904] NY CA 179 107.

[52] American Law Institute (n 47) s 4.01.

[53] See eg *Robinson and others v Smith and others* [1832] Ch NY 3 222; *Commonwealth ex rel v Anchor Building & Loan Association* [1902] Pa Super 20 101.

[54] American Law Institute (n 47) s 4.01.

[55] Eisenberg (n 41); Kershaw (n 43) 410–75.

not grossly negligent, the courts will apply the business judgement rule, which essentially means that they will not interfere and/or hold managers liable for commercial decisions. It is beyond the scope of this book to set out the difference between the conduct permitted under a negligence and gross negligence standard in the context of corporate law. However, it is important to emphasise that, currently, US courts assess the liability of corporate directors according to a considerably lower standard than the standard of care prescribed by the primary rules of tort law. Eisenberg defines the standard that the courts use in their practice as the standard of review (in Hart's terminology this would be a direct analogy of secondary rules), because this is the standard that courts use to review whether directors acted in compliance with the law and whether the courts shall hold them liable for their acts.[56]

The result of such divergence is puzzling: the care that courts require from a driver (where there is no divergence between the standard of conduct and the standard of review) is higher than the care that tribunals require from a director of a corporation (where divergence persists). The reason behind this puzzle is that the legislator and the judge want to reconcile two mutually contradictory policies. On the one hand, they want to incentivise corporate directors to make profitable but risky decisions that would increase shareholders' profits and in the long-term boost the economy (and, accordingly, apply a lower standard of review when a case is brought to make a director liable for his/her business decisions). On the other hand, they do not want to make the leash too loose to cater for any exigencies that may arise (and, accordingly, the higher standard of conduct is not brought down to a lower standard of review).[57] No such contradictory incentives exist with respect to negligent drivers, where society has a simple interest in discouraging careless behaviour. A director managing a company with the same care as the care taken by a driver would assume a risk-averse attitude with the ultimate result of shrinking the economy.[58] On balance, everybody would be worse off.

Scholars have analysed the effects of the divergence between a legally prescribed standard of conduct and a judicially applied standard of review on the first and second agency problems, ie the conflicts arising between directors having superior knowledge and information versus shareholders owning the company (the first agency problem), and the situation of a majority (controlling) shareholder with superior knowledge, economic incentives and information versus minority shareholders typically owning just a few shares per person in a big company (the second agency problem).[59]

[56] Eisenberg (n 41).
[57] ibid.
[58] Kershaw (n 43) 410–75.
[59] ibid 646–705.

C. The Third Agency Problem

The third agency problem relates to a potential conflict of interest between the companies as agents and the society as a principal. On the one hand, when companies produce goods and deliver services, they benefit society, because, due to market competition between private actors, the prices of the relevant goods decrease and their quality increases. On the other hand, by embracing a free market economy, society loses control over the production process, as companies, instead of a democratically elected government, provide essential commodities. Accordingly, there is a possibility that, rather than benefiting society as a whole, the companies would start using and/or adjusting the rules to their advantage. While a democratically elected government would be accountable to the public, and therefore would balance the interests of various stakeholders affected by industrial production, the risk is that private companies may disregard any interest other than their own.[60]

As is the case with the first and second agency problems, it is complex to strike a balance between encouraging entrepreneurs to risk their private assets to start a business that would benefit society, and regulating such business to ensure that it will not abuse the rights of individuals living in that society.[61] It is only recently, since NGOs, human rights litigators and civil society have started to publicly raise this issue, that corporate legal scholars and economists have initiated a debate about the third agency problem. While some maintain that 'the social responsibility of business is to increase its profits'[62] as society benefits already from having a free market economy, others argue that law should make companies accountable to the stakeholders affected by corporate activities.[63]

There has been no genuine effort to analyse the effects of the divergence between the standard of conduct and review as it pertains to the third

[60] Frank Easterbrook and Daniel R Fischel, *The Economic Structure of Corporate Law* (Harvard University Press, 1996) 35–39; JE Parkinson, *Corporate Power and Responsibility Issues in the Theory of Company Law* (Oxford University Press, 1995) 1–49; Bakan (n 21); Kraakman et al (n 43) 35–53. Different economic theories analyse how the relationship between companies and society works; see Muchlinski (n 3) 81–122.

[61] Kershaw (n 43) 771–87.

[62] Friedman (n 17) 173.

[63] Henry Hansmann and Reinier Kraakman, 'Toward Unlimited Shareholder Liability for Corporate Torts' (1991) 100 *The Yale Law Journal* 1879; Joseph E Stiglitz, 'Multinational Corporations: Balancing Rights and Responsibilities' (2007) 101 *Proceedings of the ASIL Annual Meeting* 3; David W Leebron, 'Limited Liability, Tort Victims, and Creditors' (1991) 91 *Columbia Law Review* 1565; Peter Muchlinski, 'Implementing the New UN Corporate Human Rights Framework: Implications for Corporate Law, Governance, and Regulation' (2012) 22 *Business Ethics Quarterly* 145.

agency problem. This book undertakes such an analysis. It argues that the divergence between the standard of conduct and the standard of review also applies to the third agency problem. The divergence increases when a business is structured as a multinational enterprise with a holding company that has multiple subsidiaries incorporated in different countries.

(i) The Standards of Conduct or Primary Rules

Both domestic and international law contribute to establishing the primary rules, or standards of conduct, regulating the conduct of multinational companies.

(a) Domestic Law

At the national level, domestic laws regulate the standard of conduct applicable to a company's territorial behaviour. When a corporation damages a stakeholder, the standard of conduct would typically be the ordinary tort law standard of care. This essentially means that a company should act as a reasonable, prudent business.[64]

Most important for the purpose of this book is the tort law concept according to which if two or more persons come together to do business they will be jointly and severally liable for such economic activity.[65] For instance, if two persons open a restaurant together and one is cooking and the other one is marketing the food, they are jointly and severally liable for any activity of the restaurant because they are jointly engaging in one economic activity. These two persons would form a partnership. This principle is also applicable if these persons are two companies: one with expertise in cooking and the other one in marketing. They would also be jointly and severally liable for their commercial activity.

There is also the possibility that an enterprise would voluntarily adopt an internal corporate code of conduct assuming additional obligations towards the stakeholders, and such a corporate code would be an additional standard of conduct that could possibly complement or replace the ordinary standard of care.[66]

(b) International Law

At the international level, the standard of conduct is determined by soft international law, human rights, or a combination of the two.

[64] SF Deakin, Angus Charles Johnston and BS Markesinis, *Markesinis and Deakin's Tort Law*, 7th edn (OUP, 2012) 99–121.

[65] ibid 880–88.

[66] Anna Beckers, *Enforcing Corporate Social Responsibility Codes: On Global Self-Regulation and National Private Law* (Hart Publishing, 2015) 149–85.

These mechanisms include some initiatives taken in the 1970s, such as the Organisation for Economic Co-operation and Development (OECD)[67] and the International Labour Organization (ILO)[68] frameworks. Others, such as the Guiding Principles on Business and Human Rights (Guiding Principles), are the outcome of the recent efforts to set out the responsibility of multinational companies for human rights abuses.[69] This book will analyse the distinctions between these different soft rules in Chapter 2. For the moment, it is sufficient to mention that, although these standards are increasingly taken into account by companies, they are soft laws and therefore unable to set up any binding obligation for multinational enterprises. They are, in this sense, quasi-legal.[70]

As it pertains to hard law, it should be mentioned that a number of scholars and academics have recently interpreted human rights as applicable between private entities, including companies. This application of human rights law is called *horizontal*, as it affects the relationship between private actor(s). Instead, the traditional application of human rights law is called *vertical*, as it affects the relationship between the state and the individual(s). The horizontal application of human rights is not yet recognised as law, but part of the academic

[67] OECD, *OECD Guidelines for Multinational Enterprises, 2011 Edition* (OECD Publishing, 2011) www.oecd-ilibrary.org/governance/oecd-guidelines-for-multinational-enterprises_9789264115415-en, accessed 22 April 2016.

[68] International Labour Office, *ILO Declaration on Fundamental Principles and Rights at Work and its Follow-Up* (ILO, 2010).

[69] John Gerard Ruggie, 'Report of the Special Representative of the Secretary-General on the Issue of Human Rights and Transnational Corporations and Other Business Enterprises' (2011) 29 *Netherlands Quarterly of Human Rights* 224; Nicola Jägers, 'UN Guiding Principles on Business and Human Rights: Making Headway towards Real Corporate Accountability' (2011) 29 *Netherlands Quarterly of Human Rights* 159; John Gerard Ruggie, 'The Construction of the UN "Protect, Respect and Remedy" Framework for Business and Human Rights: The True Confessions of a Principled Pragmatist' (2011) 2 *European Human Rights Law Review* 127; John Gerard Ruggie, 'Protect, Respect, and Remedy: The UN Framework for Business and Human Rights', in *International Human Rights Law* (Ashgate, 2010).

[70] See generally Jerbi Scott, 'Business and Human Rights at the UN: What Might Happen Next?' (2009) 31 *Human Rights Quarterly* 299; David Weissbrodt and Muria Kruger, 'Human Rights Responsibilities of Businesses as Non-State Actors' in *Non-State Actors and Human Rights* (Oxford University Press, 2005); Deva, 'Human Rights Standards' (n 4) 9–17; Celia Wells and Juanita Elias, 'Catching the Coscience of the King: Corporate Players on the International Stage' in *Non-State actors and Human Rights* (Oxford University Press, 2005); Ashley L Santner, 'A Soft Law Mechanism for Corporate Responsibility: How the Updated OECD Guidelines for Multinational Enterprises Promote Business for the Future', (2011) 43 *The George Washington International Law Review* 375; Jernej Letnar Cernic, *Human Rights Law and Business Corporate Responsibility for Fundamental Human Rights* (Europa Law Publishing, 2010) 183–216; John Gerard Ruggie and Tamaryn Nelson, 'Human Rights and the OECD Guidelines for Multinational Enterprises: Normative Innovations and Implementation Challenges' (2015) 66 *Corporate Social Responsibility Initiative Working Paper*; Gwynne Skinner et al, 'The Third Pillar: Access to Judicial Remedies for Human Rights Violations by Transnational Business | ICAR, CORE, ECCJ' (2013), http://corporatejustice.org/documents/publications/eccj/the_third_pillar_-access_to_judicial_remedies_for_human_rights_violation.-1-2.pdf; Aurora Voiculescu, 'Human Rights and the Normative Ordering of Global Capitalism', in *The Business of Human Rights: An Evolving Agenda for Corporate Responsibility* (Zed Books, 2011); Andrew Clapham, *Human Rights Obligations of Non-State Actors* (Oxford University Press, 2006) 201–11.

community is increasingly advocating for such recognition.[71] For instance, the issue of the horizontal application of human rights law to corporations was at the heart of the Alien Tort Stature (ATS) litigation in the United States. The ATS is a statute recognising the jurisdiction of US courts over tort cases alleging a violation of the *law of nations*. One of the key issues was whether or not the *law of nations*, which could be interpreted as including human rights law, would apply to corporations. After years of litigation, in *Jesner v Arab Bank*, a plurality of the US Supreme Court justices decided that human rights law has not yet prescribed obligations for corporations.[72] This debate will be analysed in more detail in Chapter 3. However, if, for now, I take for granted that international law may be directly applicable to corporations, human rights will establish yet another standard of conduct that a multinational company should comply with.

In summary, there are multiple standards of conduct, including tort law, soft international law and possibly even human rights, that apply to the actions of a multinational company.

(ii) The Standards of Review or Secondary Rules

Although the secondary rules applicable to multinational companies may be different in various jurisdictions, they are based on limited liability and territoriality, two features that substantially lower the standard of review in comparison with the standard of conduct.

(a) Domestic Law and Limited Liability

Looking back at the history of corporate and tort law, it is clear that domestic legislators established a number of rules limiting the liability of shareholders with a view to boosting the economy and enabling small businesses to flourish.[73]

[71] See Raphael Thomas, 'The Problem of Horizontal Effect' (2000) 5 *European Human Rights Law Review* 493; Dawn Oliver and Jörg Fedtke, *Human Rights and the Private Sphere: A Comparative Study* (Routledge 2007).

[72] *Jesner v Arab Bank, PLC* (n 5); *Sosa v Alvarez*, [2004] US Supreme Court 542, 692; Virginia Monken Gomez, 'The Sosa Standard: What Does it Mean for Future ATS Litigation?' (2006) 33 *Pepperdine Law Review* 469; Simon Baughen, 'Holding Corporations to Account: Crafting ATS Suits in the UK' (2013) 2 *British Journal of American Legal Studies* 533; Robert McCorquodale, 'Waving not Drowning: Kiobel outside the United States' (2013) 107 *American Journal of International Law* 846; Tyler Giannini and Susan Farbstein, 'Corporate Accountability in Conflict Zones: How Kiobel Undermines the Nuremberg Legacy and Modern Human Rights' (2010) 52 *Harvard International Law Journal* 119; Kamminga (n 5).

[73] For the history of companies' liability, see Kershaw (n 43) 3–46; Beisinghoff (n 4) 21–27; Hansmann and Kraakman (n 63); Karen Vanderkerckhove, *Piercing the Corporate Veil* (Kluwer/Aspen, 2007) 3–9; Max Gillman and Tim Eade, 'The Development of the Corporation in England, with Emphasis on Limited Liability' (1995) 22 *International Journal of Social Economics* 20. Please note that this book does not take into account the history of huge transnational trading companies enhancing colonialism, eg the East Indian Company. Although such companies were

In the nineteenth century, England started to grant limited liability to commercial enterprises.[74] At first, it granted this privilege only to groups of shareholders that would associate together in order to establish a commercial company.[75] Subsequently, corporate law allowed any shareholder, including a holding company, to benefit from the privilege of limited liability.[76] As a result, enterprises establish long chains of subsidiaries, that, despite acting as a single economic unit, can limit their liability within the group.[77] Although tort law is still applicable to companies, as to any other private actor, limited liability has established an alternative standard of review that does not take into consideration the fact that a number of enterprises make up a single economic unit even though they include multiple companies.[78]

If I apply this logic to the restaurant example used above, it is clear that limited liability creates an alternative standard applicable to companies only. Assume that two corporations, one with expertise in cooking and the other in marketing, come together to run a restaurant but, instead of doing this on their own, they create a third company with limited liability that comprises their business. Should any liability arise, the only responsible entity would be the third company. If the two corporations undercapitalise the third company to such an extent that it does not have enough resources to pay potential damages, it will be for the tort victims to bear the costs of any liability they may suffer.

The justification for this divergence between the standards of review and conduct is economic growth. Limited liability is paramount to ensure that private individuals invest in risky and profitable activities. If every investor would be liable for its entire private wealth for each company in which it invests, fewer entrepreneurs would be willing to invest in risky projects. Establishing the limited-liability regime as the standard of review applicable to companies encourages private individuals to take the risk of investing their assets in businesses.[79] Although it is true that the cost of limited liability is spread among society as a

transnational and were acting extraterritorially, they were the *mano larga* of European imperialist powers exercising public power and cannot be considered as private enterprises in modern terms. The colonial trade was regulated by colonial rules that are not taken into account in this book. For the difference between modern private enterprises and colonial companies that were the *mano larga* of the state please, see Svetlana Andrianova, Panicos Demetriades and Chenggang Xu, 'Political Economy Origins of Financial Markets in Europe and Asia' (2011) 39 *World Development* 686; M Sornarajah, *The International Law on Foreign Investment*, 3rd edn (Cambridge University Press 2010) 19–28; Olufemi Amao, *Corporate Social Responsibility, Human Rights and the Law: Multinational Corporations in Developing Countries* (Routledge 2011) 6–22.

[74] Gillman and Eade (n 73).

[75] See eg Companies Act 2006 s 6. The UK Companies Act 1862 required seven persons or more to form a company.

[76] Phillip I Blumberg, 'Limited Liability and Corporate Groups' (1985) 11 *The Journal of Corporate Law* 573, 605–11; Leebron (n 63).

[77] Vanderkerckhove (n 73) 1–9.

[78] Blumberg (n 76); Vanderkerckhove (n 73) 1–9; Muchlinski (n 3) 307–35.

[79] Blumberg (n 76); Kershaw (n 43) 3–46; Hansmann and Kraakman (n 63).

whole, it is believed that, in the long term, society benefits from the economic growth which the limited liability and the resulting investments entail.[80]

Given the divergence between the standard of conduct (ie joint and several liability for all entities running a business) and review (ie company law allowing the shareholder to limit its liability to a fixed amount) that limited liability created, domestic courts felt compelled to disregard, on a case-by-case basis, the corporate veil formed by the subsidiaries that are part of one single economic entity.[81] Although this solution entails disregarding the existence of each subsidiary as a separate company, it is important to underline that limited liability is different from the concept of separate legal personality. The divergence between the standard of conduct and review is not due to the fact that each company within an enterprise is a separate person. The problem instead is that each of these separate persons is considered as not having any liability for the obligations of its subsidiaries, even though they are part of the same economic entity.[82]

A number of corporate and international legal scholars criticise this approach and argue that, in some instances, the legislator should not transfer the cost of limited liability from shareholders to third parties. One such case is the third-party tort victims in relation to who it seems to be particularly unjust that they (rather than the shareholders) absorb the costs of the risky activities undertaken by companies.[83] These academics argue that limited liability should be applicable only in cases of adjusting (voluntary) creditors, such as, for example, banks providing finance to the corporations. In such circumstances, the creditors are believed to be sophisticated enough to take the risks deriving from limited liability into consideration and, most importantly, to assume such liabilities voluntarily (nobody forces a bank to provide credit to a corporate entity). Instead, limited liability should not be used to the detriment of involuntary creditors, such as human rights victims, who have no voluntary relationship with the company and are unable to calculate the costs of limited liability.[84] However, as Chapter 2 will demonstrate, courts have rarely listened to these criticisms.[85] As a result, the standard of conduct that multinational companies should follow according to a combination of international and domestic norms diverges substantially from the standard of review adopted by domestic courts to assess the liability of companies.

(b) International Law and Territoriality

At the international level, there is no proper standard of review, because even scholars who take the view that human rights are standards of conduct

[80] Kershaw (n 43) 771–87.

[81] See eg *Woolfson v Strathclyde Regional Council* [1978] SC 90 (HL); *DHN Food Distributors Ltd v Tower Hamlets London Borough Council Bronze Investments Ltd v Same DHN Food Transport Ltd v Same* [1976] Court of Appeal WLR 1, 852.

[82] Blumberg (n 76) 616–26.

[83] See Blumberg (n 76); Hansmann and Kraakman (n 63).

[84] See Hansmann and Kraakman (n 63).

[85] See eg *Prest v Petrodel Resources Limited and others* [2013] UKSC 34.

applicable horizontally between private parties must admit that international law does not provide a secondary rule making human rights directly enforceable against multinational companies.[86]

Therefore, the question arises as to what standard of review is applicable to corporations for a violation of human rights. The only possibility is to use domestic law and causes of actions to file complaints against corporations for a breach of international law. For instance, tort law establishes the causes of action that entitle any person to file a complaint when s/he suffers damages. This includes entitling human rights victims to file a complaint when their rights are abused. A perfect example of such a divergence between human rights as a standard of conduct and domestic causes of action as a standard of review is the ATS. As the US Supreme Court decided in *Sosa v Alvarez*,[87] the ATS refers to some violations of international law, including human rights violations. However, international law is not directly enforceable in US courts, because it does not provide the causes of action to file a complaint.[88] This essentially means that, although human rights establish the standard of conduct or the primary norm, they do not provide causes of action for domestic courts, ie the standard of review or secondary norms. For this reason, the US Supreme Court clarified that it is for the common law to provide causes of action to implement human rights law against private parties.[89]

The application of domestic causes of actions creates, however, an additional complication. Various domestic laws applicable to a multinational corporate group having a presence in different countries make the extraterritorial application of tort law often impossible.[90] The causes of action in tort are typically applicable only territorially,[91] when the human rights abuse occurs, and the

[86] For this reason, international law per se is often ill-equipped to address the concerns of private persons. Scholars theorised about transnational law as a process involving both international, domestic, private and public law; see Koh, 'Why Transnational Law Matters' (n 2); Koh, 'Trasnational Legal Process' (n 2). For an analysis of international litigation using both private and public law elements, see Giannini and Farbstein (n 72); Beth Stephens et al, *International Human Rights Litigation in US Courts* (Martinus Nijhoff, 2008) 309–33; Menno T Kamminga and Saman Zia-Zarifi (eds), *Liability of Multinational Corporations under International Law* (Kluwer, 2000) 241–305; Kamminga (n 5); Baughen (n 72); Tyler Giannini, Susan Farbstein and Anthony Clark Arend, 'The Alien Tort Statute and Corporate Liability' (2011) 160 *University of Pennsylvania Law Review*.

[87] *Sosa v Alvarez*, (n 72).

[88] Vazquez (n 40) 932–47.

[89] *Sosa v Alvarez*, (n 72).

[90] See Liesbeth Enneking, *Foreign Direct Liability and Beyond – Exploring the Role of Tort Law in Promoting International Corporate Social Responsibility and Accountability* (Eleven International Publishing, 2012) 443–522; Liesbeth Enneking, 'Crossing the Atlantic – The Political and Legal Feasibility of European Foreign Direct Liability Cases' (2008) 40 *The George Washington International Law Review* 903; Meeran (n 5); Claire Bright, 'L'accès à la justice civile en cas de violations des droits de l'homme par des entreprises multinationales' (2013) 7–114, http://cadmus.eui.eu/handle/1814/29602, accessed 15 April 2016; *Jesner v Arab Bank, PLC* (n 5); Gwynne Skinner, 'Rethinking Limited Liability of Parent Corporations for Foreign Subsidiaries' Violations of International Human Rights Law' (2015) 72 *Washington and Lee Law Review* 1769.

[91] See Enneking, 'Crossing the Atlantic' (n 90); Vazquez (n 40); Letnar Cernic (n 70) 157–80; Cees van Dam, *European Tort Law*, 2nd edn (Oxford University Press, 2013) 169–224; Bright (n 90).

perpetrator and the victim are in the same country. In this case, the victim can sue the perpetrator for abusing human rights law on the basis of the causes of action available in the national legal system. However, when the abuse occurs in multiple countries, the human rights victim has no choice other than to attempt to sue the perpetrator in a national court for conduct that took place (at least in part) extraterritorially.[92]

At the soft law level, there is only one viable mechanism that could establish an alternative standard of review applicable to companies: the OECD National Contact Points (NCPs). These are a unique system of quasi-judicial bodies that can implement the OECD Guidelines against multinational companies at the domestic level. They also overcome the limited liability and territoriality problems described above. According to the OECD Guidelines, all companies that are part of a group may be jointly responsible for an abuse. Furthermore, the OECD Guidelines are applicable everywhere in the world, with no territorial boundaries.[93] However, as further analysed in Chapter 2, there are a number of circumstances that should be taken into account while analysing the NCPs. First, although the NCPs apply international soft law, ie the OECD Guidelines, they are domestic agencies. In this sense, this creates yet another case of an international standard of conduct, established by soft law, and a national standard of review, established by national bodies. Second, being soft law mechanisms, the NCPs first have to mediate between the company and stakeholders that are parties to a dispute, and only if all fails may they assess whether the company violated the OECD Guidelines.[94] Although the decisions of the NCPs are relevant and could persuade companies to comply with the OECD Guidelines, they are non-binding and corporations are free to disregard them.[95] Therefore, the standard set-up by the NCPs could be called a quasi-standard of review for multinational corporations, because this rule is determined by quasi-judicial bodies interpreting soft laws instead of a court applying hard law.

The open question is why such standards are still soft law and are therefore unable to establish a legal standard of review. The justification for countries to adopt a number of corporate social responsibility (CSR) codes, which companies abide by on a voluntary basis only, echoes the same premise that allowed the development of limited liability,[96] ie balancing accountability with economic

[92] See Meeran (n 5); Kamminga (n 5); Jägers and Heijden (n 5); Wesche and Saage-Maaß (n 5); Enneking, *Foreign Direct Liability and Beyond* (n 90); Enneking, 'Crossing the Atlantic' (n 90); Enneking, *Foreign Direct Liability and Beyond* (n 90); Muchlinski (n 3) 125–76; Bright (n 90); Skinner et al (n 70).

[93] OECD (n 67); Ruggie and Nelson (n 70); Leyla Davarnejad, 'In the Shadow of Soft Law: The Handling of Corporate Social Responsibility Disputes under the OECD Guidelines for Multinational Enterprises' (2011) *Journal of Dispute Resolution* 351.

[94] OECD (n 67).

[95] Jerbi (n 70); Weissbrodt and Kruger (n 70) 318–35; Deva, 'Human Rights Standards and Multinational Corporations' (n 4) 9–17; Wells and Elias (n 70) 154–61; Santner (n 70); Letnar Cernic (n 70) 183–216; Ruggie and Nelson (n 70); Skinner et al (n 70); Voiculescu (n 70); Clapham (n 70) 201–211.

[96] Vanderkerckhove (n 73) 1–9; Blumberg (n 76); Kershaw (n 43) 771–87.

development. For instance, the European Commission has consistently argued that the best approach to address the accountability of multinational enterprises is to adopt CSR codes of conduct that companies will be able to follow.[97] The idea is that CSR policies will encourage multinational enterprises to adopt socially responsible behaviour while allowing them to maintain the flexibility that is necessary for globalised business models.

> Enterprises must be given the flexibility to innovate and to develop an approach to CSR that is appropriate to their circumstances. Many enterprises nevertheless value the existence of principles and guidelines that are supported by public authorities, to benchmark their own policies and performance, and to promote a more level playing field.[98]

The reason behind this approach is to reconcile two contradictory policies: on the one hand, states want to attract investors and incentivise them to take risky but profitable decisions that will boost the economy (and, accordingly, apply a lower standard of review for companies disregarding the interests of other stakeholders); but, on the other hand, states also want to encourage corporate socially responsible behaviour to avoid negative externalities that would affect their population (and, accordingly, they adopt a higher CSR standard of conduct).[99]

(iii) The Divergence between the Standards of Conduct and Review

It is clear from the analysis above that, as it pertains to the third agency problem, there is a glaring divergence between standards of conduct (or primary rules) and review (or secondary rules) at both the domestic and international level.

The standards of conduct include domestic tort law, CSR soft rules and, possibly, even human rights obligations. However, when a victim attempts to sue a multinational enterprise abusing human rights, s/he would inevitably have to meet a much higher standard of review to hold the multinational enterprise to account. This standard of review diverges from the standard of conduct both at the domestic and international level. At the domestic level, limited liability

[97] Deborah Russo, 'La promozione della responsabilitá sociale d'impresa nell'Unione europea' (2011) XVI *Il diritto dell'Unione europea* 477; Alexandra Gatto, *Multinational Enterprises and Human Rights: Obligations under EU Law and International Law* (Edward Elgar, 2011) 174–82; Giovanni Esposito and Anna Carobolante, 'Imporre o invitare? Le politiche di corporate social responsibility alla ricerca di un'identità europea' (2013) 8 *Ianus-Diritto e finanza* 5; Sébastien Touzé, 'L'approche communautaires de la responsabilité sociale des entreprises' (2009) 19 *Schweizerische Zeitschrift für internationales und europäischees Recht = Revue suisse de droit international et européen* 7; Sorcha Macleod, 'Reconciling Regulatory Approaches to Corporate Social Responsibility: The European Union, OECD and United Nations Compared' (2007) 13 *European Public Law* 671, 677–87; Antonio Gigante, 'La politica delle istituzioni comunitarie in materia di responsabilitá sociale d'impresa: voluntary o mandatory approach?' (2008) IV *Diritto pubblico comparato ed europeo* 1991.

[98] EC, 'A Renewed EU Strategy 2011–2014 for Corporate Social Responsibility' (2011) COM 681final, para 3.4.

[99] ibid.

and the territorial nature of national law restrain the possibility to hold a multinational enterprise accountable. At the international level, there is no effective standard of review applicable to corporations because there is a lack of enforcement mechanisms, except for the quasi-judicial mechanism of the OECD NCPs, which is non-binding.

Governments tend to justify such divergence between standards of conduct and review or, in Hart's language, primary and secondary rules on the basis of economic development.

III. THE AVENUES FOR LEGAL CHANGE

States are not yet willing to adopt a binding standard of review, or secondary rule, regulating the accountability of companies for human rights abuses. Therefore, scholars and activists are attempting to exploit the avenues available to them to change the current state of the law and react to the abuses committed by multinational companies extraterritorially. First, the business and human rights movement started to lobby for the creation of accountability frameworks at both the national and international level, in both developed and developing countries. Although companies are increasingly adhering to a CSR agenda, these efforts have not yet resulted in the legal changes that would be necessary to address the liability and extraterritorial issues detailed above.[100] Second, human rights litigators have filed complaints against multinational companies in domestic courts, combining arguments based on international law and causes of action in domestic tort law.[101] Against this background, this book proposes to use international courts as a tool to advance the business and human rights agenda.

A. Soft Law: Blaming and Shaming

Given the current state of the law and its inability to address the responsibility of multinational enterprises that abuse human rights, a number of scholars argue that the right approach towards multinational companies is to convince them to act responsibly towards the communities they affect. The case for this approach is that all attempts to establish binding laws detailing the human rights obligations of companies have failed so far.

[100] See Rory Sullivan, 'NGO Influence on the Human Rights Performance of Companies' (2006) 24 *Netherlands Quarterly of Human Rights* 405; Jerbi (n 70); Deva, 'Human Rights Violations' (n 4); Letnar Cernic (n 70) 127–282; Wells and Elias (n 70); Clapham (n 70) 195–270; Voiculescu (n 70), Schrempf-Stirling (n 5).

[101] See Meeran (n 5); Stephens (n 86) 309–33; Wesche and Saage-Maaß (n 5); Kamminga (n 5); Kamminga and Zia-Zarifi (n 86) 241–327; Enneking, *Foreign Direct Liability and Beyond* (n 90); Enneking, 'Crossing the Atlantic' (n 90); Enneking, 'Future of Foreign Direct Liability' (n 5); Giannini and Farbstein (n 72); Giannini, Farbstein and Arend (n 86); Skinner et al (n 70).

As it pertains to human rights law, during the past 25 years, the UN has unsuccessfully attempted to establish an international legal framework to hold multinational companies accountable for human rights abuses. One of the first attempts to establish a business and human rights legal framework was the draft of the Norms.[102] These were intended to become a binding treaty establishing the obligations of multinational companies. However, the UN Commission on Human Rights did not endorse the Norms, because a number of states did not agree to have an enforceable treaty affecting the business conduct of companies.[103] This failure caused the UN Secretary-General Kofi Annan to nominate John Ruggie as Special Representative of the UN Secretary-General on Business and Human Rights. In June 2011, Ruggie proposed a soft law framework, the Guiding Principles,[104] to the Human Rights Council, which endorsed them unanimously.[105] This led Ecuador and South Africa to propose a new resolution for the 'Elaboration of an international legally binding instrument on transnational corporations and other business enterprises with respect to human rights' at the Human Rights Council in June 2014.[106] The Human Rights Council adopted the resolution. However, a number of states voted against the adoption of such a binding treaty. It is, therefore, unclear whether the UN will succeed in establishing an international accountability framework for multinational companies.[107] The UN recently published a first draft of the potential treaty,[108] which fails to address the responsibility of companies for human rights abuses, but instead proposes to enshrine the obligations of states to protect victims of abuses against corporations. This would not be a substantial change of the current state of the law because, as this book demonstrates, states already have positive obligations to secure the rights of individuals against corporations. If this version of the treaty is adopted, its added value will be a further elaboration of existing obligations.

As it pertains to international criminal law, a number of scholars, human rights activists and countries have unsuccessfully advocated for the recognition of the international criminal responsibility of multinational companies. During

[102] UN Sub-Commission on the Promotion and Protection of Human Rights, Norms on the Responsibilities of Transnational Corporations and Other Business Enterprises with Regard to Human Rights 2003 (E/CN.4/Sub.2/2003/12/Rev.2).

[103] For the history of the norms, see Nils Rosemann, 'Business Human Rights Obligations – The Norms of the Responsibility of Transnational Corporations and Other Business Enterprises' (2005) 23 *Nordic Journal of Human Rights* 47; Weissbrodt and Kruger (n 70).

[104] Ruggie, 'Report of the Special Representative of the Secretary-General' (n 69).

[105] Jägers (n 69); Ruggie, 'Protect, Respect, and Remedy' (n 69); Ruggie, 'The Construction of the UN "Protect, Respect and Remedy" Framework for Business and Human Rights' (n 69).

[106] HR Council, 'Elaboration of an International Legally Binding Instrument on Transnational Corporations and Other Business Enterprises with Respect to Human Rights' (2014) A/HRC/26/L.22/Rev.1.

[107] Katerina Sequensova, 'Report of the Human Rights Council on its Twenty-Sixth Session' (United Nations Human Rights Council 2014) A/HRC/26/2.

[108] IGWG, Zero Draft Treaty, Legally Binding Instrument to Regulate, in International Human Rights Law, the Acvitities of Transnational Corporations and other Business Enterprises. 2018.

the negotiations concerning the draft of the Rome Treaty establishing the International Criminal Court (ICC), France proposed extending the jurisdiction of the ICC to corporations. However, the majority of the states refused this proposal and the ICC currently has jurisdiction with regard to individuals only. Similarly, the jurisdiction of the International Criminal Tribunal for the former Yugoslavia (ICTY) and the International Criminal Tribunal for Rwanda (ICTR) is also limited to individuals.[109]

By contrast, CSR voluntary frameworks are flourishing, and multinational corporations are increasingly taking them into account.[110] This was the case for the Guiding Principles. Although states have voted against the UN Norms, John Ruggie was able to convince the Human Rights Council to endorse the Guiding Principles unanimously as a soft law mechanism.[111] Such an endorsement boosted a number of soft law frameworks. First, pre-existing frameworks, such as the OECD Guidelines, were updated in line with the Guiding Principles.[112] Second, a number of NGOs are increasingly blaming and shaming companies that do not comply with any CSR framework in an attempt to raise awareness among consumers.[113] Third, some companies decided to adopt socially responsible codes of conduct voluntarily.[114] Although these initiatives have established the foundation for a cultural revolution in terms of the responsibility that multinational enterprises should have towards the global community, they are of limited use to assert the liability of companies that are not willing to adopt corporate socially responsible policies. CSR frameworks are raising the awareness of consumers and the global public as to the power of transnational corporations. However, they neither establish binding nor

[109] See French proposal 'Working Paper on Article 23, Paras 5–6, A/Conf.183/C.1/WGGP/L.5/Rev.2' (1998) Official Records of the United Nations Diplomatic Conference of Plenipotentiaries on the Establishment of an Internaitonal Criminal Court Vol III; Statute of the International Criminal Tribunal for Rwanda 1994, art 5; Statute of the International Criminal Tribunal for the Former Yugoslavia 1995, art 6; H van der Wilt, 'Corporate Criminal Responsibility for International Crimes: Exploring the Possibilities' (2013) 12 *Chinese Journal of International Law* 43; Andrew Clapham, 'Extending International Criminal Law beyond the Individual to Corporations and Armed Opposition Groups' (2008) 6 *Journal of International Criminal Justice* 899.

[110] See Jägers (n 69); Ruggie, 'Protect, Respect, and Remedy' (n 69); Ruggie, 'The Construction of the UN "Protect, Respect and Remedy" Framework for Business and Human Rights' (n 69); Davarnejad (n 93); Astrid Sanders, 'The Impact of the "Ruggie Framework" and the United Nations Guiding Principles on Business and Human Rights on Transnational Human Rights Litigation' (2014) 18 *LSE Law, Society and Economy Working Papers*; Florian Wettstein, 'Normativity, Ethics, and the UN Guiding Principles on Business and Human Rights: A Critical Assessment' (2015) 14 *Journal of Human Rights* 162.

[111] See Ruggie, 'Report of the Special Representative of the Secretary-General' (n 69).

[112] See Ruggie and Nelson (n 70).

[113] See Radu Mares, 'The Effects of CSR for the Protection of Human Rights' (2003) 7 *Mediterranean Journal of Human Rights* 113; Gilles Carbonnier, 'Corporate Responsibility and Humanitarian Action. What Relations between the Business and Humanitarian Worlds?' (2001) 83 *International Review of the Red Cross* 947; Sullivan (n 100).

[114] See Beckers (n 66); Davarnejad (n 93); Santner (n 70).

enforceable obligations; therefore, they do not directly address the liability of companies for human rights abuses.[115]

B. Litigation Against Companies in Domestic Courts

The unsatisfactory status quo detailed above caused another group of scholars and human rights activists to argue that multinational enterprises are liable in domestic courts for their extraterritorial human rights abuses. Litigators have articulated this claim in two different ways.

First, they have argued that customary international law is applicable horizontally among private parties. Therefore, it is enforceable not only against states but also against multinational companies. Their arguments combine customary international law and domestic causes of action in tort to sue multinational enterprises.[116] Specifically, in the United States, litigators have attempted to file suits on the basis of the ATS, which states: 'The district courts shall have original jurisdiction of any civil action by an alien for a tort only, committed in violation of the law of nations or a treaty of the United States.'[117] US litigators have argued that the ATS was applicable to multinational companies and referred, through the term *law of nations*, to customary international law, so that multinational enterprises should be held accountable for the violation of customary international law committed by their subsidiaries in developing countries.[118] In *Sosa v Alvarez*,[119] the US Supreme Court ruled that the ATS was a jurisdictional act, which did not create a cause of action based on customary international law, but entitled plaintiffs to bring an action in court for the violation of customary international law on the basis of a common law cause of action. Therefore, the arguments put forward against multinational companies were based in part on common law torts but also on the violation of customary international law.[120] Although this approach was successful in some cases concerning private individuals,[121] when the issue of whether customary international law and the ATS apply to foreign companies reached the US Court of Appeals for the Second Circuit and the US Supreme Court

[115] See Jerbi (n 70); Weissbrodt and Kruger (n 70) 318–35; Deva, 'Human Rights Violations' (n 4) 9–17; Wells and Elias (n 70) 154–161; Letnar Cernic (n 70) 183–216; Ruggie and Nelson (n 70); Skinner et al (n 70); Voiculescu (n 70); Clapham (n 70) 201–11; Wettstein (n 110).

[116] Giannini and Farbstein (n 72); Joseph (n 5) 21–63; Byers (n 5) 209–305; Stephens (n 86) 309–33; Giannini, Farbstein and Arend (n 86); Baughen (n 72); Enneking, 'Future of Foreign Direct Liability' (n 5).

[117] Alien's action for tort 1948 (US Code) s 1350.

[118] Giannini and Farbstein (n 72); Giannini, Farbstein and Arend (n 86); Baughen (n 72); Enneking, 'Future of Foreign Direct Liability' (n 5).

[119] *Sosa v Alvarez*, (n 72) 724.

[120] See *Kiobel v Royal Dutch Petroleum Co* [2004] Amend Cl Action Complaint Civ Action No 02 Civ 7618 KMW (SDNY); Baughen (n 72).

[121] See eg *Sarei v Rio Tinto* [2011] 9th Cir 671 F.3d 736.

in *Kiobel v Royal Dutch Petroleum*, both courts ruled in favour of the multinational company. The Second Circuit dismissed the plaintiff's claim, because it interpreted customary international law as a body of law not applicable to companies,[122] while the Supreme Court ruled in favour of the multinational company on jurisdictional grounds.[123] Furthermore, in *Jesner v Arab Bank*,[124] the US Supreme Court seemed to close the doors to parent company accountability for extraterritorial human rights abuses under the ATS. In this case, a plurality of the Supreme Court ruled that, first, in the current state of affairs, customary international law does not prescribe corporate liability for human rights abuses and, therefore, the ATS does refer to it through the term *law of nations*; and, second, domestic law could introduce corporate liability for extraterritorial human rights abuses, but Congress would have to regulate it. Litigators are using similar arguments in Canada. For instance, in the Nevsun lawsuit, victims alleged complicity of the Canadian company Nevsun in slavery, forced labour and torture crimes committed in Eritrea. The claimants argued that Nevsun violated both Canadian tort law and customary international law. Similar to the ATS litigation, one of the arguments in the Nevsun case is based on the use of private causes of actions found in Canadian tort law for the violation of customary international law. Nevsun attempted to dismiss the case on jurisdictional grounds but lost at both the district[125] and court of appeal[126] level. The appeal is currently before the Canadian Supreme Court.[127]

Second, a number of European litigators are attempting to stretch the boundaries of tort law to extend domestic causes of action to the extraterritorial human rights abuses committed by multinational companies. Although courts seem to receive this innovative approach to tort law positively, as this book will analyse in detail in Chapter 2, it is still unclear under which circumstances this line of cases applies to extraterritorial human rights abuses committed by multinational enterprises.[128]

Therefore, it is difficult to argue for the extraterritorial application of causes of action that have been designed to be applicable domestically. This approach often does not provide human rights victims with an effective remedy, because it attempts to stretch the boundaries of domestic law extraterritorially and to bypass the separate legal personality of companies.

[122] *Kiobel v Royal Dutch Petroleum* (2010) (n 5).
[123] *Kiobel v Royal Dutch Petroleum* (2013) (n 5).
[124] *Jesner v Arab Bank, PLC* (n 5).
[125] *Araya v Nevsun Resources Ltd* [2016] BCSC 1856.
[126] *Araya v Nevsun Resources Ltd* [2017] BCCA 401.
[127] 'Nevsun Lawsuit (Re Bisha Mine, Eritrea), Business & Human Rights Resource Centre', www.business-humanrights.org/en/nevsun-lawsuit-re-bisha-mine-eritrea, accessed 15 December 2018.
[128] See Meeran (n 5); Wesche and Saage-Maaß (n 5); Kamminga (n 5); Joseph (n 5); Byers (n 5) 241–305; Jägers and Heijden (n 5); Enneking, *Foreign Direct Liability and Beyond* (n 90).

C. Litigation Against States

Against this background, as an alternative avenue for legal change, this book proposes to litigate against states for their failure to secure the rights of victims against multinational enterprises. Filing suits against states would enable human rights victims to use the current state-centric structure of international law to their benefit instead of to their detriment.[129] This is for the following reasons. First, by litigating against states, the liability and extraterritorial problems would be put aside, because international law provides human rights victims with causes of action against states. This is particularly true if human rights victims attempt to file their complaints before some of the most developed human rights regional fora, such as the ECtHR or the Inter-American Court of Human Rights (IACtHR). Second, litigating against states would push for a change of the status quo. States are the only entities that have the legitimate power to change the current state of the law and recognise the role of multinational enterprises in the international arena. However, the majority of states are interested in maintaining the status quo.[130] By shifting the role of the state from a spectator to the potential perpetrator of human rights violations, victims would be able to push for the necessary changes in international and domestic laws that would acknowledge the leading role of multinational enterprises in the global arena and the responsibilities inherent in that status.

This book proposes to use the ECtHR as a tool for legal change. Specifically, it argues that, according to the ECHR, European states have a positive obligation to secure the rights of stakeholders affected by the activities of European multinational companies. This includes providing victims of extraterritorial human rights abuses with effective legal remedies and preventing multinational enterprises headquartered in Europe from abusing human rights. Therefore, victims with no effective legal remedy against European multinational enterprises in domestic courts should file cases against those states in which such companies are incorporated.

[129] Robert McCorquodale and Penelope Simons, 'Responsibility beyond Borders: State Responsibility for Extraterritorial Violations by Corporations of International Human Rights Law' (2007) 70 *MLR* 598; Olivier De Schutter, 'The Accountability of Multinationals for Human Rights Violations in European Law' in *Non-State Actors and Human Rights* (Oxford University Press, 2005); Deva, 'Human Rights Standards and Multinational Corporations' (n 4); Francesco Francioni, 'Alternative Perspectives on International Responsibility for Human Rights Violations by Multinational Corporations' in *Economic Globalisation and Human Rights* (Cambridge University Press, 2007); Nicola Jägers, *Corporate Human Rights Obligations: In Search of Accountability* (Intersentia, 2002) 137–75; Sornarajah (n 73) 155–71.

[130] See Deva, 'Human Rights Violations' (n 4); Jerbi (n 70); Weissbrodt and Kruger (n 70). As explained above, Chapter 1.III.A, recently Ecuador and South Africa proposed to adopt a binding treaty on multinational companies at the United Nations. However, a number of developed countries opposed such a treaty; see Sequensova (n 107).

This book proposes a litigation strategy that human rights activists could pursue in three main steps. First, the victims of human rights abuses should litigate their case in domestic courts. Second, if the case is unsuccessful because domestic law does not provide effective legal remedies against multinational enterprises, human rights victims should file a complaint against the relevant state at the ECtHR for its failure to secure human rights against multinational companies. The goal of this test case is to detail the responsibility of states under the ECHR. Third, once the ECtHR asserts that states have an obligation to secure the rights of victims against multinational companies, applicants could request states to provide them with effective remedies against multinationals in domestic courts. The ultimate goal of this book would be to entitle human rights victims to effective domestic remedies against multinational corporations. It advocates for the use of strategic litigation at the domestic and international level.

The role of states is fundamental to this argument, as the regulation of multinationals is within the control of the relevant states where such companies operate. States can establish effective remedies against multinational enterprises at the domestic level, and it is for the states to recognise that multinational corporations are transnational actors and, therefore, should not only have rights but also bear responsibilities towards the international community. The role of the state is to enable individuals to enjoy their rights and protect them from abuses committed by third parties.

Although international law has traditionally recognised that each state has obligations only towards its own citizens, several scholars have argued recently that states should also assume a protective role towards distant strangers.[131] In this respect, this book follows the theory proposed by Eyal Benvenisti[132] on the role of states as trustees of humanity. According to Benvenisti, although today, as never before, non-state actors are shaping and framing international law, states still hold 'the ultimate source of authority'.[133] Therefore, it is for states to act as representatives or trustees of the individuals in the international arena. Although scholars have traditionally interpreted the trust, or social contract, between states and individuals as limited to the individuals living within a certain territory, Benvenisti argues that, in a modern globalised world, states

[131] Sornarajah (n 73) 144–71; Olivier De Schutter, 'Le contrôle du respect des droits de l'homme par les sociétés transnationales: le rôle de l'état d'origine', in *Justice et mondialisation en droit du travail: du rôle du juge aux conflits alternatifs* (Dalloz, 2010); McCorquodale and Simons (n 129); Olivier De Schutter, 'Extraterritorial Jurisdiction as a Tool for Improving Human Rights Accountability for Transnational Corporations' (Business and Human Rights Resource Centre, 2006) https://www.business-humanrights.org/en/pdf-extraterritorial-jurisdiction-as-a-tool-for-improving-the-human-rights-accountability-of-transnational-corporations; Jägers (n 131) 137–75.

[132] Eyal Benvenisti, 'Sovereigns as Trustees of Humanity: On the Accountability of States to Foreign Stakeholders' (2013) 107 *American Journal of International Law* 295.

[133] ibid 296.

are constantly influencing the conduct and lives of distant strangers.[134] For these reasons, today states should act as trustees, not only of their citizens but of the whole of humanity. Benvenisti balances the statist approach, which recognises the state as the only authority in international law, and the globalist approach, according to which states are no longer at the centre of the international arena and the international community should lean towards a global constitutional system.[135] In Benvenisti's words: 'This … [approach] is not quick to endorse the demise of sovereignty. To the contrary. It regards sovereigns as key venues for policymaking. … [I]t puts faith in the power of giving voice to affected stakeholders and in the discipline of holding decision makers accountable.'[136]

Benvenisti justifies his theory with three main arguments. First, the modern world is so interconnected that the decisions taken by any state or non-state actor will influence the decision-making process of other states. As a result, domestic policies are no longer determined solely at the domestic level, but are rather defined by multiple factors outside of the democratic legislative process existing at the state level. Second, there is a democratic gap between people who have a right to vote and people who bear the consequences of such voted decisions. The policies adopted by one state affect the lives of individuals far outside its borders and, as a result, such distant strangers bear the consequences of the decisions taken by others, without being able to vote for or against such decisions. Third, many states in their domestic decision-making process often fall prey to powerful non-state actors, such as multinational enterprises. These states often lack the power to impose the will of the people whom they represent with respect to such private actors. Accordingly, non-state actors can successfully challenge, disregard or undermine the decisions of sovereign nations.[137] As a result of all these factors shaping modern international law, Benvenisti believes that modern states should have responsibilities not only towards their citizens but also towards distant strangers affected by their activities.

IV. THE PERSPECTIVE OF VICTIMS

This book investigates the remedies available to stakeholders affected by corporate activities with a particular focus on litigation.

[134] For the influence that the European Union or the United States, being some of the biggest markets in the world, have on distant strangers, see eg Joanne Scott, 'Extraterritoriality and Territorial Extension in EU Law' (2014) 62 *American Journal of Comparative Law* 87; Cedric Ryngaert, 'Whither Territoriality? The European Union's Use of Territoriality to Set Norms with Universal Effects', in *What's Wrong with International Law?: Liber Amicorum AHA Soons* (Brill/Nijhoff, 2015).

[135] Benvenisti (n 132).

[136] ibid 300.

[137] ibid.

A number of scholars have criticised this approach as often being expensive, unachievable and unfair as the power struggle between poor individuals and huge transnational companies or powerful states inevitably tends to result in a failure of the former to the benefit of the latter. Furthermore, the litigation rhetoric may polarise resources and energies through a judicialisation of social struggles, which may arguably be better resolved through the political process.[138] Despite all of these criticisms, I believe transnational litigation is a rare opportunity for people to make their voice heard at the international level. In an ever more globalised world, individuals who want to take part in the shaping of the international legal order have only a few instruments at their disposal. This is due to the fact that international law has been traditionally conceived around state sovereignty and, since the end of War World II, has also increasingly recognised the relevance of rights. Without an international sovereign, no transnational political process is possible and, therefore, the relationship between individuals and states is the preferred channel to have an impact on global law and governance.[139] Individuals have two main instruments at their disposal: pressuring their governments in order to push them to adopt a certain political agenda; or the use of rights as a legal tool to hold states accountable when they do not take their needs into consideration sufficiently. These two avenues are not contradictory, but can, and arguably should, complement each other in pushing for a change of the status quo. As this book is focused on legal, rather than political science, research, it concentrates on analysing the legal means available to individuals coming from developing countries to change the laws regulating the activities of multinational enterprises. The proposed litigation strategy aims at empowering, through the human rights language, individuals detrimentally affected by the transnational activities of corporations, with the ultimate goal of changing the laws regulating corporate conduct.

As much as this book focuses on law and the judicialisation of the social conflict between multinational enterprises and individuals, it proposes a normative agenda and demands a change in the status quo. My approach recognises that law is not neutral or apolitical but is instead a social science that serves politics.[140] The purpose of the book is to use human rights pragmatically to reconfigure the relationship between Western multinational enterprises and individuals coming from developing countries. Nevertheless, the book does not

[138] Duncan Kennedy, 'The Critique of Rights in Critical Legal Studies' in *Left Legalism/Left Critique* (Duke University Press, 2002); Susan Marks 'Human Rights in Disastrous Times' in *The Cambridge Companion to International Law* (Cambridge University Press, 2012); Amartya Sen, 'Human Rights and the Limits of Law' (2006) 27 *Cardozo Law Review* 2913.

[139] Benvenisti (n 132).

[140] Kairys (n 17); Taylor (n 17).

dismiss the concerns of companies, and it recognises that they are the fundamental tool enabling economic development.

A. Case Studies

This section analyses the following three case studies: the Bangladeshi building collapse[141] concerning workplace abuses, the Ecuadorian[142] case regarding environmental degradation, and the Nigerian case concerning militarised commerce.[143] I designed these three hypothetical case studies because they correspond to three typical human rights abuses committed by multinational companies in developing countries. In each of these case studies I assume the role of litigator representing a victim of human rights abuses from a developing country. I intentionally focus on the victims' perspective in order to demonstrate that, for various reasons, victims often suffer from a denial of justice when they attempt to sue a multinational corporate group headquartered in Europe while conducting its activities abroad through subsidiaries incorporated in developing countries. Each case study was inspired by a real case scenario which actually occurred in Bangladesh, Ecuador and Nigeria. However, this book does not take any position as it pertains to the litigation of those real-life cases.

The first case study concerns employees' rights to health and to work in a healthy environment (the 'Bangladeshi case study'). I designed the case study on the basis of the Rana Plaza building collapse in Bangladesh on 24 April 2013, and the subsequent death of more than 1,100 Bangladeshi workers. Under international law, employees' health rights are not absolute, and they may be balanced with other fundamental rights at stake in a specific case scenario. However, the members of the ILO recognise some minimum standards of protection for all workers.[144] Furthermore, in Europe, workers' rights are considered to be fundamental.[145] Finally, domestic laws regulate the rights at

[141] For a brief journalistic description of the facts, see 'Rana Plaza Tragedy: The Shocking Collapse of A Garment Factory', www.fabricoftheworld.com/rana-plaza-tragedy-collapse-of-poorly-maintained-garment-factory-in-bangladesh/, Accessed 22 June 2019.

[142] For the opposing views of NGOs and Chevron Corporation concerning the law suit, see 'ChevronToxico | The Campaign for Justice in Ecuador', http://chevrontoxico.com/, accessed 19 April 2016; 'Fraud Against Chevron | Background | Ecuador Lawsuit | Chevron', www.chevron.com/ecuador/patternoffraud/, accessed 19 April 2016.

[143] The Nigerian case is inspired by the Kiobel case discussed above: *Kiobel v Royal Dutch Petroleum Co.* (n 120); *Kiobel v Royal Dutch Petroleum* (2010) (n 5); *Kiobel v Royal Dutch Petroleum* (2013) (n 5). On militarised commerce, see also Carbonnier (n 113); Beisinghoff (n 4) 32–33.

[144] See eg International Labour Office (n 68); International Labour Office (ed), *Tripartite Declaration of Principles Concerning Multinational Enterprises and Social Policy*, 5th edn (ILO, 2017).

[145] See Jacques Velu and Rusen Ergec, *Convention européenne des droits de l'homme*, 2nd ed (Bruylant, 2014) 645–710; DJ Harris et al, *Law of the European Convention on Human Rights*,

stake in the Bangladeshi case study and provide the causes of action against each company that is part of the multinational corporate group abusing the rights of employees.

The second case study concerns the right to enjoy and live in a healthy environment (the 'Ecuadorian case study'). I designed the second case study on the basis of the environmental degradation and oil pollution which allegedly occurred in Ecuador and the litigation of the Chevron-Texaco Ecuadorian case.[146] It remains controversial whether environmental rights are the rights of the environment itself, rather than the rights of people affected by the environment.[147] However, the international community recognises that, when environmental degradation violates the rights of human beings living in a certain environment, this abuse could be labelled a human rights violation.[148]

The third case study concerns militarised commerce and the violation of absolute rights, including the right not to be tortured (the 'Nigerian case study'). The militarised commerce cases are those addressing human rights abuses in the context of '[i]ndustries retain[ing] local military forces, with known poor human rights records, to protect their operations'.[149] In these cases, multinational companies collude with the governments of developing countries to abuse the human rights of the population opposing their commercial operations.[150] I designed the case study on the basis of the alleged abuses described in *Kiobel v Royal Dutch Petroleum*. In this case, Royal Dutch Petroleum allegedly conspired with and supported the Nigerian government in committing gross human rights violations against the local population, including extrajudicial killings, crimes against humanity and torture.[151] It is recognised worldwide that some rights, such as freedom from torture, are absolute and therefore labelled *jus cogens*. These rights should never be derogated from under any circumstance in international law.[152] Despite the fact that international law forbids torture in

3rd edn (Oxford University, Press 2014) 522–90; Steve Peers et al (eds), *The EU Charter of Fundamental Rights: A Commentary* (Beck/Hart, 2014) 749–968; Sergio Bartole, Pasquale De Sena and Vladimiro Zagrebelsky (eds), *Commentario breve alla convenzione europea per la salvaguardia dei diritti dell'uomo e delle libertà fondamentali* (CEDAM, 2012) 297–370.

[146] See *Maria Aguinda Salazar y otros v Chevron Corporation* [2012] Corte Nacional de Justicia (CNJ) Judicio No 174.

[147] See Alan Boyle, 'Human Rights or Environmental Rights – A Reassessment' (2007) 18 *Fordham Environmental Law Review* 471; David R Boyd, *The Environmental Rights Revolution: A Global Study of Constitutions, Human Rights, and the Environment* (University of British Columbia Press, 2012).

[148] Boyle (n 147); Boyd (n 147); Velu and Ergec (n 145) 645–710; Harris et al (n 145) 522–90; Bartole, De Sena and Zagrebelsky (n 145) 297–370; Peers et al (n 145) 983–1003.

[149] Wells and Elias (n 70) 151; Carbonnier (n 113).

[150] See Wells and Elias (n 70).

[151] *Kiobel v Royal Dutch Petroleum Co* (n 120).

[152] See Alexidze Levan, 'Legal Nature of Jus Cogens in Contemporary International Law', *Collected Courses of the Hague Academy of International Law* (Martinus Nijhoff, 1981).

absolute terms, it is domestic law that regulates the causes of action available to victims of torture against multinational companies.[153]

I do not attempt to analyse the litigation related to the Rana Plaza,[154] Chevron or *Kiobel v Royal Dutch Petroleum* cases. The purpose of this book is to analyse what remedies would be available to human rights victims of a European multinational company with reference to these case studies. It should be noticed that, currently, a number of multinational companies are incorporated in Europe, but they establish complex supply chains in developing countries. This book will not analyse these different forms of supply chains.[155] It will focus on the easiest case of a holding company H incorporated in Europe with a fully owned subsidiary S incorporated in a developing country. The purpose of this book is to demonstrate that, even if I take into consideration the easiest and most straightforward case of incorporation aimed at limiting the liability of the holding company, European and domestic laws do not provide any effective legal remedy against H. For each case study, this book will analyse whether a human rights victim could sue the European holding company H, incorporated in the United Kingdom, for the alleged human rights abuses committed by its subsidiary S, incorporated in a developing country (being Bangladesh, Ecuador and Nigeria). In each case study, H fully owns S and controls its overall activities in the developing country.

(i) Workplace Abuses: The Bangladeshi Case Study

On 24 April 2013, the Rana Plaza building in Dhaka collapsed killing more than 1,100 and injuring thousands of Bangladeshi workers. The European and US multinational enterprises that had their production facilities in this building were allegedly paying workers less than $2 a day. According to the news reports, a few days before the collapse, some workers had noticed cracks in the wall and had alerted their employers. On 23 April, a local police inspector checked and declared the building to be unsafe and liable to collapse. However, on 24 April, a number of employers allegedly forced their employees to work against their will in the Rana Plaza building.[156]

For the purpose of this book, I do not take any position regarding the Bangladeshi building collapse and its legal consequences; instead, I will use this fact pattern and apply it to a hypothetical case study involving a British company H with subsidiary S incorporated in Bangladesh and producing

[153] See Enneking, *Foreign Direct Liability and Beyond* (n 90) 3–57; Ralph G Steinhardt, 'Corporate Responsibility and the International Law of Human Rights: The New Lex Mercatoria', in *Non-State Actors and Human Rights* (Oxford University Press, 2005); Skinner et al (n 70).

[154] See eg the criminal proceedings against Auchan that were then dismissed 'Auchan Lawsuit (Re Garment Factories in Bangladesh) | Business & Human Rights Resource Centre', http://business-humanrights.org/en/auchan-lawsuit-re-garment-factories-in-bangladesh, accessed 3 May 2016.

[155] See Sharpston (n 26).

[156] 'Rana Plaza Tragedy' (n 141).

goods in the Rana Plaza building. In this case scenario, S is undercapitalised, meaning that its capital is limited to the assets that are strictly necessary to pay for the production of goods. Every month, S distributes free cash to its parent company H so that S never holds assets beyond what is needed to ensure production in the Rana Plaza building. I will assume to be a human rights litigator representing a Bangladeshi victim, Bodhi, an employee working for S. Bodhi was working in the Rana Plaza building when it collapsed, and he was immediately rendered unconscious. Several hours later, the firefighters found him still alive under the ruins. Only after several days in hospital did Bodhi regain consciousness, but he no longer had legs, as the doctors had to amputate them in order to save his life. Bodhi is currently in need of constant medical care. Before the accident, Bodhi was working at the Rana Plaza building for the British holding company H, although he was employed by its Bangladeshi subsidiary S. A few days before the collapse, Bodhi and other employees informed their employer S that they noticed some wall cracks in the building and they did not wish to work under unsafe conditions. Their supervisor ignored these requests, reminding the workers that the Rana Plaza building was their only source of income. Bodhi was severely injured because he was forced to work under unsafe conditions.

Bodhi is seeking damages against H, the European and British holding company, as he always felt that he was an employee of the corporate group. In addition, given the limited capital of S and the number of employees seeking damages related to the Rana Plaza building collapse, Bodhi fears that S will not have enough resources to pay them all. Therefore, Bodhi decides to sue H in the UK.

(ii) Environmental Degradation: The Ecuadorian Case Study

A number of Ecuadorian indigenous people live in the territory bordering the Amazon River. Their lives depend on the river: they bathe and fish in the Amazon and drink its waters. According to the allegations filed against Chevron, in 1964 the American oil company Texaco Petroleum, which subsequently became a subsidiary of the Chevron corporate group, started to exploit oil in Ecuador with severe consequences for the Amazon rainforest and the indigenous population.[157] On the basis of these actions, some indigenous people attempted to sue Chevron in the United States, but their case was dismissed on jurisdictional grounds.[158] Therefore, they sued Chevron in Ecuador and obtained a

[157] For the opposing views of NGOs and Chevron Corporation concerning the law suit, see 'ChevronToxico' (n 142); 'Fraud Against Chevron' (n 142).

[158] *Aguinda v Texaco, Inc* [2002] US Court of Appeals 2d Cir F3d 303 470.

judgment in their favour condemning Chevron to pay several billion dollars in damages.[159] However, Chevron filed a complaint against Ecuador under the Treaty between the United States of America and Ecuador Concerning the Encouragement and Reciprocal Protection of Investment.[160] Chevron's allegations included that the Ecuadorian judgment lacked due process as it was the result of fraud and corruption. Chevron was successful, and the Permanent Court of Arbitration ruled that Ecuador should refrain from enforcing the judgment against Chevron.[161] The case is extremely complex and it is not for this book to evaluate the decisions of the US and Ecuadorian courts, or the arbitration panel. However, this case shows the lack of effective judicial remedies available to human rights victims against multinational companies.[162] After the arbitral award, the Ecuadorian plaintiffs are left with no remedies, because the US courts already dismissed their case on jurisdictional grounds[163] and the arbitration tribunal held the ruling by the Ecuadorian courts to be unenforceable.[164] Furthermore, the arbitral tribunal had no jurisdiction over human rights or environmental degradation claims, and therefore it could not assess whether Chevron abused the rights of the Ecuadorian indigenous population. Essentially, international and domestic laws provided the Ecuadorian people with a remedy only in the Ecuadorian domestic courts. Therefore, once the arbitral tribunal declared the ruling by the Ecuadorian courts unenforceable, this effectively meant that the Ecuadorian people were left without any effective remedy.

In this book, I will not take any position in relation to the Chevron litigation; instead, I will use this fact pattern and apply it to a hypothetical case study involving a European and British holding company H with subsidiary S incorporated in Ecuador. For the sake of this book, I will assume to be a human rights litigator representing an Ecuadorian victim, Elsa. Elsa is a native Ecuadorian living along the Amazon River with her family. She bathes and fishes in the Amazon, and drinks its waters. She is 50 years old and has been exposed to the Amazon River's oil degradation since childhood when S, the subsidiary of the British holding company H, started to exploit oil close to the Amazon River. Because of her constant exposure to poisoned water, Elsa suffers from severe diseases. Doctors diagnosed her with leukaemia, an illness

[159] *Maria Aguinda Salazar y otros v Chevron Corporation* (n 146).

[160] Treaty Between the United States of America and the Republic of Ecuador Concerning the Encouragement and Reciprocal Protection of Investments 1993 (Treaty Doc No 103-15).

[161] *Chevron Corporation & Texaco Petroleum Company v The Republic of Ecuador* [2018] PCA 2009–23.

[162] See Burt Neuborne, 'A Plague on Both Their Houses: A Modest Proposal for Ending the Ecuadorean Rainforest Wars' (2013) 1 *Stanford Journal of Complex Litigation* 509; Maya Steinitz and Paul Gowder, 'Transnational Litigation as a Prisoner's Dilemma' (2016) 94 *North Carolina Law Review* 751; Chiara Giorgetti, 'Mass Tort Claims in International Investment Proceedings: What Are the Lessons from the Ecuador–Chevron Dispute?' (2013) 34 *University of Pennsylvania Journal of International Law* 787.

[163] *Aguinda v Texaco, Inc* (n 158).

[164] *Chevron Corporation & Texaco Petroleum Company v The Republic of Ecuador* (n 161).

that affects most of the women living in that area. Independent experts have declared that the incidence of leukaemia in the area increased 100-fold since S started spilling oil into the Amazon River. Because of the oil exploitation by S, Elsa's life is under threat.

Elsa is seeking damages against the British company H, as she feels it was H's responsibility, as one of the largest oil corporations, to ensure that its subsidiary used sustainable technology to extract the oil. Elsa also believes that H took advantage of using an underdeveloped exploitation technology in Ecuador and made millions by exploiting the river belonging to her indigenous community.

(iii) Militarised Commerce: The Nigerian Case Study

Royal Dutch Shell has been allegedly cooperating with the Nigerian government to exploit oil in Nigeria. Specifically, the state-owned Nigerian National Petroleum Company is part of a joint venture which also includes a subsidiary of the Royal Dutch Shell Group. At the beginning of the 1990s, the Ogoni people, a population living in Nigeria in the exploited areas, started a protest against Royal Dutch Shell's oil exploitation that allegedly caused them severe health and environmental distress.[165] The Nigerian government reacted to the protest by allegedly killing, raping, torturing, and arresting the Ogoni population. Kiobel was one of the protesters who was sentenced to death. His wife was granted asylum in the United States and sued Shell in that country. The allegations against Royal Dutch Shell included a conspiracy with the Nigerian government to terrorise the Ogoni civilians and stop their demonstrations. The case went all the way to the Supreme Court, which dismissed it on jurisdictional grounds.[166]

For the purpose of this book, I will not take any position with regard to the *Kiobel v Royal Dutch Petroleum Co* litigation; instead, I will use this fact pattern and apply it to a hypothetical case study involving a British holding company H with a subsidiary S incorporated in Nigeria. I will assume to be a human rights litigator representing an Ogoni Nigerian victim. Naoki was a farmer working in Nigeria nearby the area where S was exploiting oil. Since S started extracting oil in the area close to his field, Naoki's family was no longer able to survive. Fruits or vegetables no longer grew in his field, and the entire family was starving. Neighbouring farmers were experiencing the same land degradation. One day they got together and organised a demonstration against S's oil exploitation. They sought to stop S's oil exploitation in farming areas and obtain reparation for the environmental damage inflicted on their soil. They also argued that the

[165] Fons Coomans, 'The Ogoni Case Before the African Commission on Human and Peoples' Rights' (2003) 52 *ICLQ* 749.

[166] See *Kiobel v Royal Dutch Petroleum Co* (n 120); *Kiobel v Royal Dutch Petroleum* (2013) (n 5).

Nigerian government unfairly allowed a foreign company, which never contributed to Nigeria's development, to obtain the benefits from exploiting Nigerian oil. With H's monetary support, the government answered violently and shot at the crowd. Many people were imprisoned and tortured, including Naoki. He was arrested for allegedly helping a violent person, a friend shot in the arm by the police. He spent more than a month in prison and was regularly subjected to torture until he was finally released. While Naoki was in prison, soldiers came to his farm, destroyed his home, and beat and assaulted his relatives. After the demonstrations, the entire world became aware of what had happened to Naoki and the other farmers in Nigeria. The international community and the UN expressed deep concern for the victims and sought their release. Nevertheless, H and S did not take any position against the Nigerian government's actions. Instead, they continued to finance the Nigerian government to protect their oil monopoly.

Naoki is seeking damages against the British holding company H, as he believes that H conspired with the Nigerian government to suppress the demonstrations. Naoki also believes that suing S before the Nigerian judiciary, would be useless given the alignment of interests of the Nigerian government and the multinational enterprise. Instead, Naoki is suing H in the United Kingdom, as he believes H to be the British multinational power that completely ruined his life.

(iv) The UK Home State

The main problems pertaining to holding multinational enterprises accountable are the limited liability of the parent companies for the torts committed by their subsidiary(ies) and the limited territorial reach of domestic tort and company laws. For this reason, I designed my case studies with a European parent company and a subsidiary abusing human rights outside of Europe. An important issue in this regard was where to incorporate such a European parent company, because it is on the basis of the domestic laws where such company is incorporated that this book would assess whether stakeholders affected by its corporate activities have effective remedies.

On the basis of the recent developments in the business and human rights debate in different European domestic systems,[167] I chose to incorporate H, the holding company of a multinational company group, in the United Kingdom for the following reasons.

First, with the cases *Lungowe v Vedanta*[168] and *Chandler v Cape Plc*[169], English courts have recently established the duty of care that a parent company

[167] Skinner et al (n 70).
[168] *Vedanta Resources PLC and another v Lungowe and others* [2019] UKSC 20.
[169] *Chandler v Cape Plc* [2012] (QB), X (appeal taken from Eng) EWCA Civ 525.

owes towards its subsidiaries' neighbours.[170] This jurisprudence became a persuasive body of law in a number of countries, including not only common law countries, but also civil law countries within the European Union. For example, recently Dutch courts have applied English case-law against the multinational company Royal Dutch Shell[171] with respect to the alleged torts committed by Royal Dutch Shell in Nigeria. Furthermore, the case-law concerning the duty of care of the parent company has also influenced legislative proposals in France and Switzerland. France has in fact adopted ad hoc legislation detailing the parent companies' duty of care for the torts committed by their subsidiaries,[172] while the Swiss parliament is currently assessing similar proposals.[173] Although France arguably has the most advanced piece of legislation on business and human rights, its application is unclear, as the French parliament passed the law only in 2017 after a difficult parliamentary debate lasting two years. To date, no French court has applied the law in court. Furthermore, as analysed in Chapter 5, a number of critical interpretative questions on the law are still open for debate. Therefore, this book designed the three case studies as having the parent company in the United Kingdom, because UK courts have been developing a promising jurisprudence potentially applicable to multinational enterprises abusing human rights abroad.

Second, in September 2013 the United Kingdom became the first jurisdiction to adopt the National Action Plan (NAP) to give effect to the UN Guiding Principles. Furthermore, in 2016 the United Kingdom also published an Update on its NAP. The UK NAP and its Update specifically recognised that the United

[170] See Meeran (n 5).

[171] *Akpan v Royal Dutch Shell Plc* [2015] (n 5); *Akpan v Royal Dutch Shell Plc* [2013] (n 5); Enneking, 'Future of Foreign Direct Liability' (n 5).

[172] Loi 2017-399 du 27 mars 2017 relative au devoir de vigilance des sociétés mères et des entreprises donneuses d'ordre 2017 (JORF); Bruno Le Roux, No 2578–Proposition de loi de M Bruno Le Roux relative au devoir de vigilance des sociétés mères et des entreprises donneuses d'ordre 2015; Xavier Delpech, 'Bientôt un devoir de vigilance à la charge des sociétés mères et des donneurs d'ordre' [2015] *Dalloz Actualité*; Nicolas Cuzacq, 'Le devoir de vigilance des sociétés mères et des donneurs d'ordre', in *La RSE saisi par le droit: perspectives interne et internationale* (Pedone, 2015); Renée-Claude Drouin, 'Le développement du contentieux à l'encontre des entreprises transnationales: Quel rôle pour le devoir de vigilance?' [2016] *Droit Social* 246; Pauline Dufourq, 'Devoir de vigilance des multinationales : quelles évolutions ?' [2017] *Dalloz Actualité*; Paul Mougeolle, 'Sur la conformité constitutionnelle de la proposition de loi relative au devoir de vigilance des sociétés mères et des entreprises donneuses d'ordre. Responsabilité juridique des entreprises' [2017] *La Revue des droits de l'homme*; Pierre-Louis Périn, 'Devoir de vigilance et responsabilité illimitée: Qui trop embrasse mal étreint' [2015] *Revue trimestrielle de droit commercial et de droit économique* 215.

[173] 'Conseil National Session de Printemps 2015 Neuvième Séance 11.03.15 15h00 14.3671' (2015) www.parlament.ch/fr/ratsbetrieb/amtliches-bulletin/amtliches-bulletin-die-verhandlungen?SubjectId=35082, accessed 6 June 2016; 'Responsible Business Initiative – The Initiative', http://konzern-initiative.ch/initiativtext/?lang=en, accessed 26 April 2018; RK-N, 'Eidgenössische Volksinitiative "Für verantwortungsvolle Unternehmen – zum Schutz von Mensch und Umwelt" Indirekter Gegenentwurf' 2018, https://www.parlament.ch/centers/documents/de/dok-gegenentwurf-mm-rk-n-2018-05-04.pdf; 'Tight Parliamentary Rejection of the Initiative "Clear Rules for Swiss Transnational Companies, Worldwide"', www.humanrights.ch/en/switzerland/foreign-affairs/foreign-trade/transnational/campaign-rights-borders, accessed 9 June 2016.

Kingdom has a duty to take action against human rights violations of companies that are under its jurisdiction.[174]

Third, the OECD UK NCP has the most exhaustive jurisprudence by number of specific instances taken into consideration. Although non-binding, its decisions are sophisticated and directly address both the extraterritorial and the limited liability of the parent companies.[175]

Therefore, I concluded that incorporating the parent company H for the purpose of the case studies in the United Kingdom would have provided the opportunity to analyse one of the most progressive legal regimes in Europe as it pertains to the extraterritorial liability of multinational companies. Despite the progressive nature of the UK judicial and non-judicial mechanisms, Chapter 2 concludes that, except for a limited number of cases, stakeholders affected by corporate activities do not have a significant means of redress against multinational enterprises abusing their human rights extraterritorially.

B. Normative Argument

This book builds up a normative argument to reconfigure the relationship between multinational enterprises headquartered in Europe and individuals coming from developing countries. It proposes an innovative business and human rights litigation strategy to advocate for a change of the current state of the law. The goal is to empower victims who come from developing countries to take action against European states that are not holding multinational enterprises accountable for human rights abuses. It argues that, when victims are unable to obtain redress at the national level, they could file complaints against states at the ECtHR for a lack of effective legal remedies against European multinational companies. The ultimate goal is to obtain a decision of the ECtHR detailing the positive obligation of states to secure that European corporate groups respect human rights while operating extraterritorially. Following such a decision, European states would have to provide effective remedies against multinational companies in domestic courts. This would open the door to legal reforms aimed

[174] See HM Government, 'Good Business Implementing the UN Guiding Principles on Business and Human Rights', www.gov.uk/government/uploads/system/uploads/attachment_data/file/236901/BHR_Action_Plan_-_final_online_version_1_.pdf, accessed 20 April 2016; 'UK Open Government National Action Plan 2016–18', www.gov.uk/government/publications/uk-open-government-national-action-plan-2016-18/uk-open-government-national-action-plan-2016-18, accessed 2 December 2016; Marco Fasciglione, 'Corporate Human Rights Responsibility, States' Duty to Protect and UN GPS' National Action Plans: Some Thoughts after the UK NAP Update' (2016) 1 *European Papers* 621.

[175] Ruggie and Nelson (n 70); Santner (n 70); Davarnejad (n 93); Department for Business, Innovation & Skills, 'UK National Contact Point: Procedures for Complaints Brought under the OECD Guidelines for Multinational Enterprises', www.gov.uk/government/publications/uk-national-contact-point-procedures-for-complaints-brought-under-the-oecd-guidelines-for-multinational-enterprises, accessed 22 April 2016.

at regulating the liability of European multinational enterprises for extraterritorial human rights abuses.

The book develops such a normative argument through the following steps, each corresponding to a chapter.

First, the book assesses the legal remedies currently available to the victims of human rights abuses originating in host states against a holding company incorporated in a European home state. The issue is whether, under international, EU and domestic UK law, the victims in the three case studies have an effective means of redress against the UK holding company H. I conclude that there are no such means of redress for the following reasons. International law does not provide a liability framework for holding multinational enterprises accountable for human rights abuses. The only sources that take into account the extraterritorial activities of multinational corporations are soft international law rules, which are not binding. EU law is equally failing to regulate the accountability regime applicable to multinational corporations abusing human rights. However, EU law sets out the conflict-of-laws rules applicable to extraterritorial tort law cases directed against multinational companies. These laws do not take into account human rights abuses. As a result, European courts may apply the place-of-injury law, even if that law could be a shield for the perpetrator of an extraterritorial human rights abuse. As it pertains to domestic tort and company laws, although they regulate the liability of companies within their national system, they are of limited application to multinational enterprises incorporated in a number of different countries. Only in limited cases does UK tort law hold a parent company accountable for the damage committed by its subsidiary or for its failure to prevent such damage. As a result, the victims of human rights abuses from developing countries have little chance to hold European multinational enterprises accountable successfully. European states do not provide them with effective remedies in domestic courts.

Second, the book demonstrates that the failure of European states to secure human rights protection against European multinational enterprises is a violation of the ECHR. I conduct this part of the analysis on the basis of the jurisprudence of the ECtHR on the positive obligations of states to secure human rights. I refer to the distinction between the duty to protect and fulfil to address two elements of the obligation to secure. The duty to protect requires states to establish a functioning state apparatus and therefore to provide victims of human rights abuses with effective remedies against private parties. The duty to fulfil is a *best-effort* obligation for states to progressively prevent human rights abuses. I set up such duties as obligations to provide effective remedies against multinational enterprises and to progressively prevent corporations from abusing human rights.

Third, the book argues for an extraterritorial application of the duties of European states when companies headquartered in Europe abuse human rights in developing countries. This argument includes an analysis of the

ECtHR case-law and the scholarly debate on extraterritoriality. I refer to the Maastricht Principles as a conceptual basis to understand the application of the jurisprudence of the ECtHR to the extraterritorial human rights abuses committed by multinational enterprises. My conclusion is that European states have a positive obligation to secure the human rights of distant strangers against European multinational corporations. I apply such a positive obligation to the three case studies concerning the holding company H incorporated in the United Kingdom, the subsidiaries of which abuse human rights in developing countries. I argue that, in such a hypothetical cases, the victims could file a complaint against the United Kingdom at the ECtHR for its failure to secure their rights against the holding company H.

Fourth, the book proposes some avenues for legal change that European states could implement to provide victims with effective remedies against multinational corporations and to prevent the human rights abuses committed by such companies. These proposals include either recognising multinationals as subjects of international law with responsibilities for their actions at the international level, or, in the alternative, reforming the conflict-of-laws rules, tort and company laws at the domestic level so that they will regulate the extraterritorial activities of multinational enterprises. Furthermore, I propose to reorient the trade and investment policies of European countries, so that they take into consideration the impact that the extraterritorial activities of European multinational enterprises have on human rights.

2

*The Obligations of Multinational Companies**

WHEN A SHAREHOLDER incorporates a limited liability company, it creates a separate legal person for which liability is limited to the assets the company owns. Governments grant such a privilege to companies in order to promote business. A trader is incentivised to invest its money in a business knowing that the risk is limited to the value of the shares it is willing to buy. The combination of separate legal personality and limited liability is one of the cornerstones of our modern economy, and of the financial and capital markets.[1] However, globalisation puts this economic model at risk and shows its limits. Multinational companies can take advantage of different national systems and avoid liability by establishing complex chains of subsidiaries and engaging in various contractual relationships that are subjected to different legal regimes. As a result, Western companies can take advantage of the highest standard of protection of their commercial interests in developed economies, while outsourcing their production, often according to the lowest human rights standards, in developing countries.[2] This is not to say that such outsourcing is triggered exclusively by lower human rights standards. However,

*This chapter is partly included in the following articles. Dalia Palombo, 'The Duty of Care of the Parent Company: A Comparison between French Law, UK Precedents and the Swiss Proposals' (2019) 4 *BHRJ* 265; Dalia Palombo 'Chandler v Cape: An Alternative to Piercing the Corporate Veil Beyond Kiobel v Royal Dutch Shell' (2015)4 *BJALS*, 453.

[1] See Karen Vanderkerckhove, *Piercing the Corporate Veil* (Kluwer/Aspen, 2007) 3–9; Andrew Gamble and Gavin Kelly, 'The Politics of the Company', in *The Political Economy of the Company* (Hart Publishing, 2001) 29–34; Mads Tønnesson Andenæs and Frank Wooldridge, *European Comparative Company Law* (Cambridge University Press, 2009) 109–30; David Kershaw, *Company Law in Context: Text and Materials*, 2nd edn (Oxford University Press, 2012) 3–46.

[2] See Aurora Voiculescu, 'Human Rights and the Normative Ordering of Global Capitalism', in *The Business of Human Rights: An Evolving Agenda for Corporate Responsibility* (Zed Books, 2011); Surya Deva, 'Human Rights Violations by Multinational Corporations and International Law: Where from Here?' (2003) 19 *Connecticut Journal of International Law* 1; Surya Deva, 'Human Rights Standards and Multinational Corporations: Dilemma between "Home" and "Rome"' (2003) 7 *Mediterranean Journal of Human Rights* 69; Philip Alston (ed), *Non-State Actors and Human Rights* (Oxford University Press, 2005) 141–350; Niels Beisinghoff, *Corporations and Human Rights: An Analysis of ATCA Litigation against Corporations* (Peter Lang, 2009) 13–41; Andrew Clapham, *Human Rights Obligations of Non-State Actors* (Oxford University Press, 2006) 195–270; Menno T Kamminga, 'Holding Multinational Corporations Accountable for Human Rights Abuses: A Challenge for the EC', in *The EU and Human Rights* (Oxford University Press 1999); Olufemi

lower production costs, including lower liability costs, are some of the main reasons that drive Western companies to outsource their production. This is possible because international, EU and domestic laws do not provide the victims of human rights abuses with comprehensive remedy frameworks applicable to multinational companies.[3]

The purpose of this chapter is to analyse what are (if any) the responsibilities of companies under international, EU and UK law. It will analyse the different remedies available to the victims that could be used against European multinational companies that abuse human rights extraterritorially.

I. REMEDIES IN THE HOST STATE

This section will consider the remedies available in the host state against the subsidiary S, as it may seem obvious that tort victims suffering from wrongful acts of S should first attempt to sue the subsidiary in host state courts. The reasons why the business and human rights movement, in general, and this book, in particular, focuses on the responsibility of parent companies incorporated in developed countries, rather than on the accountability of their subsidiaries incorporated in developing countries, is the lack of an effective means of redress for victims who attempt to hold such subsidiaries accountable in the host state. There are three main reasons why bringing an action against a subsidiary operating in a developing country is often, in the real world, a dead-end option.

A. Undercapitalisation

As exemplified by the Bangladeshi case study, multinational enterprises often limit the liability of their foreign subsidiary to the absolute minimum necessary to carry out a local commercial activity. The current structure of corporate law

Amao, *Corporate Social Responsibility, Human Rights and the Law: Multinational Corporations in Developing Countries* (Routledge 2011).

[3] See Antonio Gigante, 'La politica delle istituzioni comunitarie in materia di responsabilitá sociale d'impresa: voluntary o mandatory approach?' (2008) IV *Diritto pubblico comparato ed europeo* 1991; Claire Bright, 'L'accès à la justice civile en cas de violations des droits de l'homme par des entreprises multinationales' (2013) http://cadmus.eui.eu/handle/1814/29602, accessed 15 April 2016; Deva, 'Human Rights Violations' (n 2); Deva, 'Human Rights Standards' (n 2); Alexandra Gatto, *Multinational Enterprises and Human Rights: Obligations under EU Law and International Law* (Edward Elgar, 2011) 174–82; Sébastien Touzé, 'L'approche communautaires de la responsabilité sociale des entreprises' (2009) 19 *Schweizerische Zeitschrift für internationales und europäischees Recht = Revue suisse de droit internationale et européen* 7; Deborah Russo, 'La promozione della responsabilità sociale d'impresa nell'Unione europea' (2011) XVI *Il diritto dell'Unione europea* 477; Giovanni Esposito and Anna Carobolante, 'Imporre o invitare? Le politiche di corporate social responsibility alla ricerca di un'identità europea' (2013) 8 *Ianus-Diritto e finanza* 5; Sorcha Macleod, 'Reconciling Regulatory Approaches to Corporate Social Responsibility: The European Union, OECD and United Nations Compared' (2007) 13 *European Public Law* 671; Liesbeth Enneking, 'Crossing the Atlantic – The Political and Legal Feasibility of European Foreign Direct Liability

results in an incentive to pursue business by undercapitalising local subsidiaries.[4] This is beneficial to holding companies from a risk-management perspective.

Using a simple mathematical example to demonstrate how this incentive works in practice, assume that a European company, which holds assets worth €1,000,000, is interested in pursuing a business project in a developing country and pursuing that project requires an investment of €100,000. Further assume that the European company, having undertaken a careful business analysis of the project, decided that it has a 50 per cent chance of tripling its money and earning €300,000, a 20 per cent chance of losing half of its money and ending up with €50,000, and a 30 per cent chance of increasing its profit by a half, and earning €150,000. Prior to deciding whether it will invest in the project, the company would calculate the total expected return of its prospective investment, which would be equal to (1/2 × 300,000) + (1/5 × 50,000) + (3/10 × 150,000) = 150,000 + 10,000 + 45,000 = €205,000. Accordingly, the project would be a good investment, because the expected return is positive. The company invests €100,000 and has an expected return of €205,000. As a result, the expected profits are in the amount of €105,000 (€205,000 expected return minus €100,000 invested into the project). On such an investment, the company has no particular incentive to engage in additional structuring to limit its liability: this project will generate profits; it can pursue such a project in its own name.

Assume, however, that the same European company, which always owns €1,000,000, would like to invest €100,000 in a foreign project that has a negative expected return. For example, after completing its preliminary analysis of the project, the company concludes that it has a 50 per cent chance of tripling its money and earning €300,000, a 20 per cent chance of incurring a liability in the amount of €1,000,000 (because, for example, the relevant project relates to offshore oil drilling carrying substantial environmental risks), and a 30 per cent chance of losing €60,000. The company would calculate the expected return of this investment: (1/2 × 300,000) + (1/5 × –1,000,000) + (3/10 × –60,000) = 150,000 – 200,000 – 18,000 = – €68,000. Now the prospective project would be a bad investment, because the expected return is negative. The company will make an original investment of €100,000 in the project which could generate losses in the amount of €68,000, bringing its total losses related to the implementation of the project to €168,000. As a result, if the company can pursue such a project only in its own name, it will not invest and will avoid the project, which carries substantial environmental risks. However, the above economic analysis drastically changes if one permits the European company to pursue such a project not in its own name but through a locally incorporated subsidiary, a limited

Cases' (2008) 40 *George Washington International Law Review* 903; Markos Karavias, *Corporate Obligations under International Law* (Oxford University Press 2013) 68–115.

[4] Kershaw (n 1) 776–81; David W Leebron, 'Limited Liability, Tort Victims, and Creditors' (1991) 91 *Columbia Law Review* 1565; Phillip I Blumberg, 'Limited Liability and Corporate Groups' (1985) 11 *The Journal of Corporate Law* 573.

liability entity, with share capital equal to €100,000 (ie the investment required to pursue the project). The subsidiary would still have a 50 per cent chance of tripling the money and earning €300,000. However, the 20 per cent chance of incurring liability in the amount of €1,000,000 would now be limited to only the €100,000 that the European company committed to the share capital of its subsidiary. Finally, a 30 per cent chance of incurring losses in the amount of €60,000 remains the third expected scenario of how an investment may develop. The company would calculate the expected return of this investment as follows: (1/2 × 300,000) + (1/5 × –100,000) + (3/10 × – 60,000) = 150,000 – 20,000 – 18,000 = €112,000. As a result, from being significantly loss making, the project becomes revenue generating: the European company has invested €100,000 in a project that is expected to generate a return of €112,000, leaving a modest profit of €12,000. Limited liability transferred the potential losses from the investor to the third-party creditors, including local communities which ran a huge risk of environmental pollution arising in connection with the implementation of the project. It becomes evident that limited liability creates an incentive for investors to pursue economically loss-making projects by way of transferring the risks related to such projects to relevant stakeholders, ie creating negative externalities.[5]

Another effect of this corporate engineering is that an international investor is incentivised to contribute as little as possible to the assets of the subsidiary and, in any case, to contribute less than would be required to cover any potential damage that could be caused by the subsidiary. As in the above hypothetical example, an investor could have obviously contributed the total of €1,000,000, which it had to cover any potential environmental damage risks. This, however, would make the project unprofitable. It is, therefore, evident that there exists a clear economic incentive for international investors to use the limited liability of their subsidiaries to shift relevant risks related to the hazardous activities which they pursue to local communities and, by doing so, they turn potentially loss-generating projects into profitable undertakings. It is evident, however, that, in such cases, it makes no sense for victims of human rights abuses caused by such subsidiaries to file a complaint against the subsidiaries themselves: such subsidiaries would often have no assets with which to compensate the victims in full. A Bangladeshi victim of human rights abuses, such as Bodhi, would therefore not be compensated if he filed a claim against the local subsidiary S which directly abused his human rights. Accordingly, he can attempt to file a complaint against the parent company H, which will have the financial capacity to sustain the liability arising from human rights abuses committed by its subsidiary.

[5] Kershaw (n 1) 776–81; Leebron (n 4); Blumberg (n 4).

B. Investment Law

As exemplified by the Ecuadorian case, investment law may make the rulings of a host state's national courts unenforceable against investors.[6] BITs are treaties signed by developing countries with the objective of attracting foreign investors by guaranteeing them a number of core rights. They often include an arbitration clause, according to which an arbitration tribunal has jurisdiction over disputes between investors and the host state. This permits an investor to avoid any litigation in host state domestic courts, as complaints can be brought directly to arbitration tribunals.[7] In fact, BITs are usually drafted to ensure that arbitration would substitute the domestic justice system and the investor will not have to exhaust any domestic remedy in the host state prior to bringing an action before the arbitration tribunal. BITs will further typically include a guarantee against undue expropriation and of fair and equitable treatment. Historically, such provisions were introduced to prevent the host state from expropriating the assets of an investor without compensation.[8] However, a recently emerging problem is that sometimes anti-expropriation and fair and equitable treatment clauses are drafted in such terms that arbitration tribunals have interpreted them broadly as preventing host states from enforcing domestic laws or judgments which could impose any sort of monetary obligation on an investor. The rationale behind such an interpretation given by arbitration tribunals is essentially that the enforcement of any law that could result in a loss for an investor is, in fact, an expropriation or an unfair treatment.[9]

In *Starret Housing Corporation v Iran*,[10] the Iran–US Claims Tribunal decided that the term 'expropriation' included not only the nationalisation of the company's assets. In this case, Starret Housing Corporation alleged that, due to the abrupt change of the regime in Iran and the subsequent collapse

[6] See Burt Neuborne, 'A Plague on Both Their Houses: A Modest Proposal for Ending the Ecuadorean Rainforest Wars' (2013) 1 *Stanford Journal of Complex Litigation* 509; Maya Steinitz and Paul Gowder, 'Transnational Litigation as a Prisoner's Dilemma' (2016) 94 *North Carolina Law Review* 751; Chiara Giorgetti, 'Mass Tort Claims in International Investment Proceedings: What Are the Lessons from the Ecuador–Chevron Dispute?' (2013) 34 *University of Pennsylvania Journal of International Law* 787.

[7] M Sornarajah, *The International Law on Foreign Investment*, 3rd edn (Cambridge University Press, 2010) 172–235; Rudolf Dolzer and Christoph Schreuer, *Principles of International Investment Law*, 2nd edn (Oxford University Press, 2012) 130–215.

[8] Sornarajah (n 7) 172–235; Olivier De Schutter, 'Le contrôle du respect des droits de l'homme par les sociétés transnationales: le rôle de l'état d'origine', in *Justice et mondialisation en droit du travail: du rôle du juge aux conflits alternatifs* (Dalloz, 2010); Robin Broad, 'Corporate Bias in the World Bank Group's International Centre for Settlement of Investment Disputes: A Case Study of a Global Mining Corporation Suing El Salvador' (2015) 36 *University of Pennsylvania Journal of International Law* 851; Dolzer and Schreuer (n 7) 130–215; Giorgetti (n 6); Dolzer and Schreuer (n 7) 130–215.

[9] Sornarajah (n 7) 172–235; De Schutter (n 8); Broad (n 8); Dolzer and Schreuer (n 7) 130–215; Giorgetti (n 6).

[10] *Starret Housing Corporation v Iran* [1983] Iran-US CTR 4, 122.

of the Iranian banking system, the Republic of Iran effectively prevented the company from using its apartment building for commercial purposes. The Iran–US Claims Tribunal held:

> It is recognised in international law that measures taken by a State can interfere with property rights to such an extent that these rights are rendered so useless that they must be deemed to have been expropriated, even though the State does not purport to have expropriated them and the legal title to the property formally remains with the original owner.[11]

On a similar legal basis, various investors have attempted to file complaints against host states for violations of expropriation and fair and equitable treatment clauses included in BITs, even if host states did not expropriate any assets of the investor directly.[12] The argument is typically framed in a way that any law, including any public interest-oriented law, such as, for example, a law imposing higher human rights or environmental standards, could result in a loss of profit to an investor. It could, therefore, be considered an expropriation or an unfair and unequal treatment not permitted under a BIT.[13]

An example that raised great concern among human rights activists and scholars is Canadian Pacific Rim Mining Corporation's (later on acquired by OceanaGold Corporation) ownership of Pac Rim Cayman LLC, a US-based company operating in El Salvador through its foreign subsidiaries. Pac Rim Cayman LLC filed, on its own and its subsidiaries' behalf, a complaint before the International Centre for Settlement of Investment Disputes (ICSID) after El Salvador decided to limit mining concessions in order to protect its environment.[14] The allegations included that, by adopting a de facto mining ban, El Salvador violated investment law because it unfairly deprived the corporate group's investment of value. The facts of the case merit being set out in some detail. El Salvador granted to the corporate group some exploration licences that the companies had used since the beginning of the twenty-first century for mining purposes. However, the local population became disenchanted with the possibility of benefiting from the investment and increasingly rejected mining. As a result, El Salvador decided to limit mining within its territory. These limitations also affected the Pacific Rim corporations, which could not meet the requirements prescribed by El Salvadorian law to renew their exploration licences and obtain an exploitation concession. Pac Rim Cayman LLC filed a complaint at the ISCID arguing that El Salvador had banned mining in violation of investment law.[15]

[11] ibid 154.

[12] Sornarajah (n 7) 172–235; De Schutter (n 8); Broad (n 8); Dolzer and Schreuer (n 7) 130–215; Giorgetti (n 6).

[13] See Broad (n 8); Giorgetti (n 6).

[14] 'Lawsuit against El Salvador Mining Ban Highlights Free Trade Pitfalls | Guardian Sustainable Business', *The Guardian*, www.theguardian.com/sustainable-business/2015/may/27/pacific-rim-lawsuit-el-salvador-mine-gold-free-trade, accessed 11 July 2016.

[15] Broad (n 8) *Pac Rim Cayman LLC v Republic of El Salvador* [2016] ICSID ARB/09/12.

Various scholars and human rights bodies are critical of such an interpretation of BITs.[16] For instance, in its latest 2015 Report, the UN Special Rapporteur on the Right to Food expressed deep concern with respect to the adverse impact that investment arbitration has on the enjoyment of human rights in host states. Specifically, the Special Rapporteur criticised arbitration clauses entitling investors to international causes of action against states as a threat to democracy, because such arbitration proceedings undermine the public-law-oriented decisions of democratic governments. According to the Special Rapporteur, by limiting mining, the El Salvador government was implementing the will of the El Salvadorian people, and it is inconceivable that this could be overridden by a decision of an arbitration tribunal. Accordingly, investment law entitles arbitration tribunals to effectively prevent democratically elected governments from implementing public-interest-oriented regulations.[17] In the end, the ISCID arbitral tribunal decided the case in favour of El Salvador, in a decision that is possibly the first significant victory for developing countries against a multinational corporation which intended to protect its mining licences.[18] However, the proceedings are telling, as they demonstrate how multinational companies may use investment arbitration to prevent host countries from adopting public-interest-oriented legislation[19] or, as was the case in Ecuador, from enforcing a judgment against a foreign investor.[20]

It is beyond the scope of this book to address the legitimacy of the investment law regime and whether it is just in principle. However, it is important to note that investment law may, as a practical matter, limit the efficiency of bringing a lawsuit against subsidiary S incorporated in the host state which is responsible for human rights abuses, because the holding company H might be able to challenge any such domestic decision awarding damages to the victims of human rights abuses under the relevant BIT as an unfair expropriation of its assets or unfair and unequal treatment. Therefore, a victim of human rights abuses, such as, for example, the victim of environmental degradation in Ecuador, Elsa, may

[16] Sornarajah (n 7) 144–71; Fons Coomans and Rolf Künnemann (eds), *Cases and Concepts on Extraterritorial Obligations in the Area of Economic, Social and Cultural Rights* (Intersentia, 2012) 5–102; De Schutter (n 8); Olivier De Schutter, 'Extraterritorial Jurisdiction as a Tool for Improving Human Rights Accountability for Transnational Corporations' (Business and Human Rights Resource Centre, 2006) https://www.business-humanrights.org/en/pdf-extraterritorial-jurisdiction-as-a-tool-for-improving-the-human-rights-accountability-of-transnational-corporations; Joseph E Stiglitz, 'Multinational Corporations: Balancing Rights and Responsibilities' (2007) 101 *Proceedings of the ASIL Annual Meeting* 3; James Harrison, 'Human Rights Arguments in Amicus Curiae Submissions: Promoting Social Justice?', in *Human Rights in International Investment Law and Arbitration* (Oxford University Press, 2009); Ryan Suda, 'The Effect of Bilateral Investment Treaties on Human Rights Enforcement and Realization', in *Transnational Corporations and Human Rights* (Hart Publishing, 2006).

[17] Hilal Elver, 'Report of the Special Rapporteur on the Right to Food' (2015) UN Doc A/HRC/28/65.

[18] *Pac Rim Cayman LLC v Republic of El Salvador* (n 15) .

[19] Broad (n 8).

[20] *Chevron Corporation & Texaco Petroleum Company v The Republic of Ecuador* [2018] PCA 2009–23.

prefer to file a lawsuit in the home state's domestic courts, rather than in the jurisdiction in which subsidiary S operates.

C. Complicity

As exemplified by the Nigerian case study, a host state may be an accomplice of a corporate group in abusing human rights.[21] This is especially evident in cases of militarised commerce, when host states and companies jointly violate human rights. For instance, in parallel to the *Kiobel v Royal Dutch Petroleum* case filed against Royal Dutch Shell, the Ogoni people also filed a complaint against Nigeria at the African Commission on Human and Peoples' Rights (AfrCoHPR). The allegations included the active involvement of Nigeria in terrorising the local population and violating the Ogoni people's environmental rights, as well as their rights to life, property and health. The AfrCoHPR concluded that Nigeria violated the rights of the Ogoni people by actively participating in the destruction of their land and environment as an accomplice of the oil companies. Nigeria refused to take part in these proceedings, and the decisions of the AfrCoHPR are neither binding nor enforceable against African states.[22] However, it is telling that an independent international quasi-judicial body established the collusion of the government with a multinational company resulting in the violation of human rights.

Against this background, if a human rights victim, such as the Nigerian victim, Naoki, would attempt to file a complaint in Nigeria (the host state) for the human rights abuses perpetrated by subsidiary S, there would be a significant risk that his case would be unsuccessful. If the host state and the multinational company are accomplices in violating human rights, the victims have little chance of succeeding in the domestic courts of the host state and have no meaningful way to seek justice other than by filing a complaint in the home state.

Therefore, the three case studies that I proposed to illustrate the practical application of this book exemplify three situations in which filing a complaint against the subsidiary S in the host state would be useless. Often victims of human rights abuses would have little chance in real life to obtain redress against multinational companies in host states. Accordingly, this book focuses

[21] Gilles Carbonnier, 'Corporate Responsibility and Humanitarian Action. What Relations between the Business and Humanitarian Worlds?' (2001) 83 *International Review of the Red Cross* 947.

[22] Fons Coomans, 'The Ogoni Case Before the African Commission on Human and Peoples' Rights' (2003) 52 *ICLQ* 749; Giuseppe Pascale, 'Extraterritorial Applicability of the African Charter on Human and Peoples' Rights' (2014) 8(3) *Diritti umani e diritto internazionale* 644; *SERAC and CESR v Nigeria* [2001] ACoHPR 155/96; South African Institute for Advanced Constitutional, Public, Human Rights and International Law, 'The State Duty to Protect, Corporate Obligations and Extra-Territorial Application in the African Regional Human Rights System' (2010), https://www.business-humanrights.org/sites/default/files/reports-and-materials/SAIFAC-paper-re-business-human-rights-in-African-regional-system-17-Feb-2010.pdf, accessed 17 March 2019.

on an alternative solution to protect human rights: bringing an action against the holding company H, which is incorporated in the United Kingdom, for the human rights abuses perpetrated by its foreign subsidiaries S in Bangladesh, Ecuador and Nigeria, respectively.

II. REMEDIES IN THE HOME STATE

Having investigated the, often inadequate, remedies available in the host states, this section analyses those applicable to a British holding corporation H that has several foreign subsidiaries which abused human rights. It argues that the existing remedies are not effective under international, EU or UK law.

A. Soft Laws

Since the 1960s Western-based corporations have increasingly outsourced their production to developing countries. As the number of multinational companies has increased, international institutions, NGOs and governments have attempted to regulate their conduct through soft law, rather than binding obligations. At the same time, although multinational enterprises have no international legal obligations, they have increasingly assumed a number of soft law responsibilities towards the global society.[23] This section briefly introduces the main initiatives taken by the OECD, the ILO, the UN and their implementation by the UK government. Although most of these frameworks detail an international standard of conduct or primary rules applicable to multinational companies, some of them also attempt to establish a non-binding quasi-standard of review or secondary rules. As already mentioned, the OECD encouraged states to establish non-judicial bodies with a complaint mechanism assessing the activities of multinational companies. These non-judicial mechanisms shape, to a certain extent, a non-binding standard of review applicable to private parties. However, the problem with those soft law frameworks is that they are aspirational and enforceable only on a voluntary basis.[24] This became evident in a

[23] See Jerbi Scott, 'Business and Human Rights at the UN: What Might Happen Next?' (2009) 31 *Human Rights Quarterly* 299; Rory Sullivan, 'NGO Influence on the Human Rights Performance of Companies' (2006) 24 *Netherlands Quarterly of Human Rights* 405.

[24] See Jerbi (n 23); David Weissbrodt and Muria Kruger, 'Human Rights Responsibilities of Businesses as Non-State Actors' in *Non-State Actors and Human Rights* (Oxford University Press, 2005); Celia Wells and Juanita Elias, 'Catching the Conscience of the Kings: Corporate Player on the International Stage' in *Non-State Actors and Human Rights* (Oxford University Press, 2005); Jernej Letnar Cernic, *Human Rights Law and Business Corporate Responsibility for Fundamental Human Rights* (Europa Law Publishing, 2010); Leyla Davarnejad, 'In the Shadow of Soft Law: The Handling of Corporate Social Responsibility Disputes under the OECD Guidelines for Multinational Enterprises' (2011) *Journal of Dispute Resolution* 351; Ashley L Santner, 'A Soft Law

recent UK Court of Appeal case, *Okpabi v Royal Dutch Shell Plc*,[25] where the claimants argued, among other things, that the parent company was responsible for the abuses committed by its subsidiaries on the basis of CSR standards. The Court of Appeal, however, ruled that such soft law policies are inadequate to establish a duty of care of the parent company that would have hard legal consequences in case of a breach.[26] In *Lungowe v Vedanta*, although the Supreme Court delivered a decision in the victims' favour and pointed out at the fact that the guidelines established by the parent company for the group may be the basis to establish a duty of care, it did not refer to the relevance of international soft law standards in framing such duty of care.[27] Therefore, this section argues that soft laws are insufficient to hold H liable in the Bangladeshi, Ecuadorian and Nigerian case studies.

(i) The United Nations

The Guiding Principles are the most important CSR instrument, recognised at UN level. They are a soft law, non-binding mechanism and therefore 'should be read as [not] creating new international law obligations'.[28] However, the simple restatement of the already existing obligations in a coherent document established an unprecedented legal framework to encourage businesses to respect human rights.[29] The Guiding Principles set out the following three pillars. First, they establish the duty to protect human rights; second, the corporate responsibility to respect human rights; and, third, the access to remedy. The first and third pillars can be a starting point to hold states accountable for their failure to prevent multinational companies from abusing human rights and will be analysed in Chapters 3 and 4. The second pillar requires companies to respect human rights and remedy any abuse. The responsibility covers any corporate

Mechanism for Corporate Responsibility: How the Updated OECD Guidelines for Multinational Enterprises Promote Business for the Future' (2011) 43 *The George Washington International Law Review* 375; John Gerard Ruggie and Tamaryn Nelson, 'Human Rights and the OECD Guidelines for Multinational Enterprises: Normative Innovations and Implementation Challenges' (2015) 66 Corporate Social Responsibility Initiative Working Paper; Gwynne Skinner et al, 'The Third Pillar: Access to Judicial Remedies for Human Rights Violations by Transnational Business | ICAR', www.corporatejustice.org/IMG/pdf/the_third_pillar_-access_to_judicial_remedies_for_human_rights_violation.-1-2.pdf, accessed 17 March 2019.

[25] *Okpabi & Ors v Royal Dutch Shell Plc & Anor (Rev 1)* [2018] EWCA Civ 191.

[26] ibid 130.

[27] *Vedanta Resources PLC and another v Lungowe and others* [2019] UKSC 20; Robert McCorquodale, 'Parent Companies Can Have a Duty of Care for Environmental and Human Rights Impacts: Vedanta v Lungowe « Law « Cambridge Core Blog' <http://blog.journals.cambridge.org/2019/04/11/parent-companies-can-have-a-duty-of-care-for-environmental-and-human-rights-impacts-vedanta-v-lungowe/> accessed 29 April 2019.

[28] John Gerard Ruggie, 'Report of the Special Representative of the Secretary-General on the Issue of Human Rights and Transnational Corporations and Other Business Enterprises' (2011) 29 *Netherlands Quarterly of Human Rights* 224, 228.

[29] ibid 224.

action or omission that caused a human rights abuse.[30] The Guiding Principles also raise the issue of the size and economic power of multinational companies and specify that, given their influence and power in several countries, multinational corporations are especially responsible for preventing human rights abuses and promoting fundamental freedoms. Furthermore, the Guiding Principles establish the concept of *business relationship*, which includes the '[r]elationships with business partners, entities in its value chain, and any other non-State or State entity directly linked to its business operations, products or services'.[31]

A company is socially responsible for preventing human rights abuses perpetrated by any entity with which it is in a business relationship. According to the Guiding Principles, multinational corporations must not only respect local laws but also 'internationally recognised human rights, wherever they operate',[32] ie regardless of which country a company is incorporated in and/or conducts business, it must comply with the minimum human rights standards '[e]xpressed in the International Bill of Human Rights and the principles concerning fundamental rights set out in the International Labour Organization's Declaration on Fundamental Principles and Rights at Work'.[33] The Guiding Principles truly address the CSR problems by detailing the responsibility of multinational companies operating through a chain of subsidiaries in multiple countries. Specifically, they address the extraterritorial and liability problems described above in Chapter 1. First, they clarify that multinational enterprises are responsible for their transnational operations, regardless of where they operate. Second, they establish the responsibility of all companies that are part of the same supply chain, notwithstanding the fact that they may be separate legal entities and limited liability companies.

If the Human Rights Council endorsed the Guiding Principles as a binding treaty establishing legal obligations for companies, they would be an effective instrument to hold multinational corporations, such as H, accountable for the abuses committed by their subsidiaries. If I apply the Guiding Principles to the Bangladeshi, Ecuadorian and Nigerian case studies, it is clear that the holding company H would be liable for the human rights abuses perpetrated against the victims. Bodhi, Elsa, and Naoki would have to prove, first, that S abused either the International Bill on Human Rights or the ILO Work Declaration, and, second, that S is the subsidiary of and therefore, has a business relationship with, H.

However, given that the Guiding Principles are not a legally binding document, they do not establish any authoritative legal basis for the victims of human rights abuses to sue multinational companies. Currently, no victim, such as Bodhi, Elsa and Naoki, can claim in court that a holding company H is liable for the human rights abuses perpetrated by its subsidiary S on the basis

[30] ibid 236–238.
[31] ibid 238.
[32] ibid 245.
[33] ibid 237.

of the Guiding Principles. Nevertheless, a victim can argue that domestic tort and company laws, regarding the liability of companies, should be interpreted in light of the Guiding Principles. National judges may take the Guiding Principles into account as a persuasive document while interpreting domestic laws in cases concerning multinational companies abusing human rights.[34] Furthermore, the UN framework did not establish a soft law accountability mechanism, but instead it left it for states to ensure that human rights victims have access to remedies.[35]

Therefore, the Guiding Principles are one of the most advanced legal instruments available to the victims of human rights abuses by multinational companies, because they detail the obligations of states and companies towards stakeholders. However, the Guiding Principles are still a soft law mechanism and are not an authoritative legal basis for a human rights victim to claim that a multinational company is liable.

(ii) The Organisation for Economic Cooperation and Development

In 1976 the OECD adopted a set of non-binding guidelines.[36] The OECD Guidelines have been updated several times and currently include a section on human rights, specifically referring to the UN Guiding Principles, as well as a section on employment and industrial relations and one on the environment establishing that enterprises must respect human rights and environmental standards.[37] In addition to adopting the OECD Guidelines, a number of states also established NCPs. These are domestic agencies implementing the OECD Guidelines. Through a complaint mechanism, NCPs apply the OECD Guidelines to individual cases. These cases are technically called specific instances. This section briefly analyses NCPs, the OECD Guidelines and the remedies they would provide against the holding company H.

The NCPs' first function is to mediate between the parties and encourage them to come to an agreement. When this is not possible, NCPs may determine whether companies violated the OECD Guidelines and make further recommendations. The NCPs' conclusions and recommendations are not binding even when they assert a violation of the OECD Guidelines. NCPs used

[34] Nicola Jägers, 'UN Guiding Principles on Business and Human Rights: Making Headway towards Real Corporate Accountability' (2011) 29 *Netherlands Quarterly of Human Rights* 159; John Gerard Ruggie, 'Protect, Respect, and Remedy: The UN Framework for Business and Human Rights', *International Human Rights Law* (Ashgate, 2010); John Gerard Ruggie, 'The Construction of the UN "Protect, Respect and Remedy" Framework for Business and Human Rights: The True Confessions of a Principled Pragmatist' (2011) 2 *European Human Rights Law Review* 127; Letnar Cernic (n 24) 221–32.

[35] Ruggie, 'Report of the Special Representative of the Secretary-General on the Issue of Human Rights and Transnational Corporations and Other Business Enterprises' (n 28) 236–253.

[36] OECD, *OECD Guidelines for Multinational Enterprises, 2011 Edition* (OECD Publishing, 2011) www.oecd-ilibrary.org/governance/oecd-guidelines-for-multinational-enterprises_9789264115415-en, accessed 22 April 2016.

[37] ibid, part I, ss IV–VI; Ruggie and Nelson (n 24).

to focus just on the mediation process with inconclusive final statements when the mediation failed. For these reasons, scholars criticised NCPs as having various operational deficiencies, including

> [a] lack of due process … ; unequal treatment of parties; burden on complainants: unwillingness to investigate and lack of fact-finding capacity; lack of transparency, narrowing down the applicability of the guidelines; excluding company supplying chains; and an unwillingness to declare breaches of the guidelines.[38] All in all it appears that the greatest shortcoming of the OECD Guidelines is a lack of sanctioning mechanisms.[39]

However, since 1984 the OECD Member States have implemented various reforms of both the OECD Guidelines and the NCPs to address the above deficiencies. The latest reform took place in 2011 when the OECD Member States aligned the Guidelines with the newly born UN Guiding Principles. In addition to including a full chapter dedicated to human rights, the OECD Guidelines have improved the existing NCP complaint mechanism by introducing the Implementation Procedures of the OECD Guidelines for Multinational Enterprises, a set of rules of procedures regulating the application of the OECD Guidelines to individual cases.[40]

Therefore, although NCP decisions remain neither binding nor enforceable, there are encouraging reasons to file a complaint before an NCP. First, the NCP will mediate between the human rights victims and the multinational company and thereafter the victim may obtain some sort of reparation. Second, when mediation fails, the NCP may still determine whether the multinational corporation violated the OECD Guidelines. Although not binding, the NCP decision is a persuasive indication that a company violated the OECD Guidelines, which may affect its business reputation and relationship with consumers. Third, although not perfect, in addition to domestic courts, NCPs are the only mechanism available to file a complaint against a multinational corporate group for a violation of human rights law. Fourth, non-binding adjudication has some advantages over the decisions of national courts. NCPs apply the OECD Guidelines to the complaints they receive unrestrained by national laws. This effectively means that NCPs do not have to address the liability and extraterritoriality problems that domestic courts face.[41] Therefore, under the OECD

[38] Christian Aid, Amnesty International, Friends of the Earth, 'Flagship or Failure? The UK's Implementation of the OECD guidelines and approach to corporate accountability' (2007) https://corporate-responsibility.org/wp-content/uploads/2014/07/AIUK_FoE_ChristianAid_Report_Flagship_or_failureJan06.pdf.

[39] Jernej Letnar Cernic, 'Corporate Responsibility for Human Rights: A Critical Analysis of the OECD Guidelines for Multinational Enterprises' (2008) 3 *Hanse Law Review*, 71, 94; Letnar Cernic (n 24) 202.

[40] See Ruggie and Nelson (n 24).

[41] See Jerbi (n 23); Weissbrodt and Kruger (n 24) 318–355; Deva, 'Human Rights Violations by Multinational Corporations and International Law' (n 2) 9–17; Wells and Elias (n 24) 154–161;

Guidelines, each corporate group is considered a single entity, notwithstanding the fact that it may include multiple companies incorporated in different countries. Furthermore, NCPs do not have jurisdiction over a particular territory and, therefore, can consider a complaint, or specific instance, regardless of the place of injury. When the specific instance relates to corporate groups incorporated in multiple countries, the members of NCPs cooperate with their foreign colleagues, and together they elect the leading NCP which will assess the specific instance.[42]

Given that NCPs are domestic bodies, they have developed diverse practices. This section analyses a few British NCP specific instances as directly applicable to the case studies.

In *Complaint from Survival International against Vedanta Resources plc*,[43] the UK NCP held that a British company violated the OECD Guidelines, because it did not consult the indigenous community before constructing a bauxite mine. The indigenous community was living in the vicinity of the mine construction site in India. Similar to the Ecuadorian case study, the indigenous Indian community was dependent on the land and was grossly affected by the environmental degradation caused by the company.

In *Afrimex (UK) Ltd*,[44] after mediation failed, the British NCP concluded that the company had violated the OECD Guidelines. The *Afrimex (UK) Ltd* specific instance is similar to the Nigerian case study concerning militarised commerce described above. A company, incorporated in the United Kindgom, had a supplier that was allegedly paying taxes to a rebel group in the Democratic Republic of Congo. The rebel forces were using the taxes paid by the company to violate human rights in the ongoing conflict in Congo. The human rights victims alleged that the British company failed to take due care of its supply chain and prevent its suppliers from funding the rebel forces violating human rights. This specific instance analyses the relationship between the British and Congolese companies that are part of the same supply chain. Although these enterprises were not affiliated in a holding and subsidiary relationship, the NCP held the British company responsible for its failure to take due care in relation to its supply chain.

Raid & ENRC[45] is another similar case in terms of establishing the responsibility of companies for human rights violations committed through its business

Letnar Cernic (n 24) 183–216; Davarnejad (n 24); Santner (n 24); Ruggie and Nelson (n 24); Skinner, Gwynne and others (n 24); Voiculescu (n 2); Clapham (n 2) 201–211.

[42] OECD (n 36) pt II Implementation Procedures of the OECD Guidelines for Multinational Enterprises; Davarnejad (n 24); Santner (n 24); Ruggie and Nelson (n 24).

[43] *Final Statement by the UK National Contact Point for the OECD Guidelines for Multinational Enterprises Complaint from Survival International against Vedanta Resources plc* [2009] UK NCP.

[44] *Final Statement by the UK National Contact Point for the OECD Guidelines for Multinational Enterprises: Afrimex (UK) Ltd* [2008] UK NCP.

[45] *Final Statement by the UK National Contact Point for the OECD Guidelines for Multinational Enterprises: Raid & ENRC* [2016] UK NCP.

relationships. In this case, ENRC, a British company, had a business relationship with a number of Congolese companies. At first, such business relationships were contract-based, then ENRC became the shareholder of some of these companies. The NCP had to assess whether ENRC had any responsibility for numerous abuses committed by these entities in connection with mining. It declared that ENRC violated the OECD Guidelines in its capacity as a contractor first, and shareholder second.

Survival, Afrimex (UK) and *Raid & ENRC* are important specific instances for the following reasons. First, if applied to the case studies, the principles established by the UK NCP would be of help to the victims. For instance, in the Ecuadorian case study, the NCP could consider whether the indigenous community living in the vicinity of the Amazonian river was consulted before starting to exploit the land, and whether the failure to conduct such a consultation gives a right to claim damages from the offending company. Furthermore, in the Nigerian case study, the victim, Naoki, would likely be able to hold a parent company, H, responsible for the torture inflicted by the Nigerian government based on *Afrimex (UK)* and *Raid & ENRC*. In *Afrimex (UK)* and *Raid & ENRC*, the British and Congolese companies had a contractual relationship, while in the Nigerian case study, H and S have a much stronger shareholder–holding company relationship. Furthermore, the Nigerian situation is clearly more aggravated than the *Afrimex (UK)* specific instance. In *Afrimex (UK)*, the company was limiting itself to paying taxes to a group of rebels violating human rights, while in the Nigerian case study the subsidiary S actively supported and funded the terror campaign of the Nigerian government in order to continue exploiting Nigerian oil. Therefore, Naoki would likely be able to persuade the British NCP that H violated the OECD Guidelines. Second, these specific instances may persuade English courts to apply the same rules in a binding case brought before a British judge. Third, the NCP could help a victim to mediate with the offending company and come to an amicable settlement.[46]

The decisions of the British NCP are encouraging as they bypass the limited liability and extraterritoriality issues set out in Chapter 1. However, all NCP decisions are neither binding, nor able to impose any sanction on H. Therefore, the victims of human rights abuses, Bodhi, Elsa and Naoki, could approach the NCP with a specific instance only with the expectation to come to an amicable solution with the company or, as a last resort, when they have no hope of success in the British courts and would like to shame the company for its human rights abuses.

[46] See Letnar Cernic (n 24) 199–204; Larry Catá Backer, 'Rights and Accountability in Development (Raid) V Das Air and Global Witness V Afrimex: Small Steps Toward an Autonomous Transnational Legal System for the Regulation of Multinational Corporations' (2009) 10 *Melbourne Journal of International Law*.

(iii) The International Labour Organisation

The ILO adopted two CSR documents: the ILO Work Declaration[47] and the ILO Tripartite Declaration.[48] These ILO Declarations provide general guidelines addressed to both multinational companies and states concerning CSR. However, the practical implementation of the ILO Declarations is problematic for the following reasons. First, as all CSR standards, they are non-binding, and companies may adopt them on a voluntary basis only. Second, none of the ILO Declarations provides for a non-judicial implementation mechanism, such as the NCPs, as it pertains to the OECD Guidelines.[49]

The ILO Work Declaration states that, whereas governments have a duty to protect human rights victims against private actors, multinational companies have a duty to respect fundamental rights.[50] The ILO Tripartite Declaration details that, to respect fundamental rights, multinational corporations should abide by the laws of the country where they operate.[51] Specifically, as it pertains to the conditions of work, '[m]ultinational enterprises … [s]hould be not less favourable to the workers than those offered by comparable employers in the host country'.[52] Furthermore, as it pertains to safety and health, '[m]ultinational enterprises should maintain the highest standards of safety and health, in conformity with national requirements'.[53] Multinational companies have an obligation to respect human rights in the framework of the domestic law of the country where they operate. States have a duty to regulate their employment legislation in accordance with international human rights, whereas companies must comply with such regulations. In 2017 the ILO Work Declaration was updated and it now explicitly refers to the UN Guiding Principles and to the OCCD Guidelines.[54]

The ILO has two main mechanisms implementing the ILO Tripartite Declaration through a Subcommitee on Multinational Enterprises. However, both mechanisms exclude the possibility for stakeholders to file a complaint against a multinational company. The first mechanism sets out a procedure for the interpretation of the ILO Tripartite Declaration by the Subcommitee on Multinational Enterprises. If a number of parties, including governments, employers or employees, disagree on the interpretation of the ILO Tripartite Declaration, they may seek advice from the ILO, but under no circumstance will

[47] International Labour Office, *ILO Declaration on Fundamental Principles and Rights at Work and Its Follow-Up* (ILO, 2010).

[48] International Labour Office (ed), *Tripartite Declaration of Principles Concerning Multinational Enterprises and Social Policy*, 5th edn (ILO, 2017).

[49] Deva, 'Human Rights Violations' (n 2) 12–13; Weissbrodt and Kruger (n 24) 328–35; Voiculescu (n 2); Letnar Cernic (n 24) 207–16; Clapham (n 2) 211–18.

[50] International Labour Office (n 47).

[51] International Labour Office (n 48).

[52] ibid 41.

[53] ibid 44.

[54] Deva, 'Human Rights Violations' (n 2) 12–13; Weissbrodt and Kruger (n 24) 328–35; Voiculescu (n 2); Letnar Cernic (n 24) 207–16; Clapham (n 2) 211–18.

the Subcommitee on Multinational Enterprises consider whether in a particular case the employer or the government violated the ILO Tripartite Declaration. The ILO has an advisory rather than a quasi-judicial function. There is no complaint mechanism similar to the NCPs.[55] The second mechanism is a periodic survey on the implementation of the ILO Tripartite Declaration. Although stakeholders, governments and multinational companies can participate in such surveys, reports resulting from these surveys are limited to a general comment on the implementation of the ILO Tripartite Declaration and provide no possibility for stakeholders to file complaints against companies. In addition, the ILO promotes the company-union dialogue, a procedure which is confidential, based on mutual consent and which content cannot be used in any binding procedure. The role of the ILO is to facilitate dialogue, not to provide for any recommendation.[56]

Therefore, the ILO Declarations do not provide judicial or quasi-judicial remedies for the human rights victims Bodhi, Elsa and Naoki, leaving them with no option but to sue the relevant multinational companies under domestic law.

(iv) Interim Conclusion

Existing soft law instruments are an attempt by the international community to acknowledge the role of multinational enterprises as leading actors in the global arena. CSR recognises that with the power of multinational enterprises comes corresponding responsibilities towards the stakeholders affected by their corporate activities. However, the main problem with soft law frameworks is that they do not provide any enforceable mechanism against multinational enterprises. They do not go beyond requesting companies to recognise that they have human rights responsibilities. Accordingly, the soft law frameworks are unable to hold accountable those companies not willing to acknowledge their responsibility towards private actors. Despite these inherent deficiencies, soft law instruments have the advantage of promoting a CSR culture among consumers and enterprises. Furthermore, soft law instruments may persuade domestic judges to interpret corporate and tort laws in accordance with human rights standards. Therefore, soft law frameworks may be a useful tool for human rights victims to argue for a progressive interpretation of domestic tort and company laws; but they are unable to set up enforceable legal obligations against companies.

B. European Union Law

The European Union has recently put CSR on its agenda and started a serious political debate as to its role in defining the liability of multinational companies

[55] International Labour Office, Annex II, 3 (n 48).

[56] Ibid, Annex II, 2 and 3; Deva, 'Human Rights Violations by Multinational Corporations and International Law' (n 2) 12–13; Weissbrodt and Kruger (n 24) 328–335; Voiculescu (n 2); Letnar Cernic (n 24) 207–216; Clapham (n 2) 211–218.

for extraterritorial human rights abuses.[57] Some members of the European Parliament have proposed on numerous occasions to establish a European business and human rights framework that would ensure the accountability of European enterprises. However, the European Commission has always argued for a restrained voluntary approach to CSR regulations at the EU level.[58]

In the EU strategy for 2011–14 for CSR, the European Union defines CSR as 'the responsibility of enterprises for their impacts on society'.[59] The EU strategy recalls that CSR policies are non-binding and compliance is voluntary. The European Union does not regulate this area, but instead promotes dialogue between stakeholders and enterprises and encourages multinational companies to adopt CSR policies.[60]

Furthermore, the European Union abandoned its project to establish a non-binding EU CSR code of conduct. In the past, the European Union adopted some non-binding corporate codes of conducts related to specific cases of human rights abuses, such as the Code of Conduct for Companies Operating in South Africa[61] or the EU Code of Conduct on Arms Export.[62] In 1999 the European Parliament adopted the Howitt Resolution[63] calling on the European Union to adopt a legally binding document on the obligations of multinational companies. The same resolution instructed the European Commission to adopt a non-binding European Code of Conduct for Multinational Enterprises. The code would have established the European Monitoring Platform, an EU non-judicial mechanism, assessing the responsibility of European enterprises. However, the Commission did not implement the resolution. It established neither a binding nor a soft law EU mechanism applicable to multinational companies. It opted instead to boost existing CSR mechanisms, such as the ILO, the OECD and the UN Guiding Principles.[64]

On this note, the European Commission recently published a working document describing the role of the European Union in implementing the Guiding Principles in Europe. In this working document, the Commission explains that,

[57] See Kamminga (n 2); Russo, Deborah (n 3); Gigante (n 3); Esposito and Carobolante (n 3); Gatto (n 3) 174–82.

[58] See eg European Commission, 'Commission Staff Working Document on Implementing the UN Guiding Principles on Business and Human Rights – State of Play' SWD (2015) 144 final; Naomi Williamson, Astrid Stampe-Knippel and Tina Weber, 'Corporate Social Responsibility National Public Policies in the European Union – Compendium 2014' Directorate-General for Employment, Social Affairs and Inclusion Unit C.1 (Luxembourg: Publications Office of the European Union, 2014) http://ec.europa.eu/social/BlobServlet?docId=12899&langId=en.

[59] European Commission, 'A Renewed EU Strategy 2011–2014 for Corporate Social Responsibility' (2011) COM 681final, s 3.1.

[60] ibid.

[61] European Community, 'Code of Conduct for Community Companies with Subsidiaries, Branches or Representation in South Africa of 16 November 1985' (1985) 24 *International Legal Materials* 1477.

[62] European Union Code of Conduct on Arms Exports 1998 (8675/2).

[63] Richard Howitt, 'Report on EU Standards for European Enterprises Operating in Developing Countries: Towards a European Code of Conduct' [A4-0508] http://www.europarl.europa.eu/sides/getDoc.do?type=REPORT&reference=A4-1998-0508&language=EN#Contentd375815e1167.

[64] Gatto (n 3) 174–82; Touzé (n 3).

although there is no EU CSR legal instrument, the European Union has implemented some laws that influence the conduct of European enterprises.[65] These laws may be of help to implement the UN Guiding Principles' first pillar, the state's duty to protect. Among such EU laws, there is, for example, the Generalised Scheme of Preferences Plus, ie a trade policy promoting human rights in developing countries.[66] Other examples are the Accounting Directives which require certain companies to disclose information concerning their corporate policies, including CSR. Although it is clear that the European Union enacted some laws implementing the first pillar, ie the state's duty to protect, the working document does not point to any EU law implementing the second pillar, ie the responsibility of companies. The European Union limits itself to encouraging companies to abide by CSR standards, such as the OECD or ILO mechanisms.[67] Most recently, in 2019 the European Commission published another working document describing a whole range of actions the European Union put in place to promote CSR. However, such a working document confirmed the European Union's approach focused on encouraging, rather than prescribing, socially responsible business practice. A notable exception to this regime is the recent Regulation on Supply Chains Due Diligence Obligations for importers of certain metals originating from conflict and high-risk areas. However the scope of the regulation is limited to a narrow category of companies.[68]

The European Union has enacted a number of laws concerning access to justice that affect all extraterritorial cases, including those initiated against multinational companies. As it pertains to civil litigation, the European Union has enacted some regulations dealing with the conflict of laws rules, which include the cases brought by foreign stakeholders against European enterprises.[69] As it pertains to the prosecution of criminals, the European Union has also enacted laws that could be applicable in some jurisdictions where the domestic criminal system entitles public prosecutors to investigate cases against legal persons.[70] This book, however, focuses only on the tort law remedies available to human rights victims against multinational companies. It is beyond the scope of this

[65] European Commission (n 58).

[66] The EU Special Incentive Arrangement for Sustainable Development and Good Governance ('GSP+') covering the period 2014 –2015 2016 (SWD 8 final); European Commission (n 58) section 1.5.2.

[67] European Commission (n 59) s 1.2.1; Directive 2014/95/EU of the European Parliament and of th Council of 22 October 2014 Amending Directive 2013/34/EU as regards disclosure of non-financial and diversity information by large companies and groups 2014 (OJ L330).

[68] European Commission 'Commission Staff Working Document Corporate Social Responsibility, Responsible Business Conduct and Business & Human Rights': Overview of Progress SWD (2019) 143 final; Regulation (EU) 2017/821 of the European Parliament and of the Council of 17 May 2017 laying down supply chain due diligence obligations for Union importers of Tin, Tantalum and Tungsten, their ores and gold originating from conflict-affected and high risk areas [2017] OJ L130.

[69] See Regulation (EC) No 864/2007 of the European Parliament and of the Council of 11 July 2007 on the law applicable to non-contractual obligations (Rome II) [2007] OJ L199; Council Regulation (EC) No 44/2001 of 22 December 2000 on jurisdiction and the recognition and enforcement of judgments in civil and commercial matters [2001] OJ L12.

[70] See European Commission (n 58) s 3.1.2.

analysis to take into consideration the role of public prosecutors in bringing criminal proceedings against European enterprises.

This section on EU law analyses Brussels I, its Recast and Rome II establishing the conflict-of-laws rules that allow access to civil remedies within the European Union. Going back to the three case studies, the fundamental issues to take into account for the victims of human rights abuses, Bodhi, Elsa and Naoki, affected by corporate activities of the subsidiaries S in their home countries are, first, whether English courts have jurisdiction over the holding company H and, second, which law is applicable to human rights abuses committed abroad by S.

(i) Jurisdictional Issue: The European Union Brussels I Regulation

The first issue is whether a British court has jurisdiction over the holding company H for the alleged human rights abuses committed on foreign soil.

Brussels I and its Recast[71] set out the jurisdiction rules applicable to all European courts, including British courts. Brussels I and its Recast apply to all civil and commercial matters including company and tort law cases, such as a court action which the victims of human rights abuses, Bodhi, Elsa and Naoki, would bring against the holding company H. At this jurisdictional stage, it is not necessary to distinguish between workplace abuses, environmental degradation and militarised commerce,[72] because Brussels I and its Recast apply to each of the three case studies without distinction.[73]

The general rule regarding the jurisdiction of the EU courts is set out in Article 2 of Brussels I, which states: 'Subject to this Regulation, persons domiciled in a Member State shall, whatever their nationality, be sued in the courts of that Member State'.[74] Article 60(1) of Brussels I sets out the definition of domicile as it pertains to companies as follows:

> 1. For the purposes of this Regulation, a company or other legal person or association of natural or legal persons is domiciled at the place where it has its:
>   (a) statutory seat, or
>   (b) central administration, or
>   (c) principal place of business.[75]

[71] Council Regulation (EC) No 44/2001 of 22 December 2000 on jurisdiction and the recognition and enforcement of judgments in civil and commercial matters [2001] OJ L12; Regulation (EU) No 1215/2012 of the European Parliament and of the Council of 12 December 2012 on jurisdiction and the recognition and enforcement of judgments in civil and commercial matters (recast) [2012] OJ L351.

[72] See Rainer Hausmann and Ilaria Queirolo, 'Introduzione', *Regolamento Bruxelles I: Commento al Regolamento CE 44/2001 e alla Convenzione di Lugano* (IPR-Verlag, 2012) 25–30; Mathijs H Ten Wolde, Maria Elena De Maestri and Jan-Ger Knot, 'Articolo 60', *Regolamento Bruxelles I: Commento al Regolamento CE 44/2001 e alla Convenzione di Lugano* (IPR-Verlag, 2012).

[73] See Trevor C Hartley, 'Choice-of-Court Agreements, Lis Pendens, Human Rights and the Realities of International Business: Reflections on the Gasser Case', *Le droit international privé: esprit et méthodes: Mélanges en l'honneur de Paul Lagarde* (Dalloz-Sirey, 2005).

[74] Council Regulation (EC) No 44/2001 of 22 December 2000 on jurisdiction and the recognition and enforcement of judgments in civil and commercial matters art 2.

[75] ibid art 60(1).

Given that the term statutory seat has no legal meaning in common law systems, Article 60(2) of Brussels I clarifies that in common law jurisdictions '"statutory seat" means the registered office or, where there is no such office anywhere, the place of incorporation or, where there is no such place anywhere, the place under the law of which the formation took place'.[76] This would clearly apply to H, which is incorporated in London and therefore the United Kingdom is to be considered as H's domicile.

An important issue that could have potentially been problematic in this respect is the common law *forum non conveniens* doctrine, allowing domestic courts to dismiss a claim because foreign courts are better placed to decide the matter.[77] However, the Court of Justice of the European Union (CJEU) clarified in *Owusu v Jackson*[78] that such a doctrine could no longer be applicable when the defendant has its domicile in a Member State. UK courts received *Owusu v Jackson* well and implemented it in relation to multinational companies having their holding company in the United Kingdom.[79]

In this sense, it is worth taking note of the recent cases *Lungowe v Vedanta*[80] *Okpabi v Royal Dutch Shell Plc*[81] and *AAA & Others v Unilever PLC and Unilever Tea Kenya Limited*[82] that, in jurisdictional terms, are identical to the case studies analysed in this manuscript. These cases include allegations of extraterritorial torts committed by UK corporate groups through their foreign subsidiaries in Zambia, Nigeria and Kenya. In these cases, the issue was whether or not to dismiss a lawsuit on jurisdictional grounds. Either the Supreme Court or the Court of Appeal or the High Court, or all, confirmed that, under Brussels I, its Recast[83] and *Owusu v Jackson*,[84] the doctrine of *forum non conveniens* has no place in lawsuits filed against holding companies incorporated in the United Kingdom. Therefore, English courts confirmed that the *forum non conveniens*

[76] ibid art 60(2).

[77] Pippa Rogerson, *Collier's Conflict of Laws*, 4th edn (Cambridge University Press, 2013) 164–206.

[78] C-281/02 *Andrew Owusu v NB Jackson* [2005] (CJEU).

[79] For an explanation concerning the foreclosure of the doctrine of *forum non conveniens*, see John Burke, 'Foreclosure of the Doctrine of Forum Non Conveniens under the Brussels I Regulation: Advantages and Disadvantage' (2008) 3 *European Legal Forum* 121; Gilles Cuniberti, 'Forum Non Conveniens and the Brussels Convention' (2005) 54 *ICLQ* 973; CJS Knight, 'Owusu and Turner: The Shark in the Water?' (2007) 66 *CLJ* 288; Bright (n 3) 98–106.

[80] *Lungowe & Ors v Vedanta Resources Plc & Anor* [2016] EWHC TCC 975; *Lungowe & Ors v Vedanta Resources Plc & Anor* [2017] EWCA Civ 1528.

[81] *Okpabi & Ors v Royal Dutch Shell Plc & Anor (Rev 1)* [2018] EWCA Civ 191 (n 25); *Okpabi & Ors v Royal Dutch Shell Plc & Anor* [2017] EWHC TCC 89.

[82] *AAA & Ors v Unilever Plc & Anor* [2018] EWCA Civ 1532; *AAA & Ors v Unilever Plc & Anor* [2017] EWHC 371 (QB).

[83] Regulation (EC) No 864/2007 of the European Parliament and of the Council of 11 July 2007 on the law applicable to non-contractual obligations (Rome II) [2007] OJ L199; Regulation (EU) No 1215/2012 of the European Parliament and of the Council of 12 December 2012 on jurisdiction and the recognition and enforcement of judgments in civil and commercial matters (recast) [2012] OJ L351.

[84] *C-281/02 Andrew Owusu v. N.B. Jackson* (n 78); Knight (n 79).

doctrine is not a basis on which to dismiss a claim against a UK holding company controlling a foreign subsidiary.[85]

For the purpose of this book, H is incorporated in England. Therefore, under Brussels I and its Recast, English courts would certainly have jurisdiction over H in respect of all of the three case studies.

Although it does not occur in the case studies, it is worth mentioning the situation of victims suing at the same time the parent company and its foreign subsidiary in the UK. The issue is whether or not English courts would assert jurisdiction over the parent company, if the most appropriate forum to sue the subsidiary would be abroad. Assume for instance, that an English court could assert jurisdiction over H but not over S. Would the fact that a case will be litigated against S abroad prevent the court from asserting jurisdiction over H? The Supreme Court in *Lungowe v Vedanta* answered in the affirmative to such question. It held that the most appropriate forum to bring the claim against the Zambian subsidiary would normally be Zambia. Therefore, in order to avoid a duplication of judgments, if the case against the subsidiary could be filed in Zambia, the case against the parent company should be equally litigated in Zambia, unless the Zambian judicial system would be found unlikely to provide substantial justice to the victims.[86] This decision added one more burden to the victims who attempt to file a lawsuit against both the parent company and its subsidiary: they must demonstrate either that the most appropriate forum to file a suit against the subsidiary is the UK or that they would not be able to obtain substantial justice in the host country. Given the situation of injustices often occuring in host States, it may not be an impossible burden to overcome. In fact, in *Lungowe v Vedanta*, the Supreme Court asserted jurisdiction over both parent company and subsidiary because victims were unlikely to obtain substantial justice in Zambia.[87] However, this would be an additional hurdle for victims who file complaints against both a holding company and its subsidiaries. In the Bangladeshi, Ecuadorian and Nigerian case studies Bodhi, Elsa and Naoki avoid this problem by suing only the parent company H.

(ii) The Conflict-of-Laws Issue: The European Union Rome II Regulation

Once English courts asserted jurisdiction over the holding company H, it must be established whether or not UK law applies to the three case studies. Certainly, host state laws may protect human rights adequately and be the appropriate legal basis upon which to hold a multinational company accountable. However, if this is not the case, a question arises as to whether EU conflict-of-laws rules ensure the application of home state law or any other law compliant with

[85] For an analysis of the Brussels I Regulation in the framework of business and human rights, see Bright (n 3) 7–114.

[86] *Vedanta Resources PLC and another v Lungowe and others* (n 27) paras 66–87.

[87] ibid 88–101.

human rights. This issue is relevant because European multinational corporations often outsource their production to developing countries in order to benefit from legal systems which provide for lower human rights standards and weaker protection accorded to the stakeholders affected by their activities.[88]

The EU Rome II Regulation applies to '[n]on-contractual obligations',[89] including tort cases such as the lawsuits at issue here. Furthermore, it applies universally to cases arising within and outside of the European Union. Article 3 of the Rome II Regulation states: 'Any law specified by this Regulation shall be applied whether or not it is the law of a Member State.'[90] Therefore, the Rome II Regulation addresses the issue of whether or not UK law applies to the three case studies. This section analyses, first, the general rule applicable to all case studies; second, its exception applicable to environmental law; third, the forum law exception; and, finally, the provisions concerning the standards of safety and conduct.

(a) The General Rule

The general rule as set out in Article 4(1) of the Rome II Regulation states:

> Unless otherwise provided for in this Regulation, the law applicable to a non-contractual obligation arising out of a tort/delict shall be the law of the country in which the damage occurs irrespective of the country in which the event giving rise to the damage occurred and irrespective of the country or countries in which the indirect consequences of that event occur.[91]

The CJEU and scholars have consistently interpreted 'the law of the country in which the damage occurs'[92] as the law of the place of injury. They clarified that, even in cases of failure to act resulting in damage, the applicable law is the jurisdiction of the damage and not the jurisdiction where the defendant failed to act. One may think that, for example, if the holding corporation H fails to supervise its foreign subsidiary S, the failure occurs in the United Kingdom and all subsequent events are just consequences of H's failure to act.[93] However, Article 4 distinguishes between the event giving rise to the damage, such as H's failure to act, and the damage itself, such as the injuries occurred in the Bangladesh, Ecuador and Nigeria.[94] Therefore, in all of the case studies, the applicable law is the

[88] See Deva, 'Human Rights Violations' (n 2); Beisinghoff (n 2) 13–41.

[89] Regulation (EC) No 864/2007 of the European Parliament and of the Council of 11 July 2007 on the law applicable to non-contractual obligations (Rome II) [2007] OJ L199.

[90] ibid art 3.

[91] ibid art 4.

[92] ibid.

[93] Gerrit Betlem, 'Transnational Litigation against Multinational Corporations before Dutch Civil Courts', in *Liability of Multinational Corporations under International Law* (Kluwer, 2000).

[94] See Pietro Franzina, 'Il regolamento n 864/2007/CE sulla legge applicabile alle obbligazioni extracontrattuali ("Roma II")' (2008) 1 *Le nuove leggi civili commentate* 971; Karl Kreuzer, 'La comunitarizzazione del diritto internazionale privato in materia di obbligazioni extracontrattuali ("Roma II")', in *Diritto internazionale privato e diritto comunitario* (CEDAM, 2004); Ivo Bach, 'Art 4 Rome II', in *Rome II Regulation: Pocket Commentary* (Sellier, 2011); Jan von Hein, 'Article 4

law of the place of injury and not the law of the place where the alleged failure to supervise occurred. Accordingly, as a general rule, in the three case studies, the applicable laws would be Bangladeshi, Ecuadorian and Nigerian law, respectively.

(b) The Environmental Law Exception

An important exception to the general rule regarding the law applicable to tortious acts relates to environmental law. Article 7 of the Rome II Regulation states:

> The law applicable to a non-contractual obligation arising out of environmental damage or damage sustained by persons or property as a result of such damage shall be the law determined pursuant to Article 4(1), unless the person seeking compensation for damage chooses to base his or her claim on the law of the country in which the event giving rise to the damage occurred.[95]

Article 7 of the Rome II is designed to offer additional protection to the victims of environmental abuses and degradation. It entitles those victims to choose the most favourable applicable law between the place of injury or the place "in which the event giving rise to the damage occured".[96] Rome II does not entitle any other victim to the same privilege. Therefore, Article 7 of Rome II applies to the Ecuadorian case study only.

Although in cases where an action is the trigger of damage it is relatively easy to ascertain the place giving rise to the damage, being simply the place of action, in cases when a failure to act is the trigger of damage, the analysis is more complex, because an omission to act is likely to occur at different stages and, accordingly, potentially in multiple places. If the damage is caused by a failure to act, the place giving rise to the damage is 'where the responsible person should have acted'.[97] This is a relatively vague criterion. In the Ecuadorian case study, it is possible to argue that the failure to act could have occurred in the United Kingdom, where H manages its worldwide business, or in Ecuador, where subsidiary S is damaging the Ecuadorian indigenous population. However, given that Article 7 of Rome II is based on the principle of ubiquity and designed to favour the victims of environmental abuses, some scholars interpret the failure to act as arising in any plausible location where an action should have occurred.[98]

General Rule', in *Rome Regulations: Commentary on the European Rules on the Conflict of Laws* (Kluwer/Aspen, 2011).

[95] Regulation (EC) No 864/2007 of the European Parliament and of the Council of 11 July 2007 on the law applicable to non-contractual obligations (Rome II) art 7, [2007] OJ L199.

[96] Ibid; see Angelika Fuchs, 'Art 7 Rome II', in *Rome II Regulation: Pocket Commentary* (Sellier, 2011); Jan von Hein, 'Article 7 Environmental Damage', *Rome Regulations: Commentary on the European Rules on the Conflict of Laws* (Kluwer/Aspen, 2011).

[97] See von Hein, 'Article 7 Environmental Damage' (n 96) 472; Fuchs, 'Art. 7 Rome II' (n 96).

[98] See von Hein, 'Article 7 Environmental Damage' (n 96); Franzina (n 94); Kreuzer (n 94); Fuchs, 'Art. 7 Rome II' (n 96) 202–216.

Accordingly, in the Ecuadorian case study, a court may consider H's failure to monitor and control its subsidiary S as occurring in the United Kingdom, where H has its headquarters and principally manages S's business. Instead, the place of injury is clearly Ecuador. Therefore, in the Ecuadorian case study, Elsa could argue for an application of English over Ecuadorian law.

(c) The Forum Law Exception

Another exception, which may be potentially applicable to the case studies, is the overriding effect of the law of the forum. Rome II sets out two provisions addressing the issue of the law of the forum: Article 26 and Article 16.

Article 26 of Rome II, concerning the public policy (*ordre public*) of the forum, states: 'The application of a provision of the law in any country specified by this Regulation may be refused only if such application is manifestly incompatible with the public policy (ordre public) of the forum.'[99]

Article 16 of Rome II, which sets out the overriding mandatory provisions, states: 'Nothing in this Regulation shall restrict the application of the provisions of the law of the forum in a situation where they are mandatory irrespective of the law otherwise applicable to the non-contractual obligation.'[100]

This section considers two main issues arising in connection with the potential application of the forum law exception to the case studies. The first issue is whether the forum law exception applies to cases involving human rights abuses. The second issue is characterisation, ie whether applying human rights laws and recognising the responsibility of a parent company for the abuses committed by its foreign subsidiary are to be regarded as one or two separate problems.

1. First Issue: Forum Law Exception and Fundamental Human Rights

The forum law exception is rarely applicable.[101] Recital (32) of Rome II states: 'Considerations of public interest justify giving the courts of the Member States the possibility, in exceptional circumstances, of applying exceptions based on public policy and overriding mandatory provisions.'[102]

Furthermore, Rome II does not define the meaning of public policy and overriding mandatory provisions. On the basis of Rome I, which defines their scope of application as it pertains to contract obligations, national laws, jurisprudence

[99] Regulation (EC) No 864/2007 of the European Parliament and of the Council of 11 July 2007 on the law applicable to non-contractual obligations (Rome II) art 26.

[100] ibid art 16.

[101] See Andrew Dickinson, *The Rome II Regulation: The Law Applicable to Non-Contractual Obligations* (Oxford University Press, 2008) 625–41; Rogerson (n 77) 424–33; André Nollkaemper, 'Public International Law in Transnational Litigation against Multinational Corporations: Prospects and Problems in the Courts in the Netherlands', in *Liability of Multinational Corporations under International Law* (Kluwer, 2000); Kenny Chng, 'A Theoretical Perspective of the Public Policy Doctrine in the Conflict of Laws' (2018) 14 *Journal of Private International Law* 130.

[102] Regulation (EC) No 864/2007 of the European Parliament and of the Council of 11 July 2007 on the law applicable to non-contractual obligations (Rome II) r 32.

and scholars have always considered overriding mandatory rules and public policy as a set of non-negotiable rules that governments impose on contractual parties.[103] However, it is difficult to transpose such a concept to non-contractual obligations. Although, with respect to contractual obligations, the overriding mandatory laws are those rules from which the parties cannot derogate in a contract, in tort cases, public policies and overriding mandatory laws are those rules that the national legislator or judge consider more fundamental than others and applicable regardless of where the tort occurred.[104] As it is more difficult to define the latter rather than the former set of rules, the meaning of overriding mandatory rules and public policy, in the context of Rome II, is unclear.

Although Articles 26 and 16 of Rome II are similar in their application and meaning, as they both establish the law of the forum exception, there are two main distinctions.

First, whereas Article 26 of Rome II is disabling in its application, Article 16 of Rome II is enabling in its application. According to Article 26 of Rome II, a court may refuse to apply foreign law if it is contrary to its public policy. However, Article 26 of Rome II contains no rules concerning the applicable law in these cases. When a domestic court refuses to apply the foreign law on the basis of that law being contrary to its public policy, it has discretion as to which law shall apply instead: it may be the law of the forum or, for example, a different provision of foreign law. Conversely, Article 16 of Rome II is enabling in nature, as it sets out that the forum's overriding mandatory provisions are applicable instead of foreign law. Accordingly, if a court refuses to apply foreign law, it has no choice but to apply its own overriding mandatory provisions. Therefore, when a court refers to Article 26 of Rome II, it has greater discretion to choose the law applicable to the case, whereas, when the court refers to Article 16 of Rome II, it applies the law of the forum instead of foreign law.[105]

[103] Dickinson (n 101); Andrea Bonomi, 'The Role of Internationally Mandatory Rules in an European Private International Law System' [2007] *Revista de drept international privat si drept comparat* 159; Moritz Renner, 'Article 9: Overriding Mandatory Provisions', in *Rome Regulations: Commentary on the European Rules on the Conflict of Laws* (Kluwer/Aspen, 2011).

[104] See Bonomi (n 103); Arif Yascha, 'Overriding Mandatory Provisions and Administrative Authorisations According to the Rome II Regulation' [2011] *European Legal Forum* 113; Alberto Mattei, 'Prospects for Industrial Relations: Overriding Mandatory Provisions in the Transnational Labour Market' in *Labour Markets, Industrial Relations and Human Resources Management: From Recession to Recovery* (Kluwer, 2012); Veerle Van Den Eeckhout, 'Corporate Human Rights Violations and Private International Law. The Hinge-Function and Conductivity of PIL in Implementing Human Rights in Civil Proceedings in Europe: a Facilitating Role for PIL or PIL as a Complicating Factor' (2012) *Contemporary Readings in Law and Social Justice* 178; Angelika Fuchs, 'Art 16 Rome II', *Rome II Regulation: Pocket Commentary* (Sellier, 2011); Angelika Fuchs, 'Art 26 Rome II', in *Rome II Regulation: Pocket Commentary* (Sellier, 2011); Jan von Hein, 'Article 16 Overriding Mandatory Provisions', in *Rome Regulations: Commentary on the European Rules on the Conflict of Laws* (Kluwer/Aspen, 2011); Jan von Hein, 'Article 26 Public Policy of the Forum', in *Rome Regulations: Commentary on the European Rules on the Conflict of Laws* (Kluwer/Aspen, 2011).

[105] See von Hein, 'Article 16 Overriding Mandatory Provisions' (n 104); von Hein, 'Article 26 Public Policy of the Forum' (n 104); Dickinson (n 101) 625–38; Fuchs, 'Art. 16 Rome II' (n 104); Fuchs, 'Art. 26 Rome II' (n 104).

Second, the CJEU interprets the meaning of public policy and overriding mandatory rules differently. According to the jurisprudence of the CJEU, public policy belongs to fundamental principles of national law only, whereas overriding mandatory rules belong to fundamental principles of both EU and national laws.[106]

It is for the judiciary to determine the meaning of public policy on a case-by-case basis, given that no body of law has ever defined it. In the European context, the issue is then which court has the power to define the meaning of public policy. In *Dieter Krombach v André Bamberski*,[107] a case concerning the 1968 Brussels Convention on Jurisdiction and the Enforcement of Judgments in Civil and Commercial Matters[108] (now superseded by the Brussels Regulation), the CJEU clarified that '[i]t is not for the [CJEU] to define the content of the public policy of a Contracting State'.[109] It is instead for each state to define those fundamental principles that determine its public policies. However, given that the public policy exception should be used only in limited circumstances, the CJEU is '[r]equired to review the limits within which the courts of a Contracting State may have recourse to [the] … [c]oncept [of public policy]'.[110] The outcome of the case was that domestic courts were allowed to refuse to enforce a foreign judgment if such a judgment would violate the ECHR. The essence of the ruling in *Dieter Krombach v André Bamberski* is that a domestic court has the power to define the public policy of the state within certain limits. Furthermore, when the domestic court defines public policy as including the fundamental human rights guaranteed by the ECHR, such a definition of public policy would be consistent with Rome II.[111] However, whether or not its public policy should be interpreted as including the protection of fundamental human rights appears to be a choice of the state. *Dieter Krombach v André Bamberski* does not define public policy; it just restates that a court interpreting public policy as including the protection of human rights guaranteed by the ECHR does not violate Rome II.

The CJEU has not defined an EU public policy doctrine as including the ECHR; it just enables the states to refer to the ECHR as a part of their domestic public policy doctrine if they wish. When Rome II was enacted, the European Parliament proposed to add some examples of public policy exceptions to the text, including the human rights guaranteed by the ECHR. However, the European Commission and the European Council rejected such a proposal, because, although similar, public policies are still linked to the national identities

[106] See Dickinson (n 101) 625–31; Fuchs, 'Art. 16 Rome II' (n 104); von Hein, 'Article 16 Overriding Mandatory Provisions' (n 104); Fuchs, 'Art. 26 Rome II' (n 104); von Hein, 'Article 26 Public Policy of the Forum' (n 104).

[107] C-7/98 *Dieter Krombach v André Bamberski* [2000] (CJEU).

[108] 1968 Brussels Convention on jurisdiction and the enforcement of judgments in civil and commercial matters 1972.

[109] C-7/98 *Dieter Krombach v André Bamberski* (n 107) s 23.

[110] ibid.

[111] C-7/98 *Dieter Krombach v André Bamberski* (n 107); Dickinson (n 101) 626–31.

of each state.[112] The CJEU has reconfirmed this approach in its current jurisprudence, according to which the '[r]ules of public, policy … [are] for the national court to ascertain'.[113] Therefore, the definition of public policy is still unclear and remains connected to the national policy of each state. There is no such concept of European public policy including fundamental human rights.

The concept of *overriding mandatory rules* is less vague than *public policy*, as scholars can refer to the following definition of the overriding mandatory rules set out in Article 9 of Rome I:

> [p]rovisions the respect for which is regarded as crucial by a country for safeguarding its public interests, such as its political, social or economic organisation, to such an extent that they are applicable to any situation falling within their scope, irrespective of the law otherwise applicable to the contract under this Regulation.[114]

In the cases *Mazzoleni*[115] and *Arblade*,[116] the CJEU defined overriding mandatory rules as:

> [n]ational provisions compliance with which has been deemed to be so crucial for the protection of the political, social or economic order in the Member States concerned as to require compliance therewith by all person present on the national territory of that Member State and all legal relationship within that State.[117]

However, such a definition is not clear and has to be implemented on a case-by-case basis by domestic courts. It is for the courts to determine those crucial mandatory laws of a forum. In practice, national courts apply different standards. For instance, in Germany, a mandatory rule may be applicable only in the public interest of the state. The key defining factor is that the rule should be public in nature and fulfil a state interest. In France, however, mandatory laws may be rules safeguarding the interests of weaker private individuals who require additional protection, such as victims of abuses, employees and consumers.[118]

[112] See Dickinson (n 101) 625–31; von Hein, 'Article 26 Public Policy of the Forum' (n 104); Fuchs, 'Art. 26 Rome II' (n 104); Bonomi (n 103); Franzina (n 94). For an opinion as to how private international law could evolve, see Van Den Eeckhout (n 104).

[113] C-415/11 *Mohamed Aziz v Caixa d'Estalvis de Catalunya, Tarragona i Manresa (Catalunyacaixa)* [2013] CJEU ECLI:EU:C:2013:164 [52]; C-169/14 *Juan Carlos Sánchez Morcillo and María del Carmen Abril García v Banco Bilbao Vizcaya Argentaria SA* [2014] CJEU ECLI:EU:C:2014:2099 [33].

[114] Regulation (EC) No 593/2008 of the European Parliament and the Council of 17 June 2008 on the law applicable to contractual obligations (Rome I) [2008] OJL 177 art 9.

[115] C-165/98 *André Mazzoleni, and Inter Surveillance Assistance SARL, as the party civilly liable* [2001] (CJEU).

[116] Joined Cases C-369/96 and C-376/96 *Jean-Claude Arblade, Arblade & Fils SARL, as the party civilly liable (C-369/96), and Bernard Leloup, Serge Leloup, Sofrage SARL, as the party civilly liable (C-376/96)* [1999] CJEU.

[117] Bonomi (n 103) 163–64.

[118] See Jan-Jaap Kuipers and Sara Migliorini, 'Qu'est-ce que sont les lois de police? Une querelle franco-allemande après la communautarisation de la Convention de Rome' (2011) 19 *European Review of Private Law* 187.

On the issue of whether there are European overriding mandatory rules and how they shall be defined, the CJEU ruled in *Ingmar GB LtD*[119] that European overriding mandatory rules are those rules which safeguard a fundamental principle of EU law. In *Ingmar GB LtD*, the CJEU held the rule to be mandatory and applicable because it guaranteed one of European Union's most important principles, being, in this case, the protection of commercial agents.[120]

According to some scholars,[121] *Ingmar GB LtD*, *Mazzolini* and *Arblade* clarified that the CJEU applies the following two-limb test to decide if a rule is of an overriding mandatory nature. A rule is deemed to be mandatory if (1) it is a fundamental principle of a Member State or EU law, and (2) it passes a proportionality review on a case-by-case basis. In this sense, each main principle of EU or national law should be balanced and confronted with the other interests at stake and the foreign state law that would be otherwise applicable.[122] Article 16 of Rome II enables courts to apply domestic laws safeguarding fundamental human rights instead of foreign provisions. However, to determine whether such national laws shall override the foreign provisions, the Member State courts have to balance all the interests at stake. Therefore, if one applies this approach to the case studies while determining the applicable law, domestic courts will likely balance the place of injury principle, as set out in Article 4 of Rome II, with the potential violation of human rights resulting from such an application. If a court believes that the human rights at stake are of such paramount importance that the need for their protection shall override the place of injury principle, it will apply the forum law. Instead, if the court believes that the rights at stake are derogable, given the circumstances of a specific case, it would follow the general rule determining the applicable law and will apply the place of injury law.[123]

In the United Kingdom, courts are generally reluctant to apply the forum law exception in choice-of-law analysis. However, as some scholars argue, courts may be more open to apply internationally recognised public policy principles, including human rights.[124] Therefore, assuming that in the case studies the applicable Bangladeshi, Ecuadorian and Nigerian laws would violate the ECHR, the UK courts could, at least theoretically, refuse to apply such laws.[125]

[119] C-381/98 *Ingmar GB Ltd and Eaton Leonard Technologies Inc* [2000] (CJEU).

[120] See Paul Lagarde (ed), 'Les lois de police devant la Cour de Justice des Communautés Européennes', in *Richterrecht und Rechtsfortbildung in der Europäischen Rechtsgemeinschaft* (Mohr Siebeck, 2003).

[121] Bonomi (n 103).

[122] See ibid; Arif Yascha (n 104); Mattei (n 104); Piet Eeckhout, 'Opinion 2/13 on EU Accession to the ECHR and Judicial Dialogue: Autonomy or Autarky' (2015) 38 *Fordham International Law Journal* 955.

[123] See von Hein, 'Article 16 Overriding Mandatory Provisions' (n 104); Fuchs, 'Art. 16 Rome II' (n 104); Dickinson (n 101) 631–38.

[124] Chng (n 101); Jan Oster, 'Public Policy and Human Rights' (2015) *Journal of Private International Law* 542.

[125] See eg Daniel Augenstein, 'Study on the Legal Framework on Human Rights and the Environment Applicable to European Enterprises Operating Outside the European Union' (University of Edinburgh, 2010) paras 223–24, http://ec.europa.eu/DocsRoom/documents/11865/attachments/1/translations/en/renditions/native, accessed 17 March 2019.

2. Second Issue: Characterisation

The second issue is known as the characterisation problem in conflict of laws. Prior to determining which law applies to a particular case study, it must be considered within which boundaries one can choose the applicable law.[126] For example, if a fact pattern comprises several legal issues, including a mixture of claims, in part based on contract and in part based on tort law, it may be the case that the applicable law to the contractual relationship differs from the law that applies to the relationship arising on the basis of tort. The court has to determine, first, what are the different issues relevant to the case, and, second, what is the law applicable to each particular issue. As a result, the court may apply country A law as it pertains to the contract issue and country B law as it pertains to the tort issue.

This section shows how characterisation would work in the case studies. There are two main issues relevant to the case studies. The first issue is whether or not the holding company H adopted an appropriate conduct to meet the applicable human rights standard. The second issue is what standard of review applies to H for the human rights abuses perpetrated by its subsidiary S. In this instance, the difference between substantive human rights law (primary norm) and the causes of action (secondary norm) applicable against H must be considered. The human rights substantive law is the primary rule or standard of conduct, such as, for example, the employees' safety regulations in the Bangladeshi case study, the right to demonstrate freely in the Nigerian case study or the right to health in the Ecuadorian case study. Instead, the cause of action applicable against H is the standard of review or secondary norm. It determines whether H is responsible for the action of its subsidiary.[127] Even if I assume that an English court would consider the place-of-injury standard of conduct or primary norm as not meeting European human rights standards, this does not necessarily mean that the place-of-injury standard of review will not meet such human rights standards. The cause of action against H may be independent of human rights and simply determine whether or not it is possible to sue a holding company for the torts committed by its subsidiaries.

In the Bangladeshi, Nigerian and Ecuadorian case studies, an English court may consider the standard of conduct and the standard of review as two separate issues and, therefore, will conduct two independent analyses of the applicable law.[128] First, the UK court will consider the law applicable to the standard of conduct. Assuming that the UK court finds the standard of conduct in Ecuador, Nigeria and Bangladesh as violating the ECHR standards, it may apply English law as a standard of conduct. Second, the UK court will consider the standard of

[126] See Rogerson (n 77) 267–77; Bonomi (n 103); Adrian Briggs, *The Conflict of Laws* (2 edition, Oxford University Press 2008) 9–13.

[127] See Melvin Aron Eisenberg, 'The Divergence of Standards of Conduct and Standards of Review in Corporate Law' (1993) 62 *Fordham Law Review* 437.

[128] See Rogerson (n 77) 267–77; Bonomi (n 103); Briggs (n 126) 9–13.

review. According to Rome II, the UK court should apply the place-of-injury law unless it violates the law of the forum. Assuming that the place-of-injury law does not allow for suing the holding company H for the human rights abuses perpetrated by its subsidiary S, the UK court is unlikely to consider such a standard of review as contrary to the ECHR, because the separation between the legal personality of a holding company and its subsidiaries is universally accepted.[129] Accordingly, to have a claim against the parent company H, the human rights victims Elsa, Bodhi and Naoki must overcome a double burden of proof. They have to argue, first, that the unlawful conduct, such as not meeting the employee's safety regulation in Bangladesh, or violating environmental laws in Ecuador, or the military abuses against demonstrators in Nigeria, is violating fundamental human rights. Second, they also need to argue that, by preventing victims of human rights abuses from effectively bringing actions against H, the company and tort laws of Ecuador, Bangladesh or Nigeria deprive them of their right of access to justice. The second limb of this burden of proof is difficult to overcome. Given that the principles of separate legal personality and limited liability are recognised worldwide, it would be difficult to argue that preventing a victim from suing the holding company of a multinational group for the torts committed by its subsidiary would violate his/her access to justice. Therefore, UK courts may still apply the place-of-injury law to determine the standard of review applicable to the holding company H.

(d) The Rules of Safety and Conduct

The last provision of Rome II that is relevant for this analysis is Article 17, which states:

> In assessing the conduct of the person claimed to be liable, account shall be taken, as a matter of fact and in so far as is appropriate, of the rules of safety and conduct which were in force at the place and time of the event giving rise to the liability.[130]

Article 17 of Rome II is not a conflict-of-laws rule, as it does not indicate which law the court should apply. The court determines the applicable law on the basis of other provisions of Rome II. However, once the applicable law is asserted, the court may take into account what were the rules of safety and conduct in the place of injury.[131] This is not an obligation to choose the law of the place of injury, but rather a factor that the judge should consider.

[129] See Henry Hansmann and Reinier Kraakman, 'Toward Unlimited Shareholder Liability for Corporate Torts' (1991) 100 *The Yale Law Journal* 1879; Gamble and Gavin (n 1) 29–34; Vanderkerckhove (n 1) 3–9; Kershaw (n 1) 3–46; *Barcelona Traction, Light and Power Company, Limited (Belgium v Spain)* [1970] ICJ ICJ Reports 3; Andenæs and Wooldridge (n 1) 109–30.

[130] Regulation (EC) No 864/2007 of the European Parliament and of the Council of 11 July 2007 on the law applicable to non-contractual obligations (Rome II) art 17.

[131] See Dickinson (n 101) 638–41; Ivo Bach, 'Art. 17 Rome II', *Rome II Regulation: Pocket Commentary* (Sellier, 2011); Jan von Hein, 'Article 17 Rules of Safety and Conduct', *Rome Regulations: commentary on the European rules on the conflict of laws* (Kluwer/Aspen, 2011).

Scholars interpret Article 17 of Rome II as one-sided because it is likely that the place-of-injury safety rules will be more favourable to a tortfeasor than to a victim.[132] This is particularly true with respect to the case studies, where the forum is in the United Kingdom whereas the place of injury is a developing country. Therefore, although Article 17 of Rome II does not determine what the applicable law is, it may be an authoritative excuse for limiting the liability of holding companies conducting their activities in countries where the safety rules are more lenient than in Europe. For instance, in the case studies, H could argue that it should not be held accountable for the Rana Plaza building collapse as it acted in compliance with the Bangladeshi rules of safety and conduct.

(iii) Application of the Conflict-of-Laws Rules in the United Kingdom

Until recently, there were no examples of the application of the EU conflict-of-laws rules to a complex litigation filed against a UK-headquartered multinational company for extraterritorial human rights abuses. Therefore, the scholar and the litigator could only imagine how courts would apply these rules in practice. However, the cases *Lungowe v Vedanta*,[133] *Okpabi v Royal Dutch Shell Plc*[134] and *AAA & Others v Unilever PLC and Unilever Tea Kenya Limited*[135] revealed how UK courts could possibly implement these EU rules in practice. It should be noted that these were not judgments on the merits, and courts considered the question of applicable law only as a hypothetical in order to assess the arguability of the case. Nevertheless, the courts ruled that UK case-law may be relevant to assess the accountability of a British holding company for transnational torts.

Specifically, in *Lungowe v Vedanta*[136] and *AAA & Others v Unilever PLC and Unilever Tea Kenya Limited*,[137] the courts stated as common ground that Zambian and Kenyan law would apply respectively, without taking into account the exceptions under Rome II. However, the courts argued, the foreign and UK legal systems share the same notion of the common law duty of care. Therefore, UK case-law would be relevant to assess the liability of the holding company under both Zambian and Kenyan laws. In *Okpabi v Royal Dutch Shell Plc*, the High Court concluded that there were arguable grounds to apply UK law on

[132] See Symeon C Symeonides, 'Rome II and Tort Conflicts: A Missed Opportunity' (2008) 56 *The American Journal of Comparative Law* 173, 211-15; Dickinson (n 101) 638–41.

[133] *Lungowe & Ors v Vedanta Resources Plc & Anor* [2016] EWHC TCC 975 (n 80); *Lungowe & Ors v Vedanta Resources Plc & Anor* [2017] EWCA Civ 1528 (n 80); *Vedanta Resources PLC and another v Lungowe and others* (n 27).

[134] *Okpabi & Ors v Royal Dutch Shell Plc & Anor (Rev 1)* [2018] EWCA Civ 191 (n 25); *Okpabi & Ors v Royal Dutch Shell Plc & Anor* (n 81).

[135] *AAA & Ors v Unilever Plc & Anor* [2018] EWCA Civ 1532 (n 82); *AAA & Ors v Unilever Plc & Anor* [2017] EWHC 371 (QB) (n 82).

[136] *Lungowe & Ors v Vedanta Resources Plc & Anor* [2017] 1528 (n 80); *Vedanta Resources PLC and another v Lungowe and others* (n 27).

[137] *AAA & Ors v Unilever Plc & Anor* [2018] EWCA Civ 1532 (n 82).

the basis of the environmental and forum law exceptions laid out in Rome II. It further took into account the possibility to apply Nigerian law and concluded that the common law duty of care was part of Nigerian law and, therefore, the UK duty-of-care case-law would be a relevant and persuasive authority in Nigeria. Therefore, UK case-law would apply to the case by virtue of either Rome II or, alternatively, because of the commonalities between the Nigerian and British legal systems.[138]

The judgments suggest that, as long as the host states are adopting a common law legal system, the UK duty-of-care case-law would be relevant to deciding cases.[139]

Not only English courts take this approach. Interestingly enough, in *Akpan v Royak Dutch Shell*,[140] a Dutch court decided on the same facts of *Okpabi v Royal Dutch Shell Plc* and also applied UK case law. The District Court asserted jurisdiction over the case and applied Nigerian law on the basis of Dutch conflict-of-laws rules. It argued that Nigerian law is based on British common law, that the duty of care was a widely shared notion among common law countries and, therefore, the recent UK case-law concerning the parent company's duty of care was relevant to the Nigerian legal system. On this basis, the District Court applied UK case law to the facts. This approach would obviously not allow the application of UK law to a parent company when its subsidiary is incorporated in a civil law jurisdiction. Furthermore, it is questionable how courts could decide to apply their own forum law on the basis of an interpretation of host state laws. Nevertheless, this approach could serve the victims of human rights abuses that would have an additional ground to argue for the application of English law, which is currently one of the most favourable laws to them.

Beside these considerations, UK courts could possibly take into account the environmental and forum law exceptions, as mentioned in *Okpabi v Royal Dutch Shell Plc*. However, it is yet to be seen how they will implement this reasoning in practice.

(iv) Application of Host State Laws

UK courts are, therefore, likely to apply host state laws to the case studies. This section analyses what this would imply for the victims of human rights abuses. Applying host state laws may not necessarily be detrimental to victims of human rights abuses. However, the problem is that human rights are immaterial as to the choice-of-law analysis. EU conflict-of-laws rules do

[138] *Okpabi & Ors v Royal Dutch Shell Plc & Anor* (n 81).
[139] *Lungowe & Ors v Vedanta Resources Plc & Anor* [2017] 1528 (n 80) paras 122–126; *Okpabi & Ors v Royal Dutch Shell Plc & Anor* (n 81) paras 50–61.
[140] *Akpan v Royal Dutch Shell Plc* [2013] DC Hague C/09/337050/HA ZA 09-1580.

not impose the application of rules compliant with human rights standards against home or host state rules that are disrespectful of them. This results in a particularly difficult situation for victims of human rights abuses committed by multinational enterprises, because, in these cases, when corporate groups include numerous companies incorporated in different jurisdictions, the choice-of-law analysis is a fundamental step in litigation. The failure of EU choice-of-laws rules to take the respect of human rights by host and home state laws into proper consideration contributes to the victims suffering from a lack of effective remedies.

Although this book does not conduct an in-depth analysis of the liability standard available in the host states, ie Bangladesh, Ecuador and Nigeria, as it instead focuses on the remedies available in the home state, the following paragraphs will outline what could be the likely result of an application of host state laws to the three case studies.

As it pertains to Bangladesh, the Rana Plaza building collapse triggered a debate over a change in Bangladeshi labour laws and employees' protection. Multiple NGOs and local communities have been working with corporations and the Bangladeshi government to improve the extremely low standards currently applicable to situations such as the Bangladeshi case study analysed in this book.[141] Furthermore, Bangladeshi victims filed two cases for tort damages in Delaware and Canadian courts and in both cases the Delaware Superior Court[142] and the Ontario Superior Court[143] ruled that Bangladeshi law was applicable to at least some of the claims. The Delaware Superior Court decided that, under Bangladeshi law, the civil actions were barred by a one-year statute of limitations.[144] The Ontario Superior Court also decided that, under Bangladeshi law, some of the victims would be barred by the statute of limitations and, in any case, no victim would have an arguable claim.[145] In Bangladesh, criminal and labour investigations of the Rana Plaza building collapse are ongoing, but these are aimed at holding individuals to account, rather than corporations.[146] It is, however, obvious from the Delaware and Canadian judgments, as well as from the ongoing debates on the need to improve the labour and safety standards provided by Bangladeshi law, that the application of Bangladeshi laws would not guarantee an effective remedy to Bodhi against the holding company H. On the contrary, if the decision of the

[141] Dutia Raam and Erol Abdurrahman, 'Background Paper – Rana Plaza: Legal and Regulatory Responses' (2018) Asser Institute, https://www.asser.nl/doingbusinessright/blog/post/background-paper-rana-plaza-legal-and-regulatory-responses-by-raam-dutia-and-abdurrahman-erol.

[142] *Abdur Rahaman v JC Penney Corporation, Inc, The Children's Place and Wal-Mart Stores, Inc* [2016] Super Ct Del N15C-07-174.

[143] *Das v George Weston Limited* [2017] 4129 (ONSC).

[144] *Abdur Rahaman v. JC Penney Corporation, Inc., The Children's Place and Wal-Mart Stores, Inc.* (n 142).

[145] *Das v George Weston Limited* (n 143).

[146] Raam and Abdurrahman (n 141).

Ontario Superior Court is correct, under Bangladeshi law, Bodhi would have no chance in succeeding against a multinational corporation.

As it pertains to Ecuador, the application of host state law could instead be beneficial to Elsa's claim. As explained above, the Ecuadorian judiciary had the chance to assess the accountability of Chevron for environmental degradation in Ecuador. The Ecuadorian Supreme Court held Chevron liable and awarded the Ecuadorian victims damages of billions of dollars.[147] Therefore Ecuadorian law does not disregard the rights of victims of human rights abuses. Accordingly, an application of Ecuadorian law would not by itself limit Elsa's chances of success in filing a suit against the holding company H.

As it pertains to Nigeria, the application of host state law could remand to English law, leaving Naoki with potentially the same practical result, regardless of whether the UK courts would decide to apply English or Nigerian laws. As already mentioned, both UK[148] and Dutch courts have in fact suggested (in the United Kingdom) and decided (in the Netherlands) on the application of UK case-law, because the English and Nigerian systems share the same common law duty-of-care principles. It seems therefore possible that applying Nigerian law in the case study could mean a de facto application of the UK duty-of-care case-law.

Therefore, the application of host state laws may not necessarily result in a violation of human rights or in the lack of effective remedies. However, the fact that the EU choice-of-law rules do not take any human rights standards into account is by itself problematic, because it may result in denying effective remedies to the victims of human rights abuses against European multinational companies.

(v) Interim Conclusion

Under Brussels I and its Recast, it is possible to file a complaint in domestic courts against a European parent company. Instead, Rome II does not take human rights into account when determining the choice-of-law rules applicable to tort cases. The choice of law is almost universally determined by the place where an injury occurred. Therefore, Rome II effectively favours multinational companies that outsource their production to a foreign land with low human rights standards. The only meaningful exception to this general rule is the violation of environmental law, where victims may be able to sue a European company under the law of its place of incorporation. Although, in the Ecuadorian case

[147] *Maria Aguinda Salazar y otros v Chevron Corporation* [2012] Corte Nacional de Justicia (CNJ) Judicio No 174.

[148] *Okpabi & Ors v Royal Dutch Shell Plc & Anor (Rev 1)* [2018] EWCA Civ 191 (n 25); *Okpabi & Ors v Royal Dutch Shell Plc & Anor* (n 81); *Lungowe & Ors v Vedanta Resources Plc & Anor* [2016] EWHC TCC 975 (n 80); *Lungowe & Ors v Vedanta Resources Plc & Anor* [2017] 1528 (n 80); *Akpan v Royal Dutch Shell Plc* (n 140); *Akpan v Royal Dutch Shell Plc* [2015] Court of Appeal at the Hague (Den Haag) 200.126.843.

study, the human rights victim Elsa may be able to sue H under English law, in the Bangladeshi and Nigerian case studies, victims Bodhi and Naoki would likely be able to sue H only under Bangladeshi and Nigerian tort laws. In theory, Bodhi and Naoki could argue that Bangladeshi and Nigerian tort laws violate the law of the forum. However, in practice, UK courts are unlikely to apply the forum law exception.

C. Domestic Law

This section analyses the remedies available under UK domestic law to hold the parent company H to account. UK law does not provide for a framework dedicated specifically to holding multinational corporations liable for human rights abuses committed abroad. There is no law that deals directly with this matter and establishes a specific standard of review for the human rights violations perpetrated by the offshore subsidiaries of a UK-based multinational enterprise. Therefore, it is necessary to look for the areas of law of general application to establish the standard of review applicable to a multinational group of companies in such circumstances. There are two potential options where one can find the relevant rules. The standard of review or secondary norm could be potentially based on either tort law, as it pertains to civil litigation,[149] or criminal law, as it pertains to criminal justice.[150]

Tort law would be a preferable choice in this search for a standard of review or secondary norm for the following reasons. Firstly, civil litigation entitles human rights victims themselves to causes of action for any tort committed by a company incorporated in the UK. Criminal law instead does not entitle individuals to causes of action. It is for the public prosecutor to assess whether and when to initiate criminal proceedings against the perpetrator of human rights abuses. Whereas criminal justice is in the hands of the state, civil justice is instead in the hands of private persons, including individuals.[151] Secondly, traditionally, criminal justice was addressed only to individuals and not to companies. The rationale behind this reasoning is that any crime requires a particular state of mind and psychological understanding of the reality that only individuals have. Therefore, the traditional approach of criminal law is that only individuals can commit crimes.[152] Most recently, European domestic laws are increasingly recognising the possibility of holding companies criminally responsible by attributing the

[149] Kershaw (n 1) 147–55.

[150] ibid 155–65.

[151] For the distinction between criminal and civil justice, see Paul H Robinson, 'The Criminal–Civil Distinction and the Utility of Desert' (1996) 76 *Boston University Law Review* 201.

[152] Andrew Clapham, 'Extending International Criminal Law beyond the Individual to Corporations and Armed Opposition Groups' (2008) 6 *Journal of International Criminal Justice* 899; H van der Wilt, 'Corporate Criminal Responsibility for International Crimes: Exploring the Possibilities' (2013) 12 *Chinese Journal of International Law* 43.

state of mind of the directors, senior managers or employees to the company.[153] For example, the United Kingdom adopted the Corporate Manslaughter and Corporate Homicide Act in 2007.[154] According to this Act, if the state of mind of senior manager(s) is a substantial element of a homicide/manslaughter, the company may also be responsible for such a crime.[155] Another example of this recent trend is the UK Bribery Act of 2010 establishing the responsibility of companies for the failure to prevent one of their associates from committing acts of bribery.[156] However, although criminal law is opening up to the idea of holding companies responsible for criminal offences, it is still at an embryonic stage as it pertains to criminalising companies. The focus of most laws advancing this subject is typically related to the following question: under which circumstances is it possible to attribute the managers' state of mind to the company? There is still no serious intention to impose criminal liability on a parent company for the criminal offences committed by its subsidiaries.[157] Furthermore, in respect of extraterritorial criminal acts, another complication is that public prosecutors, as a general fact, do not have the possibility to conduct investigations outside their territories unless the host state government cooperates with them.[158] This is subject to international cooperation on criminal matters, which is set out in bilateral and multilateral treaties with limited application.[159] Given all these issues with the cross-border application of criminal justice, it is difficult to imagine a UK public prosecutor investigating facts occurring in another country, such as Bangladesh, Nigeria or Ecuador.

For all of the above reasons, this book focuses its analysis on the standard of review established by UK tort law. In tort, the standard of review or secondary norm includes the causes of action available to victims to file a complaint against the UK holding company H. However, to use a cause of action in domestic tort law against a company abusing human rights extraterritorially, it is necessary to analyse company law as it pertains to the liability of UK companies that are a part of a corporate group, because the specific provisions of company law can render such causes of action inefficient. This section analyses whether the combination of company and tort laws establishes a standard of review guaranteeing an effective remedy for the victims that file a complaint against the holding company H.

UK company law is based on the legal separation between shareholder(s) and the corporation.[160] As long ago as the nineteenth century, English courts

[153] Kershaw (n 1) 155–67.

[154] Corporate Manslaughter and Corporate Homicide Act 2007.

[155] ibid; Kershaw (n 1) 163–67.

[156] Bribery Act 2010 (Chapter 23); Sarah C Kaczmarek and Abraham L Newman, 'The Long Arm of the Law: Extraterritoriality and the National Implementation of Foreign Bribery Legislation' (2011) 65 *International Organization* 745.

[157] Kershaw (n 1) 155–67.

[158] Yvon Dandurand, 'Strategies and Practical Measures to Strengthen the Capacity of Prosecution Services in Dealing with Transnational Organized Crime, Terrorism and Corruption' (2007) 47 *Crime, Law and Social Change* 225.

[159] De Schutter (n 8).

[160] See Vanderkerckhove (n 1) 3–9; Kershaw (n 1) 3–46; Gamble and Gavin (n 1) 29–34.

established the concept of corporate separate legal personality in the case *Salomon v Salomon*.[161] Mr Salomon, a sole trader owning a leather shop, transferred his business to a limited liability company, where he was the majority shareholder together with other six members of his family and the only manager. Mr Salomon himself became a preferred creditor of his own company. When the company became bankrupt, he was repaid as a preferred creditor in full, with the result that other creditors were not able to obtain a discharge of their claims against the company. These creditors then sued Mr Salomon, claiming that the company was a fraud and alleging that he should be personally liable for the outstanding debts of the company. Mr Salomon rebutted this claim, stating that third-party creditors could only hold the company liable as it is a separate legal person from its shareholders. Given that the business was incorporated as a limited liability company, third-party creditors could seek a discharge of their claims only to the extent that the company had sufficient assets to pay for its liabilities. The House of Lords agreed with Mr Salomon and ruled that a company is a separate legal entity from its shareholders. Accordingly, in respect of a limited liability company, third parties may hold the company liable for its debts but will be compensated only to the extent of the assets owned by the corporation. With time, the rule that a shareholder cannot be sued for the debts of a limited liability company in which it invested gained universal application.[162]

If I apply this basic principle of company law to multinational corporate groups, it becomes evident that a holding company H will not be liable for any tort committed by its subsidiary, as they are separate legal persons. Even if I assume that the subsidiary S is liable for gross human rights abuses towards the victims Bodhi, Elsa and Naoki, the holding company H will not, as a general rule, be liable to pay with its assets for any damage related to the human rights abuses committed by S. Therefore, Bodhi, Elsa and Naoki would only be able to recover their damages against the assets held by S.

There are, however, two possible avenues to hold the parent company H liable to pay for the damage resulting from the human rights abuses committed by its subsidiary S.

Firstly, the parent company H could be held directly liable for failing to prevent human rights abuses in its corporate group. This is not, strictly speaking, an exception to the principle of limited liability. In this case, the holding company has to pay because of its own wrongful act, not because of its subsidiary. Such a liability can arise when the holding company H breaches its duty of care owed to the victim of the abuses committed by its subsidiary S. When the holding company H breaches such a duty of care, it is negligent for its own wrongful act and, therefore, a person who sustained damages as a result of such

[161] *Salomon v Salomon & Co Ltd* [1897] AC 22 (HL) 29–58.

[162] Blumberg (n 4); Max Gillman and Tim Eade, 'The Development of the Corporation in England, with Emphasis on Limited Liability' (1995) 22 *International Journal of Social Economics* 20; Leebron (n 4).

a wrongful act can file a case against H. Regardless of which human rights have been abused by the subsidiary S, the alleged tort action is based on negligence of the parent company H. It is only very recently that practitioners and scholars have begun to develop such a direct liability framework and successfully argued that it is possible to hold the parent company directly liable for a breach of its duty of care owed to the victims of human rights abuses.[163]

Secondly, it is possible to hold the parent company indirectly liable for the human rights abuses perpetrated by its subsidiary. In such a case, the victim sues the subsidiary S and, at the same time, argues that the holding company H is indirectly responsible for the abuses perpetrated by its affiliate. This is a scenario of piercing the corporate veil. The holding company is liable not because it caused damage to the victim itself, but in its capacity as a shareholder of its subsidiary S. Almost as early as corporate law recognised the limited liability of a shareholder for the acts of a company, a number of practitioners and scholars started to analyse and develop different theories on piercing the corporate veil. However, until today, piercing the corporate veil seems to be a dead end.[164] When, how and under which circumstances it is possible to pierce the corporate veil is far from established. As Lord Neuberger stated in the Supreme Court case *Prest v Petrodel Resources Ltd*: 'The lack of any coherent principle in the application of the [piercing the corporate veil] doctrine has been commented on judicially in many of the major common law jurisdictions.'[165]

UK courts established in their case-law, on the one hand, the direct corporate liability of English holding companies in respect of the acts of their subsidiaries abusing certain rights, such as, for example, the rights of employees,[166] and, on the other hand, the indirect corporate liability of English holding companies for the torts committed by their subsidiaries.[167] This section analyses the applicable UK law in the Bangladeshi, Ecuadorian and Nigerian case studies. It analyses, first, the remedies based on direct liability in tort law; and, second, the remedies based on indirect liability in corporate law (ie piercing of the corporate veil).

[163] Liesbeth Enneking, *Foreign Direct Liability and Beyond Exploring the Role of Tort Law in Promoting International Corporate Social Responsibility and Accountability* (Eleven International Publishing, 2012) 77–128; Enneking (n 3); Richard Meeran, 'Tort Litigation against Multinational Corporations for Violation of Human Rights: An Overview of the Position Outside the United States' (2011) 3 *City University of Hong Kong Law Review* 1; Sarah Joseph, *Corporations and Transnational Human Rights Litigation* (Hart Publishing, 2004) 129–43; Menno T Kamminga, 'Transnational Human Rights Litigation against Multinational Corporations Post-Kiobel', in *What's Wrong with International Law?: Liber Amicorum AHA Soons* (Brill/Nijhoff, 2015); Philipp Wesche and Miriam Saage-Maaß, 'Holding Companies Liable for Human Rights Abuses Related to Foreign Subsidiaries and Suppliers before German Civil Courts: Lessons from *Jabir and Others v KiK*' (2016) 16 *Human Rights Law Review* 370; Nicola Jägers and Marie-Jose van der Heijden, 'Corporate Human Rights Violations: The Feasibility of Civil Recourse in the Netherlands' (2008) 33 *Brooklyn Journal of International Law*, 833; Kershaw (n 1) 133–55; Bright (n 3) 65–114.

[164] See Hansmann and Kraakman (n 129); Vanderkerckhove (n 1); Kershaw (n 1) 30–78.

[165] *Prest v Petrodel Resources Limited and others* [2013] UKSC 34 [75].

[166] See *Chandler v Cape Plc* [2012] (QB), X (appeal taken from Eng) EWCA civ 525.

[167] See *Adams and Others v Cape Industries Plc and Another* [1990] Court of Appeal Ch 433.

(i) Direct Liability

This section analyses the relevant English tort law which may entitle victims to file suits against a holding company for the human rights abuses perpetrated by its foreign subsidiaries. Tort law offers an accountability framework to hold a company responsible for the acts of its affiliates. The leading case on the matter is arguably *Lungowe v Vedanta*, recently decided by the Supreme Court.[168] However, in this case, the issue of parental liability is only raised in the context of determining whether English courts had jurisdiction to hear the case. Therefore, the leading case on parental liability may still be *Chandler v Cape Plc* in which English courts have defined the standard of review applicable to a parent company for the abuses committed by its subsidiary on an employee of the group.[169] However, the Supreme Court in *Lungowe v Vedanta* clarified that *Chandler v Cape Plc* did not establish any specific parental liability regime for torts committed by subsidiaries and simply applied the principles established in *Dorset Yacht Co Ltd v Home Office*,[170] a case that was not about parental liability, to the duty of care of a parent company.[171] Given the complexity of these cases, the following sections analyse them in some details.

(a) The Supreme Court Cases on Parental Liability

Lubbe and Others v Cape Plc and *Lungowe v Vedanta* are the only House of Lords and Supreme Court cases in which the courts asserted the possibility of holding a parent company of a multinational group liable for tortious violations committed by its foreign subsidiary. However, both cases mentioned parental liability only for English courts to assert jurisdiction, and therefore their rulings are only indicative of how UK courts could decide cases on parental liability in the future. Although the cases are 19 years apart from each other, they are similar.

In *Lubbe and Others v Cape Plc*, Mr Lubbe and other employees were working for a South African subsidiary of Cape, a British holding company. The employees and a number of third parties were severely injured from exposure to

[168] *Lungowe & Ors v Vedanta Resources Plc & Anor* [2016] EWHC TCC 975 (n 80); *Lungowe & Ors v Vedanta Resources Plc & Anor* [2017] 1528 (n 80); *Vedanta Resources PLC and another v Lungowe and others* (n 27).

[169] *Chandler v Cape Plc* (n 166); Enneking, *Foreign Direct Liability and Beyond* (n 163) 77–128; Enneking, 'Crossing the Atlantic – The Political and Legal Feasibility of European Foreign Direct Liability Cases' (n 3); Meeran (n 163); Robert McCorquodale, 'Waving Not Drowning: Kiobel Outside the United States' (2013) 107 *American Journal of International Law* 846.

[170] *Home Office v Dorset Yacht Co Ltd* [1970] UKHL 2.

[171] *Vedanta Resources PLC and another v Lungowe and others* (n 27) para 56.

asbestos products and sued the UK parent company.[172] Similarly, in *Lungowe v Vedanta,* a group of Zambian claimants who were not employees of the corporate group, sued both the UK parent company Vedanta and its Zambian subsidiary KCM for transnational environmental damages caused by a mine KCM owned. In both cases, the claimants sued the holding company in the United Kingdom for the violation of a direct duty of care towards its foreign subsidiary's tort victims.[173]

In *Lubbe and Others v Cape Plc*, the House of Lords recognised in its dicta that, under certain particular circumstances, a holding company might have a direct duty of care towards the stakeholders affected by its subsidiary:

> [This case] concerns the responsibility of the defendant as a parent company for ensuring the observance of proper standards of health and safety by its overseas subsidiaries. Resolution of this issue will be likely to involve an inquiry into what part the defendant played in controlling the operations of the group, what its directors and employees knew or ought to have known, what action was taken and not taken, whether the defendant owed a duty of care to employees of group companies overseas and whether, if so, that duty was broken.[174]

Specifically, Lord Bingham of Cornhill described Mr Lubbe's claim as 'not against the defendant as the employer of that plaintiff … [but r]ather … [a]gainst the defendant as a parent compan[y]'.[175]

In *Lungowe v Vedanta*, the Supreme Court conducted a careful analysis of the previous case law and ruled as follows. First, it lowered the burden to prove the arguability of the case. It clarified, in fact, that at the jurisdictional stage, there is no need to have a trial on the relationship between parent company, subsidiary and tort victims. It is sufficient for victims to prove that the parent company may potentially owe a duty of care towards its subsidiary's neighbours. This will certainly facilitate victims in future cases.[176] Second, it clarified that 'the critical question is whether Vedanta sufficiently intervened in the management of the Mine owned by its subsidiary KCM to have incurred, itself (rather than by vicarious liability), a common law duty of care to the claimants'.[177] The answer to this question must be decided on the facts. Third, the leading case on the a duty of care is *Dorset Yacht Co Ltd v Home Office.*[178] Fourth, *Chandler v Cape* is less central than the High Court and Court of Appeal thought in previous cases because it did not establish a new category of common law

[172] *Lubbe and Others v Cape Plc and Related Appeals* [2000] UKHL 41.
[173] *Vedanta Resources PLC and another v Lungowe and others* (n 27); *Lubbe and Others v Cape Plc and Related Appeals* (n 172); Michael D Goldhaber, 'Corporate Human Rights Litigation in Non-U.S. Courts: A Comparative Scorecard' (2013) 3 *University of California Irvine Law Review* 127.
[174] *Lubbe and Others v Cape Plc. and Related Appeals* (n 172) 1555.
[175] ibid 1550.
[176] *Vedanta Resources PLC and another v Lungowe and others* (n 27) para 6–14 and 42–62.
[177] ibid para 44.
[178] ibid 54.

negligence liability.[179] *Lungowe v Vedanta* is significant because it departs from previous categorizations that were requiring a careful analysis of the circumstances of specific cases for English courts to assert jurisdiction. It, therefore, opens the door for English courts to assert jurisdiction on potentially any transnational tort committed by a UK corporate group.[180] In order to understand the importance of this ruling, it is necessary to take a step back and analyse the previous precedents.

(b) *Dorset Yacht Co Ltd v Home Office*: Two Relationships

Lungowe v Vedanta identified *Dorset Yacht Co Ltd v Home Office* as the leading case on parental liability. This case concerned the responsibility of the Home Office for failing to prevent fugitive prisoners from damaging third parties. In this case, the House of Lords analysed both the relationship between the Home Office and the prisoners and the relationship between the Home Office and the third parties. The Home Office had a controlling relationship over the prisoners, but it did not have a direct relationship towards the claimants that were just third parties holding properties in the vicinity of the Brownsea Island where the prisoners were working. The House of Lords ruled that the Home Office owed a duty of care towards the claimants who suffered from reasonably foreseeable damages inflicted by the fugitives to neighbouring Yachts.

The case did not establish a general test to find a duty of care but mentioned two fundamental pillars that courts should analyse in order to recognise the existance of a duty of care. First, the reasonable foreseeability of the chains of events[181] that resulted in damages; second, the proximity between the three parties to the case.[182] In order to determine the liability of a claimant (ie a parent company) for the torts committed by a person it controls (ie a subsidiary) towards a third party (ie a tort victim), the analysis of both the relationship between parent and subsidiary; and the relationship between parent company and tort victim is important. Although the Home Office did not have a direct relationship with the yachts' owners, it had such a controlling relationship over the prisoners in a secluded place (an island) to reasonably foresee the damages the fugitives could make to their neighbours. In the Home Office/prisoners relationship, proximity is intended as the supervision and control that the guards (Home Office's employees) had to exercise over the prisoners; while in the Home Office/tort victim relationship, the proximity between claimant and respondent is intended

[179] ibid 56.
[180] ibid 51–52.
[181] As Lord Reid argued 'When then is the dividing line? Is it foreseeability or is it such a degree of probability as warrants the conclusion that the intervening human conduct was the natural and probable result of what preceded it?' *Home Office v Dorset Yacht Co Ltd* [1970] UKHL 2 (n 170) 1028.
[182] *Home Office v Dorset Yacht Co Ltd* [1970] UKHL 2 (n 170).

as the chain of events that connects the respondent's failure to act with the damage suffered by the claimant.[183]

(c) The Relationship between the Claimant and the Respondent

Twenty years after *Dorset Yacht Co Ltd v Home Office*, the House of Lords decided another fundamental case on the duty of care: *Caparo Industries plc v Dickman and others*.[184] This case, concerned an investor who, on the basis of the false statements made by an accounting company, paid more than the value of the shares in a takeover offer. The question was whether the accounting company owed a duty of care towards the investor that relied on its statement. Put it differently: could the investor be considered a neighbour of, and in a relationship of proximity with, the accounting company? The House of Lords ruled that it could not. It focused most of its reasoning on the relationship between the accounting company (the respondent) and the investor (the claimant) rather than between the accounting company and its client (the company the investor invested in).[185] The case confirmed the *Dorset Yacht Co Ltd v Home Office*'s rejection of a test on the duty of care and its case by case analysis. In fact, in *Caparo Industries plc v Dickman and others* Lord Oliver of Aylmerton defined proximity as '[a] convenient expression so long as it is realized that it is no more than a label which embraces not a definable concept but merely a description of circumstances from which, pragmatically, the courts conclude that a duty of care exists'.[186] It is the analysis of each specific case that would allow a court to assess whether or not a claimant owes a duty of care towards a respondent. There is no general foreseeability test that could provide for an answer in this respect. *Caparo Industries Plc v Dickman and Others* also relied on the two *Dorset Yacht Co Ltd v Home Office*'s pillars: proximity and reasonable foreseeability.

However, as scholars have emphasised, *Caparo Industries Plc v Dickman and Others* introduced also an additional element, which has been defined as 'pockets of case law' approach.[187] According to this approach, different cases could be associated with various contexts to establish a duty of care. One could refer to a particular pocket of case law that would explain the application of general principles of tort law to each particular context. Therefore, the authority of each case is limited to a specific category it belongs to.

[183] Christian Witting, 'Duty of Care: An Analytical Approach' (2005) 25 *Oxford Journal of Legal Studies* 33.

[184] *Caparo Industries Plc Respondents v Dickman and Others Appellants* [1990] HL AC 2, 605.

[185] Witting (n 183).

[186] *Caparo Industries Plc. Respondents v Dickman and Others Appellants* (n 184) 633.

[187] See also Jane Stapleston, 'Duty of Care and Economic Loss: A Wider Agenda' (1991) *Law Quarterly Review* 249.

The High Court applied *Caparo Industries plc v Dickman and others* to the duty of care arguably owed by a parent company in *David Newton Sealey v ArmorGroup Services Ltd* where it dismissed an application for summary judgment. As in *Caparo Industries plc v Dickman and others*, in *David Newton Sealey v ArmorGroup Services Ltd* the court based its analysis on the relationship between the claimant (the tort victim) and the respondent (the parent company). In this case, the Armor Group, with two holding companies incorporated in the United Kingdom, had a subsidiary in Jersey. Although the holding companies were directly involved in Mr Newton Sealey's hiring process, he was employed by their Jersey subsidiary as a security agent to work in Iraq. Mr Newton Sealey was injured in Iraq and decided to sue the two Armor holding companies under English law. The issue was whether the Armor holding companies had a direct duty of care towards their subsidiary's employee. The High Court held that the holding company could arguably foresee Mr Newton Sealey's injury, because it was directly involved in both the recruitment of the employee and job operations in Iraq. Therefore, the employee had reasonable grounds to believe that he was working for the whole corporate group.[188]

From *Caparo Industries plc v Dickman and others* and *David Newton Sealey v ArmorGroup Services Ltd* it seems that the relevant relationship of proximity that is required to establish a duty of care is in between the parent company and the tort victim.

(d) The Relationship between Parent Company and Subsidiary

Chandler v Cape Plc and *Thompson v the Renwick Group Plc*, two Court of Appeal cases on the duty of care of parent companies for torts committed by their subsidiaries, changed the focus of the analysis from the relationship between parent company and victim, to the relationship between parent and subsidiary.

The facts of the cases are almost identical in terms of the relationship between parent company and tort victims, but they differ when one analyses the relationship between parent company and subsidiary. In both cases an employee of a subsidiary worked for years on the production of asbestos and sued the parent company for health damages due to abestosis. In *Chandler v Cape Plc*, the Court of Appeal explained the duty of care in the context of a parent–subsidiary relationship, arguably building up on *Caparo Industries plc v Dickman and Others* to establish a pocket of case law on parental liability. The parent company has a direct duty of care towards the subsidiary's employee when:

(1) the businesses of the parent and subsidiary are in a relevant respect the same;
(2) the parent has, or ought to have, superior knowledge on some relevant aspect of health and safety in the particular industry;

[188] *David Newton Sealey v ArmorGroup Services Ltd* [2008] EWHC (QB) 233 [26].

(3) the subsidiary's system of work is unsafe as the parent company knew, or ought to have known; and

(4) the parent knew or ought to have foreseen that the subsidiary or its employees would rely on its using that superior knowledge for the employees' protection. For the purpose of (4) it is not necessary to show that the parent is in the practice of intervening in the health and safety policies of the subsidiary. The court will look at the relationship between companies more widely. The court may find that element (4) is established where the evidence shows that the parent has a practice of intervening in the trading operations of the subsidiary, for example production and funding issues.[189]

Differently from *David Newton Sealey v ArmorGroup Services Ltd*, in *Chandler v Cape Plc*, there was no allegation that the employee had any direct relationship with the parent company. Nevertheless, the Court of Appeal held the parent company liable for its subsidiary's violation, because it assumed responsibility over its subsidiary. The liability of the parent corporation does not arise from its actions toward the subsidiary's employees, but from its '[o]mission to take steps or to give advice'[190] to the subsidiary in violation of its duty of care. Essentially, the Court of Appeal revisited the concept of *assumption of responsibility* as *attachment of responsibility*. Traditionally *assumption of responsibility* meant that a person assumes responsibility for a matter and thereafter is responsible for it. English courts interpreted the *assumption of responsibility* as voluntary and originating in a defendant's representation that would reasonably make others assume that the respondent is accountable.[191] However, in *Chandler v Cape Plc*, the Court of Appeal felt entitled to read the concept of *assumption of responsibility* no longer as a voluntary act of the parent corporation to assume responsibility over its subsidiary's employees, but rather as a legal imposition, an attachment, of responsibility that arises when the parent company knows or ought to know that the subsidiary is damaging its employees.[192] However, if it is not the voluntary assumption, what is it that establishes responsibility? It seems to be the overall influence that the parent company has over the subsidiary's activities that would result in the parent corporation knowing or being in a position to know that the subsidiary was conducting risky activities.[193] This conflation between the concepts of foreseeability, assumption and attachment of responsibility, switched the focus of the case from the relationship of proximity between parent and tort victim, to the proximity between parent and subsidiary.[194] Although the Court of Appeal stated that the simple fact of being

[189] *Chandler v Cape Plc* (n 166) 80.
[190] ibid 72.
[191] See Tim Bullimore, 'Sins of the Father, Sins of the Son' (2012) 28 *Professional Negligence* 212.
[192] *Chandler v Cape Plc* (n 166) 62–65. See also the previous case *Smith v Eric Bush* [1990] AC 1 831.
[193] See Martin Petrin, 'Assumption of Responsibility in Corporate Groups: Chandler v Cape Plc' (2013) 76 *MLR* 603.
[194] ibid.

parent and subsidiary does not necessarily entail proximity,[195] it did not clarify what the *criteria* to set proximity are. In continuty with previous case law,[196] it admitted that, given the complex structures of corporate groups, it is impossible to establish the necessary elements to prove proximity in the abstract and, therefore, courts should assess such factors on a case-by-case basis.[197] In *Chandler v Cape Plc*, the Court found proximity on multiple bases, including an exchange of information between the parent company, the subsidiary and a doctor conducting empirical research on asbestos in the factories of the corporate group; the fact that the parent company often directed the activities of the subsidiary; and the fact that the parent company set up the asbestos business and then subsequently sold it to its subsidiary. All of these elements contributed to the narrative that the parent company assumed responsibility over the group, but none of them seemed to establish such proximity on its own.[198] Therefore, it remains open to interpretation what the elements are to establish the assumption of responsibility of the parent company over its subsidiary.

In line with *Chandler v Cape Plc*, the Court of Appeal in *Thompson v the Renwick Group Plc* ruled that the duty of care depends on whether or not the holding company has more knowledge than the subsidiary on the protection of employees.[199] It, therefore, confirmed that it is the relationship between the parent corporation and its subsidiary, rather than the parent company and the employee, that matters. However, different from *Chandler v Cape Plc*, *Thompson v the Renwick Group Plc* laid out particularly demanding *criteria* for the parent company to have superior knowledge about its subsidiary. The holding company owes a duty of care when it is

> better placed, because of its superior knowledge or expertise, to protect the employees of subsidiary companies against the risk of injury and moreover where, because of that feature, it is fair to infer that the subsidiary will rely upon the parent deploying its superior knowledge in order to protect its employees from risk of injury.[200]

The Court of Appeal found a number of circumstances insufficient to establish the parent company's superior knowledge about the activities conducted by the employee. Such circumstances include the cooperation between different companies in a corporate group, the joint use of resources, the facts that the employee was driving a truck with the parent company's livery, that the parent company called a taxi on occasion for the employee and that the parent

[195] *Chandler v Cape Plc* (n 166) para 69.
[196] *Home Office v Dorset Yacht Co Ltd* [1970] UKHL 2 (n 170).
[197] ibid 67.
[198] ibid 72–81.
[199] *Thompson v The Renwick Group Plc* [2014] EWCA Civ 635 [37].
[200] ibid.

company hired the subsidiary's director who was responsible for the health and safety of the employees.[201] Most importantly the Court of Appeal found that:

> The findings of the judge on the intermingling of the businesses, the interchangeable use of depots and the shared use of resources amount to no more than a finding that these companies were operating as a division of the group carrying on a single business.[202]

This clarified that a parent company does not owe a duty of care towards the subsidiary's employees for the simple fact that it controls that subsidiary. The additional element of superior knowledge and expertise is required to establish such a duty of care.[203] It should be noted that *Thompson v the Renwick Group Plc* recognised *Chandler v Cape Plc* as the applicable law, and *Chandler v Cape Plc* ruled that there is no fixed test to determine whether a parent company and subsidiary are in a relationship of proximity.[204] If this is true, and courts must decide on a case-by-case basis, *Thompson v the Renwick Group Plc* may merely represent a situation in which, overall, the parent and the subsidiary companies were not close enough to entail the responsibility of the former for the activities of the latter. Under such a case-by-case analysis, the difference between *Thompson v the Renwick Group Plc* and *Chandler v Cape Plc* is fact-based, but it does not entail a shift of paradigm in the construction of the parent company's duty of care.

Therefore, although the Court of Appeal reached opposite conclusions in *Thompson v the Renwick Group Plc* and *Chandler v Cape Plc*, in both cases it switched its analysis from the relationship parent company/tort victim to the relationship parent company/subsidiary which would entail an attachment of responsibility of the former for the abuses committed by the latter. This change in focus, has not, however, answered to the crucial question that *Dorset Yacht Co Ltd v Home Office* and all subsequent cases left without response: who could be considered the claimant's, ie the parent company's, neighbours? How can one define the group of persons towards which the parent company owes a duty of care? It seems clear that employees may be neighbours even if they had no direct relationship with the parent company, but could a duty of care be extended also to third parties who are not employees? And could these neighbours include every person potentially damaged by a subsidiary or would this be a more limited group of people? A possible argument in favour of extending the title of neighbour to any person damaged by the subsidiary is as follows. *Chandler v Cape Plc* and *David Thompson v the Renwick Group Plc* significantly detached the duty of care from the claimant-respondent relationship.

201 ibid 34–35.

202 ibid 38.

203 Uglješa Grušić, 'Responsibility in Groups of Companies and the Future of International Human Rights and Environmental Litigation' (2015) 74 *CLJ* 30.

204 *Chandler v Cape Plc* (n 166) para 67.

Unlike in other cases,[205] in *Chandler v Cape Plc* and *Thompson v the Renwick Group Plc*, it is clear that the duty of care did not derive from the relationship between the employee and the parent company, but rather from the relationship between the subsidiary and the holding company.[206] It is this relationship that may, if close enough like in *Chandler v Cape Plc*, attach responsibility to the parent company towards the tort victim damaged by its subsidiary. Conversely, if parent and subsidiary are not connected enough like in *Thompson v the Renwick Group Plc*, the parent company is not assuming responsibility towards the employee. If the relationship between the parent and subsidiary establishes that the parent company owes a duty of care towards its subsidiary's employees, what would prevent a court from finding that the parent also has a direct duty of care towards its subsidiary's third-party victims? Arguably anyone affected by the subsidiary could be considered a neighbour provided that the parent is sufficiently in charge of the group to reasonably foresee the damages its subsidiaries could make.[207]

(e) Looking Forward: Transnational Cases

Besides *Chandler v Cape Plc* and *David Thompson v the Renwick Group Plc*, UK courts had to decide whether or not to assert jurisdiction on three transnational cases. The first one is the already mentioned *Lungowe v Vedanta*. It is by far the most significant case as the only one decided by the Supreme Court and in the victims' favour. The other two are *Okpabi v Royal Dutch Shell Plc* and *AAA & Others v Unilever PLC and Unilever Tea Kenya Limited*. These are all similar cases, because they concern multinational enterprises allegedly owing a duty of care towards involuntary tort victims who are not employees of the corporate group. They include allegations of extraterritorial environmental degradation committed by UK corporate groups through their foreign subsidiaries in Zambia and Nigeria, and the failure of the corporate group to prevent tribal violence in Kenya. Interestingly, the British courts came to different decisions as it pertains to their jurisdiction on UK multinational enterprises allegedly abusing human rights extraterritorially. In all of these cases, to assess the arguability of the claim, UK courts had to decide whether or not the parent company could arguably owe a duty of care towards the claimants. It should be noted that these assessments were part of a preliminary jurisdictional step necessary to decide

[205] *David Newton Sealey v ArmorGroup Services Ltd* (n 188).

[206] *Chandler v Cape Plc* (n 166); *Thompson v The Renwick Group Plc* (n 199).

[207] See Meeran (n 163). See eg the Dutch case *Akpan v Royal Dutch Shell Plc* that applied *Chandler v Cape* to the Nigerian subsidiary and Dutch parent company in a case involving victims who were not employees, *Akpan v Royal Dutch Shell Plc* (n 140); Liesbeth Enneking, 'The Future of Foreign Direct Liability: Exploring the International Relevance of the Dutch Shell Nigeria Case' (2014) 10 *Utrecht Law Review* 44; Nicola Jägers, Katinka Jesse and Jonathan Verschuuren, 'The Future of Corporate Liability for Extraterritorial Human Rights Abuses: The Dutch Case against Shell' (2013) 107 *The American Journal of International Law* 36.

whether the claimants had any prospect of success. There was no judgment on the merits of the cases. However, UK courts delivered opposite rulings. In *Lungowe v Vedanta*, the High Court, the Court of Appeal and the Supreme Court[208] refused a motion to dismiss the lawsuit, as Zambian tort victims had an arguable claim against the UK parent company for breach of its extraterritorial duty of care. On the contrary, in *Okpabi v Royal Dutch Shell Plc* and *AAA & Others v Unilever PLC and Unilever Tea Kenya Limited*, both the High Court and the Court of Appeal[209] dismissed the lawsuit because the parent company had no arguable duty of care towards the victims of abuses committed in Nigeria and Kenya. This may change, because the victims requested leave to appeal both *Okpabi v Royal Dutch Shell Plc* and *AAA & Others v Unilever PLC and Unilever Tea Kenya Limited*. The decision on whether or not to grant leave to appeal has been pending the ruling of *Lungowe v Vedanta*. It is now possible that the Supreme Court will grant such permission and will allow the appeal to move forward.[210] Therefore, it is crucial to understand what the implications of *Lungowe v Vedanta* may be on these cases.

In *Okpabi v Royal Dutch Shell Plc*, the High Court argued that a holding corporation does not owe a duty of care by virtue of controlling its subsidiaries, as this would de facto disregard the separate legal personality of the different companies of the group. It relied on *Thompson v the Renwick Group Plc* to state that only when a parent company has superior knowledge about the activities conducted by its subsidiaries would it have a duty of care towards the tort victims detrimentally affected by such subsidiaries.[211] The Court of Appeal confirmed the decision of the High Court, with two judges holding there was not enough evidence supporting the proximity between the parent company and its subsidiary.[212]

AAA & Others v Unilever PLC and Unilever Tea Kenya Limited may be distinguished from *Okpabi v Royal Dutch Shell Plc*, *Lungowe v Vedanta* and the case studies presented in this book because it concerns the failure of a UK multinational company to protect employees and people living in the vicinity of its industry in Kenya from tribal violence. The corporate group included a

[208] *Lungowe & Ors v Vedanta Resources Plc & Anor* [2016] EWHC TCC 975 (n 80); *Lungowe & Ors v Vedanta Resources Plc & Anor* [2017] 1528 (n 80).

[209] *Okpabi & Ors v Royal Dutch Shell Plc & Anor (Rev 1)* [2018] EWCA Civ 191 (n 25); *Okpabi & Ors v Royal Dutch Shell Plc & Anor* (n 81); *AAA & Ors v Unilever Plc & Anor* [2018] EWCA Civ 1532 (n 82); *AAA & Ors v Unilever Plc & Anor* [2017] EWHC 371 (QB) (n 82).

[210] Business & Human Rights Resource Centre, 'NGOs Support Claimants' Application to Appeal to UK Supreme Court against Unilever for Its Subsidiary's Alleged Failure to Protect Employees from Post-Electoral Violence in Kenya <https://www.business-humanrights.org/en/ngos-support-claimants-application-to-appeal-to-uk-supreme-court-against-unilever-for-its-subsidiary%E2%80%99s-alleged-failure-to-protect-employees-from-post-electoral-violence-in-kenya> accessed 30 April 2019; Business & Human Rights Resource Centre, 'Shell Lawsuit (Re Oil Spills & Ogale & Bille Communities in Nigeria – Okpabi v Shell) <https://www.business-humanrights.org/en/shell-lawsuit-re-oil-spills-ogale-bille-communities-in-nigeria-okpabi-v-shell> accessed 30 April 2019.

[211] *Okpabi & Ors v Royal Dutch Shell Plc & Anor* (n 81).

[212] *Okpabi & Ors v Royal Dutch Shell Plc & Anor (Rev 1)* [2018] EWCA Civ 191 (n 25).

parent company incorporated in the United Kingdom (Unilever) and its Kenyan subsidiary (UTKL). However, this time the subsidiary did not actively abuse human rights, but it instead failed to prevent abuses. Both the High Court[213] and the Court of Appeal[214] dismissed the case on jurisdictional grounds, because the victims did not have an arguable claim. They restated that *Chandler v Cape* did not set up a test to determine the vicinity between a parent company and its subsidiaries.[215] It is for the courts to assess proximity on a case-by-case basis. According to the Court of Appeal:

> The cases where [the assumption of responsibility] … might be capable of being alleged will usually fall into two basic types: (i) where the parent has in substance taken over the management of the relevant activity of the subsidiary in place of (or jointly with: see Vedanta Resources at [83]) the subsidiary's own management; or (ii) where the parent has given relevant advice to the subsidiary about how it should manage a particular risk.[216]

In this case, the parent had neither taken over the management of the subsidiary nor provided any advice as it pertains to situations of emergency and crisis. Therefore, the victims had no arguable claim and the case was dismissed. In determining vicinity, the Court of Appeal considered immaterial the fact that the parent and subsidiary acted as a single economic unit with the parent holding indirectly the majority of the shares in UTKL.[217]

In both *Okpabi v Royal Dutch Shell Plc* and *AAA & Others v Unilever Tea Kenya Limited* the courts attempted to detail the category of parental liability in the context of extraterritorial torts committed by its subsidiaries. However, in *Lungowe v Vedanta*, the Supreme Court disagreed with these categorisation of cases, and it argued that any parent company could potentially owe a duty of care towards tort victims affected by its subsidiary.

> I would be reluctant to seek to shoehorn all cases of the parent's liability into specific categories of that kind, helpful though they will no doubt often be for the purposes of analysis. There is no limit to the models of management and control which may be put in place within a multinational group of companies. At one end, the parent may be no more than a passive investor in separate businesses carried out by its various direct and indirect subsidiaries. At the other extreme, the parent may carry out a thoroughgoing vertical reorganisation of the group's businesses so that they are, in management terms, carried on as if they were a single commercial undertaking, with boundaries of legal personality and ownership within the group becoming irrelevant, until the onset of insolvency, as happened within the Lehman Brothers group.[218]

[213] *AAA & Ors v Unilever Plc & Anor* [2017] EWHC 371 (QB) (n 82).
[214] *AAA & Ors v Unilever Plc & Anor* [2018] EWCA Civ 1532 (n 82).
[215] ibid 36.
[216] ibid 37.
[217] ibid 16. Unilever owned 100% of a company named Brooke Bond Group Limited, which owned 88.2% of UTKL.
[218] *Vedanta Resources PLC and another v Lungowe and others* (n 27) para 51.

Furthermore, the Supreme Court clarified that *Chandler Cape Plc* is not establishing a pocket of case law on parental liability, but it is a mere example of the application of general principles of reasonable foreseeability, proximity and neighbourhood as decided in *Dorset Yacht Co Ltd v Home Office*. This seems to be, at least in part, a departure from *Caparo Industries Plc v Dickman and Others* and its pockets of case law approach. Despite this apparent departure, the Supreme Court restated that there is no fixed test to determine the existence of a duty of care. What matters is the case by case analysis of the overall relationship between parent company, subsidiary and victims, as established in *Dorset Yacht Co Ltd v Home Office*.

Therefore, the Supreme Court ruled that claims against non-employees may be arguable,[219] and it clarified that the real issue is whether parent companies 'sufficiently intervene'[220] in the business of their subsidiaries for them to assume responsibility over their actions. This seems to corroborate the argument that the focus switched from proximity between the parent company and the tort victim to proximity between parent and subsidiary. If this is true, then the duty of care could be potentially applicable to any tort victim, not a specific group of neighbours, because it is the relationship between parent and subsidiary that would define the reach of the duty of care. This approach will certainly open the door to further litigation.

The question that *Lungowe v Vedanta* has not yet answered is, however, what are the factual elements that would establish the necessary relationship between parent and subsidiary for the former to owe a duty of care towards third parties damaged by the latter. The answer to this question seems to be a matter of facts which should be decided by courts on a case by case analysis.

(f) Interim Conclusion

The tort law remedy/direct liability framework applies to the Bangladeshi, Ecuadorian and Nigerian case study, because UK case law establishes a cause of action in tort for the neighbours of a corporate group to sue the holding company. The duty of care of holding companies entitles an employee, such as Bodhi, or arguably a third-party tort victim, such as Naoki or Elsa, to file a lawsuit against a holding company H for the human rights abuses perpetrated by its subsidiary S. Therefore, Bodhi, Naoki and Elsa could benefit from a direct liability framework that would entitle them to sue H, for the human rights abuses perpetrated by S. Such direct liability, however, would be difficult to establish. It would require Bodhi, Naoki and Elsa to prove that H had control and superior knowledge about the matters which resulted in the damage caused by S. Furthermore, there is a key difference between the Bangladeshi and the

[219] *Lungowe & Ors v Vedanta Resources Plc & Anor* [2016] EWHC TCC 975 (n 80) para 115.
[220] *Vedanta Resources PLC and another v Lungowe and others* (n 27) para 44.

Ecuadorian or Nigerian case studies: while in the Bangladeshi case the victim is an employee of a Bangladeshi subsidiary of H, in the Ecuadorian and Nigerian case studies the victims of human rights abuses are not employees, but instead third parties, who do not have any relationship with S or H, but were severely damaged and affected by their corporate activities. Being an employee of the group Bodhi would arguably be in a better place than Naoki and Elsa to file such a lawsuit. While, in fact, a number of jurisdictional cases, including the Supreme Court recent decision in *Lungowe v Vedanta,* opened to the possibility to extend the parent company's duty of care to any neighbour of the corporate group, the only cases decided on the merits of the duty of care of a parent company concerned employees.

(ii) Indirect Liability

As an alternative to the direct liability cause of action in tort, a holding company could be indirectly liable for the human rights abuses perpetrated by its subsidiary. Scholars and judges have consistently set forth two main exceptions that allow the separate personality of a limited liability company to be disregarded in UK company law. The first exception is intended to prevent *evading existing legal obligations*. The second exception is based on the notion of a *single economic unit*.

(a) Evading Existing Legal Obligations

According to the *evading existing legal obligations* exception, a court is entitled to pierce the veil when a shareholder establishes a company as a sham to evade its existing legal obligations. In order to apply this exception to the limited liability of a shareholder, timing is the critical factor: the shareholder, ie the holding company, must, first, have a legal obligation towards a third party, and, second, attempt to evade it through a subsidiary. If instead the holding company first establishes its subsidiary, and subsequently its subsidiary incurred legal obligations towards third parties, the holding company is not evading any existing legal obligation. In the latter case, the holding company has never had any existing obligation towards third parties; it just established a subsidiary, which then incurred such obligations and, accordingly, the parent company cannot be held liable.[221]

English courts have constantly recognised *evading existing legal obligations* as a reason to pierce the corporate veil and hold a shareholder liable for the acts of its subsidiary. For example, in *Gilford Motor Co Ltd v Horne*,[222] a former managing director, Mr Horne, violated his non-solicitation agreement with his

[221] Kershaw (n 1) 30–78; Vanderkerckhove (n 1) 66–76.
[222] *Gilford Motor Company, Limited v Horne* [1933] Court of Appeal Ch 935.

former employer, Gilford Motor Co Ltd. Following the termination of his relationship with Gilford Motor Co Ltd, Mr Horne carried out a new business, in the name of a company established as a sham to evade its contractual obligation. In *Jones and Another v Lipman and Another*,[223] Mr Lipman agreed to sell a property first to a third party and second to his own company, in order to evade its contractual obligation. In both cases, English courts pierced the corporate veil because each defendant incorporated a company to evade his pre-existing legal obligations. Furthermore, in *Adams and Others v Cape Industries Plc*[224] the Court of Appeal confirmed that *evading existing legal obligations* is an exception to the general principle of separate corporate legal personality. Finally, in the Supreme Court case *Prest v Petrodel Resources Ltd*,[225] all the Lords agreed that, when a company is established with the purpose of *evading existing legal obligations*, a court is entitled to pierce the corporate veil and hold the shareholder accountable for the company's liabilities.

The *evading existing legal obligations* exception would hardly ever apply to multinational companies, because typically subsidiaries are the only entities that assume legal obligations towards third parties. It will rarely be the case that a holding company would, first, assume an obligation towards a third party, and, second, evade such a legal obligation through its subsidiary. Typically, a holding company would first establish its chain of subsidiaries incorporated in different countries and then run the production/activity damaging third parties. In order to evade an existing legal obligation, the holding company should first assume a legal obligation towards the victim. However, in the multinational corporate context, the holding company would typically have no relationship or obligations towards the human rights victim. Therefore, the *evading existing legal obligation* exception does not apply to the multinational corporate context, because the holding company is neither assuming, nor evading, any obligation towards the victim.

(b) Single Economic Unit

According to the *single economic unit* principle, a court is entitled to pierce the corporate veil when, in a corporate group, the holding company fully manages its subsidiaries as if they were branches of one company. Such an argument is not based on any existing liability, but on the simple fact that, under the guidance of the holding company, corporate groups act as one entity.[226]

English courts developed this line of argument in the Court of Appeal case *DHN Food Distributors Ltd v Tower Hamlets London Borough Council*.[227]

[223] *Jones and Another v Lipman and Another* [1962] Chancey Division WLR 1, 832.
[224] *Adams and Others v Cape Industries Plc. and Another* (n 167).
[225] *Prest v Petrodel Resources Limited and others* (n 165).
[226] See Vanderkerckhove (n 1) 66–76; Kershaw (n 1) 60–75.
[227] *DHN Food Distributors Ltd v Tower Hamlets London Borough Council Bronze Investments Ltd v Same DHN Food Transport Ltd v Same* [1976] Court of Appeal WLR 1, 852.

The Court of Appeal held that the DHN parent company and its subsidiaries were one entity. However, subsequent cases have limited the scope of the *single economic unit* argument. In particular, in *Woolfson v Strathclyde Regional Council*,[228] the House of Lords limited the application of *DHN Food Distributors Ltd v Tower Hamlets London Borough Council* to corporate groups where the holding company fully owns its subsidiaries. Furthermore, in *Adams and Others v Cape Plc*,[229] the Court of Appeal ruled that a court may pierce the corporate veil based on the *single economic unit* argument only when the subsidiary is a totally inactive company. In *Adams and Others v Cape Plc* the totally inactive subsidiary was a company incorporated in Lichtenstein that could be defined as a completely empty shell not conducting any activity. Finally, in *Prest v Petrodel Resources Ltd*, the Supreme Court stated that the only clear and established doctrine to pierce the corporate veil is the *evading existing legal obligations* exception and all other theories were not corroborated and confirmed by the case-law, basically disavowing the *single economic unit* doctrine as a separate exception to the principle of limited liability. Although some members of the court, such as Lord Sumption and Lord Neuberger, seemed to completely shut the door on any other piercing the corporate veil theory, other than *evading existing legal obligations*,[230] others, such as Lord Mance and Lady Hale, were more open in their dicta to alternative arguments to pierce the corporate veil.[231] However, even if I assume that *Prest v Petrodel Resources Ltd* left the door open to such other theories, it is unclear whether the *single economic unit* argument would be one of them.

Therefore, the *single economic unit* argument is unlikely to be applicable to human rights litigation against multinational corporations. Although there may be a theoretical opportunity to make a *single economic unit* argument, English courts have consistently stated that such an argument could be successful only on a case-by-case basis and under particular circumstances which require that the relevant subsidiary exists as a dormant shell company pursuing no commercial activity of its own. However, typically in human rights cases, the subsidiary is not a totally inactive company, but instead is an active business unit adversely affecting stakeholders.

(c) Interim Conclusion

The corporate law indirect liability framework is unlikely to be useful to bring a successful claim against a holding company H for the violations of human rights committed by its subsidiary S. Two rationales for piercing the corporate veil are potentially available in English law.

[228] *Woolfson v Strathclyde Regional Council* [1978] SC 90 (HL).
[229] *Adams and Others v Cape Industries Plc. and Another* (n 167).
[230] *Prest v Petrodel Resources Limited and others* (n 165) 1–83.
[231] ibid 84–102.

The first is the *evading existing legal obligations* principle, which is applicable when a shareholder assumes and evades an existing obligation towards a third party by incorporating a company. This theory is not applicable when it is the subsidiary itself that assumes an obligation towards third parties. In this case, the shareholder is not liable towards the third-party creditors. Human rights victims are not likely to be able to disregard the separate legal personality of a subsidiary on the basis of existing legal obligations because a usual scenario of multinational groups abusing human rights would not involve a pre-existing obligation of a holding company H towards the victims of such abuses. Instead, it is the subsidiary S that abuses human rights and therefore is the only responsible entity for such abuses.

The second exception permitting the corporate veil to be pierced is the *single economic unit* principle, applicable when a corporate group has a totally inactive subsidiary. The *single economic unit* does not apply to multinational companies when the subsidiary is an active business entity. Furthermore, it is unclear whether the *single economic unit* argument could be still considered alive after the dismissive Supreme Court decision in *Prest v Petrodel Resources Ltd*.

Therefore, the company law indirect liability framework is unlikely to be a useful remedy for the victims of human rights abuses in the Bangladeshi, Ecuadorian and Nigerian case studies.

III. CONCLUSION

This chapter analysed what options are available to a human rights victim, such as Bodhi, Elsa and Naoki, to bring an action against a holding company H for the human rights abuses perpetrated by its subsidiary S. It demonstrated that it would be extremely difficult for Bodhi, Elsa and Naoki to obtain any redress from the holding company H. International, EU and UK laws fail to establish a business and human rights framework providing victims with effective remedies against multinational corporations for the following reasons.

First, there is no international legal framework addressing the accountability of a European corporate group outsourcing its production to developing countries. International law established a number of soft-law frameworks that aim at regulating the leading role of multinational companies in the global economy without, however, providing for any effective remedy for human rights victims in respect of any harm resulting from such multinational corporations. Although the CSR frameworks have the advantage of promoting a business and human rights culture, they neither establish any legally binding obligation for enterprises nor provide for any enforceable mechanism to hold companies accountable.

Second, there is no EU law mechanism to hold European companies responsible for human rights abuses committed by their foreign subsidiaries. Furthermore, the EU conflict-of-laws rules limit the possibilities for human rights victims to obtain redress against a multinational company. A human rights victim would have to overcome two fundamental issues. The first issue would be to establish whether or not a European court has jurisdiction over an extraterritorial human rights abuse. Under the Brussels I and its Recast, it is clear that a European court would have jurisdiction over a legal action provided that the alleged abuse of human rights could be attributed to a European parent company. The second problem is to ensure that a law complying with human rights would apply to the case at hand. Rome II does not take possible human rights abuses into account in setting out the choice-of-law rules. Under Rome II, the applicable law to the Bangladeshi and the Nigerian case studies would, most likely, be the place of injury law, ie Bangladeshi and Nigerian law, respectively. Instead, the Ecuadorian case study would benefit from Article 7 of Rome II, which provides for a special, advantageous treatment of environmental law claims. Therefore, the Ecuadorian victim Elsa could successfully argue for the application of English law to the damage she sustained due to subsidiary S. This may possibly result in a denial of justice for the victims of human rights abuses. In fact, the application of Bangladeshi law would most likely not provide any chance of success to Bodhi. The application of Ecuadorian law may instead be favourable to Elsa's claim. As it pertains to Naoki, UK and Dutch courts have so far been open to the possibility of interpreting Nigerian law as referring to English law. This would result in Naoki being able to rely on English case-law even if the UK courts would apply Nigerian law.

Third, even if victims successfully overcome the above hurdles, the issue is whether, under the law of the forum, they have effective remedies to hold a parent company H responsible for the torts committed by its foreign subsidiary. I analysed this issue by reference to English company and tort law, which offers promising remedies in this respect.

The victims, Bodhi, Elsa and Naoki could argue that H assumed responsibility over S. Therefore, H could have reasonably foresee that the Rana Plaza building, and Bodhi's safety conditions, were not in compliance with the minimum standards of safety required under the UK Health and Safety at Work Act,[232] that the extraction of the oil in Ecuador was not meeting minimum safety and international recognised environmental standards, and that the Nigerian Government would have violated human rights in response to the demonstration organised against its mining activities. However, whether or not they will be able to demonstrate the existence and the breach of a duty of care is still very much a matter of facts and of judicial discretion. In fact, no UK court has ever found a parent company liable for a breach of its duty of care towards human rights victims abused by its foreign subsidiary. A key issue, in this regard, would be whether distant strangers such as Bodhi, Naoki and Elsa could be considered neighbours of the corporate group. Being an employee, Bodhi may arguably have

[232] Health and Safety at Work etc Act 1974 (c 37).

a better chance to qualify as proximate to H, given that previous cases where a parent company was found to owe a duty of care always concerned employees. In the Ecuadorian and Nigerian case studies, the victims could also argue for a broad application of UK case law to non-employee third-party victims. Elsa and Naoki could argue that, according to *Chandler v Cape Plc* and subsequent cases, the parent company–subsidiary relationship is fundamental to establishing the parent's duty of care. Therefore, as long as H owns, controls and supervises the activities of S, H has a duty of care towards both employees and third parties affected by the activities of S.

The other option for the victims of human rights abuses would be to pierce the corporate veil. However, in practice, it would be hardly possible to take advantage of these indirect liability doctrines. *Evading existing legal obligations*, the only established principle recognised as a basis for piercing the corporate veil in the United Kingdom, is not likely to apply to the case studies, as it requires that the holding company H has an existing legal obligation towards the human rights victim and incorporates a subsidiary S with a view to avoiding liability. Instead, holding company H had no pre-existing relationship with the victims. It first registered its subsidiaries S in Ecuador, Nigeria and Bangladesh to start business operations there. Those subsidiaries subsequently committed the alleged human rights abuses. Therefore, there would be no opportunity to argue that H established S in order to evade an existing legal obligation.

The *single economic unit* doctrine, another legal exception permitting to disregard the separate legal personality of subsidiaries in a group, is instead potentially applicable to the case studies. This would require, however, that the victim proves that S was a completely inactive company, a dormant shell, an alter ego of its holding company H. However, this would rarely be, if ever, the case in respect of the subsidiaries of multinational corporations committing human rights violations. On the contrary, such subsidiaries would almost never be empty boxes. They engage in multiple business operations, such as producing clothes in Bangladesh or exploiting oil in Ecuador and Nigeria. They hire multiple employees and have their own management. In addition, it remains unclear whether the *single economic unit* argument remains an additional ground to pierce the corporate veil after *Prest v Petrodel Resources Ltd*, in which some judges clearly indicated that the only established doctrine to pierce the corporate veil is the *evading existing legal obligation* exception.

Therefore, none of the victims, Bodhi, Elsa or Naoki, are likely to enjoy an effective remedy against the holding company H in British courts. The Bangladeshi victim Bodhi risks losing his case on conflict-of-laws grounds, as the applicable law may likely be Bangladeshi law which would hamper his possibility of obtaining any redress in court against H. The situation does not seem as problematic for Naoki and Elsa. Naoki may successfully argue for the application of UK case-law on the basis that the Nigerian and UK legal systems share common grounds. Elsa may convincingly argue under Rome II for an application of either Ecuadorian or UK law, depending on which one would be the most favourable to her case. However, if this conflict-of-laws hurdle is cleared, Elsa and Naoki may lose their cases on the merits. In fact, whereas Bodhi is an employee, and therefore in a preferred position to claim a relationship of proximity with the parent company, being third parties, Elsa and Naoki may find more difficult to argue that they are neighbours of the corporate group. The law is still unclear on this question and much would depend on whether the proximity between parent company and subsidiary is sufficient for the former to owe a duty of care towards third parties, or if instead such duty of care could be owed only towards a specific group of neighbours that are proximate enough to the group.

This chapter demonstrated that CSR, EU and domestic laws fail to provide the victims of a human rights abuse committed by a subsidiary S with effective legal remedies against its European holding company H.

3

The International Legal Obligations of States

As analysed in Chapter 2, there are no effective remedies currently available to the victims of human rights abuses to sue European multinational enterprises for the extraterritorial conduct of their foreign subsidiaries. Furthermore, there are no laws sanctioning enterprises abusing human rights transnationally. The issue is whether there is any international legal obligation on states to change the current state of the law and establish a liability regime applicable to multinational enterprises. This chapter analyses the international legal obligation of European states to ensure that corporate groups respect human rights.

Traditionally, international law was contractual in nature, as states were contracting and defining their respective obligations. International law obligations were reciprocal and defined by treaties or recognised practices among nations, while domestic law regulated the relationship between a state and its citizens.[1] Such a structure would ensure an effective human rights protection, if all states took on their role as members of the international community in good faith and, in compliance with their international legal obligations, enforced human rights standards within their territories. However, World War I and II reminded us how weak the assumption is that states enforce their international legal obligations within their territories bona fide.[2] Therefore, after World War II, international law changed profoundly. Although it maintains its contractual nature as it pertains to the relationship between states, it also assumed a public nature as it pertains to the relationship between states and individuals. The international community realised that when a state enacts domestic legislation violating human rights, international law should come into play.[3] For the

[1] See Samuel Moyn, *The Last Utopia: Human Rights in History* (Belknap Press of Harvard University Press, 2012) 11–43; Elisabet Fura-Sandstrom, 'Business and Human Rights: Who Cares?', in *Liber Amicorum Luzius Wildhaber: Human Rights – Strasbourg Views/Droits de l'homme – Regards de Strasbourg* (Engel, 2007) 159–76; Louis Henkin et al, *Human Rights*, 2nd edn (Foundation Press, 2009) 135–88; Lori Damrosch et al, *International Law, Cases and Materials*, 5th edn (West, 2009) 956–1050.

[2] Henkin et al (n 1) 135–88; Damrosch et al (n 1) 956–1050.

[3] Note that the idea of individual rights was already put forward during the Enlightenment period as it pertains to the rights of individuals within one state. After the Second World War, the rights of individuals assumed an international dimension. See Peg Birmingham, *Hannah Arendt and Human Rights: The Predicament of Common Responsibility* (Indiana University Press, 2006); Hannah

first time in history, the International Military Tribunal at Nuremberg and the International Military Tribunal for the Far East recognised that individuals also have international obligations.[4] However, more than 70 years after World War II ended, the world is still not ready to admit the horizontal application of international norms between private persons.[5] This is particularly evident if one looks at the international responsibility of multinational enterprises. Although individuals are now considered to a certain extent as duty-bearers towards their peers, and international criminal law allows victims to hold individuals responsible for perpetrating some heinous crimes, this is not the case for enterprises.[6] The Nuremberg Tribunal established that companies are not directly responsible when they abuse human rights.[7] The ICC, as well as the ICTY and the ICTR, have no jurisdiction over companies perpetrating human right abuses.[8] Despite the fact that various international organisations, including the UN,[9]

Arendt, *The Origins of Totalitarianism* (Mariner Books, 1973) 267–302; Thomas Paine, *Rights of Man* (Dover Publications, 1999); SE Barker (ed), *Social Contract: Essays by Locke, Hume, and Rousseau* (Oxford University Press, 1962); Louis Henkin, 'The Universality of the Concept of Human Rights' (1989) 506 *The Annals of the American Academy of Political and Social Science* 10; Louis Henkin, *The Age of Rights* (Columbia University Press, 1990) 13–29.

[4] See generally, A Mokhtar, 'Nullum Crimen, Nulla Poena Sine Lege: Aspects and Prospects' (2005) 26 *Statute Law Review* 41, 52–53; Hans Kelsen, 'Collective and Individual Responsibility in International Law with Particular Regard to the Punishment of War Criminals' [1943] *California Law Review* 530; Johan D van der Vyver, 'Prosecuting Offenses against the Law of Nations in the United States' (2006) 20 *Emory International Law Review* 473; Arnold Brackman, *The Other Nuremberg: The Untold Story of the Tokyo War Crimes Trials* (Harper Collins Publishers, 1988).

[5] See John H Knox, 'Horizontal Human Rights Law' [2008] *The American Journal of International Law* 1.

[6] See Carlos Manuel Vazquez, 'Direct vs Indirect Obligations of Corporations under International Law' (2005) 43 *Columbia Journal of Transnational Law* 927; Steven R Ratner, 'Corporations and Human Rights: A Theory of Legal Responsibility' (2001) 111 *The Yale Law Journal* 443.

[7] See *The IG Farben and Krupp Trials* [1949] Nuremberg Tribunal Law Reports of Trials of War Criminals, X; *Kiobel v Royal Dutch Petroleum Co* [2010] US Court of Appeals 2d Cir F3d 621 111; *Kiobel v Royal Dutch Petroleum Co* [2013] US Supreme Court 133 SCt 1659; Tyler Giannini and Susan Farbstein, 'Corporate Accountability in Conflict Zones: How Kiobel Undermines the Nuremberg Legacy and Modern Human Rights' (2010) 52 *Harvard International Law Journal* 119.

[8] See French proposal 'Working Paper on Article 23, Paras 5–6, A/Conf.183/C.1/WGGP/L.5/Rev.2' (1998) Official Records of the United Nations Diplomatic Conference of Plenipotentiaries on the Establishment of an International Criminal Court, Volume III, 251–52; Statute of the International Criminal Tribunal for Rwanda 1994, art 5; Statute of the International Criminal Tribunal for the Former Yugoslavia 1995, art 6; H van der Wilt, 'Corporate Criminal Responsibility for International Crimes: Exploring the Possibilities' (2013) 12 *Chinese Journal of International Law* 43; Andrew Clapham, 'Extending International Criminal Law beyond the Individual to Corporations and Armed Opposition Groups' (2008) 6 *Journal of International Criminal Justice* 899.

[9] See Nicola Jägers, 'UN Guiding Principles on Business and Human Rights: Making Headway towards Real Corporate Accountability' (2011) 29 *Netherlands Quarterly of Human Rights* 159; John Gerard Ruggie, 'The Construction of the UN "Protect, Respect and Remedy" Framework for Business and Human Rights: The True Confessions of a Principled Pragmatist' (2011) 2 *European Human Rights Law Review* 127; John Gerard Ruggie, 'Protect, Respect, and Remedy: The UN Framework for Business and Human Rights', in *International Human Rights Law* (Ashgate, 2010); John Ruggie Gerard, 'Report of the Special Representative of the Secretary-General on the Issue of Human Rights and Transnational Corporations and Other Business Enterprises' (2011) 29 *Netherlands Quarterly of Human Rights* 224.

supranational entities, including the European Union,[10] and influential countries, including the United Kingdom,[11] are addressing the subject of business and human rights in their current agenda, none of them has yet recognised that multinational companies have international obligations to comply with human rights.[12] As John Ruggie, the UN Special Representative for Business and Human Rights, explained, the Guiding Principles were successful among both states and private actors and unanimously endorsed by the UN Human Rights Council, because they are a traditional international legal instrument.[13] The Guiding Principles clearly establish that although under international law states have binding duties to protect human rights in the business context, companies may instead respect human rights. Such a division is crucial: while states shall ensure that businesses respect human rights, companies have no obligations under international law, as they may or may not voluntarily assume responsibility for their actions.[14] Therefore, as explained in Chapter 2, under international law, no legally binding instrument grants the victims of human rights abuses with a cause of action against multinational enterprises.

[10] See Menno T Kamminga, 'Holding Multinational Corporations Accountable for Human Rights Abuses: A Challenge for the EC', in *The EU and Human Rights* (Oxford University Press, 1999); European Commission, 'Commission Staff Working Document on Implementing the UN Guiding Principles on Business and Human Rights – State of Play' SWD(2015) 144 final; Deborah Russo, 'La promozione della responsabilitá sociale d'impresa nell'Unione europea' (2011) XVI *Il diritto dell'Unione europea* 477; Alexandra Gatto, *Multinational Enterprises and Human Rights: Obligations under EU Law and International Law* (Edward Elgar, 2011); Antonio Gigante, 'La politica delle istituzioni comunitarie in materia di responsabilita sociale d'impresa: voluntary o mandatory approach?' (2008) IV *Diritto pubblico comparato ed europeo* 1991.

[11] See 'UK Open Government National Action Plan 2016–18', www.gov.uk/government/publications/uk-open-government-national-action-plan-2016-18/uk-open-government-national-action-plan-2016-18, accessed 2 December 2016; HM Government, 'Good Business Implementing the UN Guiding Principles on Business and Human Rights', www.gov.uk/government/uploads/system/uploads/attachment_data/file/236901/BHR_Action_Plan_-_final_online_version_1_.pdf, accessed 20 April 2016; Gwynne Skinner et al, 'The Third Pillar: Access to Judicial Remedies for Human Rights Violations by Transnational Business | ICAR' www.corporatejustice.org/IMG/pdf/the_third_pillar_-access_to_judicial_remedies_for_human_rights_violation.-1-2.pdf, accessed 17 March 2019; Marco Fasciglione, 'Corporate Human Rights Responsibility, States' Duty to Protect and UN GPS' National Action Plans: Some Thoughts after the UK NAP Update' (2016) 1 *European Papers* 621.

[12] See Fura-Sandstrom (n 1); Radu Mares (ed), *The UN Guiding Principles on Business and Human Rights: Foundations and Implementation* (Martinus Nijhoff, 2011); Surya Deva, 'Human Rights Violations by Multinational Corporations and International Law: Where from Here?' (2003) 19 *Connecticut Journal of International Law* 1; Surya Deva, 'Human Rights Standards and Multinational Corporations: Dilemma between "Home" and "Rome"' (2003) 7 *Mediterranean Journal of Human Rights* 69. See the current proposition to draft a binding treaty on the obligations of multinational companies at the Human Rights Council: Katerina Sequensova, 'Report of the Human Rights Council on its Twenty-Sixth Session' (United Nations Human Rights Council 2014) A/HRC/26/2.

[13] See Ruggie, 'The Construction of the UN "Protect, Respect and Remedy" Framework for Business and Human Rights' (n 9).

[14] Ruggie, 'Report of the Special Representative of the Secretary-General' (n 9); Mares (n 12); Jägers (n 9).

Theoretically, if all states provided effective legal remedies to prevent and punish corporate human rights abuses, they would stop companies from abusing human rights because each country would ensure the respect of human rights within its own territory. However, when this is not the case, stakeholders should be permitted to bring an action against those states that fail to prevent the abuses of human rights resulting from corporate activities. The Guiding Principles have the advantage of restating that under international law states have obligations to ensure that companies respect human rights.[15] The purpose of this chapter is to set out the obligations of European home states to secure that multinational enterprises respect human rights extraterritorially. This chapter argues that the home state, which is a party to the ECHR, has three duties: the duty to respect human rights; the duty to protect human rights victims from corporate activities; and the duty to fulfil the ultimate goal to secure that companies respect human rights.

I. THE NATURE OF STATE OBLIGATIONS

Since the end of World War II, it has been widely recognised that states have international legal obligations towards individuals and such obligations are directly enforceable by the individuals against the states. As a general principle, each fundamental human right corresponds to a duty of the state. Therefore, an individual can hold the state accountable for a human rights violation.[16] However, the exact scope of the state's obligations in connection with the protection of human rights and the remedies available to the individuals against the state depend on the particular right violated and the specific factual background leading to its violation. This section analyses the relationship between the categories of human rights which can be violated, the scope of the duties of the state to secure such rights, and various remedies available to victims.

When the international community recognised that individuals were entitled to human rights and that states have corresponding international legal obligations towards individuals, different states disagreed on what those human rights were and on the scope of their international legal obligations.[17]

A. Negative Obligations

Some states believed that individuals were entitled to civil and political rights enshrined in the International Covenant on Civil and Political

[15] Ruggie, 'Report of the Special Representative of the Secretary-General' (n 9).

[16] Henkin et al (n 1) 135–88; Damrosch et al (n 1) 956–1050; Pisillo Riccardo Mazzeschi, 'Responsabilité de l'état pour violation des obligations positives relatives aux droits de l'homme', in *Collected Courses of the Hague Academy of International Law* 333 (Martinus Nijhoff, 2008) 187–223.

[17] See Henkin et al (n 1) 135–88; Damrosch et al (n 1) 956–1050; Mazzeschi (n 16) 187–223.

Rights (ICCPR).[18] States have an obligation of non-interference with such individual freedoms. Civil and political rights, also labelled first-generation rights, traditionally correspond to the state's *negative obligations*: states need do nothing other than refrain from interfering with such civil and political rights and freedoms of individuals. However, a state has to act to be in breach of its negative obligations.[19] For example, freedom of association corresponds to the state's obligation not to interfere with any association of individuals. The state may breach such an obligation only through an action of interference, eg by shutting down a demonstration. Typically, scholars label such a negative duty as an *obligation of conduct*, because the state has to adopt a specific conduct to comply with such obligations. On the one hand, the obligation of conduct is perceived as being demanding, because the state has no flexibility with regard to its actions but, instead, shall mandatorily adopt a specific conduct. On the other hand, adopting a specific conduct is relatively easy because the state is simply required to refrain from acting and interfering in the life of people or organised communities.[20] Therefore, the state complies with its negative obligations when it refrains from acting and interfering with the life of others.

B. Positive Obligations

Other states believed that individuals were entitled to social and economic rights enshrined in the International Covenant on Economic, Social and Cultural Rights (ICESCR). This is not to say that states necessarily had to choose between civil and political rights and economic, social and cultural rights. Most states signed and ratified both covenants.[21] According to social, economic and cultural rights, the state has obligations to intervene in the life of people and grant them services. These rights, also labelled second-generation rights, traditionally correspond to the states' *positive obligations* towards individuals, because to comply with their positive obligations, countries have to act. Conversely, a state violates its positive obligations when it fails to act in accordance with human rights.

A state may violate its positive obligation in multiple forms. For example, the right to healthcare corresponds to the state's obligation to build hospitals, pay doctors and nurses, and provide each individual living in a given territory

[18] International Covenant on Civil and Political Rights 1966 (999 Treaty Series) 171.

[19] See Mazzeschi (n 16) 224–233; Magdalena Sepúlveda Carmona, *The Nature of the Obligations under the International Covenant on Economic, Social, and Cultural Rights* (Intersentia, 2003) 115–248.

[20] See Mazzeschi (n 16) 271–302; Sepúlveda Carmona (n 19) 115–248; Guy S Goodwin-Gill, 'Obligations of Conduct and Result', in *The Right to Food*, Stichting Studie- en Informatiecentrum Mensenrechten (Martinus Nijhoff, 1984).

[21] For the number of countries that ratified the ICCPR and ICESCR, see OHCHR, 'Status of Ratification Interactive Dashboard', http://indicators.ohchr.org/, accessed 13 February 2017.

with the possibility to have access to healthcare. The state may breach such an obligation in a number of different ways, such as by not paying doctors and nurses, by not establishing public hospitals or by not ensuring that all individuals living in a certain territory have free public healthcare.

Typically, scholars label positive obligations as *due process*, *best-effort* or *of progressive realisation*, because the state should do everything possible, within its financial means, to ensure that the individuals can enjoy the relevant rights. A *best-effort* obligation is a duty to progressively work towards a result; it is not an obligation to achieve such a result. A state may comply with its positive obligations when it is providing the best possible services to the individuals living within its territory, even if it is not able to achieve the result it aimed for. However, it is not clear what exact specific steps the state should take to comply with its positive obligation. The answer depends on a case-by-case analysis, on the right at stake and the resources available to the state. For example, as it pertains to the right to healthcare, the result aimed for is that all individuals living in a certain state shall enjoy free healthcare. As of today, this end result is unattainable for many states and, accordingly, the question is what level of healthcare is sufficient to meet the positive obligation of each state. The answer will depend on the financial resources at the disposal of a given state. Accordingly, a developing country will comply with its obligation when it ensures that individuals have a level of healthcare commensurate with the financial resources it can reasonably be expected to spend, although it may offer a level of healthcare considerably lower than that available in developed countries. However, if the state does not act at all, it is obvious that it is in violation of its positive obligation because, in order to progressively realise an aim, a state should at least act towards the realisation of that aim.

The *best-effort* obligation is less demanding than the obligation *of conduct*, because the state has no obligation to adopt a specific conduct, but instead, has a great margin of flexibility to act. It would be often unrealistic to interpret positive duties in terms of obligations *of conduct* because, first, compliance with such obligations would often be economically demanding and in some instances impossible for states with limited resources; and, second, there is no one specific conduct that states must adopt to meet a positive obligation, but instead states may adopt a number of diverse conducts to achieve the same result. For these reasons, often negative obligations are of *conduct*, whereas positive obligations are of *best-effort*. Therefore, the procedures applicable to assess whether a state violated a certain right are different in the positive- and negative-obligation frameworks. Whereas in the negative-obligation framework the issue is whether the state acted in violation of the right, in the positive-obligation framework the issue is whether the state did enough to progressively realise the result aimed for.

Furthermore, in some cases, positive duties do not necessarily entail a *due-process* or *best-effort* obligation but require a specific result. Although states have to use their resources in order to provide healthcare or food, it is clear that, once a country already has a functioning system dedicated to these matters, meeting these obligations is no longer an issue of *progressive realisation*.

For instance, once a state has a functioning judicial system, guaranteeing effective remedies can no longer be considered a work in progress: the state shall mandatorily ensure that such institutions function properly to guarantee peoples' access to courts. In this example, it is clear that the state has sufficient resources to provide effective remedies for victims. Accordingly, the issue of whether the state has complied with its positive obligations shifts from the question of whether the state has enough resources and is able to provide effective remedies, to the question of which exact means of redress, procedures, rules and mechanisms shall the state provide for the victims. For these reasons, scholars call these duties obligations *of means* or *of result*, because the state must choose an appropriate means in order to meet a certain result. Regardless of which legislation, sanction, or judicial or quasi-judicial mechanism it adopts, the state will meet its positive obligation if it provides effective remedies to the victims. Different from the *obligation of conduct*, the *obligation of means* or *result* sets the state free to choose to adopt any conduct, provided it is appropriate to achieve the result aimed for. The *obligation of result* entails the state's obligation to implement a functioning system.[22]

Therefore, positive obligations require states to realise the result aimed for. If states do not have enough resources or opportunities, they may realise such a result only progressively. In this case, positive obligations are of *progressive realisation* or *best-effort*. If instead states have the appropriate system in place to achieve the aimed result, they should adopt a conduct that is fit for the purpose. The state will have a certain flexibility in determining which conduct to adopt. In this case, positive obligations are of *result*.

C. Overcoming the Dichotomy

With time, courts reinterpreted the concepts of positive and negative obligations as no longer being related exclusively to civil and political rights, in respect of the negative obligations, and social and economic rights, in respect of the positive obligations. The UN Human Rights Council (HRC) declared in 1981 that:

> The obligation under the [International] Covenant [on Civil and Political Rights] is not confined to the respect of human right[s]. … [S]tates parties have also undertaken to ensure the enjoyment of those rights to all individuals under their jurisdiction.[23]

[22] See Mazzeschi (n 16) 187–496; Sepúlveda Carmona (n 19) 115–248; Sandra Fredman, *Human Rights Transformed* (Oxford University Press, 2008) 65–91; Frédéric Sudre, 'Les "obligations positives" dans la jurisprudence européenne des droits de l'homme' (1995) 23 *Revue trimiestrelle des droits de l'homme* 363; Colombine Madelaine, *La technique des obligations positives en droit de la convention européenne des droits de l'homme* (Dalloz, 2014) 373–416; Goodwin-Gill (n 20).

[23] HRC, 'General Comment 3, Article 2 (Implementation at the National Level)' (1981) GEC 6632 E-2 para 1.

Since then, the HRC has reaffirmed on several occasions that it would connect civil and political rights not only with the negative obligations of the state to respect such rights but also with the positive obligation of the state to ensure the availability of such rights to the individuals.[24] In this context, international law scholars have reconsidered the positive/negative obligations divide. The modern approach is that every human right implies both negative and positive obligations for states. For example, a state breaches the human right to life if its police kills prisoners or does not prevent third parties from murdering others. In the first example, the state breaches a negative obligation, because it actively kills detainees. In the second example, the state is in breach of a positive obligation, because it does not effectively prevent third parties from killing others. The idea behind the new approach to interpreting the obligations of the state is that each state has both a negative obligation not to murder and a positive obligation to prevent third parties from killing. Whereas the obligation not to kill is an *obligation of conduct*, because the state must refrain from abusing detainees (ie a negative conduct), the obligation to protect people from murderers is positive and could entail both an *obligation of result* and *of best-effort*. For example, states have, on the one hand, an *obligation of result* to guarantee procedural rights for victims against suspected murderers and, on the other hand, a *best-effort* obligation to stop third parties from committing crimes. Although states are clearly able to guarantee procedural rights, they may not be able, but should at least make an honest and reasonable attempt, to prevent third parties from killing others.[25]

In the above example, there are two situations when a state is clearly violating its obligations. The first situation is when the state kills prisoners and, therefore, violates its negative obligations. The second situation is when the state is completely inactive with respect to private persons murdering others, and therefore violates its positive obligations to prevent such killings. These are two clear cases of a violation of the negative and positive obligations to respect and protect life. However, when the state does not actively kill and, at the same time, implements some measures to prevent third parties from committing murders, we enter a grey area of law where it is not clear whether or not the state meets its obligation. It is indisputable that the state has a positive obligation to ensure that third parties respect the lives of others. However, the issue is how exactly the state shall ensure such respect. Multiple different policies can lead to this result as, for example, establishing a set of criminal laws and sanctions against murderers or investing resources in security and law enforcement.

[24] See Sarah Joseph and Melissa Castan, *The International Covenant on Civil and Political Rights: Cases, Materials, and Commentary*, 3rd edn (Oxford University Press, 2013) 809–11; Sepúlveda Carmona (n 19) 115–248; Isabelle Hachez and Hugues Dumont, 'Les obligations positives déduites du droit international des droits de l'homme, dans quelles limites?' in *Les droits de l'homme, bouclier ou épée du droit pénal?* (Publications des Facultés Universitaires Saint-Louis, 2007).

[25] See Sepúlveda Carmona (n 19) 115–248.

In this grey area, a court will have discretion to determine whether, given the facts of a specific case, the actions undertaken by the state are effective enough to meet its obligations to ensure the human right to life.[26]

D. The Duties to Respect, Protect and Fulfil

Given the complexity of the obligations, it has recently become clear that a new framework was needed to overcome the divide between negative and positive duties, as well as obligations of *conduct*, *result* and *progressive realisation*. Therefore, a number of scholars proposed new frameworks to classify the obligations of states vis-à-vis human rights.

Scholars agreed on the concept of negative obligations, ie obligations to refrain from interfering with the rights of people. However, with regard to positive obligations, scholars were divided and proposed various classifications.

Henry Shue was the first to propose an innovative tripartite typology to classify the obligations of states with respect to human rights.[27] According to him, states must comply with three main obligations: *to avoid depriving*, *to protect from deprivation* and *to aid the deprived*, which were later simplified by some scholars and renamed as the obligations to *respect*, *protect* and *fulfil*.[28] In addition, he added later on a fourth *responsibility to take due care*. According to Shue, the obligation *to respect (avoid depriving)* includes any negative obligation of the state. The obligation *to protect (protect from deprivation)* includes a positive *obligation of result*. States with a functioning apparatus should put it to use in order to ensure the respect of human rights by private parties. The obligation to *protect* entails, first, the obligation to establish a functioning state with laws and institutions that would secure the rights of people and, second, the obligation to enforce such laws among private parties. The *obligation to fulfil (to aid the deprived)* entails a number of positive *due-process* obligations. It is an obligation of the state to help and provide assistance for those who are at a disadvantage, such as people who need special care from the state because they are in psychiatric hospitals, victims of natural disasters or victims of the state's failures to respect and protect human rights. The *responsibility to take due care* is an obligation to prevent human rights abuses which seems to encompass anything that the state could do to facilitate the enjoyment and ameliorate the standard of human rights. Furthermore, Shue was convinced that the obligations to *aid the deprived* and to *take due care* were

[26] See Ioannis Panoussis, 'L'obligation générale de protection des droits de l'homme dans la jurisprudence des organes internationaux' (2007) 70 *Revue trimestrielle des droits de l'homme* 427; Fredman (n 22) 65–91; Mazzeschi (n 16) 186–249; Sudre (n 22); Sepúlveda Carmona (n 19) 115–247.

[27] Henry Shue, *Basic Rights: Subsistence, Affluence, and US Foreign Policy*, 2nd edn (Princeton University Press, 1996).

[28] Asbjørn Eide, 'Report on the Right to Adequate Food as a Human Right' (1987) E/CN.4/Sub.2/1987/23.

somehow ancillary to the others, as there would be no need to use these obligations if states would effectively respect human rights and ensure the protection of victims of human rights abuses by private parties.[29]

A number of scholars have revisited Shue's initial classification. Asbjørn Eide proposed the currently used simplification of Shue's categories and renamed them *obligations to respect, protect and fulfil*.[30] Fried van Hoof[31] and Henry Steiner, together with Philip Alston,[32] reconsidered Shue's framework and proposed additional obligations. Although both Eide and van Hoof seem to agree broadly as to the content of the obligation to protect, they diverge as to the obligation to fulfil.

Eide proposed the inclusion of two duties within the obligation to fulfil. First, the *obligation to provide basic needs* for people at a disadvantage, which is similar to Shue's *obligation to aid the deprived*. Second, the *obligation to facilitate and assist*, which is based on Shue's *responsibility to take due care*.

Van Hoof's analysis of the obligation to fulfil includes the *obligation to ensure* and *promote*. The former broadly replicates Shue's *obligation to aid the deprived* and the Eide's *obligation to provide basic needs*. The latter adds the idea of *progressive realisation* to Shue's *responsibility to take due care* and Eide's *obligation to facilitate and assist*. The *obligation to promote* is a *due-process* obligation to improve human rights standards progressively.

Furthermore, Alston and Steiner introduced the concept of state duties to replace the previously used concept of state obligations. They revisited the obligation to protect to include *the duty to create institutional machinery essential to the realisation of rights* and the *duty to protect rights/prevent violations*. This distinction seems to replicate Shue's initial classification of the obligation to establish a functioning state apparatus and the obligation to enforce human rights among private parties. The idea is that states should, first, establish an institutional apparatus and, second, put such an apparatus into use to ensure that all individuals would effectively enjoy human rights. As it pertains to the obligation to fulfil, Alston and Steiner reconstruct it as including the *duty to provide goods and services to satisfy rights* and the *duty to promote rights*. It seems that the former corresponds to Shue's *obligation to aid the deprived*, Eide's *obligation to provide basic needs* and van Hoof's *obligation to ensure*, whereas the latter replicates van Hoof's *obligation to promote*.[33]

These categories are flexible and the boundaries between the duties can move on a case-by-case basis. Although these different classifications of human rights may seem more confusing than explanatory, this debate caused practitioners,

[29] Shue (n 27).

[30] Eide (n 28).

[31] GJH Van Hoof, 'Legal Nature of Economic, Social and Cultural Rights: A Rebuttal of Some Traditional Views' in *The Right to Food* (Martinus Nijhoff, 1984).

[32] Henry Steiner, Philip Alston and Ryan Goodman (ed), *International Human Rights in Context: Law, Politics, Morals*, 3rd edn (Oxford University Press, 2008).

[33] See Sepúlveda Carmona (n 19) 115–248.

academics and international institutions to reconsider the traditional divide between negative and positive obligations. Currently, there is a broad consensus among human rights scholars and practitioners as to the necessity to discuss states' obligations in terms of duties to respect, protect and fulfil.[34] The duty to respect corresponds to the negative obligation. It is the duty to refrain from acting in violation of a certain right. It is, therefore, an obligation of *conduct*. The duty to protect typically corresponds to a positive obligation of *result*. In respect of this duty, there is no consensus as to its precise scope. However, most scholars agree that the following elements shall be included in a duty to protect. First, the duty to protect entails the protection of individuals from human rights abuses committed by other private parties. Second, the duty to protect entails an obligation to set up a functioning state apparatus that could effectively ensure the enjoyment of human rights. Scholars are also divided as to the exact scope of the duty to fulfil. However, despite this division, there is still a common ground, as they all agree that the duty to fulfil is a *best-effort* obligation of the states to do their utmost to improve human rights standards. What shall be considered as the utmost would depend on the resources available to each state and its opportunities to improve the standard of living.[35]

One can interpret any right of an individual as triggering the corresponding duties to respect, protect or fulfil. For example, freedom from torture triggers a negative duty of the state to respect, as the state should refrain from torturing individuals; a positive duty of the state to protect, as the state should provide for each individual effective legal remedies against the perpetrators of torture; and a positive duty of the state to fulfil, ie to do its utmost to effectively stop any form of torture. Accordingly, a state clearly violates its negative duty to respect when a public agent tortures an individual (this would be a breach of a negative obligation, because the state is itself torturing the individual). The state also clearly violates its positive duty to protect when it fails to sanction and provide effective legal remedies for a victim of torture (this would be a breach of a positive obligation, because the state fails to provide an effective apparatus to protect human rights). Finally, the breach of the duty to fulfil occurs in all of those cases when the state does not do its utmost to free the country from torture. Given that the positive duty to fulfil is a *best-effort* obligation to stop torture, a court would have to determine where to draw the line on a

[34] ibid 157–248; Francesco Francioni, 'Alternative Perspectives on International Responsibility for Human Rights Violations by Multinational Corporations' in *Economic Globalisation and Human Rights* (Cambridge University Press, 2007); F Marrella, 'Regolazione internazionale e responsabilità globale delle imprese transnazionali' (2009) 3 *Diritti umani e diritto internazionale* 229; Mazzeschi (n 16) 243–49; Olivier De Schutter et al, 'Commentary to the Maastricht Principles on Extraterritorial Obligations of States in the Area of Economic, Social and Cultural Rights' (2012) 34 *Human Rights Quarterly* 1084.

[35] See Sepúlveda Carmona (n 19) 115–248; Panoussis (n 26); Fredman (n 22); Hachez and Dumont (n 24); Sudre (n 22); Mazzeschi (n 16) 186–310.

case-by-case basis. Certainly, the state must exercise its power and influence on third parties to stop or prevent them from torturing others. There may be cases when the court finds that the state did everything in its power to prevent third parties from torturing people, but it failed to ensure that no individual living in its territory suffers from torture. In those cases, the state would comply with its positive duty to fulfil because it did its utmost to prevent third parties from torturing people.

Therefore, courts currently interpret human rights as no longer linked solely to positive and negative obligations, but also to the duties to respect, protect and fulfil human rights.

II. THE POSITIVE OBLIGATION TO SECURE THAT ENTERPRISES RESPECT HUMAN RIGHTS IN THE EUROPEAN CONVENTION ON HUMAN RIGHTS

The purpose of this section is to investigate the European states' duties to protect and fulfil vis-à-vis the companies incorporated within their territories. However, before analysing the application of the ECHR in relation to corporate conduct, it is necessary to make the following two general remarks concerning the living instrument doctrine and the notion of absolute and non-absolute rights.

First, in its jurisprudence, the ECtHR has developed the doctrine of a living instrument, according to which the ECtHR is entitled to interpret and adapt the ECHR to current times. Gerald Cohen Jonathan describes: '[L]a Convention européenne est un instrument vivant considérablement enrichi par la jurisprudence de la [Cour].'[36] Although the ECtHR has no power to amend or modify the ECHR, it has a pragmatic approach and interprets the ECHR as a living instrument that should be adapted to current times.[37]

Therefore, while the text of ECHR remains the core instrument, representing the backbone of the current European human rights law structure, it is the ECHR

[36] 'The European Convention is a living instrument, enriched by the jurisprudence of the European Court of Human Rights' (translation by the author) Gérard Cohen-Jonathan, 'Quelques considérations sur l'autorité des arrêts de la Cour européenne des droits de l'homme', in *Liber amicorum Marc-André Eissen*, edition bilingue (Emile Bruylant, 1995) 39.

[37] Kanstantsin Dzehtsiarou, 'European Consensus and the Evolutive Interpretation of the European Convention on Human Rights' (2011) 12 *German Law Journal* 1730; George Letsas, 'The ECHR as a Living Instrument: Its Meaning and Legitimacy', in *Constituting Europe: The European Court of Human Rights in a National, European and Global Context* (Cambridge University Press, 2013); Frédéric Sudre, 'L'article 3bis de la Convention europóene des droits de l'homme: le droit à des conditions de déténtion conformes au respect de la dignité humaine', in *Libertés, justice, tolérance: Mélanges en hommage au Doyen Gérard Cohen-Jonathan*, vol 2 (Emile Bruylant, 2004); Khanlar Hajiyev, 'The Evolution of Positive Obligations under the European Convention on Human Rights – By the European Court of Human Rights', *La Convention européenne des droits de l'homme, un instrument vivant: mélanges en l'honneur de Christos L. Rozakis = The European Convention on Human Rights, A Living Instrument: Essays in Honour of Christos L Rozakis* (Emile Bruylant, 2011); Madelaine (n 22) 133–97; Sudre (n 22).

as interpreted by the ECtHR, which is the complete body of law currently binding on European states.

Interpreting the ECHR as a living instrument allowed the ECtHR to develop extensive jurisprudence on positive obligations.[38] The ECHR is a treaty enshrining civil and political rights and freedoms and binding states party to respect, rather than promote, protect or fulfil human rights.[39] However, the obligations arising from the ECHR may require that states act to eliminate those obstacles that effectively prevent people from enjoying their civil and political liberties.[40] In such circumstances, states have positive obligations owed to the individuals whose human rights are violated. Unlike other human rights bodies, such as the HRC or the IACtHR, the ECtHR has never explicitly developed a general theory of positive obligations.[41] However, as a practical matter, after *Airey v Ireland*[42] and *Marckx v Belgium*,[43] the ECtHR has implemented positive obligations in specific cases. The ECtHR has developed its positive obligations jurisprudence in four main steps. The first step was establishing a general positive obligation to secure the rights guaranteed under the ECHR on the basis of Article 1. Secondly, the ECtHR developed several positive obligations with respect to Article 8, which sets out *the right to respect for private and family life*. Article 8 is one of the main sources of positive obligations in European human rights law, because the ECtHR has interpreted this Article broadly as including a number of economic and social rights, such as the right to a home and to live in a healthy environment. As a third step, the ECtHR extended positive obligations to Articles 2 and 3, setting out *the right to life* and the *prohibition of torture and inhuman and degrading treatment*. In the context of its jurisprudence on positive obligations, the ECtHR considered these articles as different from Article 8, because they set out rights that can never be derogated from. Finally, the ECtHR extended its jurisprudence on positive obligations to other articles, such as, for example, Article 14 setting out the *prohibition of discrimination*.[44]

[38] See Madelaine (n 22) 133–97; Sudre (n 22); Dragoljub Popovic, *The Emergence of the European Human Rights Law: An Essay on Judicial Creativity* (Eleven International Publishing, 2011); Sudre (n 37); Cohen-Jonathan (n 36); Hajiyev (n 37).

[39] Some scholars have even argued that the ECHR is a conservative document, see eg Marco Duranti, *The Conservative Human Rights Revolution: European Identity, Transnational Politics, and the Origins of the European Convention* (Oxford University Press, 2017); Marco Duranti, 'Curbing Labour's Totalitarian Temptation: European Human Rights Law and British Postwar Politics' (2012) 3 *Humanity: An International Journal of Human Rights, Humanitarianism, and Development* 361.

[40] See Madelaine (n 22) 133–97; Sudre (n 22); Popovic (n 38); Sudre (n 37); Cohen-Jonathan (n 36); Hajiyev (n 37).

[41] See Hachez and Dumont (n 24); Popovic (n 38).

[42] *Airey v Ireland* [1979] ECHR 6289/73.

[43] *Marckx v Belgium* [1979] ECHR 6833/74.

[44] See Ellie Palmer, 'Protecting Socio-Economic Rights through the European Convention on Human Rights: Trends and Developments in the European Court of Human Rights' (2009) 2 *Erasmus Law Review* 397.

Second, to analyse the ECtHR's jurisprudence, it is important to clarify the differences between two sets of substantive rights. The ECtHR distinguishes between absolute and non-absolute human rights. The textual basis for such a divide is Article 15, which states:

1. In time of war or other public emergency threatening the life of the nation any High Contracting Party may take measures derogating from its obligations under this Convention to the extent strictly required by the exigencies of the situation, provided that such measures are not inconsistent with its other obligations under international law.
2. No derogation from Article 2, … [o]r from Articles 3, 4 (paragraph 1) and 7 shall be made under this provision.[45]

Article 15 allows states, in cases of emergency, to derogate from any ECHR obligation, except for those set out in Article 2 (Right to Life), Article 3 (Prohibition of Torture), Article 4.1 (Prohibition of Slavery), and Article 7 (No Punishment without the Law).[46] The ECtHR has construed the derogation clause set out in Article 15 narrowly. Derogation from the provisions on the basis of this Article is permitted only in cases of public emergencies, such as war or a terrorist attack.

This general provision on derogation also served another purpose: Article 15 provided a framework for the ECtHR to establish two different standards of review for absolute and non-absolute rights. It should be noted that the categories of absolute/non-absolute and derogable/non-derogable rights do not always match perfectly. However, the list of non-derogable rights provided a basis to develop the ECtHR's jurisprudence on absolute rights. Although states should always implement all rights and liberties enshrined in the ECHR, one could envisage a situation of conflict between different fundamental rights. In such circumstances, a state may have to balance different rights at stake and choose which right to protect over the others.[47] When the allegation of a violation relates to an absolute right, the ECtHR adopted a strict scrutiny test to assess whether the right was violated. Instead, when the allegation of a violation relates to a non-absolute right, the ECtHR adopted a proportionality test to balance different fundamental rights and interests at stake.[48] The proportionality review

[45] European Convention for the Protection of Human Rights and Fundamental Freedoms 1950, art 15.

[46] ibid.

[47] See Dimitris Xenos, *The Positive Obligations of the State under the European Convention of Human Rights* (Routledge 2011) 57–142.

[48] See William Schabas, *The European Convention on Human Rights: A Commentary* (Oxford University Press, 2015) 592–94; Pieter van Dijk, Fried van Hoof, Arjen van Rijn and Leo Zwaak (eds), *Theory and Practice of the European Convention on Human Rights*, 5th edn (Intersentia, 2018) 1055–59; Sergio Bartole, Pasquale De Sena and Vladimiro Zagrebelsky (eds), *Commentario breve alla Convenzione europea per la salvaguardia dei diritti dell'uomo e delle libertà fondamentali* (CEDAM, 2012) 558–60; Sudre (n 22); Julian Rivers, 'The Presumption of Proportionality' (2014) 77 *MLR* 409; Maija Pitkanen, 'Fair and Balanced Positive Obligations – Do They Exist?' [2012] *European Human Rights Law Review* 538; Alastair Mowbray, 'A Study of the Principle of Fair

determines whether, taking into consideration all the rights at stake in the case scenario, the state took appropriate measures to address a threat.

It is important to note that the ECtHR's proportionality review for non-absolute rights is not a derogation test. The proportionality test provides states with some discretion as to how to balance different rights and choose how to implement them in a particular case, provided that their choices comply with the ECHR. In this sense, it is strictly connected to the doctrine of the margin of appreciation.[49] Despite the universal nature of fundamental human rights, states are entitled to a certain discretion as to the exact application of human rights law in their national systems. Although international courts first adopted the margin of appreciation in connection with derogation cases related to national security threats, they have increasingly interpreted this doctrine as a procedural device based on the principle of subsidiarity.[50] According to the principle of subsidiarity, states are often better placed to determine how to ensure a certain result, ie the protection of fundamental human rights, in their territory. Therefore, international institutions should primarily rely on domestic legal systems to protect fundamental human rights and be ready to intervene only when states fail to ensure such protection.[51]

However, the margin-of-appreciation doctrine should not be understood as granting a state unlimited discretion to choose the appropriate policies applicable to a case of human rights violations. The margin of appreciation is limited by the boundaries of its obligations. A state may choose how to regulate private parties, provided that its choice ensures the protection of fundamental human rights. If, instead, it does not sanction private parties that perpetrate human rights abuses, the state would be in violation of its duty. Regardless of the chosen policy, by applying the margin of appreciation theory, it is clear that the state shall regulate its domestic law in accordance with human rights.[52]

A. The Obligation to Secure

Article 1 of the ECHR states: 'The High Contracting Parties shall secure to everyone within their jurisdiction the rights and freedoms defined in Section I of this Convention.'[53] To have a deeper understanding of the scope of positive

Balance in the Jurisprudence of the European Court of Human Rights' (2010) 10 *Human Rights Law Review* 289.

[49] See Eyal Benvenisti, 'Margin of Appreciation, Consensus and Universal Standards' (1999) 31 *International Law and Politics* 843; Paolo G Carozza, 'Subsidiarity as a Structural Principle of International Human Rights Law' (2003) 97 *The American Journal of International Law* 38.

[50] See Benvenisti (n 49).

[51] See Carozza (n 49).

[52] See Sudre (n 22); Bartole, De Sena and Zagrebelsky (n 48) 303–11; van Dijk (n 48) 725–50; Xenos (n 47) 57–172.

[53] European Convention for the Protection of Human Rights and Fundamental Freedoms, art 1.

obligations set out in Article 1, it is necessary to analyse the literal meaning of the English and French versions of the text. Although in the French version the obligation to secure is *l'obligation de reconnaître*, meaning, literally, the obligation to recognise, the history of the *travaux préparatoires* confirms that Article 1 was intended to enshrine an immediate obligation for states to ensure fundamental rights, rather than just to recognise them. During the negotiation of the ECHR, several countries, including France, Italy, Turkey and Ireland, thought it was best to establish a general obligation to recognise human rights, whereas other countries, including the United Kingdom, the Netherlands and Norway preferred a more precise text to make sure that states would apply the substance of the ECHR within their domestic system. Initially, the text of Article 1 proclaimed that the states *undertake to secure* human rights within their territory. However, certain contracting parties expressed concern that the verb *to undertake* could have entailed a *due process* obligation. Accordingly, it was decided to avoid reference to the word *to undertake* and refer to the obligation *to secure*.[54] The ECtHR further clarified in *Ireland v the United Kingdom*[55] that the reference in Article 1 to the verb *to secure* rather than *to recognise* has the following implications:

> By substituting the words 'shall secure' for the words 'undertake to secure' in the text of Article 1 (art 1), the drafters of the Convention also intended to make it clear that the rights and freedoms set out in Section I would be directly secured to anyone within the jurisdiction of the Contracting States. … [T]he Convention does not merely oblige the higher authorities of the Contracting States to respect for their own part the rights and freedoms it embodies; as is shown by … [t]he English text of Article 1 (art 1) ('shall secure'), the Convention also has the consequence that, in order to secure the enjoyment of those rights and freedoms, those authorities must prevent or remedy any breach at subordinate levels.[56]

Furthermore, both British and French scholars recognised that the English version using the term *to secure* is more accurate in setting out the legal meaning of Article 1.[57] The ECtHR's jurisprudence established that the ECHR enshrines both positive and negative obligations for the state to secure individual rights.[58] Although the ECtHR has never explicitly stated a general theory of duties and has developed its positive obligations jurisprudence on a case-by-case basis, it has adopted a fortiori the above-mentioned interpretation of Article 1 as a textual basis for the development of its jurisprudence on positive obligations.[59]

[54] See Madelaine (n 22) 112–13; Xenos (n 47) 10–11; Bartole, De Sena and Zagrebelsky (n 48) 13.
[55] *Ireland v the United Kingdom* [1978] ECHR 5310/71.
[56] ibid 239; Xenos (n 47) 10–11.
[57] See Madelaine (n 22) 112–19; Xenos (n 47) 10–11.
[58] See Bartole, De Sena and Zagrebelsky (n 48) 14–15.
[59] See Panoussis (n 26); Sudre (n 22).

The Article 1 obligation to secure is an independent general obligation. However, the ECtHR has consistently combined this general obligation with other substantive ECHR provisions, such as freedom from torture or slavery, to ensure that the obligations deriving from any of these rights will be interpreted in terms of a positive obligation.[60] Essentially on a first reading, besides Article 1 which clearly establishes a positive obligation to secure, the text of the other substantive provisions of the ECHR seems to refer merely to negative obligations. However, the ECtHR's jurisprudence has clarified that each right must be interpreted in conjunction with Article 1. As a result, each right entails both positive and negative obligations.[61]

A number of authors argue that there is a parallel in the interpretation of Articles 1 of the ECHR and 2 of the ICCPR. Article 2 of the ICCPR reads as follows:

> 2. Where not already provided for by existing legislative or other measures, each State Party to the present Covenant undertakes to take the necessary steps, in accordance with its constitutional processes and with the provisions of the present Covenant, to adopt such laws or other measures as may be necessary to give effect to the rights recognized in the present Covenant.
> 3. Each State Party to the present Covenant undertakes:
>   (a) To ensure that any person whose rights or freedoms as herein recognised are violated shall have an effective remedy, notwithstanding that the violation has been committed by persons acting in an official capacity;
>   (b) To ensure that any person claiming such a remedy shall have his right thereto determined by competent judicial, administrative or legislative authorities, or by any other competent authority provided for by the legal system of the State, and to develop the possibilities of judicial remedy;
>   (c) To ensure that the competent authorities shall enforce such remedies when granted.[62]

The text of Article 2 of the ICCPR clarifies that both negative and positive obligations set out in this Article are immediate in their effect, and therefore that there is no discretion to interpret a positive obligation as a limited or non-existing one.[63] Manfred Nowak explains the parallel between Article 1 of the ECHR and Article 2 of the ICCPR as follows: although they both entail the same obligation, Articles 2(2) and (3) of the ICCPR go a step further in setting out that states must take both judicial and legislative measures to meet their obligations.[64]

[60] See Madelaine (n 22) 111.

[61] ibid 112–19; Bartole, De Sena and Zagrebelsky (n 48) 14; Xenos (n 47) 10–11; David Russell, 'Supplementing the European Convention on Human Rights: Legislating for Positive Obligations' (2010) 61 *Northern Ireland Legal Quarterly* 281.

[62] International Covenant on Civil and Political Rights, art 2.

[63] See Manfred Nowak, *UN Covenant on Civil and Political Rights: CCPR Commentary*, 2nd edn (Engel, 2005) 60–62; Joseph and Castan (n 24) 39–41.

[64] Nowak (n 63) 57–62.

(i) Horizontal Application of Human Rights

Article 1 implies not only that all ECHR rights entail positive obligations of European states, but also that such obligations may be applicable horizontally between private parties.

The German constitutional court was the first to introduce the concept of *Drittwirkung*, which entails the horizontal application of human rights between private parties.[65] Although some international human rights courts, such as the IACtHR,[66] embraced this concept in their jurisprudence concerning positive obligations, the ECtHR has been reluctant to refer to the *Drittwirkung* theory. Nevertheless, the horizontal application of human rights also made its way into the ECtHR.

The European Commission of Human Rights and then the ECtHR have developed jurisprudence on positive obligations in connection with the horizontal application of human rights among private parties.[67] As the ECtHR stated for the first time in *X and Y v the Netherlands*:

> The Court recalls that although the object of Article 8 (art 8) is essentially that of protecting the individual against arbitrary interference by the public authorities, it does not merely compel the State to abstain from such interference: in addition to this primarily negative undertaking, there may be positive obligations inherent in an effective respect for private or family life (see the Airey judgment of 9 October 1979, Series A no 32, p 17, para 32). These obligations may involve the adoption of measures designed to secure respect for private life even in the sphere of the relations of individuals between themselves.[68]

There are two plausible interpretations of the horizontal application of human rights. According to the first interpretation, international law is directly applicable between private parties and, accordingly, each individual shall be permitted to enforce such provisions against the other private party. Both the ECtHR and the HRC have rejected this interpretation and clarified that states have no obligation to adopt the ECHR or the ICCPR as part of their domestic laws. It is up to each state to decide how to secure the rights enshrined in these treaties within its own legal system.[69] States may, but are not obligated to, incorporate the ECHR or the ICCPR into their laws. For example, the Human Rights Act of 1998 refers to the ECHR but does not incorporate

[65] See Raphael Thomas, 'The Problem of Horizontal Effect' (2000) 5 *European Human Rights Law Review* 493; Knox (n 5).

[66] See Antonio Augusto Cancado Trindade, 'Une ère d'avancées jurisprudentielles et institutionnelles: souvenirs de la Cour interaméricaine des droits de l'homme', in *Le particularisme interaméricain des droits de l'homme: En l'honneur du 40e anniversaire de la Convention américaine des droits de l'homme* (Editions A Pedone, 2009) 46–51.

[67] See Madelaine (n 22) 47–62; Xenos (n 47) 19–51.

[68] *X and Y v the Netherlands* [1985] ECHR 8978/80 [23].

[69] See Nowak (n 63) 57–58; Bartole, De Sena and Zagrebelsky (n 48) 15–16; Joseph and Castan (n 24) 101–03.

it directly into UK law.[70] However, the jurisprudence of the HRC and the ECtHR became increasingly demanding in terms of requiring states to ensure/secure the ECHR and the ICCPR in practical and effective terms. Therefore, some scholars argue that human rights are de facto directly applicable between private individuals.[71]

The second and more commonly embraced interpretation of the horizontal effect of human rights is the indirect application of human rights law. Both the ECtHR and HRC follow this approach, which sets out that a state has a positive obligation to ensure/secure the compliance with the ECHR or ICCPR within its jurisdiction.

According to General Comment 31 to the ICCPR:

> The legal obligation under article 2, paragraph 1, is both negative and positive in nature. States Parties must refrain from violation of the rights recognised by the Covenant. … [T]he rights specified in the Covenant are to be promoted and protected. … [A]rticle 2 requires that States Parties adopt legislative, judicial, administrative educative and other appropriate measures in order to fulfil their legal obligations. … [T]he positive obligations on States Parties to ensure Covenant rights will only be fully discharged if individuals are protected by the State, not just against violations of the Covenant rights by its agents, but also against acts committed by private persons or entities that would impair the enjoyment of Covenant rights in so far as they are amenable to application between private persons or entities.[72]

Such an interpretation extends the purpose of the ICCPR from a body of law enshrining freedoms from the state, to treaties ensuring/securing rights horizontally among private parties within the state.[73] Although the ECHR does not use the explicit language of the ICCPR, as clarified by the ECtHR's jurisprudence,[74] Article 1 also implies the existence of '[s]tate liability for the acts of private persons'.[75]

Under this approach, a state is not liable for human rights violations committed by private parties acting within its jurisdiction, but instead for its failure to address human rights abuses perpetrated by third parties.[76] This entails that the state has a certain margin of discretion in relation to which domestic policies will be implemented to secure the rights enshrined in the ICCPR and the ECHR.

[70] See Human Rights Act 1998; David Feldman, 'The Human Rights Act 1998 and Constitutional Principles' (1999) 19 *Legal Studies* 165.

[71] Nowak (n 63) 57–58.

[72] HRC, 'General Comment No 31 Nature of the General Legal Obligation Imposed on State Parties to the Covenant' (2004) CCPR/C/21/Rev 1/Add 13, paras 5–8.

[73] See Nowak (n 63) 39–40; Xenos (n 47) 47–51.

[74] *X and Y v the Netherlands* (n 68).

[75] Joseph and Castan (n 24) 101.

[76] See Nowak (n 63) 57–59; Bartole, De Sena and Zagrebelsky (n 48) 15–16; Mazzeschi (n 16) 224–33; Hachez and Dumont (n 24).

(ii) The Duties to Protect and Fulfil

As explained by Manfred Nowak, the obligation to ensure under the ICCPR, which corresponds to the obligation to secure under the ECHR, includes both the duties to protect and fulfil:

> The obligation to ensure consists of the obligation to protect individuals against interference by third parties (horizontal effect) and the obligation to fulfil, which in turns incorporates an obligation to facilitate the enjoyment of human rights and to provide services.[77]

Whereas the duty to protect entails protecting victims against private interference by third parties, the duty to fulfil requires a state to do its utmost to 'facilitate the enjoyment of human rights'.[78] The duty to protect requires states to provide procedural guarantees that will allow victims to hold the relevant perpetrators of human rights abuses accountable. It includes a procedural obligation to establish effective sanctioning mechanisms and provide the applicants with effective remedies against the perpetrators of such abuses. The duty to fulfil requires states to influence the activities of private parties in such a manner as to prevent them from abusing human rights. Whereas the duty to protect requires states to provide the victims with remedies and sanction those private parties that perpetrate abuses, the duty to fulfil requires states to do their utmost to prevent those private perpetrators from abusing human rights. In this sense, one can see the duty to protect and the duty to fulfil as two shades of a positive obligation.

The ECtHR's jurisprudence has not adopted the language of positive duties to protect and fulfil and is still using the traditional dichotomy between positive and negative obligations. Scholars have criticised this approach as it does not take into consideration the complexity of positive obligations which include multiple layers in between the duties to protect and fulfil. However, as demonstrated by Mowbray,[79] the jurisprudence of the ECtHR has become increasingly informed of the different shades of positive obligations and has de facto recognised the existence of duties to protect and fulfil. Simply, it has not adopted the language of duties, but it has instead distinguished between positive obligations of *result*, including the procedural obligation to establish a system of justice that would entitle victims of human rights abuses to fair, just and effective remedies in national courts, and *due process* or *best-effort* obligations that should be achieved progressively. This dichotomy corresponds to the positive duty to protect and fulfil affirmed by the HRC.[80]

[77] Nowak (n 63) 38.
[78] ibid.
[79] AR Mowbray, *The Development of Positive Obligations under the European Convention on Human Rights by the European Court of Human Rights* (Hart Publishing, 2004) 221–31.
[80] See Palmer (n 44); Pitkanen (n 48); Mazzeschi (n 16) 224–310; Goodwin-Gill (n 20).

(iii) Corporations

The legal personality of a company has two main effects. First, each company has the same rights and duties as any other person. Second, the home state (ie the country of incorporation) exercises the same coercive control over a company that it exercises over the individuals living in its territory. For example, the state will regulate under which circumstances a company may conduct business or how much taxes it shall pay. The application of this basic principle to the positive obligation of states to secure means that a state shall have the same obligations to enforce its laws against both individuals and companies.

States have a positive obligation to secure that private parties, including companies, respect fundamental rights. This positive obligation includes both the duty to protect third parties from human rights abuses committed by companies and the duty to fulfil the overall objective to stop companies from abusing human rights.[81]

The ECtHR has not yet directly addressed the failure of states to regulate the extraterritorial activities of multinational companies. However, the principles governing the responsibility of European states to secure the rights of individuals against enterprises are already part of the ECtHR's jurisprudence. By way of example, I will briefly summarise the facts of three cases where the ECtHR recognised that European states have positive obligations vis-à-vis corporations.

In *Fadeyeva v Russia*,[82] the ECtHR found that Russia violated the ECHR, because it did not secure the rights of Ms Fadeyeva against a polluting industry. During Soviet times, the USSR assigned to Ms Fadeyeva an apartment near a state-owned highly polluting industry. When the USSR collapsed, the industry was privatised but it continued to pollute the environment above the level permitted under Russian law. Ms Fadeyeva had no resources to move to a safe area. As a result, she suffered from severe health problems. The ECtHR ruled that the Russian government had a positive obligation to secure Ms Fadeyeva right to home and health by either ensuring that the private industry would limit its level of pollution within the margin required by law or by relocating Ms Fadeyeva to a safer area.

In *Lopez Ostra v Spain*,[83] the ECtHR ruled that Spain violated the ECHR because it did not promptly secure the rights of Ms Lopez Ostra against a private company operating a polluting waste treatment plant. Ms Lopez Ostra was living near the highly polluted plant and filed numerous complaints against the private corporation. Spain not only failed to stop the plant, but it also defended

[81] Francioni (n 34); Robert McCorquodale and Penelope Simons, 'Responsibility beyond Borders: State Responsibility for Extraterritorial Violations by Corporations of International Human Rights Law' (2007) 70 *MLR* 598; Marrella (n 34).

[82] *Fadeyeva v Russia* [2005] ECHR 55723/00.

[83] *Lopez Ostra v Spain* [1994] ECHR 16798/90.

the corporation in the various proceedings filed by Ms Lopez Ostra and her family. After years of litigation, Ms Lopez Ostra managed to win her case in the Spanish courts; the authorities temporarily shut down the waste treatment plant and relocated her to a new apartment. However, the ECtHR found that Spain was in violation of Article 8, because it acted in support of the industry and, as a result, it did not promptly secure Ms Lopez Ostra's rights.

In *Cordella and others v Italy*,[84] the ECtHR ruled that Italy failed to stop the pollution caused by the company Ilva and failed to provide victims with effective remedies. In this case, Ilva was a company producing steel near the area where the applicants lived. Despite clear evidence that Ilva's pollution harmed the living conditions of the applicants, Italy failed to respond adequately. It established a tentative environmental plan that would start only in 2023 and it meanwhile allowed the industry to continue its polluting activities. Furthermore, the victims had no way of redress in Italian courts that would have guaranteed them with either compensation for the damages suffered or a clean-up of the polluted site.

Therefore, Article 1 entails the positive obligations of European states to secure the rights of an applicant against private parties, including private industries and corporations.

B. The Procedural Duty to Protect and the Right to an Effective Remedy

The duty to protect requires states to set up functioning institutions that can protect individuals from interference by third parties. This includes providing human rights victims with effective judicial remedies against third parties, such as companies.[85]

Chapter 2 established that, in Europe, domestic laws require a high standard of conduct or primary rule from private parties that are supposed to respect human rights. Multiple laws are aimed at theoretically preventing the sort of human rights abuses which arose from the three case studies set out in this book. However, the victims of such human rights abuses do not have access to an effective remedy to protect their rights against corporate groups in the courts. Domestic laws do not establish an effective standard of review or secondary rule applicable to multinational companies. Victims often suffer from a lack of justice both in the host state, where the subsidiary S is incorporated, and in the European home state, where the holding company H is incorporated.[86] The reasons for this lack of justice are related to the structure of domestic laws. First, there is a liability issue as it pertains to company law. One of the basic

[84] *Cordella and others v Italy* [2019] ECHR 54414/13 and 54264/15.

[85] See Nowak (n 63) 39–40; Mazzeschi (n 16) 311–89; Panoussis (n 26).

[86] See Deva, 'Human Rights Standards' (n 12); Deva, 'Human Rights Violations' (n 12); Radu Mares, 'The Effects of CSR for the Protection of Human Rights' (2003) 7 *Mediterranean Journal*

principles of corporate law is that each company has a separate legal personality. Therefore, a holding company H should, generally speaking, not be liable for the abuses committed by its subsidiary S. This means that, although an applicant may file a complaint against the holding company H, domestic courts may dismiss the claim on the basis that it is S, rather than H, which committed the human rights abuse. Although there are a few exceptions to this basic principle, they are tailored to particular cases and there is no piercing the corporate veil for human rights abuses.[87] Second, there is an extraterritorial issue. Neither international nor domestic laws regulate the extraterritorial responsibility of multinational enterprises. International law does not establish any cause of action against companies, and domestic causes of action are often inadequate to sue multinational enterprises acting in multiple countries. States breach their positive duty as they fail to guarantee access to effective legal remedies and sanctions against multinational corporations.[88] This book argues that such a failure is a violation of the procedural duty to protect enshrined in the ECHR, which entitles the victims of human rights abuses to an effective remedy.

The ECtHR's, the IACtHR's and the HRC's jurisprudence on positive obligations establishes that states must not only enact laws but also provide victims with effective remedies to enforce their substantive rights.[89] The IACtHR was the first international court to recognise the concept of duty to protect as a procedural obligation to provide effective remedies for human rights victims and the efficient enforcement of substantive rights.[90] In *Velásquez-Rodríguez v Honduras*, the IACtHR held:

> An illegal act which violates human rights and which is initially not directly imputable to a State (for example, because it is the act of a private person or because the person responsible has not been identified) can lead to international responsibility of the State, not because of the act itself, but because of the lack of due diligence to prevent the violation or to respond to it as required by the Convention. … [T]he State is obligated to investigate every situation involving a violation of the rights protected

of Human Rights 113; Francesco Francioni, 'Access to Justice, Denial of Justice and International Investment Law' (2009) 20 *European Journal of International Law* 729; Claire Bright, 'L'accès à la justice civile en cas de violations des droits de l'homme par des entreprises multinationales' (PhD thesis, 2013) http://cadmus.eui.eu/handle/1814/29602, accessed 15 April 2016.

[87] See Henry Hansmann and Reinier Kraakman, 'Toward Unlimited Shareholder Liability for Corporate Torts' (1991) 100 *The Yale Law Journal* 1879; Karen Vanderkerckhove, *Piercing the Corporate Veil* (Kluwer/Aspen, 2007); Phillip I Blumberg, 'Limited Liability and Corporate Groups' (1985) 11 *The Journal of Corporate Law* 573.

[88] See Bright (n 86) 23–51; Nicola Jägers, *Corporate Human Rights Obligations: In Search of Accountability* (Intersentia, 2002) 19-37–175; Jernej Letnar Cernic, *Human Rights Law and Business Corporate Responsibility for Fundamental Human Rights* (Europa Law Publishing, 2010) 93–126; Francioni (n 86).

[89] See Panoussis (n 26); Xenos (n 47) 1–56; Madelaine (n 22) 133–97; Cancado Trindade (n 66); Nowak (n 63) 37–57; Joseph and Castan (n 24) 39–44.

[90] See Panoussis (n 26); Cancado Trindade (n 66). See eg *Panel Blanca (Paniagua Morales y otros) v Guatemala* [1998] IACHR Serie C No 23, Serie C No 37, Serie C No 76 [173]; *Castillo Páez v Peru* [1997] IACHR Serie C No 24, Serie C No 34, Serie C No 43 [90].

> by the Convention. If the State apparatus acts in such a way that the violation goes unpunished and the victim's full enjoyment of such rights is not restored as soon as possible, the State has failed to comply with its duty to ensure the free and full exercise of those rights to the persons within its jurisdiction.[91]

The ECtHR[92] and the HRC[93] subsequently adopted this jurisprudence. As already mentioned, the ICCPR enshrines the right to an effective remedy in Article 2(3), which reads as follows:

> Each State Party to the present Covenant undertakes: (a) To ensure that any person whose rights or freedoms are herein recognized are violated shall have an effective remedy, notwithstanding that the violation has been committed by persons acting in an official capacity; (b) To ensure that any person claiming such a remedy shall have his right thereto determined by competent judicial, administrative or legislative authorities, or by any other competent authority provided for by the legal system of the State, and to develop the possibilities of judicial remedy; (c) To ensure that the competent authorities shall enforce such remedies when granted.[94]

Furthermore, General Comment 31 states: 'A failure by a State Party to investigate allegations of violations could in and of itself give rise to a separate breach of the Covenant.'[95]

As to the ECHR, state parties shall establish judicial mechanisms to effectively hold the perpetrator(s) of human rights abuses accountable in court. This includes providing victim(s) with an effective legal remedy against the perpetrator(s). The ECtHR has gradually introduced the concept of procedural obligations as an element of the positive obligations to secure the protection of human rights, including the requirement to provide effective legal remedies and procedural rights for victims of human rights abuses.[96] Furthermore, the ECtHR has developed this procedural element of positive obligations on the basis of substantive rights set out in Articles 2, 3 and 8 and, later, Article 13, which specifically deals with procedural rights and defines *the right to an effective remedy*[97] as follows:

> Everyone whose rights and freedoms as set forth in this Convention are violated shall have an effective remedy before a national authority notwithstanding that the violation has been committed by persons acting in an official capacity.[98]

[91] *Velásquez-Rodríguez v Honduras* [1988] IACHR Serie C No 4 [172]–[176].

[92] See *Airey v Ireland* (n 42); *Marckx v Belgium* (n 43); *McCann v the United Kingdom* [2008] ECHR 19009/04.

[93] See HRC (n 72); *Irina Krasovskaya and Valeriya Krasovskaya v Belarus* [2012] HRC 1820/2008; *William Eduardo Delgado Páez v Colombia* [1990] HRC 195/1985; Joseph and Castan (n 24) 101–03.

[94] International Covenant on Civil and Political Rights, art 2(3).

[95] HRC (n 72) para 15.

[96] See Madelaine (n 22) 62–77; Xenos (n 47) 8–56; Sudre (n 22); Mazzeschi (n 16) 334–65; Joseph and Castan (n 24) 62–72; Panoussis (n 26); Russell (n 61).

[97] See Palmer (n 44); Madelaine (n 22) 62–77; Pitkanen (n 48); Eva Brems, 'Procedural Protection', in *Shaping Rights in the ECHR: The Role of the European Court of Human Rights in Determining the Scope of Human Rights* (Cambridge University Press, 2014).

[98] European Convention for the Protection of Human Rights and Fundamental Freedoms, art 13.

A fundamental source of procedural positive obligations, and seemingly a logical starting point for the protection of procedural rights, Article 13 has been dormant for a long time. Instead of establishing a comprehensive procedural framework as part of the positive obligation to protect human rights on the basis of Article 13, the ECtHR initially focused and took its inspiration from the provisions of the ECHR which enshrine substantive rights, such as Articles 2, 3 and 8. Article 13 then followed the jurisprudential evolution of substantive articles.[99]

For this reason, the right to an effective remedy is paradoxically both ancillary to and independent of the violation of a substantive ECHR right. The right to an effective remedy depends on whether a victim has suffered from a violation of human rights. If there is no violation, there is no need to discuss procedural rights, because the victim would simply not be able to request an effective remedy before a court. In this sense, the right to an effective remedy is ancillary to the occurrence of an actual violation of a substantive ECHR right. However, this does not mean that a violation of the right to an effective remedy is subordinated to the violation of another ECHR substantive right. When the violation is alleged, the state must entitle the victim to an effective legal remedy against the alleged perpetrator of a human rights abuse. In this sense, the right to an effective remedy is independent of a violation of the substantive rights provided under the ECHR.[100]

The ECtHR reflected on this double nature of a right to an effective remedy as being ancillary to and independent of substantive human rights violations, in the concept of an *arguable claim*. The ECtHR defines an *arguable claim* as a precondition for applying the right to an effective remedy. The *arguable claim* is the alleged violation of a substantive right. On the one hand, the right to an effective remedy is subsidiary to the alleged violation of substantive rights, because the *arguable claim* is the basis upon which a victim can claim a violation of his/her right to an effective remedy. On the other hand, the right to an effective remedy is independent of the violation of substantive rights, because, once the applicant has an *arguable claim*, the right to an effective remedy requires the state to establish additional procedural guarantees which are independent of substantive rights. It is for the ECtHR to determine when and if a claim is arguable. In *Boyle and Rice v United Kingdom* the ECtHR stated:

> The Court does not think that it should give an abstract definition of the notion of arguability. Rather it must be determined, in the light of the particular facts and the nature of the legal issue or issues raised, whether each individual claim of violation

[99] See Madelaine (n 22) 63–77; Sudre (n 22); Panoussis (n 26); Pitkanen (n 48); Palmer (n 44).

[100] See Mowbray (n 79) 205–10; David Harris et al, *Law of the European Convention on Human Rights*, 3rd edn (Oxford University Press, 2014) 766–67; van Dijk (n 48) 998–1006; Schabas (n 48) 551–52; Bartole, De Sena and Zagrebelsky (n 48) 479–94.

> forming the basis of a complaint under Article 13 (art. 13) was arguable and, if so, whether the requirement of Article 13 (art. 13) were met in relation thereto.[101]

The ECtHR further reconfirmed this interpretation, including in *Al Nashif v Bulgaria*,[102] where it made a connection between the right to an effective remedy and the state's duty to protect:

> Giving direct expression to the States' obligation to protect human rights first and foremost within their own legal system, Article 13 establishes an additional guarantee for an individual in order to ensure that he or she effectively enjoys those rights.[103]

The ancillary nature of the right to an effective remedy determines how the ECtHR interprets procedural obligations. The interpretation of the right to an effective remedy depends on the nature of the alleged violation of the substantive right.[104] The following sections analyse the procedural obligations arising from Articles 3 and 8. I specifically focus on these two Articles for the following reasons. First, Articles 3 and 8 apply to the Bangladeshi, Ecuadorian and Nigerian case studies, which I use as practical examples to illustrate the argument set out in this book. Second, while the ECtHR's jurisprudence on Article 8 established the basis for procedural positive obligations in cases of non-absolute rights, the ECtHR developed its jurisprudence on procedural obligations in cases of absolute rights on the basis of Articles 3 and 2.

(i) Article 8 and the Duty to Regulate Private Industries

This section analyses the ECtHR's case-law on the obligation to provide an effective remedy in connection with Article 8, which states:

> 1. Everyone has the right to respect for his private and family life, his home and his correspondence.
> 2. There shall be *no interference* by a public authority with the exercise of this right *except such as is in accordance with the law and is necessary in a democratic society* in the interests of national security, public safety or the economic wellbeing of the country, for the prevention of disorder or crime, for the protection of health or morals, or for the protection of the rights and freedoms of others.[105]

[101] *Boyle and Rice v the United Kingdom* [1988] ECHR 9659/82, 9658/82 [55].

[102] *Silver and others v the United Kingdom* [1983] ECHR 5947/72, 6205/73, 7052/75, 7061/75, 7107/75, 7113/75, 7136/75; *Aksoy v Turkey* [1996] ECHR 21987/93; *Bubbins v the United Kingdom* [2005] ECHR 50196/99; *Rotaru v Romania* [2000] ECHR 28341/95; *Z and others v the United Kingdom* [2001] ECHR 29392/95; *Hatton and others v the United Kingdom* [2003] ECHR 36022/97; *Al-Nashif v Bulgaria* [2002] ECHR 50963/99.

[103] *Al-Nashif v Bulgaria* (n 102) para 132.

[104] See Mowbray (n 79) 205–10; Harris and others (n 100) 766–67; van Dijk (n 48) 998–1006; Schabas (n 48) 551–52; Bartole, De Sena and Zagrebelsky (n 48) 479–94.

[105] European Convention for the Protection of Human Rights and Fundamental Freedoms, art 8 (emphasis added).

Paragraph 1 determines the scope of application as including the protection of private life, family life, home and correspondence. In addition, the ECtHR has expanded each of these four areas of private life. This is consistent with the interpretation of the ECHR as a living instrument. As a result of this interpretation, Article 8 currently protects an increasing number of fundamental rights, which have evolved over time, including cases of sexual orientation, ethnic and religious identity, healthcare, freedom of press, police search and seizure, child adoption, childcare, immigration, and prisoners' rights.[106]

Against this background, this book focuses on one of Article 8's most innovative interpretations as also including the duty of states to regulate private industries. The ECtHR has increasingly interpreted Article 8 as requiring states to regulate private industries in accordance with fundamental human rights. Traditionally, scholars have analysed the duty to regulate private industries primarily in connection with environmental rights, as most of the cases related to the failure of states to regulate companies arose in connection with environmental pollution. Although the ECtHR has established this obligation primarily in the context of environmental abuses, it expressly recognised that such a duty is a broader concept that may overlap with, but shall not be limited to, environmental rights.[107]

Article 8 applies to the three case studies which are used as hypotheticals. First, the duty of the state to regulate private industries is clearly applicable to the abuse of rights of the indigenous people that occurred as a result of environmental pollution in Ecuador. However, it is also applicable to the human rights abuses that took place in Bangladesh, because of the collapse of the production facilities resulting in various injuries to the people who were working there. Finally, the duty to regulate private industries also includes preventing companies from colluding with states to abuse human rights, as occurred in the Nigerian case study.

According to the jurisprudence of the ECtHR, the obligations deriving from Article 8 include such a wide variety of potential scenarios of application that it is often impossible to determine whether in a particular case the state has a positive or negative obligation. A state may allow private industries to abuse human rights by its action or its failure to act. For example, a state may enact laws promoting irresponsible behaviour of companies resulting in the violation of human rights, while another state may fail to regulate the responsibility of companies for human rights abuses and, by such an omission to regulate,

[106] See Mowbray (n 79) 127–87; Harris et al (n 100) 522–91; van Dijk (n 48) 663–750; Bartole, De Sena and Zagrebelsky (n 48) 299–303; Olivier De Schutter, 'Reasonable Accommodations and Positive Obligations in the European Convention on Human Rights', in *Disability Rights in Europe: From Theory to Practice* (Hart Publishing, 2005).

[107] See *Hatton and others v the United Kingdom* (n 102) paras 96–104; Popovic (n 38).

contribute to the violation of human rights. In the real world, it is often impossible to determine with certainty whether the violation of Article 8 is the result of a failure of the state to regulate business and human rights issues or an action of the state that promotes and contributes to unethical business policies. Traditionally, one could analyse the former as a breach of the state's positive duty and the latter as a breach of state's negative duty. However, the ECtHR has consistently ruled that, regardless of whether one interprets the state's duty in terms of positive or negative obligations, Article 8 applies in the same way.[108] For example, in *Hatton v the United Kingdom*[109] and *Moreno Gomez v Spain*,[110] the ECtHR stated:

> Whether the case is analysed in terms of a positive duty on the State to take reasonable and appropriate measures to secure the applicants' rights under paragraph 1 of Article 8 or in terms of an interference by a public authority to be justified in accordance with paragraph 2, the applicable principles are broadly similar. In both contexts regard must be had to the fair balance that has to be struck between the competing interests of the individual and of the community as a whole.[111]

Therefore, there is no practical difference if one interprets the duty of a state in terms of positive or negative obligations.

Furthermore, different rights and interests may be at stake in a particular case.[112] When non-absolute rights are in conflict, a state party has to choose which right should take precedence and what shall be the exact limitation on the other rights. When trying to reconcile conflicting rights, a state party shall consider all the rights at stake and strike a fair balance between competing interests. While preferring one right over another, the state interferes with the right of an individual to favour the interest of others. To prevent arbitrary actions of the state in such circumstances, paragraph 2 of Article 8 sets out a procedural safeguard as states may limit the rights of individuals only if such interference is '[i]n accordance with the [law]'.[113]

This obligation based on paragraph 2 of Article 8 is parallel to Article 13, which sets out an obligation of the state to provide the victims of human rights violations with effective legal remedies.[114] For this reason, the ECtHR often interprets the procedural obligations deriving from Articles 8 and 13 together.

[108] See van Dijk (n 48) 739–44; Xenos (n 47) 57–73; Harris and others (n 100) 531–35; Popovic (n 38).
[109] *Hatton and others v the United Kingdom* (n 102).
[110] *Moreno Gomez v Spain* [2005] ECHR 4143/02, para 55.
[111] *Hatton and others v the United Kingdom* (n 102) para 98.
[112] See van Dijk (n 48) 739–44; Xenos (n 47) 57–73; Harris et al (n 100) 531–35.
[113] European Convention for the Protection of Human Rights and Fundamental Freedoms, art 8.
[114] See Mowbray (n 79) 181–86 and 205–20; Harris and others (n 100) 522–36 and 764–82; van Dijk (n 48) 1021–23; Xenos (n 47) 57–172; Bartole, De Sena and Zagrebelsky (n 48) 474–518.

In *Silver and Others v the United Kingdom*,[115] an historical case dated 1983, the ECtHR laid down some initial guidelines for interpreting Article 13 in conjunction with non-absolute rights. First, non-judicial bodies can meet the effective remedy requirements set out in Article 13. Therefore, a state will comply with Article 13 as long as it provides the victim with an effective legal remedy before a domestic authority, which may not necessarily be a court. Second, the ECtHR ruled that '[a]lthough no single remedy may itself entirely satisfy the requirements of Article 13 (art. 13), the aggregate of remedies provided for under domestic law may do so'.[116] Therefore, the proportionality review under Article 13 applies only to the aggregate of remedies and not against each individual remedy. Third, the state has a margin of appreciation to implement Article 13. Furthermore, in *Klass v Germany*[117] and *Leander v Sweden*,[118] the ECtHR set out that, in cases of national security related to a system of secret surveillance, '[a]n effective remedy under Article 13 … [m]ust mean a remedy that is *as effective as can be*, having regard to the restricted scope for recourse inherent in any system of secret surveillance'.[119]

Therefore, in its initial jurisprudence, the ECtHR adopted a low standard of review against states violating a procedural obligation. According to this case-law, a state complies with Article 13 as long as it provides remedies '[a]s effective as can [be]'.[120] However, in its subsequent jurisprudence, the ECtHR tightened the standard: although states have a margin of appreciation when implementing Article 13 in conjunction with non-absolute rights, they '[m]ust make available to the individual concerned the effective possibility of challengin[g]'[121] the human rights abuse before a national authority. In particular, the ECtHR limited the application of *Klass v Germany* and *Leander v Sweden* to national security cases, such as those involving secret surveillance. In addition, the ECtHR offered a reminder that the scrutiny system adopted in *Klass v Germany* provided the applicant with the possibility of recourse and an independent review. However, when such a possibility of recourse is not present, the state is in violation of Article 13, notwithstanding the alleged national security threat:

> While procedural restrictions may be necessary to ensure that no leakage detrimental to national security would occur and while any independent authority dealing with an appeal against a deportation decision may need to afford a wide margin of appreciation to the executive in matters of national security, that can by no means justify doing away with remedies altogether whenever the executive has chosen to invoke the terms 'national security'.[122]

[115] *Silver and others v the United Kingdom* (n 102).
[116] ibid 113.
[117] *Klass and others v Germany* [1978] ECHR 5029/71, para 69.
[118] *Leander v Sweden* [1987] ECHR 9248/81, para 84.
[119] ibid; *Klass and others v Germany* (n 117) para 69 (emphasis added).
[120] *Klass and others v Germany* (n 117) para 69; *Leander v Sweden* (n 118) para 84.
[121] *Al-Nashif v Bulgaria* (n 102) para 133.
[122] ibid 137.

Nowadays, the ECtHR interprets this procedural safeguard as an obligation of the state to provide an effective remedy both for the party who was adversely affected by such an interference and the beneficiary of such an interference.[123]

(a) Rights of an Adversely Affected Party

This section considers the effective remedies that should be available to a party adversely affected by the interference of a state. The ECtHR interprets paragraph 2 of the Article 8 requirement to act '[i]n accordance with the [law]'[124] as entitling the victims of human rights violations to an effective legal remedy against any act or omission of the state. Each state is free to favour one interest over others, and therefore has certain discretion to limit some rights. However, an individual who is adversely affected by the state's decision to limit his/her rights must be able to challenge such a decision in court. The limitations of human rights may take the form of either an action of the state, such as, for example, a regulation allowing a company to build its factory close to a residential neighbourhood, or an omission of the state, such as, for example, the failure to adopt environmental laws that would prevent companies from emitting poisonous gases affecting the health of the population living in the vicinity of such industries. In any of these cases, the state must entitle the adversely affected party to the real-life opportunity to challenge the state's actions and failures to act.[125] As the ECtHR stated in *Ockan and others v Turkey*[126] and *Taskin v Turkey*:[127]

> [T]he individuals concerned must … [be] able to appeal to the courts against any decision, act or omission where they consider that their interests or their comments have not been given sufficient weight in the decision-making [process].[128]

Furthermore, in *Hatton and others v the United Kingdom*,[129] the ECtHR ruled that under UK law the standard of review applicable to the regulation of night flights at Heathrow airport was too low to meet the requirements of Article 13. *Hatton and others v the United Kingdom* is a case setting out the obligation of states when their laws allow a private company to abuse non-absolute rights. In its first judgment, the ECtHR held that the United Kingdom was in violation of both Articles 8 and 13.[130] As it pertains to

[123] See Sudre (n 22); van Dijk (n 48) 745–50; Xenos (n 47) 57–172; Bartole, De Sena and Zagrebelsky (n 48) 303–11.
[124] European Convention for the Protection of Human Rights and Fundamental Freedoms, art 8.
[125] See Mowbray (n 79) 181–86 and 205–20; Harris et al (n 100) 522–36 and 764–82; van Dijk (n 48) 745–50 and 1021–23; Xenos (n 47) 57–172; Bartole, De Sena and Zagrebelsky (n 48) 303–11 and 474–518; Sudre (n 22).
[126] *Ockan and others v Turkey* [2006] ECHR 46771/99, para 43.
[127] *Taskin and others v Turkey* [2005] ECHR 46117/99, para 119.
[128] ibid.
[129] *Hatton and others v the United Kingdom* (n 102).
[130] *Hatton and others v the United Kingdom* [2001] ECHR 36022/97.

Article 13, the ECtHR ruled that the standard of review or secondary norm applicable to the UK regulations of night flights was limited to '[c]oncepts … [of] … [i]rrationality, unlawfulness and patent unreasonableness … [which do not appropriately take into c]onsideration … [w]hether the claimed increase in nights flights … [was j]ustifiable'.[131] The ECtHR stated that, under Article 13, a victim of human rights violations is entitled to an effective remedy to challenge the policies pursued by the state. In this context, an *effective remedy* means a standard of review or secondary norm that would effectively allow such a victim to challenge the state regulation allegedly violating his/her right before a national authority. Such a standard should include a proportionality review that would determine whether, under Article 8, the state's regulation adequately balances the adversely affected rights of the victim and of the community as a whole. A few years after the first *Hatton and others v the United Kingdom* judgment, the Grand Chamber of the ECtHR reconsidered the case and found no violation of Article 8. However, the Grand Chamber confirmed that the United Kingdom violated Article 13, because it failed to provide the victims with an appropriate standard of review that would allow UK courts to determine whether the night flight regulation complied with Article 8.[132]

Hatton and others v the United Kingdom detailed the meaning of the proportionality test applicable when the alleged violations relate to non-absolute rights. In respect of such a category of human rights, states have a margin of appreciation when they determine how to meet their non-absolute obligations under the ECHR. They may choose to meet their obligation by implementing a number of different policies. However, under Articles 8 and 13, each state has an obligation to provide the victim of human rights violations with an effective standard of review that would permit domestic courts to rule whether the state is in breach of the ECHR. In particular, domestic courts must be able to determine, under a proportionality test, whether the choice made by a state struck a fair balance between all conflicting rights.[133] If, as in *Hatton and others v the United Kingdom*, the choice made by the state meets such a balance, national authorities will find the state in compliance with the national law and the ECHR. However, even if the state is in full compliance with the ECHR substantive rights, under Article 13, each state has a procedural obligation to provide the victim with an effective remedy.

If a domestic remedy is available on paper but, as a practical matter, it does not provide the victims of human rights violations with effective judicial review, the state is in breach of Article 8. This principle was confirmed in *Connors v the United Kingdom*,[134] in which members of gipsy communities were theoretically entitled to a judicial review against an eviction from their properties, but, in practice, the judicial procedure was such that domestic courts

[131] *Hatton and others v the United Kingdom* (n 102) para 141.
[132] *Hatton and others v the United Kingdom* (n 102).
[133] See Mowbray (n 79) 181–86 and 205–20; Harris et al (n 100) 522–36 and 764–82; van Dijk (n 48) 1021–23; Xenos (n 47) 57–172; Bartole, De Sena and Zagrebelsky (n 48) 474–518.
[134] *Connors v the United Kingdom* [2004] ECHR 66746/01.

could not review the merit of the eviction. The ECtHR ruled that: 'The power to evict without the burden of giving reasons liable to be examined as to their merits by an independent tribunal has not been convincingly show[n].'[135] Therefore, in *Connors v the United Kingdom,* the ECtHR held the United Kingdom to be in breach of its obligations to provide effective remedies under Article 8. Similarly, in *Keegan v United Kingdom,*[136] according to the black-letter law, the applicants were entitled to seek damages from the police for a search carried out in their house. However, the standard of review was limited to whether or not the police acted with malice. The ECtHR ruled that the standard based on malice was in favour of the police and did not comply with the ECHR, because, as a practical matter, the applicant had limited possibilities to prove such malice and, accordingly, to obtain damages in English courts.

In *Lopez Ostra v Spain*, the ECtHR found Spain to be in violation of Article 8, because it entitled Ms Lopez Ostra to a remedy against a polluting industry in theory but not in practice. Ms Lopez Ostra lived in the town of Lorca where a waste-treatment plant (built on a piece of land owned by the town municipality) polluted the air with gas, fumes and smells. When Ms. Lopez Ostra and her family initiated proceedings against the waste treatment plant, the Lorca municipality supported the polluting industry in court. Furthermore, the remedies were not promptly available, as Ms Lopez Ostra's family was able to relocate to a safe area and obtain a temporary shutdown of the waste treatment plant only after years of painful litigation.[137]

One reasoning behind this procedural obligation is that domestic courts should be the first institutions to safeguard the rights set out in the ECHR. It is for domestic courts to implement the ECHR in practice and prevent further litigation before the ECtHR. As established in *Keegan v the United Kingdom*, '[t]he question the Court must ... [a]ddress is whether the applicants had a remedy at national level to "enforce the substance of the Convention right[s]"'.[138] When national authorities adopt a low standard of review or secondary norm, the state is in violation of Article 13, because no effective legal remedy is available to the person whose human rights are allegedly violated.[139]

(b) Rights of a Beneficiary

When a state takes some measures favouring the rights of an individual over the rights of other members of the community, it has to guarantee that the beneficiary of such measures has effective access to courts to protect his/her interests. A state establishing a number of human rights policies that are not

[135] ibid 94.

[136] *Keegan v the United Kingdom* [2006] ECHR 28867/03.

[137] *Lopez Ostra v Spain* (n 83).

[138] ibid 41.

[139] See Mowbray (n 79) 181–86 and 205–20; Harris et al (n 100) 522–36 and 764–82; van Dijk and Arai (n 48) 1021–23; Xenos (n 47) 57–172; Bartole, De Sena and Zagrebelsky (n 48) 474–518.

actionable in court violates the ECHR because it implements the ECHR in theory but not in practice.[140] For example, if the home state enacts an environmental law that entitles the human rights victim Elsa to an environmental right potentially applicable against the holding company H, Elsa would be considered to be a beneficiary of such a domestic environmental law. However, to comply with the duty to protect, the home state would also have to ensure that the beneficiary Elsa has effective remedies in courts allowing her to enforce such an environmental law. As stated in *Moreno Gomez v Spain*, '[r]egulations to protect guaranteed rights serve little purpose if they are not duly enforced and the Court must reiterate that the Convention is intended to protect effective rights, not illusory ones'.[141]

Therefore, states fail to secure the duty to protect when they enact laws that the victims of human rights violations cannot enforce in domestic courts. If the home state's domestic law entitles Elsa to some environmental rights, but with no effective remedies against H, the home state would violate the duty to protect.

The ECtHR stated the obligation of states to provide effective remedies to the beneficiaries of public policies on numerous occasions.[142] As long ago as 1979, the ECtHR confirmed this principle when it ruled in *Airey v Ireland*[143] that Ireland violated Article 8, as it did not make recourse to courts '[e]ffectively accessible to the applicant',[144] and therefore her right existed only in theory and not in practice. Furthermore, in a 1985 case *X and Y v the Netherlands*,[145] the ECtHR found the Netherlands to be in violation of Article 8, as Dutch criminal law did not provide the applicant '[w]ith practical and effective protection'[146] in court.

The ECtHR reconfirmed this approach in *Cordella and others v Italy*.[147] In this case, the ECtHR found Italy violated Articles 13 and 8 as, despite providing the applicant with administrative and criminal proceedings theoretically actionable against the polluting company Ilva, it did not guarantee any remedy that would have allowed victims to obtain compensation for the environmental damage, or a clean-up of the polluted site where they lived. This recent case confirmed once again that states must provide remedies that are effective in practice and able to relieve victims from the harm they suffered.

[140] See Mowbray (n 79) 181–87 and 205–20; Harris et al (n 100) 522–36 and 764–82; van Dijk and Arai (n 48) 745–50 and 1006–26; Bartole, De Sena and Zagrebelsky (n 48) 297–311 and 474–98. See also *Ledyayeva, Dobrokhotova, Zolotareva and Romashina v Russia* [2007] ECHR 53157/99, 53247/99, 53695/00 and 56850/00; *Guerra and others v Italy* [1998] ECHR 116/1996/735/932.

[141] *Moreno Gomez v Spain* (n 110) para 61.

[142] See Mowbray (n 79) 181–87 and 205–20; Harris et al (n 100) 522–36 and 764–82; van Dijk and Arai (n 48) 745–50 and 1006–26; Bartole, De Sena and Zagrebelsky (n 48) 297–311 and 474–98.

[143] *Airey v Ireland* (n 42).

[144] ibid 33.

[145] *X and Y v the Netherlands* (n 68).

[146] ibid 30.

[147] *Cordella and others v Italy* (n 84).

Therefore, when states enact domestic substantive laws, they must also guarantee effective remedies connected with the enforcement of such laws. Articles 8 and 13 require European states to establish effective legal remedies. Article 8 sets out non-absolute rights, and states therefore have discretion as to how to balance the conflicting rights of the parties protected and the interests of society as a whole. The state should strike a balance between those competing interests. However, both the beneficiary and the party adversely affected by such policies shall have a procedural right to challenge any state's decision.

(ii) Article 3 and the Duty to Prevent Torture and Inhuman and Degrading Treatment

This section analyses the right to an effective remedy in connection with absolute rights. It focuses on the violations of Article 3, as it is the main Article applicable to the Nigerian case study. Article 3 states: 'No one shall be subjected to torture or to inhuman or degrading treatment or punishment.'[148] The obligation to ensure that no one suffers from torture, or inhuman or degrading treatment is absolute and straightforward. It also includes the procedural obligation to entitle the victim of alleged torture, or inhuman or degrading treatment to effective remedies in court.[149] An effective legal remedy must entitle the victim to a right to compensation and include an effective investigation.[150] In *Aksoy v Turkey*, concerning the violation of Article 13 brought in conjunction with Article 3, the ECtHR ruled:

> The nature of the right safeguarded under Article 3 of the Convention (art. 3) has implications for Article 13 (art. 13). Given the fundamental importance of the prohibition of torture ... [and] the especially vulnerable position of torture victims, Article 13 (art. 13) imposes, without prejudice to any other remedy available under the domestic system, an obligation on States to carry out a thorough and effective investigation of incidents of torture. ... [This includes] ... [i]n addition to the payment of compensation where appropriate, a thorough and effective investigation capable of leading to the identification and punishment of those responsible and including effective access for the complainant to the investigatory procedure. It is true that no express provision exists in the Convention such as can be found in Article 12 of the 1984 United Nations Convention against Torture and Other Cruel, Inhuman or Degrading Treatment or Punishment, which imposes a duty to proceed to a 'prompt and impartial' investigation whenever there is a reasonable ground to believe that an act of torture has been committed. However, in the Court's view, such a requirement is implicit in the notion of an 'effective remedy' under Article [13].[151]

[148] European Convention for the Protection of Human Rights and Fundamental Freedoms, art 3.

[149] See Mowbray (n 79) 205–10; Harris et al (n 100) 766–67; van Dijk (n 48) 998–1006; Schabas (n 48) 191–94 and 551–52; Bartole, De Sena and Zagrebelsky (n 48) 479–94; Popovic (n 38).

[150] See eg *Assenov and others v Bulgaria* [1998] ECHR 90/1997/874/1086; *Aksoy v Turkey* (n 102); *Z and others v the United Kingdom* (n 102).

[151] *Aksoy v Turkey* (n 102) para 98.

The Court clarified that, with respect to the violation of an absolute right, the state's duty to provide the victim with an effective remedy should be interpreted as '[a] duty to proceed to a "prompt and impartial" investigation'[152] as set out in the UN Convention against Torture and Other Cruel, Inhuman or Degrading Treatment or Punishment.[153]

Previously, the ECtHR seemed to follow the *Silver and Others v the United Kingdom*'s[154] line of precedents when interpreting Article 13 in conjunction with Article 3. For example, in a 1996 case, *Chahal v United Kingdom*,[155] the ECtHR ruled that, in theory, a state could also comply with Article 13 by legislating for a non-judicial investigation authority to address the cases falling within Article 3. However, in *Aksoy v Turkey*,[156] the ECtHR clarified that such an alternative domestic authority would be consistent with an obligation of a state to provide an effective remedy only if it entitles the victims of human rights violations to the full range of guarantees required by absolute rights such as Article 3. The ECtHR specifically distinguished between such cases as *Klass and others v Germany*[157] and *Leander v Sweden*,[158] and *Chahal v the United Kingdom*,[159] as the former were cases related to non-absolute rights, whereas the latter pertained to absolute rights set out in Article 3.

The ECtHR interpreted Article 13 in conjunction with an absolute right as requiring the state: (1) to conduct '[a] thorough and effective investigation capable of leading to the identification and punishment of those responsible';[160] (2) to provide '[e]ffective access for the complainant to the investigatory procedure';[161] and (3) to provide the victim with a remedy '[o]n the liability in damages',[162] and eventually entitle him/her to the payment of compensation including both pecuniary and non-pecuniary damages.[163] This strict scrutiny test has two main effects. On the one hand, states must conduct an effective investigation. Typically, in most states, such an investigation corresponds to a criminal investigation permitting the identification and punishment of a perpetrator of human rights abuses. On the other hand, states must provide the victim with a cause of action to seek damages. Typically, in most states, such a remedy corresponds to a cause of action in tort against the perpetrator of human rights abuses.

[152] ibid.
[153] Convention against Torture and Other Cruel, Inhuman or Degrading Treatment or Punishment 1984.
[154] *Silver and others v the United Kingdom* (n 102).
[155] *Chahal v the United Kingdom* [1996] ECHR 22414/93.
[156] *Aksoy v Turkey* (n 102).
[157] *Klass and others v Germany* (n 117).
[158] *Leander v Sweden* (n 118).
[159] *Chahal v the United Kingdom* (n 155).
[160] *Z and others v the United Kingdom* (n 102) para 109.
[161] *Aksoy v Turkey* (n 102) para 98.
[162] *Bubbins v the United Kingdom* (n 102) para 170.
[163] *Z and others v the United Kingdom* (n 102) para 109; *Bubbins v the United Kingdom* (n 102) para 171.

Therefore, in cases of absolute rights, the state has two parallel obligations as it pertains to companies abusing human rights. First, it must conduct an effective investigation against the corporate group abusing fundamental rights. Second, the state must provide the victim of human rights abuses with a cause of action to claim damages against the corporate group.[164]

The ECtHR defines the exact meaning of an *effective remedy in practice* on a case-by-case basis. However, it is possible to infer the following general principle from the ECtHR's case-law. Establishing a remedy that a victim could use in theory against the perpetrator of human rights abuses is not sufficient for the state to meet its obligations under Article 3. The remedy must be available to the victim in practice. In *Assenov v Bulgaria*,[165] *Labita v Italy*[166] and *Boicenco v Moldova*,[167] the ECtHR has consistently ruled:

> If … [the remedy would not be effective] …[t]he general legal prohibition of torture and inhuman and degrading treatment and punishment, despite its fundamental importance …[w]ould be ineffective in practice and it would be possible in some cases for agents of the State to abuse the rights of those within their control with virtual impunity.[168]

This requires at a minimum that domestic courts dealing with such cases of human rights abuses must be impartial, show their commitment to addressing any complaint related to the abuse of the rights enshrined by Article 3, and submit such cases

> [t]o the careful scrutiny … [s]o that the deterrent effect of the judicial system in place and the significance of the role it is required to play in preventing violations of the right to life and the prohibition of ill-treatment are not undermined.[169]

For example, in the case of *97 members of the Gldani Congregation of Jehovah's witnesses and four others v Georgia*,[170] the ECtHR found Georgia to be in violation of Article 3 because, despite video records of violence against Jehovah's Witnesses, domestic authorities asserted that they were incapable of conducting an investigation, as it was not possible to identify the perpetrators. Similarly, in *MC v Bulgaria*,[171] the ECtHR found Bulgaria to be in violation of

[164] See Harris et al (n 100) 275–78 and 764–82; Xenos (n 47) 57–172; Mowbray (n 79) 43–65 and 205–20; Bartole, De Sena and Zagrebelsky (n 48) 72–87; Schabas (n 48) 191–94 and 546–52; van Dijk (n 48) 1011–16; Popovic (n 38).

[165] *Assenov and others v Bulgaria* (n 150).

[166] *Labita v Italy* [2000] ECHR 26772/95.

[167] *Boicenco v Moldova* [2006] ECHR 41088/05.

[168] *Assenov and others v Bulgaria* (n 150) para 102; *Labita v Italy* (n 166) para 131; *Boicenco v Moldova* (n 167) para 120.

[169] *Beganovic v Croatia* [2009] ECHR 46423/06, para 77; *Okkali v Turkey* [2007] ECHR 52067/99, para 66.

[170] *97 members of the Gldani Congregation of Jehovah's witnesses and 4 others v Georgia* [2007] ECHR 71156/01.

[171] *MC v Bulgaria* [2004] ECHR 39272/98.

Article 3, because the prosecutor in a rape case did not duly consider the factual circumstances of the case (a fourteen-year-old girl having sex for the first time with two men) that, if duly considered, would have likely caused the prosecutor to assert that the victim did not have consensual sex. In *Labita v Italy*,[172] the ECtHR held Italy to be in violation of Article 3, because, despite the victim being able to start a proceeding, the court did not allow him to participate in a screening check of the suspects that would have given him the opportunity to recognise the policemen who allegedly tortured him. In *Okkali v Turkey*,[173] the ECtHR found a violation of Article 3, because domestic courts considered the confession of police officers as a mitigating element and did not hold them responsible for the maltreatment of the prisoners.

The main difference between providing effective remedies under Article 8 and Article 3 is as follows: while Article 8 sets out a non-absolute right entitling the state to limit the rights of individuals when required to advance a public interest, states are not allowed to curtail the human rights protected by Article 3. Therefore, while Article 8 establishes two distinct procedural obligations, Article 3 simply entitles any victim with an arguable claim to an effective remedy. Article 8 provides both an individual who was adversely affected by the state's conduct with a right to challenge it and the beneficiary of such conduct with a right to enforce it in domestic courts. This entails that the state must protect the rights of both the adversely affected individual and the beneficiary of any governmental policy. Instead, under Article 3, the state may not limit the rights of an individual protected by this Article, as every person should benefit from absolute protection. Therefore, Article 3 entitles everyone to the same protection against torture and the right to an effective remedy in court.[174]

Furthermore, in addition to an obligation to guarantee effective remedies in court, the state has a duty to penalise those who abuse absolute human rights. States have a margin of discretion in choosing the appropriate form to implement such sanctions in practice. However, when the sanctioning mechanism does not appropriately deter the perpetrators of torture, or inhuman or degrading treatment, the state is in breach of its obligations under Article 3.[175] This sanctioning obligation is applicable only to absolute rights, because the overriding importance of protecting such rights requires that states take all possible measures to prevent any abuse.

[172] *Labita v Italy* (n 166).

[173] *Okkali v Turkey* (n 169).

[174] See Harris et al (n 100) 275–78 and 764–82; Xenos (n 47) 57–172; Mowbray (n 79) 43–65 and 205–20; Bartole, De Sena and Zagrebelsky (n 48) 72–87; Schabas (n 48) 191–94 and 546–52; van Dijk (n 48) 1011–16; Popovic (n 38).

[175] See Harris et al (n 100) 275–78; Xenos (n 47) 142–72; Michael K Addo and Nicholas Grief, 'Does Article 3 of the European Convention on Human Rights Enshrine Absolute Rights?' (1998) 9 *European Journal of International Law* 510; Uğur Erdal and Hasan Bakirci, *Article 3 of the European Convention on Human Rights: A Practitioner's Handbook* (OMCT, 2006) 212–28.

Therefore, with respect to non-absolute rights, states are entitled to favour the rights of some individuals over others. States do not have an absolute obligation to penalise anyone abusing human rights, but instead, they must strike a fair balance between competing interests. Instead, with respect to absolute rights, states must, first, sanction any abuse of such rights, and, second, entitle the victims to an effective recourse in court against the perpetrator of such abuses.

(iii) The Relationship between the State and the Private Company

The original meaning of the right to an effective remedy was guaranteeing a remedy against the state.[176] However, with the evolution of the ECHR from an instrument focused on negative obligations of the state, to positive obligations that the State must implement to ensure the protection of human rights, the meaning of the term *effective remedy* also changed. The ECtHR explains this evolution of the concept of effective remedy from a right to challenge the decision of the state to a right to challenge the failure to act of the state in *Z and others v UK*[177] and *Paul and Audrey v the United Kingdom*.[178] In both cases the ECtHR held that:

> Where alleged failure by the authorities to protect persons from the acts of others is concerned, Article 13 may not always require that the authorities undertake the responsibility for investigating the allegations. There should, however, be available to the victim or the victim's family a mechanism for establishing any liability of State officials or bodies for acts or omissions involving the breach of their rights under the Convention.[179]

Furthermore, the ECtHR stated in *Ockan and others v Turkey*[180] and *Taskin v Turkey*:[181]

> The individuals concerned must … [b]e able to appeal to the courts against any decision, act or omission where they consider that their interests or their comments have not been given sufficient weight in the decision-making process.[182]

Recently, the ECtHR has also reaffirmed that states are liable both for their actions and failures to act.[183] When the ECtHR deals with the negative obligations of

[176] See Bartole, De Sena and Zagrebelsky (n 48) 474–518; Madelaine (n 22) 63–77; Harris et al (n 100) 764–82.
[177] *Z and others v the United Kingdom* (n 102).
[178] *Paul and Audrey Edwards v the United Kingdom* [2002] ECHR 46477/99.
[179] *Z and others v the United Kingdom* (n 102) para 109; *Paul and Audrey Edwards v the United Kingdom* (n 178) para 97.
[180] *Ockan and others v Turkey* (n 126).
[181] *Taskin and others v Turkey* (n 127).
[182] ibid 119; *Ockan and others v Turkey* (n 126) para 43.
[183] See e.g. *Meryem Celik and others v Turkey* [2013] ECHR 3598/03 .

a state with respect to human rights, the right to an effective remedy is the right to challenge the decision made by the state which resulted in the alleged violation of human rights. This was confirmed in *Hatton v United Kingdom*[184] in which the United Kingdom adopted a regulation allowing airline companies to fly during the night hours and, as a result of this legislation, private companies started to fly at night, allegedly abusing the right to a home of the people living in the vicinity of Heathrow airport.[185] The ECtHR set out that the concept of effective remedies shall permit the affected people to challenge such a regulation in court.

Instead, when a claimant alleges the breach of a positive obligation of the state to ensure human rights, the effective remedy cannot be equivalent to a right to challenge a decision made by the state, because typically a violation of a positive obligation is related to a failure of a state to take action. With respect to a positive obligation of the state to secure human rights, the right to an effective remedy means the right to challenge the failure of the state to prevent an act of a private party which resulted in the violation of human rights.[186]

But how to entitle a victim with an effective remedy against a state's failure to act which resulted in a private party abusing human rights? The most straight forward avenue is to provide such a victim with a cause of action directly against the private party. When challenging the actions committed by the private party in domestic courts, the relevant victims will give courts the chance to either confirm the choice made by the government, by holding the third party's actions lawful, or to penalise the state's failure to prevent or stop a private actor from abusing human rights. By engaging in this analysis, domestic courts review not only the third party's alleged illegal act resulting in the abuse of human rights, but also, indirectly, the state's failure to prevent such abuse perpetrated by a third party.[187]

The ECtHR established such a positive obligation of the state to provide effective remedies against private parties abusing human rights on the basis of Article 1.[188] For example, in *97 members of the Gldani Congregation of Jehovah's witnesses and four others v Georgia*[189] and *Beganovic v Croatia*,[190] the ECtHR ruled that the '[p]ositive obligation to conduct an official investigation … [c]annot be considered in principle to be limited solely to cases of ill-treatment by State agents'.[191]

[184] *Hatton and others v the United Kingdom* (n 102).
[185] ibid; Mowbray (n 79) 181–87.
[186] See Harris and others (n 100) 764–82; Mowbray (n 79) 205–20; Bartole, De Sena and Zagrebelsky (n 48) 474–518; van Dijk (n 48) 1024–26; Brems (n 97).
[187] Brems (n 97); Palmer (n 44); Madelaine (n 22) 62–77.
[188] See Xenos (n 47) 59–73; Madelaine (n 22) 63–77.
[189] *97 members of the Gldani Congregation of Jehovah's witnesses and 4 others v Georgia* (n 170).
[190] *Beganovic v Croatia* (n 169).
[191] *97 members of the Gldani Congregation of Jehovah's witnesses and 4 others v Georgia* (n 170) para 97.

Furthermore, in *Z and others v the United Kingdom*,[192] *MC v Bulgaria*,[193] *97 members of the Gldani Congregation of Jehovah's witnesses and four others v Georgia*,[194] and *Beganovic v Croatia*,[195] the ECtHR ruled:

> [T]he obligation on the High Contracting Parties under Article 1 of the Convention to secure to everyone within their jurisdiction the rights and freedoms defined in the Convention, taken together with Article 3, requires States to take measures designed to ensure that individuals within their jurisdiction are not subjected to torture or inhuman or degrading treatment or punishment, including such ill-treatment administered by private individuals.[196]

In *Cordella and others v Italy*,[197] the ECtHR ruled Italy violated Article 13 because it did not provide the applicant with a cause of action to enforce the clean-up of the polluted site and/or to obtain compensation for the damage suffered. The fact that the applicants could initiate administrative or criminal proceedings that the state would have to fulfil on its own was not considered sufficient to constitute an effective remedy. The ECtHR seemed to suggest that the state had to entitle the victim directly with a cause of action against the polluting industry to obtain compensation and/or the clean-up of the area.

The ECtHR's jurisprudence has not yet addressed the application of the right to an effective remedy in relationship to the human rights abuses committed by multinational enterprises. However, the Guiding Principles have established such a connection. They have a full section detailing access to remedy as part of the duty to protect the victims of human rights abuses against multinational companies. Guiding Principles 25 and 26 set out as follows:

> [A]s part of their duty to protect against business-related human rights abuse, States must take appropriate steps to ensure, through judicial, administrative, legislative or other appropriate means, that when such abuses occur within their territory and/or jurisdiction those affected have access to effective remedy.[198]
>
> States should … [r]educe legal, practical and other relevant barriers that could lead to a denial of access to remedy.[199]

The UN Human Rights Council's commentary to Guiding Principle 26 provides a number of examples of the legal barriers that could deny justice, including, first, when '[t]he way in which legal responsibility is attributed among members of a corporate group under domestic criminal and civil laws facilitates the

[192] *Z and others v the United Kingdom* (n 102).

[193] *MC v Bulgaria* (n 171).

[194] *97 members of the Gldani Congregation of Jehovah's witnesses and 4 others v Georgia* (n 170).

[195] *Beganovic v Croatia* (n 169).

[196] ibid 70; *Z and others v the United Kingdom* (n 102) para 73; *97 members of the Gldani Congregation of Jehovah's witnesses and 4 others v Georgia* (n 170) para 96; *MC v Bulgaria* (n 171) para 149.

[197] *Cordella and others v Italy* (n 84).

[198] Ruggie, 'Report of the Special Representative of the Secretary-General' (n 9) 246.

[199] ibid 247–48.

avoidance of appropriate accountability';[200] and, second, when '[c]laimants face a denial of justice in a host State and cannot access home State courts regardless of the merits of the claim'.[201] Accordingly, providing legal remedies requires establishing an effective standard of review, or secondary norm, against multinational enterprises abusing human rights.

The Guiding Principles are of particular importance as they have been endorsed by a number of international institutions including the European Union[202] and the Council of Europe, which is the main political institution in the ECHR legal order. The Council of Europe published the Recommendation of the Committee of the Ministers to Member States on Human Rights and Business (the 'Recommendation') setting out the policies which the state parties to the ECtHR should implement to comply with the Guiding Principles.[203] The Recommendation includes a detailed appendix on the responsibility of European states as it pertains to business and human rights. The appendix analyses the Third Pillar of the Guiding Principles dealing with the Access to Remedy extensively. Specifically, paragraphs 15 and 35 of the Recommendation state:

> 15. Within their jurisdiction, member States have a duty to protect individuals against human rights abuses by third parties, including business enterprises. This includes their positive and procedural obligations under the European Convention on Human Rights, as applied and interpreted by the European Court of Human Rights. Such obligations consist of requirements to prevent human rights violations where the competent authorities had known or ought to have known of a real risk of such violations, to undertake an independent and impartial, adequate and prompt official investigation where such violations are alleged to have occurred; to undertake an effective prosecution, and to take all appropriate measures to establish accessible and effective mechanisms which require that the victims of such violations receive prompt and adequate reparation for any harm suffered. …
>
> 35. Member States should consider allowing their domestic courts to exercise jurisdiction over civil claims concerning business-related human rights abuses against subsidiaries, wherever they are based, of business enterprises domiciled within their jurisdiction if such claims are closely connected with civil claims against the latter enterprises.[204]

The Recommendation focuses on the jurisdiction that the states should assert over the extraterritorial activities conducted by European multinational corporate groups through their foreign subsidiaries. It specifically links the Guiding Principles' duty to protect to the ECHR-based positive obligations to provide effective remedies for the victims of human rights abuses against private actors.

[200] ibid 248.
[201] ibid.
[202] European Commission (n 10).
[203] Committee of Ministers, 'Recommendation of the Committee of Ministers to Member States on Human Rights and Business' (2016) CM/Rec 3.
[204] ibid 15, 35.

Furthermore, the Recommendation confirms that the right to an effective remedy should be interpreted as the obligation to guarantee an effective remedy for a victim of human rights abuses, not only against the state but also against any private actor allegedly abusing human rights. The Recommendation links Article 13 with the obligation to provide an effective remedy against multinational enterprises. Paragraphs 31 and 34 of the Recommendation set out this interconnection as follows:

> 31. Member States should ensure the effective implementation of their obligations under Articles 6 and 13 of the European Convention on Human Rights and other international and European human rights instruments, to grant to everyone access to a court in the determination of their civil rights, as well as to everyone whose rights have been violated under these instruments, an effective remedy before a national authority, including where such violation arises from business activity. …
>
> 34. Member States should apply such legislative or other measures as may be necessary to ensure that their domestic courts have jurisdiction over civil claims concerning business-related human rights abuses against business enterprises domiciled within their jurisdiction.[205]

This is the first document establishing a direct connection between the Guiding Principles' duty to protect and the ECHR-based procedural positive obligations to provide effective remedies. It is beyond any reasonable doubt that, when assessing the responsibility of a European state in one of the hypothetical case studies, the ECtHR will have high regard for the Recommendation, which, although non-binding, is a persuasive instrument of interpretation for any party to the ECHR. It is particularly noteworthy that paragraph 15 of the Recommendation, where the Committee of Ministers establishes an interconnection between the Guiding Principles and the ECHR-based positive procedural obligations, sets out a persuasive interpretation of both the Guiding Principles and the ECHR. In this respect, it is arguable that the recommendations by the Committee of Ministers have a different authority when they relate to the ECHR rather than any other international legal instrument.[206] When the Committee of Ministers discusses an international law instrument, such as, for example, the Guiding Principles, it provides an opinion on the matters set out in such an instrument. However, when the Committee of Ministers opines on the meaning of the ECHR, it interprets a treaty that has been accepted by all members of the Council of Europe. For this reason, the interpretation of the ECHR by the Committee of Ministers would have a special status and higher authority in comparison to the interpretation of any other international treaty.[207]

[205] ibid 31–34.

[206] See Gregor Puppinck, 'Status of the Recommendations of the Committee of Ministers in the Legal Field of the Council of Europe – Synthesis', European Centre for Law and Justice, www.academia.edu/2083218/Status_of_the_recommendations_of_the_Committee_of_Ministers_in_the_legal_field_of_the_Council_of_Europe_Synthesis, accessed 9 December 2016.

[207] ibid.

In accordance with such an interpretation, the Vienna Convention on the Law of Treaties Article 31(3)(c) states: 'There shall be taken into account, together with the context: … [a]ny relevant rules of international law applicable in the relations between the parties'.[208] A recommendation of the Council of Europe would clearly fit within Article 31(3)(c) as, while non-binding, it is a '[r]elevant rule … [a]pplicable … [b]etween the parties'.[209] Scholars, as well as the jurisprudence of the ECtHR, have in fact clarified that soft rules of international law would qualify in terms of Article 31(3)(c).[210] Accordingly, it is unlikely that the ECtHR would disregard a recommendation coming from the Council of Europe as it pertains to the interpretation of the ECHR.

C. The Duty to Fulfil

The sole availability of effective legal remedies against corporations may not prevent them from abusing human rights. Multinational enterprises may find an alternative way to evade liability or may just assume the risk of liability, given that only a very limited number of victims will have the financial means, time and expertise to sue in court. Accordingly, the issue is whether, in such circumstances, the state has further duties to stop companies from abusing human rights.

The answer will depend on whether a state made its *best-effort* by providing effective legal remedies to the victims or is in a position to take further steps to stop companies from abusing human rights. Such an additional further obligation is a duty of the state to do everything feasible to promote and facilitate the respect of human rights by companies. In Manfred Nowak's words, it is an obligation to '[f]acilitate the enjoyment of human rights and an obligation to provide services'.[211] The duty to fulfil is applicable in the following two main cases. First, states must prevent the abuses and promote the respect of human rights between private parties when they have the power to influence their conduct. Second, states must progressively provide services, such as education or healthcare, to those in need. In both cases, the duty to fulfil is a positive obligation, because states have an obligation to act. However, whereas, in the former case, the positive obligation requires states to influence third parties, in the latter, states act independently from any other person.[212] This book focuses on the former case, as it analyses the positive obligation of states to influence the conduct of multinational companies.

[208] Vienna Convention on the Law of Treaties 1969 (Vol 115, I-18232) 331, art 31(3).
[209] ibid art 31(3).
[210] See Oliver Dörr and Kirsten Schmalenbach (eds), *Vienna Convention on the Law of Treaties: A Commentary* (Springer, 2012) 560–68; *Demir and Baykara v Turkey* [2008] ECHR 34503/97.
[211] Nowak (n 63) 38.
[212] ibid 37–39; Sepúlveda Carmona (n 19) 115–248.

To some degree, scholars associate the duty to fulfil with a *due diligence* obligation. The concept of *due diligence* is unclear, because it is a framework potentially applicable across all duties to respect, protect and fulfil. However, the core definition of *due diligence* is an obligation of *best-effort* or *progressive realisation* that requires states to prevent acts committed by third parties and/or influence private parties so that they respect human rights. Although there may be instances when states have *due diligence* obligations related to their duties to respect and protect, it is clear that in most cases *due diligence* obligations will be part of the duty to fulfil and would require states to promote human rights among private parties or prevent them from abusing human rights.[213] However, associating the duty to fulfil to a *due diligence* obligation may also be dangerous, as companies and states often use the language of *due diligence* to argue that they do not have a legally binding obligation at all.[214] This book takes the position that, although the duty to fulfil entails a *best-effort* and *progressive realisation* type of obligation, it is legally binding as it requires states to act and do their utmost to attain the desired outcome. In this sense, it is true that the duty to fulfil is not an obligation *of result*, as achieving a certain outcome is not the benchmark to test whether or not a state meets its obligations. It is also not a simple obligation of *conduct*, as the state has not one, but a wide range, of possibilities as to the actions that it can take towards achieving a certain result. In fact, these actions, taken to attain a future goal, are the benchmark to determine the state's liability. Furthermore, it should be noted that there is a difference between the CSR *due diligence* obligation of companies and the human rights *due diligence* obligation of states. Whereas the former is usually constructed as an obligation of holding companies to ensure that the entities within their supply chains respect human rights or environmental standards, the latter is a standard that states should follow to meet their human rights obligations.[215]

It should be noted that the separation between the duty to protect and the duty to fulfil is not always straightforward, especially as it pertains to the influence that states exercise over private actors. For instance, this book considers the duty to fulfil in terms of Eide's *obligations to provide basic needs* and to *facilitate and assist*, Shue's *obligations to aid the deprived* and *responsibility to take due care*, Van Hoof's *obligations to ensure and promote*, as well as Alston and Steiner's *duties to provide goods and services* and *to promote rights*.[216] The common ground in all of these obligations is for the state to do its utmost to promote or facilitate the enjoyment of rights. This essentially means that, in

[213] See Mazzeschi (n 16) 390–496; Duncan French and Tim Stephens, 'ILA Study Group on Due Diligence in International Law First Report' (International Law Association, 2014).

[214] See Menno T Kamminga, 'Due Diligence Mania', *The Women's Convention Turned 30* (Intersentia, 2012).

[215] See Fasciglione (n 11) 630–33.

[216] See Sepúlveda Carmona (n 19) 115–248; Mazzeschi (n 16) 242–56.

so far as the state has the possibility to influence the conduct of third parties, it has a responsibility to use its influence to facilitate the enjoyment of human rights.[217]

Whatever analytical approach one adopts with regard to the duty to protect or fulfil, a number of scholars agree that states have an obligation to influence the activities of private parties in order to facilitate the enjoyment of human rights.[218] For instance, the Maastricht Principles classify the obligation to influence others in general terms as a duty to protect. Principle 26 of the Maastricht Principles sets out:

> States that are in a position to influence the conduct of non-State actors even if they are not in a position to regulate such conduct, such as through their public procurement system or international diplomacy, should exercise such influence, in accordance with the Charter of the United Nations and general international law, in order to protect economic, social and cultural rights.[219]

However, when it comes to the obligations to influence others in the international sphere, the Maastricht Principles classify them under the duty to fulfil. The Maastricht Principles construe the duty to fulfil in narrow terms as an obligation to engage extraterritorially to influence the conduct of other actors that abuse human rights.

Therefore, this book argues that states should use their power to influence the activities of multinational enterprises to prevent human rights abuses. This power will vary depending on the given state. Whereas the duty to protect applies to any state, in so far as it can provide effective legal remedies for victims against companies, the duty to fulfil applies only to those states that are capable of effectively taking further steps to influence the conduct of companies. It is impossible to detail the exact content of the duty to fulfil on a general basis. This obligation does not set an absolute benchmark applicable to all countries. Each state may implement different policies to meet its duty, provided that it does its utmost to achieve the result to stop private parties (including companies) from abusing human rights. States are not measured by the same yardstick, rather the duty is tailored to their economic and political reality. The ECtHR considers various factors that are relevant to determine whether states comply with their duty to fulfil. The first factor is the geopolitical situation of the country that could effectively place it in a position to influence other actors. The second factor is the nature of the rights at stake in each particular case. The third factor is the factual circumstances in which a violation of the ECHR arises. In this sense, one should take into account the differences between absolute and

[217] See Mazzeschi (n 16) 242–49; Sepúlveda Carmona (n 19) 115–248; Eyal Benvenisti, 'Sovereigns as Trustees of Humanity: On the Accountability of States to Foreign Stakeholders' (2013) 107 *American Journal of International Law* 295, 313–26.

[218] See Mazzeschi (n 16) 242–49; Sepúlveda Carmona (n 19) 115–248; Benvenisti (n 217) 313–26.

[219] De Schutter et al (n 34) pt 26.

non-absolute rights. As already analysed above, although states can never derogate from absolute rights, they may balance non-absolute rights within certain limits defined by the ECtHR's case-law.[220]

(i) Article 8 and the Fair Balance Test

Given that Article 8 sets out non-absolute rights, paragraph 2 entitles states to balance the opposing interests that arise in a particular case. With respect to the regulation of human rights violations addressed in this book, such conflicting interests include, on the one hand, the rights of companies, and, on the other hand, the rights of stakeholders adversely affected by the activities of corporate groups. For instance, the home state could favour the interests of enterprises over stakeholders affected by their operations with a view to promoting economic development and, by doing so, benefit society as a whole. There is no clear and perfect balance for the state to strike. Therefore, when addressing the question of whether a state has managed to balance the interests of the conflicting parties in a manner consistent with its obligations under the ECHR, the ECtHR never reviews the substantive choices made by the state, but rather focuses on its decision-making process.[221] As a consequence of this approach, certain scholars have labelled the ECtHR review 'as "proceduralisation" or "proceduralisation movement"',[222] because the review is not related to the choice itself, but instead to '[m]ethodological framework through which the whole set of pertinent interests can be taken into account in an equitable and impartial manner'.[223] According to the ECtHR's case-law, the state's decision-making process must include the following steps.

First, the state must prove that there are competing interests at stake in the case at hand. Paragraph 2 of Article 8 states: 'There shall be no interference by a public authority with the exercise of this rights except such as … [i]s necessary in a democratic society.'[224] The ECtHR interprets the term necessity strictly as a 'pressing social need'.[225] If there is no *pressing social need* to interfere with the rights of an individual or to allow a private party to interfere with such rights, the state is in breach of Article 8. For example, in *Christine Goodwin v the*

[220] See Sudre (n 22); Bartole, De Sena and Zagrebelsky (n 48) 303–11; van Dijk (n 48) 725–30 and 739–50.

[221] See Harris et al (n 100) 522–85; Xenos (n 47) 57–172; van Dijk (n 48) 725–50; Bartole, De Sena and Zagrebelsky (n 48) 297–369; Mowbray (n 79) 181–87; Palmer (n 44); Popovic (n 38); De Schutter (n 106); Loukis Loucaides, 'Environmental Protection through the Jurisprudence of the European Convention on Human Rights' (2005) 75 *British Yearbook of International Law* 249; Schabas (n 48) 401–406.

[222] Xenos (n 47) 67; Françoise Tulken and Sebastien Van Drooghenbroeck, 'L'évolution des droits garantis et l'interprétation jurisprudentielle de la CEDH' (Collection Les Conférences Publiques du Pôle européen Jean Monnet, 2002).

[223] Xenos (n 47) 68; Tulken and Van Drooghenbroeck (n 222).

[224] European Convention for the Protection of Human Rights and Fundamental Freedoms, art 8.

[225] *Keegan v the United Kingdom* (n 136) para 30.

United Kingdom,[226] a case concerning the recognition of the gender assigned to a transsexual applicant, the ECtHR ruled that the United Kingdom was in violation of Article 8, because there was no competing interest weighing against the recognition of the applicant's gender.

> Since there are no significant factors of public interest to weigh against the interest of this individual applicant in obtaining legal recognition of her gender re-assignment, ... [the ECtHR] reaches the conclusion that the fair balance that is inherent in the Convention now tilts decisively in favour of the applicant.[227]

Similarly, in another case concerning gender assignment, *L v Lithuania*,[228] the ECtHR ruled that, given the limited number of people in need of gender-reassignment surgery, enabling transsexuals to have the surgery would not adversely affect the state's budget. There was no competing interest at stake that would justify avoiding gender-reassignment surgeries in Lithuania. Therefore, when enabling an individual to enjoy human rights does not adversely affect the competing interests of others, the state should entitle him/her to fundamental rights.

Accordingly, applying this line of analysis to the situation when a state allows an enterprise to disregard minimum safety/environmental standards for the sake of encouraging entrepreneurial activities and boosting the economy, the ECtHR could find that requiring the respect of a certain minimum standard does not adversely affect the rights of corporations. Therefore, the state may not have compelling reasons to allow companies to disregard environmental and minimum safety standards for the sake of increasing their profits. Instead, states could require companies to adopt minimum safety and environmental standards while conducting their industrial activities.

Second, the ECtHR must consider whether the state violated its own domestic regulations when striking a balance in a given case. Assume, for the purpose of illustration of how this second limb applies, the case of a company's poisonous emissions, which exceed the threshold permitted under domestic law. If domestic authorities do not sanction such a company, given that its industrial production is fundamental to the national economy, this action of the domestic authorities would constitute a breach of paragraph 2 of Article 8.[229] This hypothetical example occurred in fact in *Moreno Gómez v Spain*,[230] *Ledyayeva v Russia*[231] and *Fadeyeva v Russia*,[232] when the ECtHR recognised

[226] *Christine Goodwin v the United Kingdom* [2002] ECHR 28957/95.
[227] ibid 93.
[228] *L v Lithuania* [2008] ECHR 27527/03.
[229] See Harris et al (n 100) 522–85; Xenos (n 47) 57–172; van Dijk (n 48) 725–50; Bartole, De Sena and Zagrebelsky (n 48) 297–369; Mowbray (n 79) 181–87; Pitkanen (n 48); Popovic (n 38); Loucaides (n 221); Schabas (n 48) 401–06.
[230] *Moreno Gómez* (n 110).
[231] *Ledyayeva, Dobrokhotova, Zolotareva and Romashina v Russia* (n 140).
[232] *Fadeyeva v Russia* (n 82).

that the state was in breach of Article 8. Although the ECtHR considered the importance of the economic activities conducted by the relevant industries in each of the above cases, the state should have complied with its own domestic law which prohibited such activities. However, in these cases, Spain and Russia did not apply their domestic laws in practice, given the importance of the industries at issue. For example, in *Fadeyeva v Russia*, Russian law prohibited the construction of residential homes in the vicinity of an industry reaching a certain threshold of poisonous emissions. Despite this prohibition, the home of Ms Fadeyeva was located near a polluting industry, in violation of domestic law.[233] The ECtHR ruled that Russia should have ensured the application of its own domestic environmental law. In particular, Russia could have chosen to either limit the poisonous emissions of the relevant industries or provide Ms Fadeyeva with an option to relocate to a different location that would not be subject to such pollution. By failing to ensure any of these options and, more generally, by failing to ensure the compliance with its domestic laws, Russia violated the ECHR.[234]

Third, states must make an informed decision. In cases concerning companies, the ECtHR has consistently ruled that the decision-making process must include preliminary investigations of the effects that the industrial activity may have on the rights of individuals.[235] For instance, in *Taskin v Turkey* and *Hatton v the United Kingdom*, the ECtHR held that:

> [t]he decision-making process must firstly involve appropriate investigations and studies in order to allow them to predict and evaluate in advance the effects of those activities which might damage the environment and infringe individuals' rights and to enable them to strike a fair balance between the various conflicting interests at stake.[236]

In *Cordella and others v Italy*,[237] the ECtHR also held Italy violated Article 8 on the basis of the copious, yet not sufficiently taken into consideration, scientific evidence pointing at the negative effects Ilva's activities had on the health of people living nearby. Therefore, Article 8 requires states to effectively investigate the industrial activities conducted by companies within their jurisdiction and to assess, on the basis of scientific studies, whether such activities may prejudice fundamental rights.

Furthermore, the ECtHR requires states to adjust their policies to the changing circumstances affecting human rights. For example, in *Christine Goodwin v*

[233] The Soviet Union assigned a home to Ms Fadeyeva when the environmental laws regulating industrial pollution were not in place.

[234] *Fadeyeva v Russia* (n 82).

[235] See Harris et al (n 100) 522–85; Xenos (n 47) 57–172; van Dijk (n 48) 725–50; Bartole, De Sena and Zagrebelsky (n 48) 297–369; Mowbray (n 79) 181–87; Pitkanen (n 48); Popovic (n 38); Loucaides (n 221); Schabas (n 48) 401–06.

[236] *Taskin and others v Turkey* (n 127) para 119; *Hatton and others v the United Kingdom* (n 102) para 128.

[237] *Cordella and others v Italy* (n 84).

the United Kingdom,[238] the ECtHR demanded that the United Kingdom bring its laws on transsexuals up to the level of the advanced recognition of such rights arising in the twenty-first century. The ECtHR requires states to increase the protection of vulnerable groups of individuals in accordance with evolving human rights standards. In connection with this requirement to adjust the level of domestic protection in relation to the evolution of human rights, it is clear that the international community is increasingly recognising the responsibility of multinational enterprises for human rights abuses.[239] Although the ECtHR has not yet applied this principle to the evolving nature of the business and human rights relationship, it is arguable that, in striking a fair balance between different competing interests, the state should, in accordance with its obligations under the ECHR, consider, on the one hand, the benefits that the current structure of multinational companies bring to society as a whole, and, on the other hand, the human rights abuses that multinational enterprises are able to commit due to the current structure of company law. To strike a fair balance between such conflicting interests, states should conduct an effective investigation into the potentially harmful activities of multinational enterprises, taking into consideration the evolving business and human rights framework. As demonstrated in Chapter 2, it is clear that, the choice of the European legislators of where the balance between the interests of enterprises and stakeholders lies is currently skewed in favour of the companies.

Therefore, the duty to fulfil requires states to adopt an efficient decision-making process in striking a fair balance between competing interests. To achieve this objective, the state must, first, identify the competing interests as stake, second, act in accordance with its own domestic laws, and, third, make informed decisions that should be adjusted in accordance with the constantly evolving standards of human rights protection.

(ii) Article 3 as an Absolute Duty to Fulfil

It is difficult to reconcile the concepts of an absolute obligation arising from Article 3 and the *best-effort* duty to fulfil. On the one hand, Article 3 sets out an absolute obligation requiring the state to protect any individual from any abuse

[238] *Christine Goodwin v the United Kingdom* (n 226).

[239] See Mares (n 12); Jägers (n 9); Anna Beckers, *Enforcing Corporate Social Responsibility Codes: On Global Self-Regulation and National Private Law* (Hart Publishing, 2015); John Gerard Ruggie, 'Business and Human Rights: The Evolving International Agenda' (2007) 101 *The American Journal of International Law* 819; Aurora Voiculescu, 'Human Rights and the Normative Ordering of Global Capitalism', in *The Business of Human Rights: An Evolving Agenda for Corporate Responsibility* (Zed Books, 2011); David Weissbrodt and Muria Kruger, 'Human Rights Responsibilities of Businesses as Non-State Actors' in *Non-State Actors and Human Rights* (Oxford University Press, 2005); Fura-Sandstrom (n 1); David Bilchitz, 'The Ruggie Framework: An Adequate Rubric for Corporate Human Rights Obligations?' (2010) 7 *SUR* 199; Astrid Sanders, 'The Impact of the "Ruggie Framework" and the United Nations Guiding Principles on Business and Human Rights on Transnational Human Rights Litigation' (2014) 18 *LSE Law, Society and Economy Working Papers*.

by private parties. On the other hand, there is no way a state can possibly control the life of all private individuals and ensure that nobody will ever commit an act of torture prohibited under Article 3.[240] Therefore, the duty to ensure that third parties respect human rights, even when this obligation relates to absolute rights, is not an obligation of *result*, as it would constitute an unreasonable burden on the state. Instead, it is a *best-effort* duty to fulfil. However, it is possible to reconcile the apparent conflict between absolute rights and *best-effort* obligations if one interprets the duty to fulfil as the state's absolute obligation to do its utmost to stop any violation of Article 3. In this sense, the state does not have an absolute obligation to stop torture, but it has an absolute obligation to do its best to ensure that no person suffers from torture or inhuman and degrading treatment. The ECtHR clarified the concept of the absolute *best-effort* obligation in *Beganovic v Croatia*:

> [I]t goes without saying that the obligation on the State under Article 1 of the Convention cannot be interpreted as requiring the State to guarantee through its legal system that inhuman or degrading treatment is never inflicted by one individual on another.[241]

The difficulty in the cases arising in connection with Article 3, like *Beganovic v Croatia*, is to set out exactly what are the steps a state should take to meet its duty to fulfil. The answer to this question depends on a case-by-case analysis, as it is impossible to establish in general terms what the best policies are that a state must adopt in order to ensure that no ill-treatment occurs in a given situation.

Furthermore, it should be noted that the application of the duty to fulfil is limited in cases of absolute rights, because most of the obligations imposed on the states are of either *conduct* or *result* and not of *progressive realisation*. As explained above, where an absolute right is at stake, states shall provide human rights victims with both effective recourse to justice in court and sanction any conduct abusing fundamental rights. Assuming that the state complies with both of these obligations, there is not much left that the state could possibly do to progressively ensure that no victim would suffer from torture or inhuman and degrading treatment.

However, in its jurisprudence, the ECtHR encountered a few scenarios in which, in addition to sanctioning the human rights abuses and providing the victim with an effective remedy, it required the state to take additional steps to ensure the application of Article 3 progressively.[242] Such additional steps usually related to the effective protection of the victim of human rights violations. For example, in *Opuz v Turkey*,[243] the ECtHR held Turkey to be in violation of

[240] See Harris et al (n 100) 275–78; Xenos (n 47) 142–72; Addo and Grief (n 175); Erdal and Bakirci (n 175) 212–28.

[241] *Beganovic v Croatia* (n 169) para 71.

[242] See Harris et al (n 100) 275–78; Xenos (n 47) 142–72; Addo and Grief (n 175); Erdal and Bakirci (n 175) 212–28.

[243] *Opuz v Turkey* [2009] ECHR 33401/02.

Article 3, because Turkish law failed to protect a victim of domestic violence against her husband, as it did not entitle her to the right to live in a state guest-house. In this case, it is clear that the requirement to permit the victim to live in a guest-house requires the state to take additional steps in addition to sanctioning domestic violence against women and entitling them to an effective remedy in national court. This is a *best-effort* duty to fulfil, as the state has an obligation to do its utmost to neutralise the husband's violence effectively. The meaning of *best-effort* would depend on the country's economic resources and the possibility to allocate them to the protection of the victim. In the case of Turkey, the ECtHR ruled that it should have ensured a safe home for the applicant who was suffering from domestic violence.

Therefore, Article 3 requires states to do their utmost to progressively ensure that companies respect human rights.

(iii) Trade and Investment

The specific policies that a state shall implement to meet its duty to fulfil will need to be decided on a case-by-case basis. For instance, in *Opuz v Turkey*,[244] the ECtHR held that Turkey could offer public accommodation to protect a victim from domestic violence. Instead, in *Fadeyeva v Russia*,[245] an environmental degradation case which resulted in an abuse of rights of Ms Fadeyeva, the ECtHR held that Russia could either ensure that Russian companies respect environmental standards or provide alternative housing for people living in an environmentally unsafe area. These cases are useful because they provide at least some general guidance as to the policies a state should implement to meet its duty to fulfil. The ECtHR has not yet opined on the scope of the duty to fulfil as it pertains to extraterritorial human rights abuses committed by European multinational companies, such as a UK-based holding company H. However, as established in *Opuz v Turkey*, when the ECtHR implements the duty to fulfil, it relies on specialised international treaties and practices established in a specific area:

> In interpreting the provisions of the Convention and the scope of the State's obligations in specific cases … [t]he Court will also look for any consensus and common values emerging from the practices of European States and specialised international instruments, such as the CEDAW, as well as giving heed to the evolution of norms and principles in international law through other developments such as the Belém do Pará Convention, which specifically sets out States' duties relating to the eradication of gender-based violence.[246]

[244] ibid.
[245] *Fadeyeva v Russia* (n 82).
[246] *Opuz v Turkey* (n 243) para 164.

Accordingly, with respect to the obligation of states to secure human rights victims against the abuses committed by companies, the ECtHR should follow the current evolution of the international business and human rights standards to clarify the scope of the states' duty to fulfil. This would be in compliance with Article 31(3)(c) of the Vienna Convention on the Law of the Treaties, because soft law qualifies as '[r]elevant rules of international law … [which s]hall be taken into account'[247] to interpret the ECHR.[248] The Guiding Principles provide some guidance in this respect:

> States must protect against human rights abuse within their territory and/or jurisdiction by third parties, including business enterprises. This requires taking appropriate steps to prevent, investigate, punish and redress such abuse through effective policies, legislation, regulations and adjudication.[249]

The commentary to the Guiding Principles clarifies the above-quoted obligation as follows:

> [S]tates are not per se responsible for human rights abuse by private actors. However, States may breach their international human rights law obligations … [w]here they fail to take appropriate steps to prevent, investigate, punish and redress private actors' abuse. While States generally have discretion in deciding upon these steps, they should consider the full range of permissible preventative and remedial measures, including policies, legislation, regulations and adjudication.[250]

Certain measures that the Guiding Principles refer to would clearly fit within the duty to protect, as they would depend on the capacity of the state apparatus to sanction and regulate the activities of multinational companies. However, a number of policies would fit within the duty to fulfil, as defined in this book, as they would require states to influence multinational companies that are not directly under the state's control.[251] These measures include preventing companies from abusing human rights by influencing their conduct on a global scale.

The Recommendation clarifies the application of the Guiding Principles as they pertain to the obligations of states. Consistent with the Guiding Principles, the Recommendation does not expressly set out the duty to fulfil as distinct from the duty to protect. However, the Recommendation refers to the state's obligation to enable companies to respect human rights. This rather vague duty is followed by a list of prospective measures, which states should implement to enable businesses to respect human rights. More specifically, the Recommendation sets

[247] Vienna Convention on the Law of Treaties, art 31(3).
[248] See Dörr and Schmalenbach (n 210) 560–68; *Demir and Baykara v Turkey* (n 210).
[249] Ruggie, 'Report of the Special Representative of the Secretary-General' (n 9) 229.
[250] ibid.
[251] See Chapter 3.I.D and Chapter 3.II.A(ii).

out two foreign policies that European states should adopt in compliance with human rights: trade and investment.[252]

> 23. When concluding and during the term of trade and investment agreements or other relevant conventions, member States should consider possible human rights impacts of such agreements and take appropriate steps, including through the incorporation of human rights clauses, to mitigate and address identified risks of adverse human rights impacts.
>
> 24. In order not to facilitate the administration of capital punishment or torture in third countries by providing goods which could be used to carry out such acts, member States should ensure that business enterprises domiciled within their jurisdiction do not trade in goods which have no practical use other than for the purpose of capital punishment, torture, or other cruel, inhuman or degrading treatment or punishment.
>
> 25. Member States should, when business enterprises … are represented in a trade mission to member States and third countries, address and discuss possible adverse effects future operations might have on the human rights situation in those countries and require participating companies to respect the UN Guiding Principles or the Guidelines for Multinational Enterprises of the Organisation for Economic Co-operation and Development (OECD).[253]

The Recommendation establishes the obligation of a state to influence the conduct of multinational enterprises in a way that would prevent corporate human rights abuses. In fact, foreign trade and investment policies are some of the most powerful instruments available to states to influence the activities of non-state actors overseas. Both states and companies are actively participating in foreign trade and investment. Whereas states use trade and investment policies to increase their weight in the global economy, companies need global markets to increase their revenues by selling their products worldwide.[254] For this reason, through foreign trade and investment policies, European home states could influence the extraterritorial conduct of multinational enterprises. The obligation specifically requires investigating what human rights negative externalities could arise out of an investment or trade treaty.[255] It is important to note that the Recommendation refers to the OECD Guidelines as another cornerstone that states should rely on in requiring multinational companies involved in trade missions to respect human rights.[256] The Recommendation recognises and sets out in detail a duty to positively influence the conduct of multinational corporations through investment and trade laws.

[252] Committee of Ministers (n 203).

[253] ibid paras 23–25.

[254] See generally Gro Nystuen, Andreas Føllesdal and Ola Mestad (eds), *Human Rights, Corporate Complicity and Disinvestment* (Cambridge University Press, 2011).

[255] Committee of Ministers (n 203) paras 23–25.

[256] OECD, *OECD Guidelines for Multinational Enterprises, 2011 Edition* (OECD Publishing, 2011) www.oecd-ilibrary.org/governance/oecd-guidelines-for-multinational-enterprises_9789264115415-en, accessed 22 April 2016; Committee of Ministers (n 203) para 25.

III. THE APPLICATION TO THE CASE STUDIES

In the case studies, Bodhi, Elsa and Naoki could claim that the United Kingdom violated the ECHR by failing to secure their rights against private companies.

Under Article 1, the United Kingdom has positive obligations to secure the rights of the applicants against both actions and omissions by the state. The omissions include the failure of the UK to provide effective remedies to potential victims against companies domiciled within its territories (duty to protect) and to influence the conduct of corporations in order to prevent them from abusing human rights (duty to fulfil).

As it pertains to the duty to protect, the United Kingdom has an obligation to provide victims with effective remedies which should guarantee not only a symbolic access to court, but an effective remedy in practice. Bodhi and Elsa, who claim a violation of environmental and health rights under Articles 8, 13 and 1, are entitled to an effective remedy to challenge the UK policy which allows UK corporations to adopt low health and safety or environmental standards when they act through their foreign subsidiaries. Naoki, who claims a violation of Article 3 (freedom from torture) in connection with Articles 13 and 1, is entitled not only to challenge the state's failure to prevent corporate complicity in torture, but also to require the United Kingdom to set up effective sanctioning mechanisms to prevent UK companies from abusing Article 3. However, as demonstrated in Chapter 2, it would be difficult, if not impossible, for Bodhi, Elsa or Naoki to file a suit against H in UK courts. No claimant has so far succeeded in such a transnational tort case against a UK company. The steps that a victim of human rights abuses would have to take and the hurdles that would be involved in such fight are so insurmountable that Bodhi, Elsa and Naoki would likely be unable to file a successful complaint in the United Kingdom. They are therefore unable to benefit from effective remedies in UK courts. The United Kingdom's failure to provide Bodhi, Elsa or Naoki with effective remedies against a UK corporation, such as H, may result in a violation of Articles 13 and 1 in conjunction with Article 8, as it pertains to the cases of Bodhi and Elsa, and with Article 3 as it pertains to the case of Naoki. Therefore, if unsuccessful in UK courts, Bodhi, Elsa and Naoki could attempt to file a complaint against the United Kingdom with the ECtHR.

As it pertains to the duty to fulfil, the United Kingdom has an obligation to do its utmost to prevent corporations from violating human rights. However, as demonstrated by Chapter 2, the only actions taken in this sense by European states, including the UK, are soft law based. The United Kingdom enacted a national action plan in 2013 and its update in 2016.[257] However, other than declaratory statements in favour of the development of a business and human rights framework, the United Kingdom has not taken any substantive steps in

[257] 'UK Open Government National Action Plan 2016–18' (n 11); HM Government (n 11).

terms of regulating the activities of UK corporations. The 2016 Update of the National Action Plan mentions, as the only relevant laws that would contribute to a business and human rights agenda, the Bribery Act,[258] the Modern Slavery Act,[259] and section 172 of the Companies Act 2006.[260]

The Bribery Act is an effective piece of legislation applicable to corporations worldwide, but it only criminalises acts of bribery, leaving unsecured any human rights abuse.

The Modern Slavery Act does not regulate, let alone sanction, the conduct of private companies and merely introduced a reporting obligation for UK corporations. Such an obligation may certainly be helpful in terms of exposing companies that contribute to slavery, but it is by no means an appropriate tool to prevent corporations from abusing human rights, given that it neither regulates, nor sanctions corporate conduct. Furthermore, the Modern Slavery Act is limited to the crime of slavery, and it does not include a wide range of human rights abuses, such as those suffered by the victims of the case studies, Bodhi, Elsa and Naoki, namely torture, inhuman and degrading treatment, environmental degradation, and bodily harm.

Section 172 of the Companies Act 2006 requires directors to consider the interest of various stakeholders while making decisions in the interest of shareholders. Multiple scholars have convincingly demonstrated that the United Kingdom is a shareholder primacy jurisdiction and its laws, including section 172, unequivocally require corporations to act in the primary interest of shareholders.[261] Other states have instead adopted a pluralistic approach, requiring corporate officers to act in the best interest of the company which could coincide with the interest of various stakeholders, including but not limited to, shareholders.[262] The United Kingdom has not taken this approach. Therefore, section 172 of the Companies Act 2006 does not require corporate officers to make their choices in accordance with human rights law and cannot be considered a significant step in this regard.

In sum, Bodhi, Elsa and Naoki could argue that there has been no meaningful attempt by the United Kingdom to engage with corporations to prevent human rights abuses. The United Kingdom's failure to prevent corporations from abusing human rights may result in a violation of Articles 8, as it pertains to the cases of Bodhi and Elsa, and with Article 3 as it pertains to the case of Naoki. Therefore, if unsuccessful in UK courts, Bodhi, Elsa and Naoki could attempt to file a complaint against the United Kingdom with the ECtHR.

[258] Bribery Act 2010, c 23.

[259] Modern Slavery Act 2015, c 30.

[260] Companies Act 2006, s 172.

[261] David Kershaw, *Company Law in Context: Text and Materials*, 2nd edn (Oxford University Press, 2012) 334–86.

[262] See eg New York Business Corporation Law 1961, s 717.

IV. CONCLUSION

Domestic laws applicable to multinational companies violate the ECHR in two respects.

First, the standard of review or secondary norm applicable to multinational corporations does not guarantee the victims of human rights abuses access to justice. The procedural duty to protect, as it is recognised by the ECtHR, requires states to provide the victims of human rights abuses with an effective remedy in domestic courts. Whereas Article 13 establishes a general procedural obligation to provide for effective remedies, Articles 3 and 8 detail how states should implement such a procedural obligation in practice. As it pertains to the violation of non-absolute rights, states may balance the rights of the private parties whose human rights enshrined in Article 8 have been adversely affected by the state's policies, with the interests of other individuals who benefit from such policies. The state may decide to interfere with the human rights of a person for the benefit of others. Nevertheless, Article 8 requires the state to provide both the victim and beneficiary of such interference with effective recourse to a court. The victim of the interference must be able to challenge the choice made by the state, while the beneficiary must have effective recourse to a court to ensure that his/her rights are protected in practice. As it pertains to absolute rights, under no circumstance may states interfere with the rights of individuals. Under Article 3, the state has two parallel obligations. First, it must conduct its own effective investigation and establish its own sanctioning mechanisms against the perpetrators of a human rights abuse. Second, it must provide the victim with a cause of action to claim civil damages against the corporate group which abused human rights. However, under the company law regimes analysed in Chapter 2, the victims of human rights abuses do not have an effective legal remedy against corporate groups responsible for such abuses. There is no practically accessible way to make a holding company accountable for the human rights abuses perpetrated by its subsidiary. This lack of judicial remedies arguably violates Articles 13, 8 and 3.

Second, domestic laws do not attempt to prevent companies from abusing human rights. The duty to fulfil requires states to progressively realise a given aim. In the context of business and human rights, the purpose of the duty to fulfil is to stop companies from abusing fundamental rights. The ECtHR interpreted the duty to fulfil differently in cases of non-absolute and absolute human rights abuses. In cases of non-absolute rights, such as the rights arising from Article 8, states are required to adopt an efficient decision-making process to balance the competing interests of several parties entitled to the protection of their human rights. The state must identify such competing interests, make an informed decision, act in compliance with its own national laws, and ensure that any such balance is adjusted in accordance with evolving human rights standards. With respect to absolute human rights, under no circumstances may a state favour the interests of a company over the absolute rights of an individual.

Article 3 requires states to do their utmost to ensure that private parties respect human rights. The duty to fulfil requires states to take concrete steps to stop companies from abusing human rights. The ECtHR defines the exact scope of such additional measures on a case-by-case basis. The Recommendation has already recognised the duty to fulfil as applicable to business and human rights cases. Such a duty to fulfil entails an obligation of the state to conclude BITs and trade agreements and pursue its foreign trade and investment policies in a manner that would encourage the protection of human rights.

Therefore, the United Kingdom arguably has a duty to guarantee effective remedies against British multinational enterprises (duty to protect) for the victims of human rights abuses and to take into account in its investment and trade policies the interests of foreign stakeholders affected by UK corporate activities (duty to fulfil).

4

Extraterritoriality

CHAPTER 3 DEMONSTRATED that the ECHR obliges states to secure the rights of human rights victims against private persons, including private industries and corporations. The remaining question is, however, whether such an obligation is also applicable extraterritorially when European-headquartered corporate groups abuse human rights in developing countries through their foreign subsidiaries. The ECtHR has not yet decided such a case and therefore there is no straightforward answer to this question. However, the following analysis suggests that, on the basis of its current jurisprudence, the ECtHR would be likely to recognise the extraterritorial jurisdiction of European states in future cases.

First, I would like to clarify the position of European states with respect to the extraterritorial abuses committed by multinational corporations. The positive obligations of European states would be territorial. European states, such as the United Kingdom, would have to secure the effective remedies of victims (duty to protect) against the parent company H incorporated within its territory. This procedural duty would be confined to the territory of the United Kingdom. As it pertains to the duty to fulfil, European states would have to do their utmost to prevent human rights abuses committed by corporations headquartered in Europe. This obligation includes a wide range of actions which would always be based on the control that the European states, in this case the United Kingdom, exercise over parent corporations such as H incorporated within their territory. These situations differ substantially from cases in which European states act abroad, such as in foreign military operations. In the case studies, the only entity acting transnationally is the corporate group, while victims request the United Kingdom to act territorially. This is a peculiar situation for the ECtHR to analyse, because it implies territorial actions of European states which would have an effect on the transnational activities of non-state actors.

Second, although the ECtHR has not yet decided a case related to a European parent corporation abusing human rights extraterritorially through its subsidiaries, it has developed a complex and detailed jurisprudence in a number of similar situations. This chapter argues that, on the basis of this jurisprudence, the ECHR obliges European states to secure the rights of victims against parent companies incorporated in Europe even when they abuse human rights extraterritorially. My argument is strictly construed around the role of holding corporations and the control that European States exercise over such companies. I do not argue for universal jurisdiction, as I do not believe the ECtHR would require states to assert jurisdiction over enterprises that have no links to Europe.

Third, the ECtHR's jurisprudence does not develop in a vacuum. Cross-fertilisation and judicial dialogue are some of the reasons that drive the ECtHR to interpret the ECHR as a living instrument. Therefore, this chapter also analyses the case-law of other human rights regional courts and committees as well as the UN Treaty Bodies. Each of these human rights bodies has developed a jurisprudence based on the same premises that the ECtHR has used in terms of both extraterritoriality and the positive obligations of states vis-à-vis the conduct of corporations. Some of them reproduce a jurisprudence substantially similar to the ECtHR, while some go a step further in terms of providing extraterritorial protection to victims of human rights abuses, and some have extensively analysed states' obligations in relation to the extraterritorial human rights abuses committed by multinational enterprises. All of them, however, base their jurisprudence on the same principles used by the ECtHR and all of them refer to the ECtHR's jurisprudence as the persuasive authority for their decisions. It is therefore likely that the ECtHR would take the jurisprudence of other human rights courts and treaty bodies into consideration in developing its own case-law on business and human rights.

Therefore, this chapter analyses, first, the *lex lata*: the current law under the ECHR; and, second, the *lex ferenda*: how the ECtHR's jurisprudence could evolve given the rulings of other human rights courts, committees and treaty bodies on business and human rights.

I. *LEX LATA*: EXTRATERRITORIALITY IN THE EUROPEAN CONVENTION ON HUMAN RIGHTS

Over the past 20 years, the ECtHR has developed extensive jurisprudence on the extraterritorial application of human rights law. The topic is controversial as it touches on two unresolved issues in international law: the universality of human rights and the exterritorial application of a regional treaty. Scholars and courts have analysed each issue separately, but the ECtHR had the burden of connecting them, being at the head of both a regional treaty and a human rights institution. The result has been an inconsistent jurisprudence. Some cases, such as *Bankovic and others v Belgium*,[1] limited the possibility to extend the jurisdiction of states beyond their territories, whereas others, such as *Ilascu and others v Moldova and Russia*,[2] *Nikolaus and Jurgen Treska v*

[1] *Bankovic and others v Belgium and others* [2001] ECHR 52207/99.
[2] *Ilascu and others v Moldova and Russia* [2004] ECHR 48787/99.

Albania and Italy[3] and *Vrioni and others v Albania and Italy*,[4] broadened the concept of jurisdiction.[5]

Scholars have attempted to reconcile these different sets of cases by proposing various extraterritoriality theories. Some scholars focus on the need to broaden the jurisdiction of the court in light of the universality of human rights, whereas others are emphasising the limited regional reach of the ECHR. The following section outlines the current debate.

As a general principle, states are responsible for securing the areas within their jurisdiction. Traditionally, states have jurisdiction over their territory only. This general principle is reflected in the letter of Article 1 of the ECHR: 'The High Contracting Parties shall secure to everyone within their jurisdiction the rights and freedoms defined in Section I of this Convention.'[6]

According to a literal interpretation of Article 1, states have jurisdiction only over those victims who are within their territory, notwithstanding where and who the perpetrators of extraterritorial human rights abuses are. This interpretation distinguishes the issues of jurisdiction and human rights obligations. Essentially, the ECtHR would have to assess first whether a state had jurisdiction over the victims, and, only in the affirmative, decide whether it violated its obligations. A number of scholars embrace this approach, arguing that jurisdiction is a precondition to human rights. For instance, Samantha Besson wrote:

> [The] … very question of the concrete feasibility of duties only arises once jurisdiction has been established and the abstract rights recognized. There can be no human rights duties without human rights, and the existence of human rights depends on jurisdiction in the first place. Jurisdiction cannot therefore be directly equated with the feasibility of human rights duties.[7]

The ECtHR embraced this approach in the seminal case *Bankovic and others v Belgium*. The facts of the case are as follows. During the war in Yugoslavia, NATO bombed a radio station in Belgrade. Sixteen people died in the attack. The relatives of the victims filed a complaint against the European states that are members of NATO and, therefore, participated in the bombings. The ECtHR ruled that there was no jurisdictional link between the foreign victims and the European states that were party to NATO, because the victims were outside of

[3] *Nikolaus and Jurgen Treska v Albania and Italy* [2006] ECHR 26937/04.

[4] *Vrioni and others v Albania and Italy*, Applications [2009] ECHR 35720/04 and 42832/06.

[5] See Michał Gondek, *The Reach of Human Rights in a Globalising World: Extraterritorial Application of Human Rights Treaties* (Intersentia, 2009) 123–203; Gerard Gonzalez, 'La responsabilité des états parties à la Convention européenne des droits de l'homme du fait de leurs actions extraterritoriales' [2007] *Annuaire de Droit Européen* 755.

[6] European Convention for the Protection of Human Rights and Fundamental Freedoms 1950, art 1.

[7] Samantha Besson, 'The Extraterritoriality of the European Convention on Human Rights: Why Human Rights Depend on Jurisdiction and What Jurisdiction Amounts To' (2012) 25 *Leiden Journal of International Law* 857, 868.

their territories. Furthermore, the ECtHR could not become a world human rights court assessing any violation worldwide, and it could only decide cases within the *espace juridique européen*, meaning the territory of those states that are signatories of the ECHR.[8] This territorial approach recognises a strict test based on effective control over foreign territories and authority and control over persons as a sole basis to exercise extraterritorial jurisdiction.[9]

At the opposite side of the spectrum, there is the universalist view, embraced by the concurring opinion of Judge Bonello in the case of *Al-Skeini and others v the United Kingdom* and, in different versions, by a number of scholars.[10] According to this view, jurisdiction and human rights obligations are inherently connected. Therefore, if we take the universality of human rights seriously, as Yuval Shany argues,[11] the ECtHR should apply a functional test, holding a state responsible when it can prevent a human rights violation. This approach has a number of different versions. For example, Yuval Shany sees a foreseeability test as a limit to the capability of the state: a European state would be responsible for the human rights abuses committed extraterritorially when such violations are direct, significant and foreseeable. He therefore excludes unforeseeable events that may still be attributed to the state's action, such as, for instance, climate change.[12] Judge Bonello provided a more liberal interpretation of the functional test in a concurring opinion to *Al-Skeini and others v the United Kingdom*: 'The duties assumed through ratifying the Convention go hand in hand with the duty to perform and observe them. Jurisdiction arises from the mere fact of having assumed those obligations *and from having the capability to fulfil them* (or not

[8] *Bankovic and others v Belgium* (n 1); Loukis Loucaides, *The European Convention on Human Rights: Collected Essays* (Martinus Nijhoff, 2007) 73–94; Rick Lawson, 'Life after Bankovic: On the Extraterritorial Application of the European Convention on Human Rights', in *Extraterritorial Application of Human Rights Treaties* (Intersentia, 2004); Cedric Ryngaert, 'Clarifying the Extraterritorial Application of the European Convention on Human Rights' (2012) 28 *Merkourios: Utrecht Journal of International and European Law* 57.

[9] *Bankovic and others v Belgium* (n 1); *Al-Skeini and Others v The United Kingdom* [2011] ECHR 55721/07.

[10] Fons Coomans and Menno T Kamminga, 'Comparative Introductory Comments on the Extraterritorial Application of Human Rights Treaties', in *Extraterritorial Application of Human Rights Treaties* (Intersentia, 2004); Fons Coomans and Rolf Künnemann (eds), *Cases and Concepts on Extraterritorial Obligations in the Area of Economic, Social and Cultural Rights* (Intersentia, 2012); Olivier De Schutter, 'The Accountability of Multinationals for Human Rights Violations in European Law', in *Non-State Actors and Human Rights* (Oxford University Press, 2005); Olivier De Schutter, 'Extraterritorial Jurisdiction as a Tool for Improving Human Rights Accountability for Transnational Corporations' (Business and Human Rights Resource Centre, 2006) https://www.business-humanrights.org/en/pdf-extraterritorial-jurisdiction-as-a-tool-for-improving-the-human-rights-accountability-of-transnational-corporations; Olivier De Schutter, 'Le contrôle du respect des droits de l'homme par les sociétés transnationales: le rôle de l'état d'origine', in *Justice et mondialisation en droit du travail: du rôle du juge aux conflits alternatifs* (Dalloz, 2010); Marko Milanovic, *Extraterritorial Application of Human Rights Treaties: Law, Principles, and Policy* (Oxford University Press, 2011).

[11] Yuval Shany, 'Taking Universality Seriously: A Functional Approach to Extraterritoriality in International Human Rights Law' (2013) 7 *The Law & Ethics of Human Rights* 47, 67–70.

[12] Shany (n 11).

to fulfil them).'[13] He proposes a jurisdictional test, which is far away from the authority and control test defined in *Bankovic and others v Belgium*. He believes that the ability to fulfil an obligation entails jurisdiction.[14]

From a different perspective, Nehal Bhuta criticised the extraterritorial application of the ECHR as it imposes a regional treaty on countries that have never agreed to it. According to him, extraterritoriality would certainly improve the European human rights system, but it would not help to develop other judicial systems. The priority should be the improvement of judicial systems in developing countries, instead of the extraterritorial application of the ECHR which has no political legitimacy outside of Europe. Therefore, he concurs with the territorial approach and argues that the ECHR should apply only within the territories of those states that have agreed to it.[15]

The literature on the extraterritorial application of the ECHR discusses the issue of jurisdiction in between these different views, with some emphasising universality and others the regional nature of the ECHR. None of these perspectives is wrong. Different scholars have simply focused on different cases and, as it is impossible to reconcile all of the case-law of the ECtHR within one single extraterritoriality theory, each perspective is right but fails to explain extraterritoriality comprehensively.

Against this background, this chapter argues that the most comprehensive scholarly approach that could help in analysing the ECtHR's jurisprudence on extraterritoriality are the Maastricht Principles. In 2011, a group of scholars adopted the Maastricht Principles. Despite their focus on economic, social and cultural rights, their analysis of the extraterritorial obligations of human rights law is relevant to the jurisprudence of the ECtHR. In fact, the Maastricht Principles have, among other things, proposed to connect the issue of jurisdiction and obligations in a unique way: the territorial and extraterritorial jurisdiction of a state would depend on the type of obligation that such a state ought to meet. With their clear-cut approach linking diverse obligations with different jurisdictional tests, the Maastricht Principles are the most appropriate doctrinal framework to reconceptualise the jurisprudence of the ECtHR. They establish and interrelate two fundamental elements: obligations and jurisdiction.

> 8. Definition of extraterritorial obligations
>
> For the purposes of these Principles, extraterritorial obligations encompass:
>
> a) obligations relating to the acts and omissions of a State, within or beyond its territory, that have effects on the enjoyment of human rights outside of that State's territory; and

[13] *Al-Skeini and Others v The United Kingdom* (n 9) para Concurring Opinion of Judge Bonello, para 13.

[14] ibid Concurring Opinion of Judge Bonello.

[15] Nehal Bhuta, 'The Frontiers of Extraterritoriality – Human Rights as Global Law', in *The Frontiers of Human Rights* (Oxford University Press, 2016).

b) obligations of a global character that are set out in the Charter of the United Nations and human rights instruments to take action, separately, and jointly through international cooperation, to realize human rights universally[16]

9. Scope of jurisdiction

A State has obligations to respect, protect and fulfil economic, social and cultural rights in any of the following:

a) situations over which it exercises authority or effective control, whether or not such control is exercised in accordance with international law;
b) situations over which State acts or omissions bring about foreseeable effects on the enjoyment of economic, social and cultural rights, whether within or outside its territory;
c) situations in which the State, acting separately or jointly, whether through its executive, legislative or judicial branches, is in a position to exercise decisive influence or to take measures to realize economic, social and cultural rights extraterritorially, in accordance with international law.[17]

The Commentary to the Maastricht Principles links Principles 8(a), concerning the obligations deriving from the acts and omissions of states, meaning the duties to respect and protect, with 9(a) and (b), detailing, as a basis to assert jurisdiction, authority, effective control and foreseeable effects. Instead, Principle 8(b), concerning obligations of a global character, is connected to Principle 9(c), detailing, as a basis for jurisdiction, the state's 'position to exercise decisive influence'.[18] One may wonder why the threshold to assert jurisdiction in 9(c) is much lower than in 9(a) and (b). The answer is that 9(c) applies to the obligations described in 8 (b), which are known as the duty to fulfil, ie '[o]bligations of a global character … [t]o realize human rights universally'.[19] These are *best-efforts* duties that no state can achieve by itself, but they entail constant cooperation with other actors. It is clear that authority and control over persons and effective control over territories cannot be the bases to achieve this kind of far-reaching obligation.[20] Therefore, the applicable test to assert extraterritorial jurisdiction is necessarily different from 9(a) and (b).

I believe the distinction between Principles 8(a), 9(a) and (b) on the one side, and Principles 8(b) and 9(c) on the other, matches the jurisprudence of the ECtHR as it pertains to the extraterritorial application of the ECHR.

[16] Olivier De Schutter et al, 'Commentary to the Maastricht Principles on Extraterritorial Obligations of States in the Area of Economic, Social and Cultural Rights' (2012) 34 *Human Rights Quarterly* 1084, pt 8.

[17] ibid pt 9.

[18] ibid.

[19] ibid pt 8(b).

[20] See Riccardo Pisillo Mazzeschi, 'Responsabilité de l'état pour violation des obligations positives relatives aux droits de l'homme', in *Collected Courses of the Hague Academy of International Law*, 333 (Martinus Nijhoff, 2008) 390–496; Magdalena Sepúlveda Carmona, *The Nature of the Obligations under the International Covenant on Economic, Social, and Cultural Rights* (Intersentia, 2003) 115–248; Eyal Benvenisti, 'Sovereigns as Trustees of Humanity: On the Accountability of States to Foreign Stakeholders' (2013) 107 *The American Journal of International Law* 295, 313–26.

The first basis to assert jurisdiction, detailed in Principle 9(a), ie authority and/or control over persons and/or territories, applies to cases when a European state acts extraterritorially and exercises power over foreigners or overseas territories.[21] I will label this basis *extraterritorial control*, because in these cases the jurisdictional test depends on the control that the state exercises extraterritorially. These are typically cases of military occupations, where states control an overseas territory or of foreign prisoners held in captivity abroad. This basis applies to extraterritorial actions and omissions of the state and, therefore, to the extraterritorial duties to respect and protect.

The second basis to assert jurisdiction, detailed in Principle 9(b), ie 'State acts or omissions bring about foreseeable effects … [o]utside its territory',[22] applies to those cases when the state's territorial conduct has extraterritorial effects. I will label this basis *territorial control with extraterritorial effects*, because, in these cases, the jurisdictional test depends on the state's territorial control which affects individuals living abroad. For instance, a state is failing to prevent its nationals from abusing human rights extraterritorially. These are typically cases of procedural rights which the state guarantees territorially but which will have a foreseeable extraterritorial effect. This basis applies to both territorial actions (duty to respect) and failures to act (duty to protect) which would secure the rights of individuals abroad.

The third basis to assert jurisdiction, detailed in Principle 9(c), ie '[t]he State, … [i]s in a position to exercise decisive influence or to take measures to realiz[e] … [r]ights extraterritorially',[23] applies to those cases when the state is in a position to influence foreign actors. These may be either other states or non-state actors. Here the logic shifts completely from the necessity to exercise authority or control over other actors to the capability to influence them. I will label this basis as *ability to influence*, because, in these cases, the jurisdictional test depends on the direct or indirect influence that a state exercises over foreign actors.

The following sections analyse the three bases to assert jurisdiction in the jurisprudence of the ECtHR: *extraterritorial control*, *territorial control with extraterritorial effects* and the *ability to influence*.

A. Extraterritorial Control

These are cases when a state acts or fails to act abroad. These relate both to the duties to respect, or negative obligations, as well as the duties to protect, or positive obligations of result. The literature has analysed these cases extensively in the context of extraterritorial military operations and detentions when

[21] De Schutter et al (n 16) pt 9(a).
[22] ibid pt 9(b).
[23] ibid pt 9(c).

states have either acted in violation of human rights (duty to respect) or have failed to prevent a human rights violation that was within their control (duty to protect).

According to the leading case, *Al-Skeini and others v the United Kingdom*, states have jurisdiction over extraterritorial conduct in the following two instances. Firstly, a state has jurisdiction outside its territory when it has effective control over a foreign land. In such circumstances, the state must ensure the ECHR's standards in the occupied foreign territory as if the territory was part of its own.[24] Secondly, a state has jurisdiction when it has authority and control over both the perpetrator and victim of an act that is in breach of the ECHR. The ECtHR sets out three main scenarios when a state has authority over the perpetrator(s) and victim(s) of human rights abuses.[25]

The first scenario relates to the conduct of consular agents and diplomats who are in a foreign territory. Despite being physically present in a foreign land, diplomats and counsels remain within the jurisdiction of their home state, which is, accordingly, responsible for their extraterritorial actions.[26]

The second scenario relates to the conduct of state agents having authority and control over an individual in a foreign territory. A typical example of such control is when state agents take people into custody in a foreign territory. For instance, in *Ocalan v Turkey*,[27] Turkish authorities arrested Mr Ocalan in Kenya, and in *Issa v Turkey*,[28] Turkish soldiers took some civilians into custody and executed them in Iraq. To establish a jurisdictional link in such cases, it is necessary to prove double control. First, the state must exercise control over its agents. This control is presumed as the agents represent the country abroad. Second, the state agents must exercise authority and control over the victims of human rights violations. This form of extraterritorial jurisdiction is typically invoked in cases of negative obligations when a state agent violates human rights. In these cases, the key issue is whether the state agent has control over the victim.[29]

The third established scenario relates to those cases in which the State 'exercises all or some public powers'[30] over the foreign land by consent or invitation of the foreign government.[31] Scholars sometimes misinterpret this exception as being based on territorial control rather than on authority and control over persons.[32] However, it is possible to clarify the scope of this exception and

[24] *Al-Skeini and Others v The United Kingdom* (n 9) paras 138–40.
[25] ibid paras 133–37.
[26] ibid para 134.
[27] *Ocalan v Turkey* [2005] ECHR 46221/99.
[28] *Issa and others v Turkey* [2005] ECHR 31821/96.
[29] *Al-Skeini and Others v The United Kingdom* (n 9) paras 121–33.
[30] ibid para 135.
[31] See Shanta Bhavnani, 'ECtHR Extends Application of Convention beyond Council of Europe Borders' [2011] 16 *EHRAC Bulletin* 1; Barbara Miltner, 'Revisiting Extraterritoriality after Al-Skeini: The ECHR and its Lessons' (2012) 33 *Michigan Journal of International Law* 693; Ryngaert (n 8).
[32] See M Milanovic, 'Al-Skeini and Al-Jedda in Strasbourg' (2012) 23 *European Journal of International Law* 121; Bhavnani (n 31).

distinguish it from the situation in which a state has jurisdiction on the basis of having control over the territory, by considering the nature of negative and positive obligations.

When a state controls a territory, it will have jurisdiction over any conduct of either state agents or third parties within that territory, regardless of whether the state's responsibility is claimed in connection with positive or negative obligations. However, when a case relates to authority and control over persons, the distinction between negative and positive obligations is necessary. The state controls its agents, but it is more difficult to imagine how it could have control over private individuals in a foreign territory. In cases of state agents, there is a clear jurisdictional link between the agent and the state. However, when the state has a positive obligation to ensure that third parties respect human rights, the issue is whether it is possible to establish a jurisdictional link between the state and a third party. According to *Al-Skeini and others v the United Kingdom*, such a jurisdictional link exists when the state exercises some public function in a foreign land, without necessarily controlling the foreign territory. The jurisdictional link lies in the authority and control that the state agents exercise over the third-party perpetrator and victim of the human rights abuse.[33] Usually, a state has jurisdiction over an abuse when both the perpetrator and the victim are in its territory. In an extraterritorial context, this territorial element boils down to whether the state has authority and control over the perpetrator and the victim of a human rights abuse. Such control over private individuals will be present when the state exceptionally exercises certain public authority over them.

The ECtHR applied this rule in the *Al-Skeini and others v the United Kingdom* case in which the United Kingdom was exercising public power in Iraq, and was therefore responsible for the casualties in a military operation. Although some victims died because of the action of British soldiers, at least one victim died under uncertain circumstances. An unknown person shot the applicant's wife. Although it was not clear whether British troops or a private party killed the victim, the UK control over the military operation was enough to establish a jurisdictional link, irrespective of who shot the victim. It was immaterial whether the shooter was a private individual or a member of the military.[34]

In *Jaloud v The Netherlands*,[35] the ECtHR also applied the 'exercise of all or some public powers'[36] exception. In this case, the Netherlands was conducting military operations in Iraq under the general military command of the United Kingdom and the United States. Although the coalition forces were occupying Iraq, the role of the Dutch military was limited: it was supervising and providing

[33] *Al-Skeini and Others v The United Kingdom* (n 9) paras 135–50.
[34] ibid.
[35] *Jaloud v The Netherlands* [2014] ECHR 47708/08.
[36] *Al-Skeini and Others v The United Kingdom* (n 9) para 135.

military advice to the Iraqi Civil Defence Corps. On 21 April 2004, while a group of Iraqi guards was at a checkpoint, an unidentified vehicle approached them and shot at them several times. The guards fired back and the vehicle drove away. The Iraqi guards informed the Dutch coalition forces, who sent over a Dutch lieutenant to investigate the incident. A few minutes after the initial shooting, another vehicle approached the checkpoint at high speed and drove into numerous barrels establishing the checkpoint. At this point, the guards and the Dutch lieutenant shot the front passenger, Mr Jaloud, dead. Like in *Al-Skeini and others v the United Kingdom*, it was not clear whether a state agent (ie, the Dutch lieutenant) or a third party (ie, one of the Iraqi guards) shot Mr Jaloud. However, regardless of who fired, the Netherlands had jurisdiction, because it had authority to supervise the actions of the Iraqi army. Even assuming that it was a member of the Iraqi guards who killed Mr Jaloud, the Netherlands was supervising the checkpoint and, therefore, had jurisdiction over the perpetrator (ie the Iraqi guard) and the foreign victim.[37] Therefore, when a state exercises public power over a foreign territory, without necessarily reaching the level of effective control, it is responsible for ensuring that not only its agents, but also third parties respect fundamental rights.[38]

As stated in the Maastricht Principles 8(a) and 9(a), the cases of *extraterritorial control* concern those obligations linked with the extraterritorial actions or omissions of states. The theory behind these cases is quite conservative, as it was first established in *Bankovic and others v Belgium*: the jurisdiction depends on the control and authority that states exercise extraterritorially. The ECtHR has certainly developed this test from its first definition, as it now includes the following four scenarios: cases when state agents have extraterritorial authority and control over an individual; the responsibility of states for the conduct of their consular services and diplomats; cases of military occupation; and cases when a state 'exercises all or some public powers'[39] over a foreign land by consent or invitation of the foreign government.[40] The two latest scenarios permit the ECtHR to broaden the jurisdiction of the state, not only over its actions but also over its failures to prevent the extraterritorial human rights abuses committed by third parties. However, regardless of how far the ECtHR went, the core of the jurisdictional test is always inevitably linked to the elements of authority and control, which leaves a number of situations, such as bombing abroad, outside of the jurisdiction of the state.

Marko Milanovic explains this jurisdictional link by separating negative and positive obligations. According to Milanovic, the ECtHR attributes the action of state agents to the state, because they represent the state abroad and this entails that the state has extraterritorial negative obligations. Instead, with regard to

[37] *Jaloud v The Netherlands* (n 35).
[38] *Al-Skeini and Others v The United Kingdom* (n 9) paras 135–50.
[39] ibid para 135.
[40] See Bhavnani (n 31); Miltner (n 31).

private perpetrators of human rights abuses, the state must have some degree of control over the territory where such a perpetrator is located to assume a positive obligation.[41]

It is important to underline that, at the time Milanovic wrote his theory, the ECtHR had not yet decided *Al-Skeini and others v the United Kingdom*. Therefore, Milanovic did not distinguish, as the ECtHR does, between the case of 'effective control over an area'[42] that occurs in cases of military occupation, from the lower degree of 'exercise [of] all or some of the public powers'[43] over a territory, which, in *Al-Skeini and others v the United Kingdom*, the court classifies as part of the authority and control over persons test. However, Milanovic's analysis of positive and negative obligations is fundamental to understand *Al-Skeini and others v the United Kingdom*. According to Milanovic, the state always has extraterritorial negative obligations. In addition, the state also has extraterritorial positive obligations when it has a certain degree of control over a territory.[44] To this extent, Milanovic's theory is helpful to analyse the extraterritorial control cases. States may be responsible for their acts or omissions only when they have control over the alleged violation. Such control is presumed when a state agent acts or when the state has a certain degree of control over the territory where a private perpetrator acts.

B. The Duty to Protect: Territorial Control with Extraterritorial Effects

The ECtHR's jurisprudence concerning the extraterritorial control over foreign territory/persons is not directly applicable to multinational enterprises abusing human rights extraterritorially. Neither the overseas territories, where the relevant abuses occur, are under the control of the state, nor can a company perpetrating such abuses be considered as performing any public function in such territories. Accordingly, it may be argued that states cannot be responsible under the ECHR for the failure to prevent overseas human rights abuses committed by companies. However, such an argument is based on an erroneous perspective overlooking the truth of the matter: in cases of multinational enterprises abusing human rights overseas, the wrongful conduct of the state is not extraterritorial, it is instead territorial with extraterritorial effects.[45] In the Bangladeshi, Ecuadorian and Nigerian case studies, which I set out at the beginning of this book to show its practical application to the real-world abuses of

[41] Milanovic (n 10) 209–22.
[42] *Al-Skeini and Others v The United Kingdom* (n 9) paras 137–38.
[43] ibid para 135.
[44] Milanovic (n 10) 209–22.
[45] Daniel Augenstein, 'Study on the Legal Framework on Human Rights and the Environment Applicable to European Enterprises Operating Outside the European Union' (University of Edinburgh, 2010) paras 32–42, http://ec.europa.eu/DocsRoom/documents/11865/attachments/1/translations/en/renditions/native, accessed 17 March 2019.

human rights, the United Kingdom does not, and is not required to, conduct any extraterritorial activity to provide effective remedies against the holding company H. According to the procedural duty to protect, states have an obligation to provide the victim of human rights abuses with effective remedies against the holding company H incorporated within their national borders. States have no obligation to act extraterritorially. The only entity acting extraterritorially is the corporate group H, which is controlling its subsidiary S incorporated in a foreign land. It is true that, by regulating the activities of the corporate group H acting extraterritorially, the United Kingdom regulates corporate activities that may occur in the foreign land. However, this does not mean that the state is acting extraterritorially. The state's actions or failures to act are territorial with potential extraterritorial effects.

This section will analyse the situation of territorial state conduct having extraterritorial effects and show its application to the overseas human rights abuses committed by European multinational enterprises. It analyses the ECtHR's case-law concerning territorial conduct with extraterritorial effects by focusing on three considerations: (i) whether the applicant is within the state's control; (ii) whether the perpetrator of the human rights abuse is within the state's control; and (iii) whether the state's conduct has any extraterritorial effect.

By applying each of the above considerations to the three hypothetical case studies, it is clear that, acts occurring in Bangladesh, Ecuador or Nigeria are outside the jurisdiction of the United Kingdom, as it has neither control over the foreign territory nor control over the subsidiaries S incorporated in each of these jurisdictions. However, the United Kingdom has full control over the holding company H, which is incorporated in the UK and controls 100% of the share capital of each subsidiary S. In this context, the issue is whether the state (being the United Kingdom in the hypothetical case studies) is responsible for providing effective remedies against the holding company (being H in the case studies) with extraterritorial effects.

(i) Control Over the Victim but not the Perpetrator

The first ruling of the ECtHR on territorial conduct with extraterritorial effects was *Soering v the United Kingdom*.[46] The United States requested the United Kingdom to extradite Mr Soering to the State of Virginia for murder charges. Virginia is one of the states in which the death penalty is in place. Therefore, by handing Mr Soering over to the Virginian authorities, the United Kingdom would have exposed him to potential death. The applicant alleged that the United Kingdom would violate the ECHR by extraditing him to the United States.

[46] *Soering v the United Kingdom* [1989] ECHR 14038/88.

The issue was whether the United Kingdom was in breach of the ECHR for the potential death and inhuman and degrading treatment of Mr Soering occurring outside its jurisdiction. The ECtHR had to weigh the following considerations. On the one hand, Mr Soering was under UK authority. If the United Kingdom did not hand Mr Soering over to the United States, he would not be exposed to the risk of death penalty and to the inhuman and degrading treatment of the death row. On the other hand, after the extradition and at the time of potential death, the United Kingdom would no longer have jurisdiction over Mr Soering.

The ECtHR ruled that the United Kingdom would violate the ECHR if it extradited Mr Soering to the United States. The United Kingdom had full control over the applicant, as he was detained there. Therefore, Mr Soering was within UK jurisdiction. Accordingly, the United Kingdom's territorial decision to extradite Mr Soering would have exposed him to potential death and inhuman and degrading treatment in a foreign land where the ECHR was not applicable. However, the United Kingdom had no control over the prospective perpetrator of a human right abuse, being, in this case, the State of Virginia, which could potentially execute Mr Soering.

Soering v the United Kingdom established the following test with respect to the territorial actions of a state related to an extraterritorial violation of human rights: when a state acts territorially and has control over the victim of a potential or actual human rights violation, there is a jurisdictional link between the state and the human right abuse, even if the actual or prospective perpetrator of that abuse is located outside the jurisdiction of the state.

In a number of subsequent cases, such as *Saadi v Italy*,[47] the ECtHR reconfirmed the *Soering v the United Kingdom* ruling. Scholars have called this interpretation *protection par ricochet*,[48] which could be translated as *consequential protection*. In these cases, the ECHR protects persons from a prospective violation occurring outside the jurisdiction of the state and, therefore, theoretically outside the state's control. The rationale for this approach is that such a violation would be the direct consequence of actions occurring within the jurisdiction of the state party: it is clear that, in these cases, the relevant state party to the ECHR controls whether or not a third country would be able to violate human rights.[49] Therefore, *Soering v the United Kingdom* established the jurisdictional link between a country and a human rights violation when the state has control over the victim.[50]

[47] *Saadi v Italy* [2008] ECHR 37201/06.

[48] See Sergio Bartole, Pasquale De Sena and Vladimiro Zagrebelsky (eds), *Commentario breve alla Convenzione europea per la salvaguardia dei diritti dell'uomo e delle libertà fondamentali* (CEDAM, 2012) 16.

[49] ibid 16–17; William Schabas, *The European Convention on Human Rights: A Commentary* (Oxford University Press, 2015) 194–96.

[50] *Soering v the United Kingdom* (n 46).

(ii) Control Over the Perpetrator but not the Victim

Referring to *Soering v the United Kingdom*, the ECtHR held in the case *Ilascu and others v Moldova and Russia* that: 'A State's responsibility may also be engaged on account of acts which have sufficiently proximate repercussions on rights guaranteed by the Convention, even if those repercussions occur outside its jurisdiction.'[51] It is clear from *Soering v the United Kingdom* that, when a state has control over a victim, it has jurisdiction over the human rights violation. However, after *Soering v the United Kingdom*, the issue remained whether, in the circumstances when a state party to the ECHR has control over a perpetrator, it also has jurisdiction over the human rights abuse.

The cases in which the ECtHR opined as to the jurisdiction of European states for human rights abuses committed by a European national abroad include *Ben el Mahi and others v Denmark*,[52] *Markovic v Italy*[53] and *Rantsev v Cyprus and Russia*.[54]

In *Ben el Mahi and others v Denmark*, a Danish newspaper published a series of cartoons with caricatures of the Prophet Muhammed. The publication triggered a diplomatic crisis, with a number of countries requesting an audience with the Danish government. However, the Danish government refused, because the Danish newspaper enjoyed the freedom to express critical views on Islam. Furthermore, a group of Moroccan citizens residing and living in Morocco and a number of Moroccan Muslim organisations filed several complaints of defamation against the Danish newspaper in Danish domestic courts. They also reported the facts to the Danish police in the hope that this could lead to a criminal proceeding against the newspaper. All of their attempts to obtain redress in Denmark were unsuccessful. Therefore, the applicants filed a case in the ECtHR, alleging that Denmark discriminated against them and violated their freedom of religion. The ECtHR dismissed the case on jurisdictional grounds, on the basis that the applicants were Moroccan, living and residing in Morocco, and therefore Denmark had no jurisdiction over them.

Another fundamental case is *Markovic v Italy*. This case had the same facts as *Bankovic and others v Belgium*[55] and was decided by the ECtHR in 2006, six years after the *Bankovic and others v Belgium* decision. However, whereas in *Bankovic and others v Belgium* the ECtHR ruled that there was no jurisdictional link between the extrajudicial killings that occurred during NATO bombings in Belgrade and the European states participating in that military operation, in *Markovic v Italy* the ECtHR found such a jurisdictional link.[56] The only meaningful difference between the two cases is that, unlike in *Bankovic and others v Belgium*, in *Markovic v Italy*, the applicants filed a tort

[51] *Ilascu and others v Moldova and Russia* (n 2) para 317.
[52] *Ben El Mahi and others v Denmark* [2006] ECHR 5853/06.
[53] *Markovic and others v Italy* [2006] ECHR 1398/03.
[54] *Rantsev v Cyprus and Russia* [2010] ECHR 25965/04.
[55] *Bankovic and others v Belgium* (n 1).
[56] See Gonzalez (n 5).

law complaint for civil damages in Italian domestic court against the Italian government for providing an Italian military base for NATO to attack the radio station in Belgrade.[57]

As discussed, in *Bankovic and others v Belgium*, the ECtHR dismissed the case on jurisdictional grounds. The states acted extraterritorially, the human rights violation occurred in a foreign land, the perpetrator of the human rights abuses was NATO, an entity that is not a party to the ECHR, and the victims were in a foreign territory.[58] In *Markovic v Italy*, the first section of the ECtHR dismissed the complaints alleging a violation of Articles 2, 10 and 17 of the ECHR on jurisdictional grounds for the very same reasons that caused the ECtHR to dismiss the complaints in *Bankovic and others v Belgium*. Furthermore, it dismissed the violation of Article 13, as it was deemed to be absorbed by the alleged violation of Article 6. This is understandable, as Articles 13 and 6 represent two sides of the same coin: the right to an effective legal remedy and the related procedural right to a fair trial. It declared the complaints alleging a violation of Article 6 admissible and referred it to the Grand Chamber.[59]

The issue is why the ECtHR found the complaint based on Article 6 to be admissible after *Bankovic and others v Belgium*. The answer is rather straightforward: the complaint based on Article 6 requested the Italian government to provide the victim with fair proceedings within the Italian territory. In the complaints based on Articles 2, 10 and 17, the issue at stake was whether the state had jurisdiction over its extraterritorial actions; however, in the complaints based on Articles 6 and 13, the issue was whether Italy had jurisdiction over its territorial conduct with extraterritorial effects. In *Markovic v Italy*, the conduct which allegedly resulted in the violation of the ECHR by Italy was territorial; the alleged perpetrator of the human rights abuse was the government of Italy itself, but the victims of the human rights abuse were outside Italian authority and control. The ECtHR ruled that Article 6 applied to any action occurring within the Italian territory, even though the victims, whose rights were violated as a result of such an act, were resident overseas and the human rights violation occurred extraterritorially. The ECtHR ruled as follows:

> Although the extraterritorial nature of the events alleged to have been at the origin of an action may affect the applicability of Article 6 and the outcome of the proceedings, it cannot under any circumstances affect the jurisdiction ratione loci and ratione personae of the State concerned. If civil proceedings are brought in the domestic courts, the State is required by Article 1 of the Convention to secure in those proceedings respect for the rights protected by Article 6. The Court considers that, once a person brings a civil action in the courts or tribunals of a State, there indisputably exists, without prejudice to the outcome of the proceedings, a 'jurisdictional link' for the purposes of Article 1.[60]

[57] *Markovic and others v Italy* (n 53) paras 13–19.
[58] *Bankovic and others v Belgium* (n 1); Loucaides (n 8) 73–94; Lawson (n 8).
[59] *Markovic and others v Italy* (n 53) para 4; *Markovic and others v Italy* [2003] ECHR 1398/03.
[60] *Markovic and others v Italy* (n 53) para 54.

Therefore, once an applicant files a complaint in domestic court, the state asserts jurisdiction over the case and has to guarantee effective remedies and fair proceedings for the victims of human rights abuses.[61]

There are two fundamental elements of this decision. First, *Markovic v Italy* recognises a particular role for procedural rights, as they require the state to take purely territorial actions that could have extraterritorial effects. Second, these rights are conditioned on the fact that the state has control over the perpetrator of the human rights abuse.[62]

It has to be noted that, after asserting jurisdiction over the case, the ECtHR ruled in Italy's favour, because Italian courts handled the complaints against the government in compliance with the ECHR. More specifically, the Italian Court of Cassation dismissed the claim on the basis of a political question doctrine, given that the issue at stake was the responsibility of the Italian government for an act of war. This aspect, however, is irrelevant for the purposes of this book, because it pertains to the merits of the case. What is important to retain from *Markovic v Italy* is, instead, that the ECtHR asserted jurisdiction over the complaint about the violation of the applicant's procedural rights occurring outside the territory of Italy.[63]

In *Rantsev v Cyprus and Russia*,[64] a Russian citizen was allegedly a victim of human trafficking. She left Russia with the expectation of finding a job in Cyprus, but, in fact, she became a prostitute and, under unclear circumstances, involving her employer and the Cyprus police, she died. Aside from the obvious question as to whether Cyprus failed to protect the victim, the issue of interest in relation to extraterritoriality was whether Russia had to conduct an effective investigation into the matter. Although the ECtHR found that Russia had no obligation to investigate Ms Rantseva's death, because neither the victim nor the perpetrator were under Russian authority or control, it held Russia accountable for failing to investigate cross-border human trafficking resulting in Ms Rantseva's death in Cyprus. Specifically, '[t]he failure to investigate the recruitment aspect of alleged trafficking would allow an important part of the trafficking chain to act with impunity'.[65]

The interesting aspect of this case is that, very much like extraterritorial human rights abuses perpetrated by corporations, human trafficking is transnational. The abuse was perpetrated both in Russia and in Cyprus in a transnational chain and therefore each country must conduct an investigation within its boundaries that would have extraterritorial effects. The ECtHR views the fight against human trafficking as an issue of cooperation, where Cyprus and Russia would both have to investigate the matter. In this case, Russia had control

[61] See Gondek (n 5) 199–201.
[62] See Gonzalez (n 5).
[63] *Markovic and others v Italy* (n 53) paras 92–116.
[64] *Rantsev v Cyprus and Russia* (n 54).
[65] ibid 307.

over at least some of the traffickers, ie the perpetrators, who were conducting a transnational criminal business, even though the victim was de facto abused and forced into prostitution only after she left Russian territory. By analogy, the home state would have the obligation to investigate the activities of the parent company in respect of the human rights abuses perpetrated transnationally. Instead, Russia had no obligation to investigate the death of Ms Ratnseva, as both the victim and perpetrator of the human rights abuse were outside of its territory. Therefore, *Rantsev v Cyprus and Russia*[66] recognised that Russia had an obligation to investigate the chain of human trafficking which was under its authority and control.

Given their different outcomes, it is not straightforward to reconcile *Ben el Mahi and others v Denmark*, *Markovic v Italy* and *Rantsev v Cyprus and Russia*. However, the following considerations may help.

First, in *Ben el Mahi and others v Denmark*, the ECtHR found that Denmark lacked jurisdiction under Article 1, because there was no link between the Danish newspaper and the applicants. The newspaper acted only within the territory of Denmark, as it published the caricatures in Denmark, targeting the Danish market. Neither the Danish government nor the Danish newspaper acted extraterritorially. Therefore, this situation differs from those in which a citizen abuses human rights in a foreign territory. In *Ben el Mahi and others v Denmark*, the Danish newspaper could not possibly foresee the effect on the rights of Moroccan people living in Morocco by its publication in Denmark. However, in *Rantsev v Cyprus and Russia*, the human traffickers had obviously orchestrated the victim's travel to Cyprus; and in *Markovic v Italy*, Italy allowed NATO to use its base for the attack. Certainly, in these latter cases, the extraterritorial violation of human rights abuses was, to say the least, foreseeable.

Second, in *Ben el Mahi and others v Denmark*, the applicants did not argue that Denmark violated their right to an effective remedy. This is an important factor to be taken into account, because in *Markovic v Italy* the ECtHR distinguished between substantive and procedural claims. Although, under Article 1, European states may not exercise extraterritorial jurisdiction over certain foreign abuses, once the applicant has filed a complaint in domestic courts, the state has jurisdiction, as it pertains to the domestic proceedings addressing the extraterritorial case. In other words, once proceedings are initiated, a state must guarantee the applicant a fair and effective remedy. Interestingly, *Rantsev v Cyprus and Russia* also concerns the procedural obligation of Russia to conduct an effective investigation into the human trafficking chain which resulted in Ms Rantseva's death in Cyprus.

Therefore, once an applicant files a complaint in domestic courts, the state must guarantee the procedural rights enshrined in Articles 6 and 13, because, by filing a complaint, the applicant establishes a sufficient jurisdictional link

[66] *Rantsev v Cyprus and Russia* (n 54).

between the state and the lawsuit at stake. This rule is conditional on the fact that the state has control over either the perpetrator or the victim of the human rights abuse.

(iii) Control Over Neither the Victim nor the Perpetrator

When a state has no control over either the victim or the perpetrator, it may still exercise universal jurisdiction. Universal jurisdiction is a theory according to which any country is entitled to prosecute the perpetrator of those violations of *jus cogens* that are recognised as aberrant everywhere in the world. International law is not settled on the question of whether universal jurisdiction is an accepted means for establishing jurisdiction over a case.[67] There are a number of cases based on universal jurisdiction, such as the Eichmann case, in which Eichmann committed crimes in the Third Reich against European citizens, but he was prosecuted in Israel;[68] or the Pinochet case, where Pinochet committed crimes in Chile, but Spain requested that the United Kingdom extradite him for the violation of *jus cogens* norms.[69] However, following the ICJ's ruling in *Democratic Republic of the Congo v Belgium*,[70] holding that the Belgian universal jurisdiction statute violated the international law on immunity, the number of cases based on universal jurisdiction has decreased significantly. The main issue as it pertains to universal jurisdiction is whether it is possible to disregard the immunity of state officials or states to assert universal jurisdiction over a case concerning foreign victims and perpetrators.[71]

The ECtHR has been confronted with a few universal jurisdiction cases including *Al-Adsani v the United Kingdom*,[72] *Jones and others v the United Kingdom*,[73] *Nait-Liman v Switzerland*[74] and, to a certain extent, *Rantsev v Cyprus and Russia.*

[67] See Kenneth Roth, 'The Case for Universal Jurisdiction' (2001) 80 *Foreign Affairs New York* 150; Henry A Kissinger, 'The Pitfalls of Universal Jurisdiction' (2001) 80 *Foreign Affairs New York* 86; Devika Hovell, 29 'The Authority of Universal Jurisdiction' (2018) *EJIL* 427.

[68] Covey Oliver, 'The Attorney-General of the Government of Israel v Eichmann' (1962) 56 *The American Journal of International Law* 805; *Attorney General of the Government of Israel v Eichmann* [1962] Supreme Court of Israel 336/61.

[69] *Regina v Bartle and the Commissioner of Police for the Metropolis and others ex parte Pinochet Regina v Evans and another and the Commissioner of Police for the Metropolis and others Ex Parte Pinochet* [1999] 2 WLR 827; Michael Byers, 'English Courts and Serious Human Rights Violations Abroad: A Preliminary Assessment', in *Liability of Multinational Corporations under International Law* (Kluwer, 2000).

[70] *Arrest Warrant of 11 April 2000 (Democratic Republic of the Congo v Belgium)* [2002] ICJ ICJ Reports 3.

[71] See Lee M Caplan, 'State Immunity, Human Rights, and Jus Cogens: A Critique of the Normative Hierarchy Theory' (2003) 97 *The American Journal of International Law* 741; Lorna McGregor, 'State Immunity and Human Rights Is there a Future after Germany v Italy?' [2013] 11 *Journal of International Criminal Justice* 125; Andrea Bianchi, 'Immunity versus Human Rights: The Pinochet Case' (1999) 10 *European Journal of International Law* 237.

[72] *Al-Adsani v the United Kingdom* [2001] ECHR 35763/97.

[73] *Jones and others v the United Kingdom* [2014] ECHR 34356/06 and 40528/06.

[74] *Nait-Liman v Switzerland* [2018] ECHR 51357/07.

The facts of the first two cases are similar. In both, the issue was whether, under the ECHR, the applicant had a right to universal jurisdiction. British citizens filed tort law complaints in the United Kingdom against Kuwait and Saudi Arabia, because Kuwaiti and Saudi authorities allegedly tortured them. The victims requested that the United Kingdom provide them with effective legal remedies in UK courts against Kuwait, Saudi Arabia and the perpetrators of torture (state officials), arguing that such acts constituted a breach of *jus cogens* norms and, accordingly, every state should bring the perpetrators of such acts to justice in its domestic courts. At the time the alleged violations occurred, the United Kingdom had no jurisdiction over either the victim or the perpetrator of the human rights abuses and all the facts took place in a foreign territory. Furthermore, these cases were brought against foreign states and states' officials and therefore there was an issue as to the jurisdictional immunity of Kuwait and Saudi Arabia. On this basis, the UK courts refused to accept the legal actions of the applicants. Following this refusal, the applicants filed complaints against the United Kingdom, because of its failure to provide them with an effective legal remedy against Kuwait and Saudi Arabia. The issue was whether the United Kingdom had sufficient jurisdictional links with the alleged human rights violation. In both cases, the United Kingdom did not have control over Kuwait, Saudi Arabia, the victims or the perpetrators. In *Al-Adsani v the United Kingdom*, the ECtHR specifically distinguished the case from *Soering v the United Kingdom*, because there was no causal connection between the United Kingdom and the alleged torture.[75] Furthermore, in both cases, the United Kingdom acted in compliance with the customary international law principle of immunity, which was a procedural bar to the claims against Saudi Arabia, Kuwait and their officials.[76] Therefore, the ECtHR held in favour of the United Kingdom.

However, the ECtHR did not recognise an obligation to assert universal jurisdiction even in cases where the immunity of a foreign state or foreign official was not at stake. This was certainly the case in the already mentioned *Rantsev v Cyprus and Russia*, where the ECtHR held that

> [t]he applicant relies on the fact that Ms Rantseva was a Russian national. However, the Court does not consider Article 2 requires member States' criminal laws to provide for universal jurisdiction in cases involving the death of one of their nationals.[77]

Essentially, Russia was under no obligation to investigate the death of a citizen abroad, although, as already analysed above, it had the obligation to investigate her recruitment by human traffickers in Russia.

[75] *Al-Adsani v the United Kingdom* (n 72) para 40.

[76] *Al-Adsani v the United Kingdom* (n 72); *Jones and others v the United Kingdom* (n 73); Byers (n 69).

[77] *Rantsev v Cyprus and Russia* (n 54) para 244.

Furthermore, in *Nait-Liman v Switzerland*,[78] the Chamber and Grand Chamber did not consider the issue of immunity, because Swiss domestic courts decided they first had to assess whether or not they had jurisdiction over the case and they would have considered immunity only with a decision in the affirmative. The ECtHR, which reviewed the decisions of Swiss domestic courts, adopted the same approach focusing only on the issue of jurisdiction.[79] The facts of the case are as follows. The applicant was a Tunisian national who has been allegedly tortured in Tunisia on the orders of the Ministry of the Interior. He then obtained asylum in Switzerland and lived there. In February 2001, he learned that the Tunisian Minister of the Interior was hospitalised in Geneva and filed a criminal complaint with the Geneva police for the torture he suffered in Tunisia. By the time the police attempted to arrest the Minister, he had already left Switzerland. The applicant then filed a civil complaint with Swiss courts against the Ministry of the Interior and the Tunisian state. Swiss courts dismissed his case on jurisdictional grounds, and he filed a complaint with the ECtHR. The Grand Chamber took the opportunity to explain in detail the concept of universal jurisdiction and its application in accordance with the ECHR. It clarified that, under the ECtHR, states are under no obligation to assert universal jurisdiction because, in such cases, they have control neither over the victim nor over the perpetrator of an extraterritorial human rights abuse.

Interestingly, the ECtHR distinguished *Nait-Liman v Switzerland* from the *Akpan v Royak Dutch Shell*[80] case where Dutch courts asserted jurisdiction over a foreign subsidiary of Shell for extraterritorial human rights abuses. The ECtHR ruled that

> [a]t least in the Akpan case, there existed a solid connecting link with the Netherlands, in that the entity against which proceedings were brought before the Netherlands courts was a subsidiary of a company established under the authority of that State. It is not therefore possible to speak of universal jurisdiction in an absolute sense in respect of that case.[81]

This is very relevant to the case studies, because the ECtHR ruled that, even in those cases filed against a foreign subsidiary, the state could exercise authority and control over the parent corporation and, therefore, a jurisdictional link could still be established indirectly. This logic seems to suggest that when, as in the case studies analysed in this book, victims would file a lawsuit against parent corporations the jurisdictional link would certainly be established, because the home state would exercise full authority and control over the holding companies.

[78] *Nait-Liman v Switzerland* [2016] ECHR 51357/07; *Nait-Liman v Switzerland* (n 74).
[79] *Nait-Liman v Switzerland* (n 74) paras 98–99.
[80] *Akpan v Royal Dutch Shell Plc* [2013] DC Hague C/09/337050/HA ZA 09-1580.
[81] *Nait-Liman v Switzerland* (n 74) para 183.

To date, under the ECHR, there is no case-law recognising sufficient links to hold a state accountable on the basis of universal jurisdiction (ie when the human rights violation occurs abroad and both the human rights victim and the perpetrator are outside of the state's jurisdiction).

(iv) *Scholarly Debate*

According to Maastricht Principles 8(a) and 9(b), the cases of *territorial control with extraterritorial effects* relate to territorial actions or omissions of states that have repercussions abroad. These cases apply to both the duty to respect and the duty to protect, as both the actions and failures to act of the state may have a detrimental extraterritorial impact on human rights. They concern a territorial obligation of states to provide procedural guarantees in relation to foreseeable extraterritorial violations of human rights. The ECtHR sets a limit in relation to these cases of *territorial control with extraterritorial effects*: a state must exercise authority and control over either the victims or the perpetrators of human rights abuses. This entails that states have no obligation to accept cases where victims use national courts to file complaints against foreign perpetrators for abuses committed abroad. The ECtHR enforced this principle even in cases of torture where a state could invoke universal jurisdiction. Essentially, under the jurisprudence of the ECtHR, a state can, but has no obligation to, assert universal jurisdiction if it has control neither over the victim nor the perpetrator of an extraterritorial abuse of human rights.

The *territorial control with extraterritorial effects* test could be reduced to the concept of foreseeability. In essence, a European state has to guarantee procedural rights for victims in order to sanction the perpetrators of human rights abuses (*Markovic v Italy*) or prevent future violations (*Soering v the United Kingdom*, *Rantsev v Cyprus and Russia*) only when it could foresee potential extraterritorial damages. If, instead, a human rights abuse is outside of the state's control, such as in *Jones and others v the United Kingdom*, *Al-Adsani v the United Kingdom*, *Nait-Liman v Switzerland* and *Ben el Mahi and others v Denmark*, it has no jurisdiction over unforeseeable foreign violations. This limit is in line with the theory of Yuval Shany, who embraces a functional approach, arguing that the jurisdiction of European states depends on their capability to meet their obligations, but only when the human rights violations are a direct, significant and foreseeable consequence of the state's conduct. It would be unreasonable, Shany argues, to require states to prevent a human rights violation that they could not foresee, even though such a violation could be potentially connected to their conduct, such as, for example, global warming.[82] The ECtHR adopts this approach as it pertains to the cases of *territorial control with extraterritorial effects*, where states have jurisdiction only when their territorial conduct has foreseeable extraterritorial effects.

[82] Shany (n 11) 67–70.

The theory underlying these cases is more liberal than the one the ECtHR followed for cases of pure *extraterritorial control*. In fact, whereas the cases of *extraterritorial control* require the State to exercise authority and control over both the perpetrator and the victim of human rights abuses or effective control over the foreign territory, in cases of *territorial control with extraterritorial effects* it is sufficient for the state to exercise authority and control either over the victim or the perpetrator of human rights abuses. One could justify this different approach with the following two reasons.

First, in cases of *territorial control with extraterritorial effects* the state acts territorially and, therefore, is presumed to be able to control the conduct of perpetrators or victims who are within its territory. This situation differs from a state acting abroad where the control over foreign persons is usually limited. It is, therefore, logical to apply a stricter jurisdictional test to those situations where states act extraterritorially before holding European states accountable for conduct outside of their control.

Second, the cases of *territorial control with extraterritorial effects* have so far concerned the obligation to provide procedural guarantees to victims. This creates a particular category of cases, where European states have a positive obligation of result to guarantee procedural rights for foreign victims: guaranteeing these rights is a territorial conduct for the state but has extraterritorial effects. Marko Milanovic identified this category of procedural obligations as distinct from the others. According to him, positive obligations include substantive and procedural duties. Whereas a state has a positive, substantive obligation only when it has a certain degree of control over a territory entailing control over a private perpetrator, it always has the procedural obligation to prosecute a perpetrator of human rights abuses within its own state borders.[83] This distinction is convincing because, as the ECtHR ruled in *Markovic v Italy*,[84] the procedural obligation of the state to provide the victim of human rights abuses with an effective remedy against the perpetrator of such abuses is territorial in nature and the state always has control over procedural guarantees provided in its own courts. However, Milanovic also distinguishes between the positive procedural obligation deriving from the violations committed by a state agent and the positive procedural obligation deriving from the violations committed by a private party. According to Milanovic, the ECHR requires states to provide effective legal remedies against state agents perpetrating human rights abuses abroad, but not against private nationals perpetrating the same abuses.[85] This aspect of Milanovic's theory is highly problematic, because, if I assume that procedural obligations are territorial in nature, as it was decided in *Markovic v Italy*, and that the state has authority and control over a perpetrator of human rights abuses, the same legal reasoning shall justify providing

[83] Milanovic (n 10) 209–22.
[84] *Markovic and others v Italy* (n 53).
[85] Milanovic (n 10) 209–22.

an effective remedy against a state agent or against a private perpetrator who is under the control of the state. Milanovic's artificial distinction, denying an effective remedy in the circumstances that private parties commit human rights abuses, does not take into account the evolving jurisprudence of all international courts, including the ECtHR, that is increasingly blurring the distinction between positive and negative obligations.[86] It is interesting to note that, in a later article analysing *Al-Skeini and others v Italy*, Milanovic admits that his theory no longer fits within the jurisprudence of the ECtHR:

> The scope of *positive* obligations is likewise unclear. Would, for example, the UK … [h]ave had the procedural positive obligation to investigate if one of the killings was purely private in nature, i.e., if there was no involvement by UK soldiers?[87]

Yuval Shany provides the best critique of Milanovic's approach in his analysis of the *Herbicide* case[88] between Ecuador and Colombia, in which Ecuador accused Colombia of spraying some toxic herbicides on Colombian territories that would also contaminate the Ecuadorian sky. Milanovic comments on this case as follows:

> [C]olombia would be responsible for violating the rights of Ecuadorian residents adversely affected by its spraying operation, as the operation was conduct by its own agents or on its own behalf. Colombia would not, however, have the same obligation under human rights treaties with regard to pollution or herbicides used by purely private actors operating within its territory and having effects in Ecuador.[89]

Shany responds:

> But why shouldn't Colombia protect foreigners from harms caused by private actors operating from within its own borders? … [I]ndividuals should be protected from all right infringements regardless of whether the harm originates from private and public actors.[90]

Shany's approach is convincing. If, as Milanovic admits himself, a state has obligations when it has control over a person or a territory, in the *Herbicide* case, Colombia would have control over a private party and this case would not be substantially different from *Al-Skeini and others v Italy*, where the state controlled both public and private individuals allegedly abusing human rights.[91] Under this approach, it is clear that states are responsible only if they fail to protect individuals from the activities that they can control and that result in an abuse of rights. If a state cannot control the activity of a private company,

[86] Besson (n 7) 879; Shany (n 11) 62.

[87] Milanovic (n 32) 132.

[88] *Case concerning aerial herbicide spraying (Ecuador v Colombia): order of 13 September 2013* [2013] ICJ Reports 278.

[89] Milanovic (n 10) 218.

[90] Shany (n 11) 62.

[91] Shany (n 11); *Al-Skeini and Others v The United Kingdom* (n 9) paras 135–50.

it would not have any duty to protect human rights victims from the actions of such a private entity. A state should be liable solely for its failure to control private companies incorporated within its territories.[92]

C. The Duty to Fulfil: The Ability to Influence

The core of the duty to fulfil is for states to make their best effort to improve the human condition. This includes influencing the behaviour of third parties so that they respect human rights and providing services and assistance for individuals. With regard to the role of states in the international arena, the duty to fulfil includes all of those obligations of a global character, defined by Maastricht Principle 8(b), that aim at improving the human condition globally. These are *best-effort* duties that can be progressively accomplished in cooperation with other states and may include both territorial and extraterritorial actions.

To comply with such obligations of a global character, states inevitably have to act extraterritorially while not exercising either control or authority over a given territory or person. The nature of these obligations, therefore, singles out these cases as distinct from those of *extraterritorial control*, such as *Al-Skeini and others v the United Kingdom* and *Bankovic and others v Belgium*, and of *territorial control with extraterritorial effects*, such as *Soering v the United Kingdom* and *Markovic v Italy*, where the applicable test is always related to the level of authority and control that the state exercises over the victim, the perpetrator or a foreign territory. Therefore, the ECtHR developed limited jurisprudence applicable to such residual cases concerning the positive obligations of states that do not exercise any form of authority or control over a foreign territory or person. In these cases, the bases to assert jurisdiction are not authority or control but instead the *ability to influence* other actors.[93]

In *Ilascu and others v Moldava and Russia*,[94] a fundamental case on positive obligations, the Transdniestrian region declared itself independent from Moldova in 1991. The newly proclaimed, but not internationally recognised, Transdniestrian Republic and the Russian troops, which were supporting the Transdniestrian separatists, were in conflict with the Moldovian government. The Supreme Court of the Transdniestrian Republic held the applicants responsible for anti-Soviet activities and two murders. It sentenced one applicant to death and the others to imprisonment. The applicants filed a complaint before the ECtHR against both Russia and Moldova. The decision of the ECtHR is complex and holds both Russia and Moldova responsible. The case

[92] See Shany (n 11).
[93] De Schutter et al (n 16) pts 8–9.
[94] *Ilascu and others v Moldova and Russia* (n 2).

against Moldova is important, as it addresses the issue of whether the ECHR is applicable when states act without any control or authority over territories or persons.

Although legally the Transdniestrian Republic was part of the territory of Moldova, it was clear that the Republic of Moldova did not exercise authority over that region, as it was jointly controlled by a group of separatists and Russia. As to the decisions of the Transdniestrian judicial bodies, Moldova could consider the Transdniestrian region as a foreign territory. None of the elements of territoriality was present in this case. Moldova did not have control either over the applicants or the perpetrators of the human rights abuses, because they were under the authority of the Transdniestrian region. The human rights abuses occurred outside the territory controlled by Moldova. The applicant argued that the ECHR required Moldova to take actions in a territory outside its control. The ECtHR acknowledged that Moldova did not have control over Transdniestria and, therefore, held that it did not have an obligation of result towards the victims, as it was not able to ensure the protection of their fundamental rights. However, the ECtHR ruled that Moldova violated a duty to fulfil, because it could have influenced the Transdniestrian separatists to respect human rights. The ECtHR ruled that

> even in the absence of effective control over the Transdniestrian region, Moldova still has a positive obligation under Article 1 of the Convention to take the diplomatic, economic, judicial or other measures that it is in its power to take and are in accordance with international law to secure to the applicants the rights guaranteed by the Convention.[95]

The ECtHR held that Moldova violated its *best-effort* obligations to act outside of the territory it controlled in order to prevent human rights abuses. Some scholars considered this landmark case as territorial. They argued that the ECtHR ruled in the victim's favour because it interpreted the concept of territorial jurisdiction in formal, instead of effective, terms. According to them, the Transdniestrian region was formally a part of Moldova as it was not internationally recognised as a separate country.[96] However, other scholars, such as Michał Gondek and Gerard Gonzalez, rebutted this interpretation of the concept of jurisdiction on the basis of the subsequent case-law of the ECtHR.[97]

In *Nikolaus and Jurgen Treska v Albania and Italy*,[98] the Albanian government first confiscated a property located in Albania belonging to the applicant and then sold it to Italy. The applicants filed a complaint against both Italy and

[95] ibid 331.

[96] See Julie Tavernier, 'Compétence ratione loci: extraterritorialité et recevabilité', in *Quel filtrage des requêtes par la Cour européenne des droits de l'homme?* (Council of Europe, 2011); Loucaides (n 8) 73–94; Milanovic (n 10) 106–10.

[97] See Gonzalez (n 5); Gondek (n 5) 185–98.

[98] *Nikolaus and Jurgen Treska v Albania and Italy* (n 3).

Albania for violations of the ECHR. They complained that Albania confiscated the property without due process and fair compensation. Furthermore, they argued that Italy violated their right to property by taking over their building which Albania had unlawfully confiscated. The complaint against Italy is important for the analysis of the extraterritorial application of the ECHR.

This application is similar to the *Ilascu and others v Moldava and Russia* case, because the applicants requested that Italy undertake actions in a place outside of its control. The case mirrors *Ilascu and others v Moldava and Russia* with a significant difference: whereas the Transdniestrian region was formally part of Moldova and, therefore, one could argue that Moldova should have had authority over its territory,[99] this was not the case in respect of Italy and the relevant part of the territory of Albania where an alleged breach of human rights occurred.[100] Accordingly, the issue that the ECtHR had to address was whether, despite this absence of control over the Albanian territory, Italy still had jurisdiction on the basis of the influence it could exercise over the Albanian government, allegedly perpetrating a human rights abuse. The absence of effective control over Albanian territory was not a sufficient ground for the ECtHR to dismiss Italian jurisdiction over the case, because

> even in the absence of effective control of a territory outside its borders, the State still has a positive obligation under Article 1 of the Convention to take the diplomatic, economic, judicial or other measures that it is in its power to take and are in accordance with international law to secure to applicants the rights guaranteed by the Convention.[101]

It is important to note that, although in *Nikolaus and Jurgen Treska v Albania and Italy* the ECtHR cited *Ilascu and others v Moldava and Russia*, it added the wording '[t]erritory outside … [the State's] borders'.[102] This confirms that, even when states have no control over a foreign territory, they still have an obligation to do their utmost to protect human rights.[103] This principle applies not only to particular cases, such as *Ilascu and others v Moldava and Russia*, when a state lost control over its own territory but also to cases such as *Nikolaus and Jurgen Treska v Albania and Italy*, where a state had no control over a '[t]erritory outside its borders'.[104]

[99] *Ilascu and others v Moldova and Russia* (n 2); Milanovic (n 10) 106–10; Tavernier (n 96); Loucaides (n 8) 73–94.

[100] *Nikolaus and Jurgen Treska v Albania and Italy* (n 3); Gondek (n 5) 185–98; Gonzalez (n 5).

[101] *Nikolaus and Jurgen Treska v Albania and Italy* (n 3) (b) Complaint under Article 1 of Protocol No 1, (ii) The Court's assessment.

[102] ibid.

[103] See Gondek (n 5) 197–98; Gonzalez (n 5).

[104] *Nikolaus and Jurgen Treska v Albania and Italy* (n 3) (b) Complaint under Article 1 of Protocol No 1, (ii) The Court's assessment.

On the merits, the ECtHR ruled in Italy's favour, because Italy did not have any influence over Albania. Specifically, it was for the Albanian courts to decide on the confiscation of the applicant's land. According to the ECtHR:

> It is clear from the circumstances of the present case that the applicants were not within Italian jurisdiction. It must, therefore, be acknowledged that that State did not exercise jurisdiction over the applicants; the proceedings in issue were conducted exclusively in Albanian territory; the Albanian courts alone had sovereign authority in the applicants' case; and the Italian authorities had no direct or indirect influence over decisions and judgments delivered in Albania.[105]

The ECtHR ruled that Italy did not have jurisdiction over the alleged violation of human rights that occurred in Albania, also because it did not have 'direct or indirect influence over decisions and judgments delivered in Albania'.[106] The *Nikolaus and Jurgen Treska v Albania and Italy* judgment suggests that, even in those cases when there is neither control over a territory, nor authority over the people, a state may have extraterritorial jurisdiction when it can influence foreign actors, which is to say, it has a duty to fulfil. The key point here is that the basis for Italy to exercise jurisdiction was the influence that it could exercise over Albania. However, if the state is not in such a position to influence another actor, it does not owe a duty to fulfil and, therefore, it does not have jurisdiction over the human rights abuse. This effectively means that a state has to meet the following two conditions to assert extraterritorial jurisdiction: first, the state must have assumed human rights obligations arising from the ECHR; and, second, the state must be able to influence the extraterritorial conduct of another state or private actor in order to prevent a possible human rights violation. Italy did not have jurisdiction over the alleged violation of human rights, because it did not have the *ability to influence* the Albanian judiciary and therefore it did not owe a duty to fulfil to the Albanian applicant.[107]

The ECtHR confirmed this approach in another case, *Vrioni and others v Albania*,[108] which applied the *Nikolaus and Jurgen Treska v Albania and Italy* judgment to an almost identical case also concerning the expropriation of land in Albania sold thereafter to Italy. Therefore, even when a state party to the ECHR has no authority over a person or effective control over a territory, it nevertheless has extraterritorial jurisdiction if it is in a position to influence the conduct of another state or private actor.

Scholars have traditionally focused on *Al-Skeini and others v the United Kingdom* and *Bankovic and others v Belgium* as the leading cases to assert jurisdiction over a foreign territory,[109] and often disregarded *Ilascu and others*

[105] ibid.
[106] ibid.
[107] *Nikolaus and Jurgen Treska v Albania and Italy* (n 3); Gonzalez (n 5) 766–70.
[108] *Vrioni and others v Albania and Italy* (n 4).
[109] See Loucaides (n 8) 73–94; Lawson (n 8); Miltner (n 31); Bhavnani (n 31).

v Moldova and Russia, *Nikolaus and Jurgen Treska v Albania and Italy* and *Vrioni and others v Albania and Italy*. However, these five cases establish different tests to assert extraterritorial jurisdiction.[110] Whereas, according to the majority opinion in *Al-Skeini and others v the United Kingdom*, the test is effective control over a territory or authority and control over a person, according to *Ilascu and others v Moldova and Russia*, *Nikolaus and Jurgen Treska v Albania and Italy* and *Vrioni and others v Albania and Italy*, the test is the capability of the state to influence the conduct of foreign actors. The extraterritoriality theory behind these cases is the functional approach brought forward by Judge Bonello in his concurring opinion in *Al-Skeini and others v the United Kingdom*.[111] In Judge Bonnello's words:

> States ensure the observance of human rights in five primordial ways: firstly, by not violating (through their agents) human rights; secondly, by having in place systems which prevent breaches of human rights; thirdly, by investigating complaints of human rights abuses; fourthly, by scourging those of their agents who infringe human rights; and, finally, by compensating the victims of breaches of human rights. These constitute the basic minimum functions assumed by every State by virtue of its having contracted into the Convention. A 'functional' test would see a State effectively exercising 'jurisdiction' whenever it falls within its power to perform, or not to perform, any of these five functions. … [T]he duties assumed through ratifying the Convention go hand in hand with the duty to perform and observe them. Jurisdiction arises from the mere fact of having assumed those obligations and from having the capability to fulfil them (or not to fulfil them).[112]

Judge Bonnello refers to authority and control as the basis to assert jurisdiction. However, he does not refer to the *Al-Skeini and others v the United Kingdom* test on effective control over a territory or authority and control over a person. Instead, he refers to a more general notion of control that the state has if it exercises one of the following functions: *controlling its state agents*, *preventing human rights abuses*, *investigating complaints*, *sanctioning the perpetrators of human rights abuses* and *compensating the victims*.[113] In *Ilascu and others v Moldova and Russia*, the state had jurisdiction on the basis of the *preventing human rights abuses* function. Given that Moldova was in the position, through diplomatic means, to prevent human rights abuses in the Transdnistrian region, it had jurisdiction over the case.[114]

Shany correctly explains such approach as universalism or functionalism, because, given that human rights are universally applicable, if a state is in a position to prevent a human rights abuse, the state has jurisdiction. Besson analyses Judge Bonnello's approach in terms of capability. A state has jurisdiction if it

[110] Gondek (n 5) 185–98.
[111] Shany (n 11) 67–71.
[112] *Al-Skeini and Others v The United Kingdom* (n 9) Concurring Opinion of Judge Bonello, paras 10–13.
[113] ibid, para 10.
[114] *Ilascu and others v Moldova and Russia* (n 2).

has the capability to prevent, influence or stop an abuse. Both authors criticise Judge Bonello's approach as being too demanding on the state. Although Shany admits that the approach is compelling as a matter of principle, he believes that such an overbroad notion of jurisdiction could, as a practical matter, put States in difficult situations when compliance with such obligations would not be feasible.[115] Besson's critique is more radical. She disagrees with a universal application of human rights in principle. She believes that jurisdiction is a precondition to human rights and the related obligations of the state to respect such rights. According to her, unless there is a treaty, such as the ECHR, detailing the conditions upon which a state has jurisdiction over a certain territory/person, there are neither human rights nor human rights obligations. Human rights are conditioned upon the state's jurisdiction.[116]

Therefore, whereas it is true that in *Al-Skeini and others v the United Kingdom* the ECtHR rejected the capability test, as Michał Gondek and Gerard Gonzalez noted, the ECtHR applied the capability test in *Ilascu and others v Moldova and Russia*, *Nikolaus and Jurgen Treska v Albania and Italy* and *Vrioni and others v Albania and Italy*.[117] The open question is why there is such a different standard in *Al-Skeini and others v the United Kingdom*, *Bankovic and others v Belgium*, *Jaloud v the Netherlands*, *Soering v the United Kingdom*, *Rantsev v Cyprus and Russia* and *Markovic v Italy*, on the one side, and in *Ilascu and others v Moldova and Russia*, *Nikolaus and Jurgen Treska v Albania and Italy* and *Vrioni and others v Albania and Italy*, on the other. I believe the discrepancy between these standards depends on the nature of the obligations taken into account in these different cases. Whereas in the former cases the issue was whether the state violated its duties to respect and protect, in the latter the issue was whether the state violated its duty to fulfil. In the wording of the Maastricht Principles, in *Al-Skeini and others v the United Kingdom*, *Bankovic and others v Belgium*, *Jaloud v the Netherlands*, *Soering v the United Kingdom*, *Rantsev v Cyprus and Russia* and *Markovic v Italy*, the obligation at stake was a Principle 8(a), ie '[o]bligations relating to the acts and omissions of a State, within or beyond its territory, that have effects on the enjoyment of human rights outside of that State's territory',[118] whereas in *Ilascu and others v Moldova and Russia*, *Nikolaus and Jurgen Treska v Albania and Italy* and *Vrioni and others v Albania and Italy*, the obligation was a Principle 8(b), ie '[o]bligations of a global character … [t]o realize human rights universally'.[119] It is clear that, whereas the former obligations are particularly demanding and, therefore, such duties are considered within the state's reach only when it exercises authority and control

[115] Shany (n 11).

[116] Besson (n 7).

[117] See Gondek (n 5) 185–98; *Ilascu and others v Moldova and Russia* (n 2); *Nikolaus and Jurgen Treska v Albania and Italy* (n 3); *Vrioni and others v Albania and Italy* (n 4); Gonzalez (n 5).

[118] De Schutter et al (n 16) pt 8(a).

[119] ibid pt 8(b).

over territories or persons, the latter obligations are so far-reaching that if states implemented them only when they had full authority and control, they would become hardly useful.[120] In other words, given that the duties to respect and protect are demanding obligations of conduct and result in requiring the state to adopt precise conduct or meet a certain goal, the ECtHR felt that it would be unreasonable to hold states accountable on a functional basis. Therefore, it restricted the basis to assert jurisdiction according to the *Al-Skeini and others v the United Kingdom*'s test on authority and control over persons and effective control over territory.

It is true that, in cases of *territorial control with extraterritorial effects*, such as *Soering v the United Kingdom*, *Markovic v Italy* and *Rantsev v Cyprus and Russia*, the ECtHR adopted a more liberal test given the presence of a strong territorial element, but such test is nevertheless based on authority and control over either the victim or the perpetrator. Instead, given that the duty to fulfil is a less demanding obligation of a global character to influence the conduct of third parties through diplomatic means, the standard to assert jurisdiction where such a duty is concerned is substantially lower. In order to assert jurisdiction on a breach of the duty to fulfil, it is enough for the state to have the power to influence foreign activities.

II. *LEX FERENDA*: THE STATE'S DUTIES AND MULTINATIONAL ENTERPRISES

The sections above have analysed the jurisprudence of the ECtHR as it pertains to the application of positive obligations and extraterritoriality. The ECtHR has not yet applied the ECHR to a case where a state failed to secure the extraterritorial rights of victims vis-à-vis a holding company, such as, H. Nevertheless this book argues that it is perfectly possible for the ECtHR to apply its jurisprudence to such cases in the future. This section justifies such an interpretation of the ECtHR's case-law on the basis of an already-developed jurisprudence of other human rights adjudicative bodies and soft laws applicable to business and human rights.

It is important to note that the ECtHR's jurisprudence does not develop in a vacuum. A number of scholars have studied and explained the phenomenon of cross-fertilisation and judicial dialogue in international and human rights law. International courts are listening to each other and are increasingly attempting to develop consistent jurisprudence across different jurisdictions.[121]

[120] See Mazzeschi (n 20) 224–49 and 311–496; Sepúlveda Carmona (n 20) 115–248; Benvenisti (n 20) 313–26; Guy S Goodwin-Gill, 'Obligations of Conduct and Result', in *The Right to Food*, Stichting Studie- en Informatiecentrum Mensenrechten (Martinus Nijhoff, 1984).

[121] Antonio Augusto Cancado Trindade, 'The Merits of Coordination of International Courts on Human Rights' (2004) 2 *Journal of International Criminal Justice* 309; Olga Frishman,

This is particularly true for human rights bodies and courts as they all refer to some principles that, although incorporated in different treaties, have universal aspirations.[122] In order to understand the jurisprudence of the ECtHR and its possible developments, it is, therefore, fundamental to take into account the jurisprudence of the other human rights bodies and courts. Before analysing their decisions on the positive obligations of states to secure that enterprises respect human rights extraterritorially, it is important to distinguish the different roles that human rights courts, bodies and instruments have in such a judicial dialogue.

First, human rights adjudication includes three regional courts, ie the ECtHR, the IACtHR and the AfrCtHPR, and two regional commissions, ie the IACoHR and the African Commission on Human and Peoples' Rights (AfrCoHPR). All human rights courts are able to decide on individual complaints and deliver advisory opinions. The decisions and opinions of all human rights courts are binding. However, whereas in the European system individuals can file complaints directly with the ECtHR,[123] in the American system the individual complaints have to be filed with the IACoHR which may then refer them to the IACtHR. The IACoHR is a body with numerous functions, in addition to hearing individual complaints. This is due to the structure of the American human rights system, including both the American Declaration on Human Rights (ADHR), initially a non-binding document, which the IACtHR and the IACoHR have increasingly recognised as binding, and the American Convention on Human Rights (ACHR). As a result, the IACoHR publishes general reports, makes onsite visits, writes recommendations, and hears individual complaints related to violations of both the ADHR and the ACHR. If the complaints pertain to the ACHR, it can refer them to the ACtHR.[124] In the African system, the AfrCtHPR can receive cases referred by the AfrCoHPR, by other states, as well as by individuals and NGOs, provided that the state against which the complaint is brought has agreed to the individual complaint procedure.[125] The AfrCoHPR is instead a quasi-judicial body which, in addition to hearing

'Transnational Judicial Dialogue as an Organisational Field' (2013) 19 *European Law Journal* 739; Anne-Marie Slaughter, 'Judicial Globalization' (2000) 40 *Virginia Journal of International Law* 1103.

[122] Paolo G Carozza, 'Human Dignity and Judicial Interpretation of Human Rights: A Reply' (2008) 19 *European Journal of International Law* 931; Jeremy Waldron, 'Is Dignity the Foundation of Human Rights?' in *Philosophical Foundations of Human Rights* (Oxford University Press, 2015); Louis Henkin, 'The Universality of the Concept of Human Rights' (1989) 506 *The Annals of the American Academy of Political and Social Science* 10.

[123] Registry of the Court (ECtHR), 'Rules of Court' (2019).

[124] IACoHR, 'Rules of Procedure of the Inter-American Court of Human Rights'; IACoHR, 'Rules of Procedure of the Inter-American Commission on Human Rights'; OAS, 'Basic Documents in the Inter-American System' (1 August 2009), www.oas.org/en/iachr/mandate/Basics/intro.asp, accessed 25 January 2019.

[125] 'Welcome to the African Court', www.african-court.org/en/index.php/12-homepage1/1-welcome-to-the-african-court, accessed 25 January 2019; AfrCtHPR, 'Rules of Court'.

individual complaints, has the functions to promote human rights and interpret the African Charter on Human and People's Rights (AfrChHPR).[126] Whereas the jurisprudence of the ECtHR and IACtHR is highly developed and the two courts often refer to each other as persuasive authorities, the AfrCtHPR has so far decided a limited number of cases, given that it was established only in 2004. In contrast, the AfrCoHPR, which came to existence in 1986, has decided several cases. However, the AfrCoHPR is a quasi-judicial body delivering non-binding decisions.[127]

Second, the UN human rights system includes a number of quasi-judicial Treaty Bodies, such as the ICCPR, the International Covenant on Economic, Social and Cultural Rights (ICESCR), the Convention on the Elimination of all Forms of Discrimination Against Women, and the Convention on the Rights of the Child, each one specialised to interpret its respective covenant. All of these covenants are binding on the signatory states, whereas the interpretations by the Treaty Bodies is not binding. The Treaty Bodies decide individual complaints and deliver General Comments and Concluding Observations on the conduct of the signatory states. Whereas the individual complaints apply the covenants to specific cases, the Concluding Observations address all the human rights violations committed by a state in a certain timeframe. They, therefore, typically dedicate a few generally worded paragraphs per human rights violation. They also deliver general comments on topical human rights issues, which explain in detail how states ought to implement the UN Treaties.[128] It is noteworthy that both the CESCR and the CRC have released a General Comment specifically addressing state obligations with respect to corporate abuses.[129]

In this judicial dialogue, each human rights adjudicative body has a different function. The regional courts and commissions are typically less activist in their interpretation of their founding treaties, because they are concerned with the enforcement of their binding decisions. Instead, quasi-judicial bodies are generally willing to propose innovative interpretations of their treaties to advance the development of international law. At the same time, when an adjudicating body delivers an Advisory Opinion or a General Comment, it will typically engage in a more creative interpretation of the relevant treaty, knowing that the opinion or comment will not be directly enforceable in a specific case but will instead

[126] ACoHPR, 'Rules of Procedure of the African Commission on Human and Peoples' Rights' (2010); ACoHPR 'History', www.achpr.org/about/history/, accessed 25 January 2019.

[127] Giuseppe Pascale, 'Extraterritorial Applicability of the African Charter on Human and Peoples' Rights' (2014) 8 *Diritti umani e diritto internazionale* 644.

[128] Philip Alston and James Crawford (eds), *The Future of UN Human Rights Treaty Monitoring* (Cambridge University Press, 2000); Helen Keller and Geir Ulfstein (eds), *UN Human Rights Treaty Bodies: Law and Legitimacy* (Cambridge University Press, 2012).

[129] CESCR, 'General Comment No 24 on State obligations under the International Covenant on Economic, Social and Cultural Rights in the Context of Business Activities' (2017); CRC, 'General Comment No 16 (2013) on State obligations regarding the impact of the business sector on children's rights' (2013).

establish a general principle of interpretation.[130] Therefore, a General Comment from a Treaty Body will usually go further in establishing the obligations of states than a decision of a regional court on an individual complaint.

However, despite these differences in their general approach, the jurisprudence of regional courts and quasi-judicial bodies is complementary in shaping and framing human rights law. Quasi-judicial bodies are often the pioneers in developing an activist interpretation of their founding treaties. Their decisions become persuasive precedents for regional human rights courts which may rely on them to develop their own jurisprudence.[131]

The case-law on multinational enterprises seems to follow the same pattern. Quasi-judicial bodies have already delivered several Concluding Observations and two General Comments on the accountability of home states for the extraterritorial human rights abuses committed by multinational enterprises, and regional courts are increasingly developing jurisprudence on extraterritoriality and private industries that is potentially applicable to transnational corporations. In this regard, it should be noticed that none of the human rights treaties was conceived having in mind the obligations of states in connection with corporate abuses. However, the progressive jurisprudence of human rights courts, commissions and Treaty Bodies has increasingly incorporated the positive obligations of states in relation to private industries.

Furthermore, there are several soft law instruments that explicitly mention the positive obligations of states with respect to the human rights abuses committed by multinational corporations. The starting point of all of these soft law mechanisms is always that companies are private legal persons that should be treated by states as private individuals.[132] The most important soft law instruments will include the following.

First, the Guiding Principles revisit the tripartite duties to respect, protect and fulfil, and adapt them to the business and human rights framework. The main dichotomy in the Guiding Principles is the state's duty to protect and the companies' responsibility to respect. States have positive obligations to protect individuals against multinational companies, whereas companies have a negative responsibility to refrain from abusing human rights. In this sense, the Guiding Principles use the dichotomy between positive and negative obligations to

[130] Alston and Crawford (n 128); Keller and Ulfstein (n 128).

[131] Carla Buckley and others, *Towards Convergence in International Human Rights Law: Approaches of Regional and International Systems* (Brill/Nijhoff, 2017).

[132] See Robert McCorquodale and Penelope Simons, 'Responsibility Beyond Borders: State Responsibility for Extraterritorial Violations by Corporations of International Human Rights Law' (2007) 70 *MLR* 598; Francesco Francioni, 'Alternative Perspectives on International Responsibility for Human Rights Violations by Multinational Corporations', in *Economic Globalisation and Human Rights* (Cambridge University Press, 2007); Nicola Jägers, *Corporate Human Rights Obligations: In Search of Accountability* (Intersentia, 2002) 137–75; De Schutter, 'Le contrôle du respect des droits de l'homme par les sociétés transnationales' (n 10); Jernej Letnar Cernic, *Human Rights Law and Business Corporate Responsibility for Fundamental Human Rights* (Europa Law Publishing, 2010) 93–125.

establish different duties and responsibilities for states and companies. However, whereas under general human rights law the negative and positive duties of the states are both binding legal obligations, according to the Guiding Principles, companies have no binding obligations but instead mere voluntarily assumed responsibilities to refrain from abusing human rights.[133] Therefore, the Guiding Principles are a soft law instrument restating the hard obligations of states and the soft responsibilities of companies. It should be noted that the Guiding Principles do not set out a distinction between the duties to fulfil and protect. For example, they include both the duty to enforce laws[134] as well as the duty to promote the respect for human rights by enterprises.[135] As set out above, according to the tripartite classification, the former is part of the duty to protect, whereas the latter is part of the duty to fulfil. However, the Guiding Principles do not adopt the language of the duty to fulfil. Furthermore, the Guiding Principles add a section dedicated only to access to remedy as part of the state's duty to protect.[136] Accordingly, states must provide human rights victims with effective judicial remedies against multinational enterprises. The United Kingdom, the European Union and the Council of Europe have all published a document on the implementation of the Guiding Principles. The UK government adopted a document in 2013 in which it recognised its duty to protect human rights against companies that are under UK jurisdiction.[137] This commitment was reconfirmed in 2016.[138] The European Commission also published two documents in 2015 and 2019 in which it recognised that states have a duty to protect victims from human rights abuses committed by multinational enterprises.[139]

Second, the ILO sets out that all states parties have a positive duty to prevent companies from abusing the ILO principles and conventions. This obligation

[133] See John Gerard Ruggie, 'The Construction of the UN "Protect, Respect and Remedy" Framework for Business and Human Rights: The True Confessions of a Principled Pragmatist' (2011) 2 *European Human Rights Law Review* 127; John Gerard Ruggie, 'Protect, Respect, and Remedy: The UN Framework for Business and Human Rights', in *International Human Rights Law* (Ashgate, 2010); John Gerard Ruggie, 'Business and Human Rights: The Evolving International Agenda' (2007) 101 *The American Journal of International Law* 819; Nicola Jägers, Katinka Jesse and Jonathan Verschuuren, 'The Future of Corporate Liability for Extraterritorial Human Rights Abuses: The Dutch Case against Shell' (2013) 107 *The American Journal of International Law* 36; John Gerard Ruggie, 'Report of the Special Representative of the Secretary-General on the Issue of Human Rights and Transnational Corporations and Other Business Enterprises' (2011) 29 *Netherlands Quarterly Human Rights* 224.

[134] Ruggie, 'Report of the Special Representative of the Secretary-General' (n 133) 230.

[135] ibid 233.

[136] ibid 246–47.

[137] HM Government, 'Good Business Implementing the UN Guiding Principles on Business and Human Rights', www.gov.uk/government/uploads/system/uploads/attachment_data/file/236901/BHR_Action_Plan_-_final_online_version_1_.pdf, accessed 20 April 2016.

[138] 'UK Open Government National Action Plan 2016–18', www.gov.uk/government/publications/uk-open-government-national-action-plan-2016-18/uk-open-government-national-action-plan-2016-18, accessed 2 December 2016.

[139] European Commission, 'Commission Staff Working Document on Implementing the UN Guiding Principles on Business and Human Rights – State of Play' SWD (2015) 144 final; European Commission, 'Commission Staff Working Document Corporate Social Responsibility, Responsible Business Conduct and Business & Human Rights: Overview of Progress' SWD (2019) 143 final.

may be inferred from two fundamental ILO documents: the ILO Work Declaration[140] and the ILO Tripartite Declaration.[141] The ILO Work Declaration restates that states have a negative obligation to respect, and a positive obligation to promote and realise the ILO fundamental principles. Those principles include the ILO Tripartite Declaration, which is the main ILO document concerning CSR. The ILO Tripartite Declaration addresses both states and multinational enterprises. Although both ILO Declarations are non-binding documents, they restate that states, as primary actors of international law, have an obligation to ensure that companies respect the ILO principles.

Although none of these instruments is binding, they corroborate the interpretation of human rights treaties in terms of positive obligations of states to secure and ensure the rights of individuals against multinational corporations.[142] Human rights treaty bodies and courts are, therefore, increasingly taking them into account when interpreting the respective covenants and conventions in cases of human rights abuses committed by corporations.

As analysed with respect to the ECHR, human rights adjudication has ruled quite extensively on both the extraterritoriality and positive obligations of states to prevent abuses by private industries. More recently, however, human rights adjudication has combined these two bodies of case-law to recognise the existence of an extraterritorial positive obligation of states to secure the human rights of victims against multinational enterprises. The following sections analyse the jurisprudence of regional human rights courts and the treaty bodies on (A) extraterritoriality, (B) the positive obligations of states to prevent abuses from private enterprises, (C) the duty to protect, and (D) the duty to fulfil in relation to the activities of multinational enterprises.

A. Extraterritoriality

Like the ECHR, the ACHR and most UN human rights treaties include a jurisdiction clause stating that they apply within the jurisdiction of the contracting states. However, the ADHR, AfrChHPR, ICESCR and the Convention on the

[140] International Labour Office, *ILO Declaration on Fundamental Principles and Rights at Work and its Follow-Up* (ILO, 2010).

[141] International Labour Office (ed), *Tripartite Declaration of Principles Concerning Multinational Enterprises and Social Policy*, 5th edn (ILO, 2017).

[142] See Ruggie, 'The Construction of the UN "Protect, Respect and Remedy" Framework for Business and Human Rights' (n 133); Ruggie, 'Protect, Respect, and Remedy' (n 133); Ruggie, 'Business and Human Rights' (n 133); Nicola Jägers, 'UN Guiding Principles on Business and Human Rights: Making Headway towards Real Corporate Accountability' (2011) 29 *Netherlands Quarterly of Human Rights* 159; Radu Mares (ed), *The UN Guiding Principles on Business and Human Rights: Foundations and Implementation* (Martinus Nijhoff, 2011); Astrid Sanders, 'The Impact of the "Ruggie Framework" and the United Nations Guiding Principles on Business and Human Rights on Transnational Human Rights Litigation' (2014) 18 *LSE Law, Society and Economy Working Papers*; David Bilchitz, 'The Ruggie Framework: An Adequate Rubric for Corporate Human Rights Obligations?' (2010) 7 *SUR* 199.

Elimination of all Forms of Discrimination Against Women have no jurisdiction clause.[143] This omission may arguably allow a wider extraterritorial application of human rights law for these treaties. However, this textual difference does not seem to have a substantial impact on the extraterritorial application of human right treaties. In fact, the IACoHR and the ACtHR have applied the same extraterritoriality theory for both the ACHR and the ADHR, notwithstanding that the former has a jurisdiction clause whereas the latter does not.[144] The AfrCoHPR and the AfrCtHPR have not decided a substantial number of extraterritorial cases yet, although some decisions did refer to extraterritoriality.[145] The treaty bodies have developed a detailed jurisprudence on extraterritoriality with numerous Concluding Observations and General Comments specifically on the obligations of home and host states of multinational enterprises.[146] In this context, despite some treaties not including any jurisdiction clause, the jurisprudence of the various treaty bodies does not significantly differ.

Given the developed jurisprudence of the treaty bodies on the extraterritorial application of human rights to home and host states of transnational corporations, their General Comments and Concluding Observations will be analysed in sections C and D specifically focused on the duty to protect and fulfil. This section on extraterritoriality will instead analyse the jurisprudence of the American and African human rights courts and commissions.

[143] See eg European Convention for the Protection of Human Rights and Fundamental Freedoms, art 1; American Convention on Human Rights 1969, art 1; International Convention on the Elimination of All Forms of Racial Discrimination 1969, art 3; Convention on the Rights of the Child 1990, art 2; International Covenant on Civil and Political Rights 1966, art 2.

[144] *Advisory Opinion on the Environment and Human Rights* [2017] IACHR OC-23/17; *Alejandre Jr v Cuba* [1999] IACoHR 86/99; *Franklin Guillermo Aisalla Molina Ecuador v Colombia* [2010] IACoHR 112/10; *Danny Honorario Bastidas Meneses and others v Ecuador* [2011] IACoHR 153/11; Helena De Vylder, 'The Territorial Scope of the American Convention on Human Rights' (2014) 1 *Inter-American and European Human Rights Journal* 204; Alejandra Gonza, 'Integrating Business and Human Rights in the Inter-American Human Rights System' (2016) 1 *Business and Human Rights Journal* 357; María Carmelina Londoño-Lázaro, Ulf Thoene and Catherine Pereira-Villa, 'The Inter-American Court of Human Rights and Multinational Enterprises: Towards Business and Human Rights in the Americas?' (2017) 16 *The Law and Practice of International Courts and Tribunals* 437.

[145] Pascale (n 127); South African Institute for Advanced Constitutional, Public, Human Rights and International Law, 'The State Duty to Protect, Corporate Obligations and Extra-Territorial Application in the African Regional Human Rights System' (2010), www.business-humanrights.org/sites/default/files/reports-and-materials/SAIFAC-paper-re-business-human-rights-in-African-regional-system-17-Feb-2010.pdf, accessed 17 March 2019; Takele Soboka Bulto, 'Patching the "Legal Black Hole": The Extraterritorial Reach of States' Human Rights Duties in the African Human Rights System' (2011) 27 *South African Journal on Human Rights* 249.

[146] See eg CERD, 'Concluding Observations on the Combined Seventh to Ninth Periodic Reports of the United States of America' (2014) CO 7–9; CRC, 'Concluding Observations on the Combined Third and Fourth Periodic Report of Canada, Adopted by the Committee at its Sixty-First Session' (2012) CO 3–4; HRC, 'Concluding Observations on the Sixth Periodic Report of Germany, Adopted by the Committee at its 106th Session' (2012) CO 6; CRC, 'Concluding Observations on the Combined Second to Fourth Periodic Reports of Switzerland' (2015) CO 2–4; CESCR, 'Concluding Observations on the Fourth Periodic Report of Austria' (2013) CO 4; CESCR, 'Concluding Observations on the Fifth Periodic Report of Norway' (2013) CO 5; CESCR, 'General Comment No 24' (n 129); CRC, 'General Comment No 16' (n 129).

The IACtHR has recently released an unprecedented *Advisory Opinion on Environment and Human Rights* which clarified the meaning of extraterritoriality in the American human rights system.

> States must ensure that their territory is not used in any way that may cause significant damage to the environment of other States or of areas outside their territorial limits. Consequently, States have the obligation to prevent causing transboundary damage.
>
> States are obligated to adopt all necessary measures to avoid that activities carried out *on their territory or under their control* affect the rights of individuals *within or outside their territory*.
>
> Regarding transboundary damage, a person is subject to the jurisdiction of the State of origin, if there is a *causal connection between the incident that took place on its territory and the violation of the human rights of persons outside its territory*. The exercise of jurisdiction arises when the State of origin exercises *effective control of the activities* that caused the damage and consequent violation of human rights.[147]

The IACtHR uses the notion of effective control differently from the ECtHR. Instead of describing it as an authority *and* control test, the IACtHR has analysed it as an authority *or* power *or* control test. For the IACtHR, effective control means a de facto control that a state exercises over a certain conduct, instead of the de jure control required by the ECtHR.[148] According to the Advisory Opinion, first, the conduct causing extraterritorial human rights abuses does not necessarily have to be unlawful, it could be a lawful action or omission resulting in extraterritorial abuses.[149] Second, such conduct could be either territorial or extraterritorial. A state may exercise effective control in situations when it acts extraterritorially or in situations where a territorial conduct has extraterritorial effects.[150] Third, it could be a state conduct, as well as the conduct of private actors. Remarkably the IACtHR addressed in the Advisory Opinion, the positive obligations of states to prevent transnational environmental damage committed by private persons, including corporations.[151] The state has an obligation to prevent any extraterritorial human rights violations. However, these extraterritorial obligations are limited by a double test of causality and foreseeability: states are accountable only if their actions or omissions have caused foreseeable and significant extraterritorial damage. The IACtHR explains this limitation on the basis that states should not meet an impossible

[147] *Advisory Opinion on the Environment and Human Rights* (n 144) 104 (emphasis added).

[148] De Vylder (n 144) 212–13; Angeliki Papantoniou, 'Advisory Opinion on the Environment and Human Rights' (2018) 112 *The American Journal of International Law* 460; 'EJIL: Talk! – Human Rights and the Protection of the Environment: The Advisory Opinion of the Inter-American Court of Human Rights', www.ejiltalk.org/human-rights-and-the-protection-of-the-environment-the-advisory-opinion-of-the-inter-american-court-of-human-rights/, accessed 15 October 2018.

[149] *Advisory Opinion on the Environment and Human Rights* (n 144) para 103.

[150] ibid paras 93–94.

[151] ibid paras 143–51.

burden that would hold them accountable even for conduct that would cause unforeseeable detrimental effects.[152]

The IACtHR justified its decision by overwhelmingly quoting the ECtHR's case-law on extraterritoriality.[153] It seems, in fact, that the IACtHR attempted to incorporate the three different tests developed by the ECtHR, and discussed above, as it pertains to the duty to respect, protect and fulfil.[154] The IACtHR's decision broadly agrees with Yuval Shany's extraterritorial analysis of the ECtHR's jurisprudence. As the reader may recall, the capability analysis, used by the ECtHR as it pertains to violations of the duty to fulfil, entails that a state would be responsible for extraterritorial human rights abuses when it is capable of preventing them.[155] However, Shany believes that such a test would put an extremely heavy burden on the state which could be responsible for unforeseeable events that could be associated with its conduct. He therefore proposes to limit the capability approach only to violations that are direct, significant and foreseeable.[156] Such a limitation seems close to the test used by the IACtHR, which confines the extraterritorial jurisdiction to situations when a state controls conduct that can cause foreseeable extraterritorial human rights abuses.

Interestingly, in 2017, the HRC released its General Comment No 36 on Article 6 of the ICCPR, on the right to life. The General Comment includes a paragraph on the extraterritorial application of the right to life which addresses states' conduct that has a 'direct and reasonably foreseeable impact'[157] outside of their territories. There seems, therefore, to be a common ground between the HRC and the IACtHR in the development of a foreseeability test as a basis to assert extraterritorial jurisdiction.

But how did the IACtHR come to this progressive interpretation of extraterritoriality? To understand this, it is necessary to analyse the jurisprudence of the IACoHR on extraterritoriality. On multiple occasions, the IACoHR applied the ECtHR's *authority and control* test stated in *Bankovic and others v Belgium* and revisited in *Al-Skeini and others v the United Kingdom*. However, the IACoHR interpreted it as a de facto, instead of a de jure, control test.[158] This is particularly evident in *Alejandre Jr v Cuba*,[159] where the IACoHR ruled that Cuba was accountable for an extraterritorial military strike, using the effective-control test to prove that Cuba exercised control over the military action. This decision contradicts *Bankovic and others v Belgium*, where the ECtHR used the effective control test, instead, in terms of the de jure control exercised over Belgrade.

[152] ibid paras 118–20.

[153] ibid fn 128, 135, 136, 137, 138, 139, 146, 147, 167, 168, 169, 170, 184.

[154] See Chapter 4.I.

[155] *Al-Skeini and Others v The United Kingdom* (n 9) Concurring Opinion of Judge Bonello.

[156] Shany (n 11).

[157] HRC, 'General Comment No 36 on Article 6 of the International Covenant on Civil and Political Rights, on the Right to Life' (2018) CCPR/C/GC/36, para 22.

[158] De Vylder (n 144); Papantoniou (n 148); 'EJIL: Talk! – Human Rights and the Protection of the Environment' (n 148).

[159] *Alejandre Jr v Cuba* (n 144).

However, a few details are important to distinguish the two cases. First, in *Bankovic and others v Belgium*, the military strike was carried out by NATO, an international organisation that is clearly not a party to the ECHR. This differs from the *Alejandre Jr v Cuba* case, where the Cuban military was the only body responsible for the strike. Second, in *Alejandre Jr v Cuba*, the strike was in international waters, a territory not controlled by any state, whereas in *Bankovic and others v Belgium*, the strike was in Belgrade, which was at that time part of the Yugoslavian territory.[160] Although these factual circumstances may explain the divergent application of the effective control test by the ECtHR and the IACoHR in this particular case, the IACtHR has continued to apply a de facto test in its jurisprudence. For instance, in *Franklin Guillermo Aisalla Molina Ecuador v Colombia*, a case concerning a military operation that Colombian forces undertook in Ecuador, which resulted in extrajudicial killings, the IACoHR interpreted the test of effective control in terms of causality. According to the IACoHR, Colombia exercised extraterritorial jurisdiction, because the conduct of its agents caused an alleged extraterritorial violation of human rights.[161] Furthermore, in *Danny Honorio v Ecuador*, a case concerning the responsibility of Ecuador for the death of a Colombian citizen in Colombia, the IACoHR confirmed that the *authority and control* test is based on causality.[162]

The African system is, instead, still at an embryonic stage in terms of the development of its extraterritorial jurisprudence. In fact, the AfrCtHPR has not yet decided a case on extraterritoriality, and the AfrCoHPR did not set out an extraterritorial theory or test but decided one significant case on extraterritoriality. In the *Democratic Republic of Congo v Burundi, Rwanda, Uganda*,[163] it held Burundi, Rwanda and Uganda responsible for their military activities in Congo on the basis of the 'effective control' exercised over the foreign territory without explaining its meaning. Although this is only one case, certain scholars considered it as the starting point for the development of a jurisprudence on extraterritoriality by the AfrCoHPR. This argument is particularly convincing if one considers the absence of a jurisdiction clause in the AfrChHPR and the inclusion of such rights, as a right to peace and security, which are inherently transnational.[164]

B. Positive Obligations and Private Enterprises

Like the ECtHR, the other human rights regional institutions have all developed jurisprudence on the positive obligations of states to prevent abuses by corporations.

[160] De Vylder (n 144) 214–15.
[161] *Franklin Guillermo Aisalla Molina Ecuador v Colombia* (n 144).
[162] *Danny Honorario Bastidas Meneses and others v Ecuador* (n 144); De Vylder (n 144) 218–19.
[163] *Democratic Republic of Congo v Burundi, Rwanda, Uganda* [1999] ACoHPR 227/99.
[164] Pascale (n 127); Takele Soboka (n 145).

The IACoHR and IACtHR have developed the most advanced jurisprudence with respect to protecting indigenous people. In the Americas, in fact, states have often allowed foreign companies to take advantage of the natural resources belonging to indigenous people. As a result, indigenous groups have retaliated against multinational enterprises and have accused states of violating their positive obligations to protect them against foreign investors. The IACoHR and the IACtHR approached these cases, first, from the perspective of a violation of the right to property, which they interpreted as a collective right of indigenous peoples; and, second, as a violation of the right to life, as indigenous people could not survive as a people without exercising control over their lands and natural resources.[165] The apparently innovative interpretation of these two rights does nothing other than apply the states' positive obligations to protect and fulfil also in terms of guaranteeing fundamental rights against corporations. This includes both providing effective remedies to the indigenous peoples seeking redress against corporations (duty to protect), as well as improving the conditions of indigenous people by preventing corporations from abusing their rights (duty to fulfil).

The IACtHR and IACoHR clarified that the rights to effective remedies against corporations require states to set up domestic procedures to allow indigenous people to claim their ancestral territories, as well as to sanction corporations abusing indigenous people's rights.[166] In this sense, the IACoHR and the IACtHR have developed jurisprudence that is similar to the ECtHR as it pertains to its interpretation of Article 13 in combination with Article 1

[165] Efrén C Olivares Alanís, 'Indigenous Peoples' Rights and the Extractive Industry: Jurisprudence from the Inter-American System of Human Rights' (2013) 5 *Goettingen Journal of International Law* 187; Thomas Antkowiak, 'A Dark Side of Virtue: The Inter-American Court and Reparations for Indigenous Peoples' (2014) 25 *Duke Journal of Comparative and International Law* 1; Thomas Antkowiak, 'Rights, Resources, and Rhetoric: Indigenous Peoples and the Inter-American Court' (2013) 35 *University of Pennsylvania Journal of International Law* 113; Diana Contreras-Garduño and Sebastiaan Rombouts, 'Collective Reparations for Indigenous Communities before the Inter-American Court of Human Rights' (2011) 27 *Utrecht Journal of International and European Law* 4; Valerio De Oliveira Mazzuoli and Dilton Ribeiro, 'Indigenous Rights before the Inter-American Court of Human Rights: A Call for a Pro Individual Interpretation' (2015) 2 *The Transnational Human Rights Review* 32; Mario Melo, 'Recent Advances in the Justiciability of Indigenous Rights in the Inter-American System of Human Rights' (2006) 4 *SUR* 31; Jo M Pasqualucci, 'The Evolution of International Indigenous Rights in the Inter-American Human Rights System' (2006) 6 *Human Rights Law Review* 281; Aniko Raisz, 'Indigenous Communities before the Inter-American Court of Human Rights – New Century, New Era' (2008) 5 *Miskolc Journal of International Law* 35; Vasiliki Saranti, 'International Justice and Protection of Indigenous Peoples – the Case-Law of the Inter-American Court of Human Rights' (2012) 9 *US-China Law Review* 427.

[166] See eg *Kichwa Indigenous People of Sarayaku v Ecuador* [2012] IACHR 245; *Sawhoyamaxa Indigenous Community v Paraguay* [2006] IACHR 146; *Yakye Axa Indigenous Community v Paraguay* [2005] IACHR 125; *Maya indigenous communities of the Toledo District v Belize* [2004] IACoHR 40/04; IACoHR, 'Indigenous Peoples, Afro-Descendent Communities, and Natural Resources: Human Rights Protection in the Context of Extraction, Exploitation, and Development Activities' (2015) OEA/SerL/V/II Doc 47/15; *Kalina and Lokono Peoples v Suriname* [2015] IACHR 309.

(ie the positive obligation to provide effective remedies against private parties).[167] However, the IACoHR and the IACtHR have even gone a step further than the ECtHR by developing jurisprudence on reparations which should include more than monetary sanctions and compensation for damage. The IACoHR and the IACtHR took into consideration the condition of indigenous peoples who do not value money in the same way as other communities do and that seek instead to enjoy their ancestral lands. Reparations must, therefore, include the restitution of indigenous peoples' lands or the offer to move to another territory where the indigenous people can live in accordance with their own way of life.[168]

As it pertains to the duty to fulfil, the IACoHR and the IACtHR explained in detail the additional steps that states must take beyond the duty to protect. They ruled that states must balance the interests of the corporation and the indigenous peoples. To strike a fair balance, they need to conduct impact assessment analyses, taking into consideration the economic development of the areas, the property rights of corporations as well as the indigenous peoples' communal rights to their lands and natural resources. The IACtHR explained the steps of such an assessment process: (1) states must guarantee the participation of the indigenous community in any decision-making process concerning land exploration or the exploitation of natural resources; (2) states must ensure that indigenous peoples would get some benefit as a result of industrial activities conducted on their ancestral lands; and (3) states must conduct a scientific environmental and social impact assessment before granting any concession to a private industry.[169] Step (3) is particularly detailed. The environmental and social impact assessments:

> (i) … [m]ust be performed by independent and competent teams; (ii) they are a prior condition to being able to award any concession; (iii) they must always be performed prior to the start of any investment or development project; (iv) they must evaluate the real risks of a project in such a way as to minimize them if the project is executed; (v) they must be required by internal law and supervised by the State; and (vi) they must respect the culture and traditions of local communities.[170]

These are prior conditions that the state must meet before approving an investment project that would have an impact on the indigenous population. Interestingly, the IACtHR also recalled the obligation to conduct such an environmental impact assessment in its recent *Advisory Opinion on Environment and Human Rights*. This entails that states must also conduct such an assessment when

[167] See eg *Z and others v the United Kingdom* [2001] ECHR 29392/95; *Paul and Audrey Edwards v the United Kingdom* [2002] ECHR 46477/99; *Ockan and others v Turkey* [2006] ECHR 46771/99; *Taskin and others v Turkey* [2005] ECHR 46117/99; *Hatton and others v the United Kingdom* [2003] ECHR 36022/97; *Hatton and others v the United Kingdom* [2001] ECHR 36022/97.

[168] Antkowiak, 'A Dark Side of Virtue' (n 165); Contreras-Garduño and Rombouts (n 165).

[169] Gonza (n 144); Londoño-Lázaro, Thoene and Pereira-Villa (n 144).

[170] Londoño-Lázaro, Thoene and Pereira-Villa (n 144) 453.

private industries might cause environmental degradation with extraterritorial effects.[171]

This analysis is similar to the one adopted by the ECtHR in *Fadeyeva v Russia*, *Hatton and others v the United Kingdom*, *Moreno Gomez v Spain*, and *Cordella and others v Italy* where it ruled that Article 8 prescribed striking a fair balance between, on the one hand, the opposite environmental and health rights of people living in the vicinity of an industry or airport, and, on the other hand, the economic development such industries may bring to the wider community. The ECtHR has also referred to an environmental impact assessment that the state must conduct in striking such a fair balance.[172] Certainly, the situation of indigenous peoples cannot be equated to that of common citizens, and therefore the ECtHR did not go as far as the IACtHR in defining how such an impact assessment must be conducted and instead left a wider margin of appreciation to the states. Nevertheless, the reasoning of two regional courts is similar in terms of balancing different interests, such as environmental safety and economic development through environmental and social impact assessments.

The African regional system had limited opportunities to adjudicate cases involving indigenous people and corporations. However, it did hold African states to account on the basis of similar standards to those established by the ECtHR and the IACtHR.

The most famous case is the already discussed *SERAC and CESR v Nigeria*, where Nigeria was accused of contributing to the destruction of indigenous peoples' land and environment perpetrated by a Shell subsidiary (Shell Petroleum Development Corporation, 'SPDC') and a state-owned Nigerian corporation (Nigerian National Petroleum Company, 'NNPC').[173] The complainant argued that the Nigerian government covered up the environmentally disruptive corporate activities though military and legal action directed to protect SPDC and NNPC to the detriment of the Ogoni people. This case is different from the IACtHR and ECtHR case-law, because Nigeria was not only responsible for failing to prevent SPCD and NNPC from abusing human rights, but it had actively violated the rights of the Ogoni peoples itself by protecting and aiding SPCD and NNPC with military action. The AfrCoHPR held Nigeria responsible for the violations of multiple rights, including the right to health, housing, food, and the right of people to dispose of their natural resources. It found such violations not only on the basis of the duty to respect, or negative obligations, but also of the duties to protect and fulfil. The Nigerian government had to prevent private corporations, such as SPDC and NNPC, from abusing

[171] *Advisory Opinion on the Environment and Human Rights* (n 144) 156–70.

[172] *Fadeyeva v Russia* [2005] ECHR 55723/00; *Moreno Gomez v Spain* [2005] ECHR 4143/02; *Hatton and others v the United Kingdom* [2003] (n 167); *Hatton and others v the United Kingdom* [2001] (n 167).

[173] *SERAC and CESR v Nigeria* [2001] ACoHPR 155/96.

human rights, instead of aiding them. This included specifically an obligation to conduct an environmental and social impact assessment prior to allowing corporations to invest in a particular project. Interestingly, the AfrCoHPR referred to both the IACtHR's and the ECtHR's jurisprudence to justify its analysis of the positive duties in relation to the conduct of private corporations.[174]

Another relevant case, *Zimbabwe Human Rights NGO Forum v Zimbabwe*, dealt primarily with political violence in Zimbabwe that occurred in 2000 following a constitutional referendum. Although the case did not deal with corporations, the AfrCoHPR dedicated a large section of its decision to non-state actors, and it specifically held

> they are not limited to individuals since some perpetrators of human rights abuses are organisations, corporations or other structures of business and finance, as the research on human rights impacts of oil production or the development of power facilities demonstrates.[175]

By referring again to the ECtHR's and IACtHR's jurisprudence, the AfrCoHPR declared that states have positive duties to protect victims against non-state actors and a duty to fulfil the actual realisation of human rights. These obligations would very much depend on the foreseeability of human rights abuses perpetrated by non-state actors and the ability of states to organise their apparatus to address such abuses. This includes an obligation to conduct a proper investigation and provide effective remedies, as well as an obligation to take the necessary steps to avoid and prevent human rights abuses by non-state actors.[176]

C. The Duty to Protect and Multinational Enterprises

Pursuant to the duty to protect, states must ensure that domestic substantive and procedural laws comply with human rights. Domestic procedural laws shall entitle individuals to effective legal remedies against corporate groups.

However, the ECtHR's jurisprudence has not yet detailed the scope of such an obligation of the state when it relates to effective remedies against multinational enterprises abusing human rights extraterritorially, rather than within the territory of the states parties to the ECHR. The ECtHR has not yet decided a case similar to the case studies, in which a holding company H is incorporated in a European state and its wholly owned subsidiaries, which are incorporated in various developing countries, abuse human rights extraterritorially.

[174] Fons Coomans, 'The Ogoni Case before the African Commission on Human and Peoples' Rights' (2003) 52 *ICLQ* 749; *SERAC and CESR v Nigeria* (n 173).

[175] *Zimbabwe Human Rights NGO Forum v Zimbabwe* [2006] ACoHPR 245/02 136.

[176] ibid 135–64; South African Institute for Advanced Constitutional, Public, Human Rights and International Law (n 145).

Instead, the Treaty Bodies, and recently the IACtHR in its *Advisory Opinion on Environment and Human Rights*, did set out the procedural duty to protect the victims of human rights abuses against multinational enterprises in various Concluding Observations and two General Comments.[177]

In the *Advisory Opinion on Environment and Human Rights* the IACtHR ruled that the states' extraterritorial obligation to protect is also applicable to private actors, including corporations, abusing human rights. Specifically, it declared that states must adequately sanction private actors for their extraterritorial abuses and ensure that they indemnify victims.[178] Furthermore, referring to the jurisprudence of the ECtHR, it ruled that states have an obligation to provide effective remedies and access to justice to the victims of human rights abuses committed by private entities, even in extraterritorial cases.[179] The IACtHR further referred to the already-established jurisprudence of the Treaty Bodies on the obligations of home states to regulate the conduct of companies incorporated within its territory, even when such companies act extraterritorially.[180]

The Treaty Bodies issued multiple Concluding Observations and General Comments which set out the positive duty of states to protect the victims of human rights abuses against multinational enterprises.

In the last Concluding Observations with respect to Germany, the HRC found that the measures taken by Germany were insufficient to address the human rights abuses committed by German companies abroad. According to the HRC:

> The State party is encouraged to set out clearly the expectation that all business enterprises domiciled in its territory and/or its jurisdiction respect human rights standards in accordance with the Covenant throughout their operations. It is also encouraged to take appropriate measures to strengthen the remedies provided to protect people who have been victims of activities of such business enterprises operating abroad.[181]

Although the Concluding Observations are, by their nature, general and broad, they nevertheless address specific issues raised by individuals or NGOs with

177 See eg HRC (n 146) para 16; CESCR, 'Concluding Observations on the Fourth Periodic Report of Austria' (n 146) para 12; CRC, 'General Comment No 16' (n 129) paras 38–44; CRC, 'Concluding Observations on the Combined Second to Fourth Periodic Reports of Switzerland' (n 146) paras 22–23; CRC, 'Consideration of Reports Submitted by States Parties under Article 44 of the Convention Concluding Observations: Australia' (2012) CO 4, paras 27–28; CERD, 'Concluding Observations on the Combined Seventh to Ninth Periodic Reports of the United States of America' (n 146) para 10; CRC, 'Concluding Observations on the Combined Third and Fourth Periodic Report of Canada' (n 146) paras 28–29; CERD, 'Consideration of Reports Submitted by States Parties under Article 9 of the Convention Concluding Observations of the Committee on the Elimination of Racial Discrimination Canada' (2012) CO 19–20, para 14; CERD, 'Consideration of Reports Submitted by States Parties under Article 9 of the Convention Concluding Observations of the Committee on the Elimination of Racial Discrimination United Kingdom of Great Britain and Northern Ireland' (2011) CO 18–20, para 29; CESCR, 'General Comment No 24' (n 129).

178 *Advisory Opinion on the Environment and Human Rights* (n 144) paras 117–18.

179 ibid paras 233–40.

180 ibid para 151.

181 HRC (n 146) para 16.

the HRC. In this respect, it is noteworthy that the HRC made the Concluding Observations set out above referring to a real-life case which was very similar to the hypothetical cases set out in this book. Specifically, the Concluding Observations addressed the report submitted by Global Initiative for Economic, Social and Cultural Rights, an NGO, concerning the activities of a Ugandan company, Kaweri Coffee Plantation Ltd. The company is a subsidiary of Neumann Kaffee Gruppe, a German multinational enterprise. According to the report, the Ugandan government evicted more than 2,000 people from their homes to vacate the territory for Kaweri Coffee Plantation Ltd in order to grow crops of coffee subsequently sold by Neumann Kaffee Gruppe. The report argues that Germany did not comply with its extraterritorial obligation to protect the human rights of Ugandans against the German company, Neumann Kaffee Gruppe. It focuses on the failure of Germany to provide effective legal remedies for the victims of the eviction against Neumann Kaffee Gruppe.[182] The HRC took note of this issue in its Concluding Observations, in which it encouraged Germany to supervise the activities of multinational enterprises investing abroad. The Concluding Observations state that Germany has a positive duty to protect the victims of human rights abuses committed by foreign-based companies affiliated with German corporate groups. They also indirectly confirmed that states have a duty to provide effective remedies against multinational companies to the victims, whose rights have been abused by such corporations.[183]

The CESCR is the Treaty Body that has delivered the most advanced comment on states' obligations to ensure human rights vis-à-vis business. General Comment No 24 on State Obligations under the ICESCR in the Context of Business Activities defines in detail the extraterritorial obligations of home and host states in holding corporations to account when they abuse human rights transnationally. It specifically describes the states' duties to respect, protect and fulfil as well as their extraterritorial application. As it pertains to the duty to protect, it stated:

> 16. The obligation to protect entails a positive duty to adopt a legal framework requiring business entities to exercise human rights due diligence in order to identify, prevent and mitigate the risks of violations of Covenant rights, to avoid such rights being abused, as well as to account for the negative impacts caused or contributed to by their decisions and operations and those of entities they control on the enjoyment of Covenant rights. States should adopt measures such as imposing due diligence requirements to prevent abuses of Covenant rights in a business entity's supply chain and by subcontractors, suppliers, franchisees, or other business partners. …

[182] Neumann Kaffee Gruppe, 'About Us', www.nkg.net/aboutus, accessed 27 November 2016; The Global Initiative for Economic, Social and Cultural Rights (GI-ESCR), 'Parallel Report Submitted by the Global Initiative for Economic, Social and Cultural Rights (GI-ESCR) to the Country Report Task Force of the Human Rights Committee on the Occasion of the Consideration of List of Issues Related to the Sixth Periodic Report of Germany during the Committee's 105th Session' (2012) http://tbinternet.ohchr.org/Treaties/CCPR/Shared%20Documents/DEU/INT_CCPR_NGO_DEU_105_8525_E.pdf, accessed 27 November 2016.

[183] HRC (n 146).

> 33. In discharging their duty to protect, States Parties should also require corporations to deploy their best efforts to ensure that entities whose conduct these corporations may influence, such as subsidiaries (including all business entities in which they have invested, whether registered under the State party's laws or under the laws of another State) or business partners (including suppliers, franchisees or subcontractors) respect Covenant rights. Corporations domiciled in the territory and/or jurisdiction of States Parties should be required to act with due diligence to identify, prevent and address abuses to Covenant rights by such subsidiaries and business partners, wherever they may be located. The Committee underlines that, although the imposition of such due diligence obligations does have impacts on situations located outside these States' national territories since potential violations of Covenant rights in global supply chains or in multinational groups of companies should be prevented or addressed, this does not imply the exercise of extraterritorial jurisdiction by the States concerned. Appropriate monitoring and accountability procedures must be put in place to ensure effective prevention and enforcement. Such procedures may include imposing a duty on companies to report on their policies and procedures to ensure respect for human rights and providing effective means of accountability and redress for abuses to Covenant rights.[184]

The duty to protect would, therefore, entail an obligation of a home state to provide victims with effective remedies against parent corporations. According to the CESCR, this is not an exercise of extraterritorial jurisdiction. Instead, these are domestic procedural guarantees that would have extraterritorial effects on transnational business activities.

In General Comment No 24, the CESCR detailed the content of obligations it has already applied in previous Concluding Observations. For example, it requested Austria to adopt appropriate legislation to ensure that Austrian companies would respect human rights while acting extraterritorially. In its 2013 Concluding Observations on Austria, the CESCR held:

> The Committee is concerned at the lack of oversight over Austrian companies operating abroad with regard to the negative impact of their activities on the enjoyment of economic, social and cultural rights in host countries. … The Committee urges the State party to ensure that all economic, social and cultural rights are fully respected and rights holders adequately protected in the context of corporate activities, including by establishing appropriate laws and regulations, together with monitoring, investigation and accountability procedures to set and enforce standards for the performance of corporations, as underlined in the Committee's statement on the obligations of States parties regarding the corporate sector and economic, social and cultural rights.[185]

Furthermore, in 2016, it requested France to adopt a due-diligence obligation law[186] that, at the time, was still under consideration by the French parliament.

[184] CESCR, 'General Comment No 24' (n 129) paras 16 and 33.

[185] CESCR, 'Concluding Observations on the Fourth Periodic Report of Austria' (n 146) para 12.

[186] Loi 2017-399 du 27 mars 2017 relative au devoir de vigilance des sociétés mères et des entreprises donneuses d'ordre 2017 (JORF).

The French law is the first ever providing victims of human rights abuses with remedies in civil courts against French parent corporations that fail to exercise appropriate due diligence in their supply chains. The CESCR decided:

> 13 The Committee urges the State party to take measures to prevent business enterprises domiciled in its territory or under its jurisdiction from committing human rights violations abroad. In that connection, the Committee encourages the State party to expedite the adoption of a law which would impose a binding obligation on such enterprises to fulfil their duty of care with respect to human rights and would guarantee victims of human rights violations resulting from activities of these enterprises abroad with access to redress in the courts of the State party.[187]

The CRC also wrote a ground-breaking General Comment No 16, on State Obligations Regarding the Impact of the Business Sector on Children's Rights. The Comment specifically addresses the human rights abuses committed by multinational enterprises and the home State's duty to protect.

> Business enterprises increasingly operate on a global scale through complex networks of subsidiaries, contractors, supplies and joint ventures. Their impact on children's rights, whether positive or negative, is rarely the result of the action or omission of a single business unit, whether it is the parent company, subsidiary, contractor, supplier or others. Instead, it may involve a link or participation between businesses units located in different jurisdictions. ... [T]here are particular difficulties for States in discharging their obligations to respect, protect and fulfil the rights of the child in this context owing, among other reasons, to the fact that business enterprises are often legally separate entities located in different jurisdictions even when they operate as an economic unit which has its centre of activity, registration and/or domicile in one country (the home State) and is operational in another (the host State).[188]

The CRC implemented and anticipated General Comment No 16 in several Concluding Observations. For instance, in the 2015 Concluding Observations on Switzerland and in the 2012 Concluding Observations on Australia and Canada, the CRC criticised the lack of effective legal remedies in home states for victims of corporate human rights abuses. The Committee consistently held that adopting voluntary CSR measures is not sufficient for a state to meet the requirements of the duty to protect. According to the 2015 Concluding Observations related to Switzerland:

> [T]he Committee is concerned that the State party solely relies on voluntary self-regulation and does not provide a regulatory framework which explicitly lays down the obligations of companies acting under the State's party jurisdiction or control to respect the rights of the child in operations carried out outside the State party's territory. In the light of its general comment No 16 (2013) on State obligations regarding the impact of the business sector on children's rights, the Committee recommends that the State party: (a) Establish a clear regulatory framework for industries operating

[187] CESCR, 'Concluding Observations on the Fourth Periodic Report of France' (2016) CO 4, para 13.
[188] CRC, 'General Comment No 16' (n 129) para 38.

> in the State party, including through expediting the adoption of the Ruggie Strategy for Switzerland, to ensure that their activities do not negatively affect human rights or endanger environmental, labour and other standards, especially those relating to children's rights, and ensure its effective implementation; (b) Ensure that business enterprises and their subsidiaries operating in or managed from the State party's territory are legally accountable for any violations of children's rights and human rights.[189]

According to the 2012 Concluding Observations on Australia:

> 27. … [W]hile acknowledging the existence of a voluntary code of conduct on a sustainable environment by the Australian Mining Council … the Committee notes the inadequacy of this in preventing direct and/or indirect human rights violations by Australian mining enterprises.
>
> 28. … the Committee recommends that the State party: … [e]xamine and adapt its legislative framework (civil, criminal, administrative) to ensure that legal accountability of Australian companies and their subsidiaries regarding abuses to human rights, especially child rights, committed in the territory of the State party or overseas and establish monitoring mechanisms, investigation, and redress of such abuses, with a view to improving accountability, transparency and prevention of violations.[190]

According to the 2012 Concluding Observations on Canada:

> 28. … [T]he Committee is particularly concerned that the State party lacks a regulatory framework to hold all companies and corporations from the State party accountable for human rights and environmental abuses committed abroad.
>
> 29. The Committee recommends that the State party establish and implement regulations to ensure that the business sector complies with international and national human rights, labour, environment and other standards, particularly with regard to child rights. … [The Committee] recommends that the State party ensure: (a) The establishment of a clear regulatory framework for, inter alia, the gas, mining, and oil companies operating in territories outside Canada to ensure that their activities do not impact on human rights or endanger environment and other standards, especially those related to children's rights; (b) The monitoring of implementation by companies at home and abroad of international and national environmental and health and human rights standards and that appropriate sanctions and remedies are provided when violations occur with a particular focus on the impact on children.[191]

The CRC recognised that home states owe an extraterritorial positive duty to protect children affected by the activities of multinational enterprises. Furthermore, it set up the conditions that trigger a home state's duty to protect foreign nationals affected by corporate human rights abuses.

[189] CRC, 'Concluding Observations on the Combined Second to Fourth Periodic Reports of Switzerland' (n 146) paras 22–23.

[190] CRC, 'Consideration of Reports Submitted by States Parties under Article 44 of the Convention Concluding Observations: Australia' (n 177) paras 27–28.

[191] CRC, 'Concluding Observations on the Combined Third and Fourth Periodic Report of Canada' (n 146) paras 28–29.

> 43. Home States … have obligations, arising under the Convention and the Optional Protocols thereto, to respect, protect and fulfil children's rights in the context of businesses' extraterritorial activities and operations, provided that there is a reasonable link between the State and the conduct concerned. A reasonable link exists when a business enterprise has its centre of activity, is registered or domiciled or has its main place of business or substantial business activities in the State concerned.[192] …
>
> 44. States should enable access to effective judicial and non-judicial mechanisms to provide remedy for children and their families whose rights have been violated by business enterprises extraterritorially when there is a reasonable link between the State and the conduct concerned. Furthermore, States should provide international assistance and cooperation with investigations and enforcement proceedings in other States.[193]

The identification of such a link is a defining factor of the duty to protect. Home states have a duty as long as they can control the activities of private actors. Such control is present when a multinational group, such as the group controlled by H, has its holding company incorporated in the home state. Furthermore, the CRC set out the elements of the duty to protect. Home states must, first, adopt clear laws sanctioning multinational enterprises abusing human rights and, second, provide effective remedies for the victims of such abuses. As long as the home state has a reasonable link with a multinational enterprise, it owes a duty to protect to any victim, regardless of its nationality or residence.

The Committee on the Elimination of Racial Discrimination (CERD) also recognised the home state's duty to protect any victim of human rights abuses committed by private enterprises. For instance, in its 2014 Concluding Observation on the United States, the CERD held:

> [The Committee] reiterates its previous concern regarding the adverse effects of economic activities related to the exploitation of natural resources in countries outside the United States by transnational corporations registered in the State party on the rights to land, health, environment and the way of life of indigenous peoples and minority groups living in these regions. …
>
> The Committee calls upon the State party to … [t]ake appropriate measures to prevent the activities of transnational corporations registered in the State party which could have adverse effects on the enjoyment of human rights by local populations in other countries, especially by indigenous peoples and minorities.[194]

Furthermore, in its 2012 Concluding Observations on Canada, the CERD held:

> [T]he Committee is concerned that the State party has not yet adopted measures with regard to transnational corporations registered in Canada whose activities negatively impact the rights of indigenous peoples outside Canada. … The Committee recommends that the State party take appropriate legislative measures to prevent

[192] De Schutter et al (n 16) pt 25.

[193] CRC, 'General Comment No 16 (2013)' (n 129) paras 43–44; De Schutter et al (n 16) pt 25.

[194] CERD, 'Concluding Observations on the Combined Seventh to Ninth Periodic Reports of the United States of America' (n 146) para 10.

> transnational corporations registered in Canada from carrying out activities that negatively impact on the enjoyment of rights of indigenous peoples in territories outside Canada, and hold them accountable.[195]

As it pertains to the UK, the CERD set out in its 2011 Concluding Observations:

> The Committee is concerned at reports of adverse effects of operations by transnational corporations registered in the State party but conducted outside the territory of the State party that affect the rights of indigenous peoples to land, health, environment and an adequate standard of living. … The Committee encourages the State party to take appropriate legislative and administrative measures to ensure that acts of transnational corporations registered in the State party comply with the provisions of the Convention. In this regard, the Committee recommends that the State party should ensure that no obstacles are introduced in the law that prevent the holding of such transnational corporations accountable in the State party's courts when such violations are committed outside the State party.[196]

Therefore, there is a consensus among the Treaty Bodies to recognise that home states owe a positive duty to protect foreign stakeholders affected by the extraterritorial activities of multinational groups. The positive obligation is based on the notion of control that a home state can exercise over multinational enterprises when their holding companies are registered within its territory. Such a duty to protect entails, first, an obligation to adopt domestic laws sanctioning multinational enterprises abusing human rights abroad, and, second, the requirement to provide the stakeholders with effective remedies in domestic courts against such multinationals.

D. The Duty to Fulfil and Multinational Enterprises

As explained in Chapter 3 and in the preceding sections of this chapter in more detail, the duty to fulfil requires states to do their utmost to prevent or limit human rights abuses and ameliorate the human condition.

The ECtHR, as well as other regional courts and commissions, often interprets such a duty as an obligation to strike a fair balance between the opposing interests at stake in a case. The main avenue regional courts suggest for striking such a balance is through environmental, human rights and social impact assessment. In cases involving private industries, states must assess all the liabilities and risks that industrial activities may imply, evaluate them through a cost–benefit analysis, and assess whether such activities would be acceptable from

[195] CERD, 'Consideration of Reports Submitted by States Parties under Article 9 of the Convention Concluding Observations of the Committee on the Elimination of Racial Discrimination Canada' (n 177) para 14.

[196] CERD, 'Consideration of Reports Submitted by States Parties under Article 9 of the Convention Concluding Observations of the Committee on the Elimination of Racial Discrimination United Kingdom of Great Britain and Northern Ireland' (n 177) para 29.

the human rights perspective.[197] This impact assessment analysis works well in territorial cases concerning a company operating within the territory of one state. However, an open question is how to apply such a cost–benefit analysis to transnational cases. In cases unrelated to corporate conduct, as it pertains to the extraterritorial application of the duty to fulfil, the ECtHR refers to the ability to influence and the possibility for states to ameliorate the human rights conditions abroad through diplomatic or economic means.[198] Given that the ECtHR's jurisprudence has not yet dealt with a case on an extraterritorial breach of a duty to fulfil in connection with the abuses of private industries, it is difficult to imagine how to combine these two sets of jurisprudence on enterprises and extraterritoriality. However, the recent *Advisory Opinion on Environment and Human Rights* by the IACtHR and multiple comments of the Treaty Bodies have provided some avenues to interpret the duty to fulfil in connection with multinational enterprises abusing human rights extraterritorially. These decisions by the IACtHR and the Treaty Bodies would be a persuasive authority in a future case on the extraterritorial application of the ECHR in relation to the human rights abuses committed by private enterprises.

In the *Advisory Opinion on Environment and Human Rights*, the IACtHR has, for the first time ever, connected its jurisprudence on the positive obligation of states to prevent environmental and human rights abuses by private parties, including corporations, with its case-law on extraterritorial jurisdiction.[199] As it pertains to the duty to fulfil, the IACtHR has detailed an obligation to cooperate and negotiate at the international level to prevent extraterritorial environmental damage. Such an obligation includes a duty to keep other states informed and consult with them before engaging or allowing private parties to engage in activities that may have a significant environmental impact.[200]

The UN Treaty Bodies went one step further in defining the meaning of the obligation to cooperate at the international level as it pertains to the extraterritorial human rights abuses committed by corporations. They have applied the state's duty to fulfil to the cases of multinational companies by specifically referring to foreign trade and investment policies.

The decisions of the Treaty Bodies clarify the duty to fulfil as the home state's obligation to influence the conduct of multinational companies abroad.

[197] See eg *Ledyayeva, Dobrokhotova, Zolotareva and Romashina v Russia* [2007] ECHR 53157/99, 53247/99, 53695/00 and 56850/00; *Fadeyeva v Russia* (n 172); *Hatton and others v the United Kingdom* [2003] (n 167); *Hatton and others v the United Kingdom* [2001] (n 167); *Moreno Gomez v Spain* (n 172); *Lopez Ostra v Spain* [1994] ECHR 16798/90; *Taskin and others v Turkey* (n 167); *Kichwa Indigenous People of Sarayaku v Ecuador* (n 166); *Sawhoyamaxa Indigenous Community v Paraguay* (n 166); *Yakye Axa Indigenous Community v Paraguay* (n 166); *Maya indigenous communities of the Toledo District v Belize* (n 166); *Kalina and Lokono Peoples v Suriname* (n 166); *SERAC and CESR v Nigeria* (n 173).

[198] See eg *Nikolaus and Jurgen Treska v Albania and Italy* (n 3); *Vrioni and others v Albania and Italy* (n 4).

[199] *Advisory Opinion on the Environment and Human Rights* (n 144) paras 71–151.

[200] ibid paras 181–210.

The defining factor for the application of the duty to fulfil is the consideration that, although states have neither authority nor control over the overseas subsidiaries of their home companies, they nevertheless have the power to influence such subsidiaries through foreign policies.[201] For example, in the 2014 Concluding Observations on China, the CESCR stated:

> The Committee calls upon the State party to adopt a human rights-based approach to its policies of international cooperation, by: (a) Undertaking a systematic and independent human rights impact assessment prior to making funding decisions; (b) Establishing an effective monitoring mechanism to regularly assess the human rights impact of its policies and projects in the receiving countries and to take remedial measures when required; (c) Ensuring that there is an accessible complaint mechanism for violations of economic, social and cultural rights in the receiving countries.[202]

This definition of the duty to fulfil clarifies that home states should take human rights into account in all of their foreign policy considerations. Given the impact that foreign trade and investment policies have on the transnational conduct of multinational enterprises, the Treaty Bodies have focused many of their decisions on foreign trade and investment. For instance, in the General Comment No 24 on State Obligations under the ICESCR in the Context of Business Activities, the CESCR stated:

> States Parties should identify any potential conflict between their obligations under the Covenant and trade or investment treaties, and refrain from entering into such treaties where such conflicts are found to exist,[203] as required under the principle of the binding character of treaties.[204] The conclusion of such treaties should therefore be preceded by human rights impact assessments, taking into account both the positive and negative human rights impacts of trade and investment treaties, including their contribution to the realization of the right to development. Such impacts on human rights of the implementation of the agreements should be regularly assessed,

[201] See CESCR, 'Concluding Observations on the Second Periodic Report of China, Including Hong Kong, China, and Macao, China' (2014) CO 2, para 12; CRC, 'General Comment No 16 (2013)' (n 129) para 46; CESCR, 'Consideration of Reports Submitted by States Parties under Articles 16 and 17 of the Covenant Concluding Observations of the Committee on Economic, Social and Cultural Rights Switzerland' (2010) CO 2–3, para 24; HR Council, 'Report of the Working Group on the Universal Periodic Review, Switzerland' (2012) 22/11, para 123.85; CRC, 'Consideration of Reports Submitted by States Parties under Article 44 of the Convention Concluding Observations: Republic of Korea' (2012) CO 3–4, paras 26–27; CESCR, 'Concluding Observations on the Fifth Periodic Report of Norway' (n 146) para 6; CESCR, 'Consideration of Reports Submitted by States Parties under Articles 16 and 17 of the Covenant Concluding Observations of the Committee on Economic, Social and Cultural Rights Germany' (2011) CO 5, para 10; Global Initiative for Economic, Social and Cultural Rights (GI-ESCR), 'UN Pronouncements on Extra-Territorial Obligations' (2015) Human Rights Law Sources Working Paper, http://globalinitiative-escr.org/wp-content/uploads/2015/11/151027-Human-Rights-Law-Sources-ETOs.pdf, accessed 17 March 2019.

[202] CESCR, 'Concluding Observations on the Second Periodic Report of China, Including Hong Kong, China, and Macao, China' (n 201) para 12.

[203] See A/HRC/25/54/A001, paras 55 and 59–63.

[204] Articles on Responsibility of States for Internationally Wrongful Acts, Art 5.

> to allow for the adoption of any corrective measures that may be required. The interpretation of trade and investment treaties currently in force should take into account the human rights obligations of the State, consistent with Article 103 of the Charter of the United Nations and with the specific nature of human rights obligations.[205] States Parties cannot derogate from the obligations under the Covenant in trade and investment treaties they may conclude. They are encouraged to insert a provision explicitly referring to their human rights obligations in future treaties, and to ensure that mechanisms for the settlement of investor–State disputes take human rights into account in the interpretation of investment treaties or of investment chapters in trade agreements.[206]

Furthermore, the CRC established the following obligation in its General Comment No 16 on State Obligations Regarding the Impact of the Business Sector on Children's Rights:

> Home States should ensure that there are effective mechanisms in place so that the government agencies and institutions with responsibility for implementation of the Convention and the Optional Protocols thereto coordinate effectively with those responsible for trade and investment abroad. They should also build capacity so that development assistance agencies and overseas missions that are responsible for promoting trade can integrate business issues into bilateral human rights dialogues, including children's rights, with foreign Governments.[207]

The states' business and human rights government agencies should work together to ensure that investment and trade policies respect human rights.

Furthermore, in the 2012 Universal Periodic Review on Switzerland, the Report of the Human Rights Council Working group stated that Switzerland should 'undertake an impact assessment on the possible consequences of its foreign trade policies and investment agreements on the enjoyment of economic, social and cultural rights by the population of its partner countries'.[208]

A number of Concluding Observations have also detailed the duty to fulfil in terms of trade and investment policies. For instance, in its 2010 Concluding Observations on Switzerland, the CESCR held: 'The Committee recommends that the State party comply with its Covenant obligations and take into account its partner countries' obligations when negotiating and concluding trade and investment agreements.'[209]

Furthermore, the CESCR stated in its last Concluding Observations on France that states are responsible for negative human rights externalities that EU trade and investment treaties may have in host countries.[210]

[205] *Sawhoyamaxa Indigenous Community v Paraguay* (n 166) para 140.

[206] CESCR, 'General Comment No 24' (n 129) para 13.

[207] CRC, 'General Comment No 16' (n 129) para 46.

[208] HR Council (n 201) para 123.85.

[209] CESCR, 'Consideration of Reports Submitted by States Parties under Articles 16 and 17 of the Covenant Concluding Observations of the Committee on Economic, Social and Cultural Rights Switzerland' (n 201) para 24.

[210] CESCR, 'Concluding Observations on the Fourth Periodic Report of France' (2016) CO 4.

9. The Committee is concerned by the failure to devote sufficient attention to the impact that bilateral or multilateral trade or investment agreements concluded or being negotiated by the State party or the European Union have or will have on the enjoyment of Covenant rights in the other countries that are party to those agreements. The Committee is particularly concerned by the fact that the mechanisms for settling disputes between States and investors provided for in several agreements could reduce the State's ability to protect and achieve some of the Covenant rights (art 2 (1)).

10. The Committee calls upon the State party to fully assume its obligations under the Covenant in regard to the negotiation and implementation of bilateral and multilateral trade and investment agreements. The Committee encourages the State party, in particular, to:

(a) Ensure that consultations with stakeholders, including the communities concerned, are undertaken in the course of the drafting, negotiation and ratification of such agreements, on the basis of an assessment of the expected impact;
(b) Ensure that an impact assessment is systematically carried out during the implementation of agreements with a view to making adjustments, where appropriate, to the terms of the commitments; and
(c) Ensure that the dispute settlement mechanisms do not jeopardize the State party's ability to fulfil its obligations under the Covenant.[211]

While this provision establishes a rather general obligation, the Treaty Bodies have also detailed in more specific terms both the trade and investment policies that states should adopt to meet their duty to fulfil. As it pertains to trade, the Treaty Bodies set out two main obligations with which states should comply. First, they should conduct preliminary and ongoing impact assessments of the human rights standards adopted in host countries with which they wish to trade. An ongoing impact assessment requires that states should monitor whether the victims of human rights abuses are guaranteed effective remedies in the host countries. In other words, home states should effectively monitor whether host states comply with their duty to protect the host states' people against the home states' investors. The rationale for this requirement is that, if home states boycott trade with countries that are not complying with basic human rights, this will encourage host states to increase their business and human rights record. Second, states should prevent the goods produced by the companies abusing human rights from having access to the home states' markets. This measure should effectively encourage companies to organise their commercial activities in compliance with human rights standards.[212]

[211] ibid 9–10.

[212] See CESCR, 'Concluding Observations on the Second Periodic Report of China, Including Hong Kong, China, and Macao, China' (n 201) para 12; CRC, 'General Comment No 16' (n 129) para 46; CESCR, 'Consideration of Reports Submitted by States Parties under Articles 16 and 17 of the Covenant Concluding Observations of the Committee on Economic, Social and Cultural Rights Switzerland' (n 201) para 24; HR Council (n 201) para 123.85; CRC, 'Consideration of Reports Submitted by States Parties under Article 44 of the Convention Concluding Observations: Republic of Korea' (n 201) paras 26–27; CESCR, 'Concluding Observations on the Fifth Periodic Report

For instance, the CRC held in its 2012 Concluding Observations on the Republic of Korea:

> 26. …[t]he Committee … notes with concern that: (a) The State party is importing products from countries which are under investigation by the International Labour Organization (ILO) (and the European Parliament) for reportedly using forced child labour, thus becoming complicit with a serious breach to child rights; … [(b)] No human rights impact assessment seems to have preceded negotiations for free trade agreements that the State party has entered into or is pending entry into.
>
> 27. … [T]he Committee recommends that the State party: … [(a)] Monitor the entry of products to prevent the importation of those which are produced with forced child labour and to use its trade agreements and national legislation to require that the products entering its market are child labour free; … [(b)] Ensure that prior to the negotiation and conclusion of free trade agreements, human rights assessments including child rights are conducted and measures adopted to prevent violations.[213]

The Treaty Bodies also took similar decisions with respect to foreign investment policies made to protect companies headquartered in home states. These decisions focus on the support that home states provide for their nationals that outsource their production abroad. The Treaty Bodies argued that, while protecting investors, home states should have regard to the rights of foreign stakeholders. For instance, the CESCR wrote the following on the overseas activities of German companies:

> The Committee expresses concern that the State party's policy-making process in, as well as its support for, investments by German companies abroad does not give due consideration to human rights. … [T]he Committee calls on the State party to ensure that its policies on investments by German companies abroad serve the economic, social and cultural rights in the host countries.[214]

In this case, although the CESCR recognised the efforts of Germany to promote fundamental rights, it found that its foreign investment policies protect German companies, while they are not ensuring that the same companies respect human rights. Furthermore, in its opinion on Norway the CESCR wrote:

> The Committee recommends that the State party ensure that investments by the Norges Bank Investment Management in foreign companies operating in third countries are subject to a comprehensive human rights impact assessment (prior to and during the investment). The Committee also recommends that the State party adopts policies and other measures to prevent human rights contraventions abroad

of Norway' (n 146) para 6; CESCR, 'Consideration of Reports Submitted by States Parties under Articles 16 and 17 of the Covenant Concluding Observations of the Committee on Economic, Social and Cultural Rights Germany' (n 201) para 10.

[213] CRC, 'Consideration of Reports Submitted by States Parties under Article 44 of the Convention Concluding Observations: Republic of Korea' (n 201) paras 26–27.

[214] CESCR, 'Consideration of Reports Submitted by States Parties under Articles 16 and 17 of the Covenant Concluding Observations of the Committee on Economic, Social and Cultural Rights Germany' (n 201) para 10.

> by corporations that have their main offices under the jurisdiction of the State party, without infringing the sovereignty or diminishing the obligations of the host States under the Covenant.[215]

According to the CESCR, the home state has an obligation to control the overseas activities of its multinational corporations with a view to preventing human rights abuses. This goal can be achieved through investment policies that home states should take only after conducting an impact assessment on the enjoyment of human rights in the relevant host states and ensuring the ongoing monitoring of such investment policies as to their compliance with the obligations of the states to protect human rights.[216]

Therefore, the Treaty Bodies have developed a quite detailed jurisprudence on the home states obligations to adopt trade and investment policies that would influence the conduct of multinational enterprises in order to prevent human rights abuses in host countries. This jurisprudence is providing a tangible definition of the duty to fulfil with respect to the transnational conduct of multinational enterprises.

III. THE EXTRATERRITORIAL APPLICATION TO THE CASE STUDIES

This section sets out a possible scenario of the ECHR extraterritorial application to the three case studies, when a foreign subsidiary S, of a corporate group headquartered in the United Kingdom, abuses human rights in the host states, namely Bangladesh, Ecuador and Nigeria.

As it pertains to the duty to protect, the United Kingdom would have to provide effective remedies to victims against the parent company H for the abuses committed by its subsidiary S. This would be a territorial positive obligation of the United Kingdom with extraterritorial effect. The United Kingdom exercises authority and control over the parent company and would have to provide effective remedies within its territory, but this would have extraterritorial repercussions. As it pertains to the duty to fulfil, the United Kingdom would have to do its utmost to influence the extraterritorial conduct of multinational enterprises headquartered in the United Kingdom. This would include taking diplomatic and economic measures at both the national and international level.

[215] CESCR, 'Concluding Observations on the Fifth Periodic Report of Norway' (n 146) para 6.

[216] See CESCR, 'Concluding Observations on the Second Periodic Report of China, Including Hong Kong, China, and Macao, China' (n 201) para 12; CESCR, 'Consideration of Reports Submitted by States Parties under Articles 16 and 17 of the Covenant Concluding Observations of the Committee on Economic, Social and Cultural Rights: Switzerland' (n 201) para 24; CESCR, 'Concluding Observations on the Fifth Periodic Report of Norway' (n 146) para 6; CESCR, 'Consideration of Reports Submitted by States Parties under Articles 16 and 17 of the Covenant Concluding Observations of the Committee on Economic, Social and Cultural Rights Germany' (n 201) para 10.

A. Duty to Protect

The procedural duty to protect requires that the United Kingdom shall guarantee victims effective legal remedies within its territory. However, the application of the duty to protect in the context of multinational groups is complicated by various extraterritorial effects of their activities. In principle, the United Kingdom shall provide an effective legal remedy against the UK holding company H. Such state conduct is territorial in nature. The United Kingdom has authority over the holding company H controlling the subsidiaries S which allegedly perpetrates human rights abuses abroad. However, the United Kingdom does not have jurisdiction over the victims of human rights abuses Bodhi, Elsa and Naoki, who are nationals and residents of Bangladesh, Ecuador and Nigeria, respectively. The issue is whether the United Kingdom has sufficient link to H's failure to exercise effective control over the human rights abuses committed by its foreign subsidiaries S. This chapter proved, on the basis of the relevant case-law of the ECtHR, that the United Kingdom has such a jurisdictional link for the following reasons.

First, the ECtHR confirmed in *Markovic v Italy*[217] that, once the state has jurisdiction over a perpetrator of a human rights abuse, the ECHR is applicable. According to *Markovic v Italy*, the state is under an obligation to ensure foreign applicants with the right of access to domestic courts against the perpetrator of extraterritorial human rights abuses, as long as the respondent is within the state's jurisdiction. The ECtHR asserts jurisdiction over the victim once s/he files a complaint in domestic courts.[218] In the Bangladeshi, Nigerian and Ecuadorian case studies, H failed to regulate its corporate group from the United Kingdom in a manner which would ensure that its overseas subsidiaries respect human rights. This failure to regulate the activities of its subsidiaries in accordance with human rights is an act which occurred within the jurisdiction of the United Kingdom, where H is incorporated. The United Kingdom must ensure effective legal remedies against H as it is the head of a British corporate group.

Second, the ECtHR could protect the human rights victims Bodhi, Elsa and Naoki *par ricochet*. Similar to *Soering v the United Kingdom*,[219] in the hypothetical case studies a territorial conduct occurring within the United Kingdom has as a direct consequence an extraterritorial violation of the human rights of victims Bodhi, Elsa and Naoki in Bangladesh, Ecuador and Nigeria, respectively. In *Soering v the United Kingdom*, the extradition of Mr Soering by the United Kingdom to the United States would have exposed Mr Soering to a potential death penalty in Virginia. In the case studies, H's failure to exercise *due diligence* over its corporate group results in human rights abuses occurring overseas.

[217] *Markovic and others v Italy* (n 53).
[218] ibid 54.
[219] *Soering v the United Kingdom* (n 46).

The only substantial difference between the two cases is that, while *Soering v the United Kingdom* dealt with a negative obligation, ie the conduct of state authorities which would have sent Mr Soering to the United States,[220] the case studies deal with a positive obligation, ie the failure of the state to regulate the activities of a third party. However, this difference between positive and negative obligations is no longer substantial, as the ECtHR has consistently ruled that the ECHR is equally applicable in both cases. Thus, the protection *par ricochet* applies to the victims of human rights violations in all three case studies.[221]

Third, in *Rantsev v Cyprus and Russia*, the ECtHR ruled that Russia had an obligation to investigate the Russian cell of a transnational human traffick which resulted in the death of a Russian citizen in Cyprus. Although the ECtHR clarified that Russia had no obligation to investigate the death of Ms Rantseva occurring in Cyprus, because both the victim and the perpetrators of the murder where outside of Russia's authority and control, it held Russia accountable for failing to investigate the Russian cell of that transnational chain. By analogy, the parent company incorporated in the United Kingdom is part of a transnational corporate chain. The United Kingdom should, therefore, investigate its links and relationships to the extraterritorial abuses committed by its foreign subsidiary.

For the avoidance of doubt, the above obligation does not require that the United Kingdom should provide an effective legal remedy against foreign corporations, because the United Kingdom has no control over them. This conclusion follows from *Al-Adsani v the United Kingdom*,[222] *Jones and others v the United Kingdom*[223] and *Nait-Liman v Switzerland*,[224] in which the ECtHR ruled that the states have no obligation to provide for universal jurisdiction when both the victims of human rights abuses and the perpetrators of such acts are outside of the states' jurisdiction and the human rights abuse occurred in a foreign land.

Therefore, under the ECHR, the United Kingdom has a procedural duty to provide foreign victims of human rights abuses, such as Bodhi, Elsa and Naoki, with an effective legal remedy against the holding company H, being a multinational company incorporated within its territory.

This analysis of the ECtHR's case-law is corroborated by the rulings, Concluding Observations and General Comments of the regional American and African committees and courts, as well as the Treaty Bodies. Although there are differences in terms of the level of details these bodies have achieved in developing the positive obligations of states to provide effective remedies against corporations abusing human rights extraterritorially, they all agree on a possible extraterritorial application of their treaties, even in cases involving private

[220] ibid.
[221] See Bartole, De Sena and Zagrebelsky (n 48) 16–17.
[222] *Al-Adsani v the United Kingdom* (n 72).
[223] *Jones and others v the United Kingdom* (n 73).
[224] *Nait-Liman v Switzerland* (n 74); *Nait-Liman v Switzerland* (n 78).

actors and positive obligations. The Treaty Bodies are the most advanced in this respect with numerous Concluding Observations and General Comments dedicated specifically to the positive obligations of home States to provide effective remedies to victims of human rights abuses committed in the host states.[225] Furthermore, the IACtHR has also reiterated the same concept, although in more general terms, in its *Advisory Opinion on Environment and Human Rights*.[226]

Therefore, the United Kingdom has a duty to protect victims Bodhi, Elsa and Naoki against H, for the human rights abuses committed by its subsidiary S in Bangladesh, Ecuador and Nigeria. However, for the reasons set out in Chapter 2, currently, the United Kingdom does not provide effective legal remedies for victims Bodhi, Elsa and Naoki against the holding company H. Furthermore, it does not establish any domestic law sanctioning the extraterritorial human rights abuses committed by British multinational enterprises.

B. Duty to Fulfil

The duty to fulfil requires states to influence private parties to respect human rights and may include both territorial and extraterritorial measures. The key point in the cases of multinational companies is that the home states' measures would have to influence the behaviour of the subsidiary S which is abusing human rights extraterritorially. Therefore, through the control that it exercises over the holding company H, the home state should attempt to influence the activities of S. The ECtHR developed a *best-effort* obligation to '[t]ake the diplomatic, economic, judicial or other measures … [t]o secure to applicants the rights guaranteed by the Convention'.[227] It also clarified that European States have jurisdiction for the purpose of Article 1 when they have the ability to influence a foreign actor through such 'diplomatic, economic, judicial or other measures'.[228]

[225] HRC (n 146) para 16; CESCR, 'Concluding Observations on the Fourth Periodic Report of Austria' (n 146) para 12; CRC, 'General Comment No 16' (n 129) paras 38–44; CRC, 'Concluding Observations on the Combined Second to Fourth Periodic Reports of Switzerland' (n 146) paras 22–23; CRC, 'Consideration of Reports Submitted by States Parties under Article 44 of the Convention Concluding Observations Australia' (n 177) paras 27–28; CERD, 'Concluding Observations on the Combined Seventh to Ninth Periodic Reports of the United States of America' (n 146) 10; CRC, 'Concluding Observations on the Combined Third and Fourth Periodic Report of Canada' (n 146) paras 28–29; CERD, 'Consideration of Reports Submitted by States Parties under Article 9 of the Convention Concluding Observations of the Committee on the Elimination of Racial Discrimination Canada' (n 177) para 14; CERD, 'Consideration of Reports Submitted by States Parties under Article 9 of the Convention Concluding Observations of the Committee on the Elimination of Racial Discrimination United Kingdom of Great Britain and Northern Ireland' (n 177) para 29; CESCR, 'General Comment No 24' (n 129).

[226] *Advisory Opinion on the Environment and Human Rights* (n 144).

[227] *Nikolaus and Jurgen Treska v Albania and Italy* (n 3) 12 (b) Complaint under Article 1 of Protocol No 1 (ii) The Court's assessment.

[228] ibid.

Accordingly, applying this principle to the case studies, the United Kingdom should arguably take territorial or extraterritorial diplomatic, economic and judicial measures to prevent S, the subsidiaries of the UK holding company H, from abusing human rights. The ECtHR has not yet determined the measures that should be taken by a state to stop multinational enterprises from abusing human rights extraterritorially. However, its jurisprudence has already established the duty for governments to conduct human rights impact assessments when they adopt various policies, including those allowing private industries to harm the health of people or the environment.[229] The IACtHR ruled in its recent unprecedented *Advisory Opinion on Environment and Human Rights* that such an impact assessment analysis should also be conducted in extraterritorial cases, when the activities conducted by private actors, such as corporations, may have an extraterritorial detrimental effect.[230]

Arguably, all measures taken by a state may require such a human rights impact assessment. However, trade and investment policies seem particularly relevant to the case of corporations abusing human rights extraterritorially. In fact, the Treaty Bodies, as well as the ECHR Committee of Ministers, have already emphasised that investment and trade policies could be a fundamental tool to influence the conduct of multinational enterprises.[231] The open question is how the ECtHR would assess the influence that states may have on trade and investment agreements in terms of measures that they could take to secure the applicant's rights in a concrete case. This section conducts such an analysis in respect of the BITs signed by the United Kingdom with the host states of the case studies: Bangladesh, Ecuador and Nigerian.

The United Kingdom has signed 110 BITs, including with Bangladesh,[232] Nigeria[233] and Ecuador,[234] to protect British investors.[235] According to these

[229] See eg *Lopez Ostra v Spain* (n 197); *Fadeyeva v Russia* (n 172); *Ledyayeva, Dobrokhotova, Zolotareva and Romashina v Russia* (n 197); *Hatton and others v the United Kingdom* [2003] (n 167); *Hatton and others v the United Kingdom* [2001] (n 167); *Taskin and others v Turkey* (n 167).

[230] *Advisory Opinion on the Environment and Human Rights* (n 144).

[231] See CESCR, 'Concluding Observations on the Second Periodic Report of China, Including Hong Kong, China, and Macao, China' (n 201) para 12; CRC, 'General Comment No 16' (n 129) para 46; CESCR, 'Consideration of Reports Submitted by States Parties under Articles 16 and 17 of the Covenant Concluding Observations of the Committee on Economic, Social and Cultural Rights Switzerland' (n 201) para 24; HR Council (n 201) para 123.85; CRC, 'Consideration of Reports Submitted by States Parties under Article 44 of the Convention Concluding Observations: Republic of Korea' (n 201) paras 26–27; CESCR, 'Concluding Observations on the Fifth Periodic Report of Norway' (n 146) para 6; CESCR, 'Consideration of Reports Submitted by States Parties under Articles 16 and 17 of the Covenant Concluding Observations of the Committee on Economic, Social and Cultural Rights Germany' (n 201) para 10; De Schutter et al (n 16) pt 29; Committee of Ministers, 'Recommendation of the Committee of Ministers to Member States on Human Rights and Business' (2016) CM/Rec(2016)3 paras 23–25.

[232] Agreement between the Government of the United Kingdom of Great Britain and Northern Ireland and the Government of the People's Republic of Bangladesh for the Promotion and Protection of Investments 1980 (Treaty Series No 73).

BITs, the definition of an 'investment' always includes shares in companies. Investors may be either individuals or corporations. Therefore, the BITs between the United Kingdom and Bangladesh, Nigeria and Ecuador apply to the three case studies: H is a British company and a shareholder investing respectively in the Bangladeshi, Ecuadorian and Nigerian subsidiaries S. Accordingly, the BITs will protect H investing in Bangladesh, Nigeria and Ecuador through its subsidiaries. Such protection includes provisions requiring Bangladesh, Nigeria and Ecuador to compensate any losses which are incurred by H due to wars, revolutions or national emergencies, and not to expropriate the assets of the UK holding company H without fair compensation.

The UK BITs could be fundamental to determine the content of the United Kingdom's duty to fulfil. Although the United Kingdom is committed to protect British companies investing abroad, it is not equally committed to protecting the rights of individuals living in foreign jurisdictions against the wrongful acts of UK investors. None of these BITs includes any provision acknowledging the rights of stakeholders and the human rights obligations of multinational companies. Arguably, the ECtHR could find the United Kingdom to be in violation of a duty to fulfil because, while it has successfully negotiated the recognition of the investors' rights, it fails to consider any meaningful protection of human rights which can be abused by its investors. This essentially means that the United Kingdom could influence, through its foreign policy, the attitude of investors towards human rights, but it fails to do so.

It goes without saying that, in the first place, BITs are meant to protect investors and not human rights. However, it is striking to note that, although the United Kingdom, and European states in general, successfully protect their investors abroad, they have not ensured a comparable level of protection for the stakeholders detrimentally affected by the industrial activities of such investors.[236]

[233] Agreement between the Government of the Federal Republic of Nigeria and the Government of the United Kingdom of Great Britain and Northern Ireland for the Promotion and Protection of Investments 1991 (Treaty Series No 66).

[234] Agreement between the Government of the United Kingdom of Great Britain and Northern Ireland and the Government of the Republic of Ecuador for the Promotion and Protection of Investments 1996 (Treaty Series No 18).

[235] 'United Kingdom | Bilateral Investment Treaties (BITs)', http://investmentpolicyhub.unctad.org/IIA/CountryBits/221, accessed 29 December 2016.

[236] See M Sornarajah, *The International Law on Foreign Investment*, 3rd edn (Cambridge University Press, 2010) 144–71; Coomans and Künnemann (n 10) 5–102; De Schutter, 'Le contrôle du respect des droits de l'homme par les sociétés transnationales' (n 10); De Schutter, 'Extraterritorial Jurisdiction' (n 10); Joseph E Stiglitz, 'Multinational Corporations: Balancing Rights and Responsibilities' (2007) 101 *Proceedings of the ASIL Annual Meeting* 3; Patrick Dumberry and Gabrielle Dumas-Aubin, 'How to Impose Human Rights Obligations on Corporations under Investment Treaties?' (2011) 4 *Yearbook on International Investment Law and Policy* 569; Ryan Suda, 'The Effect of Bilateral Investment Treaties on Human Rights Enforcement and Realization', in *Transnational Corporations and Human Rights* (Hart Publishing, 2006).

IV. CONCLUSION

The ECtHR applies a three-pillar approach to analysing the issue of extraterritoriality.

The first pillar includes the cases when a state acts extraterritorially and establishes extraterritorial jurisdiction over a foreign territory. In these cases, the ECHR applies to a foreign land. *Bankovic and others v Belgium* and *Al-Skeini and others v the United Kingdom* set out the following two tests when a state exercises extraterritorial jurisdiction: first, when a state has effective control over a foreign territory; and, second, when a state has authority and control over a person located in a foreign land.

The second pillar includes the cases when a state acts territorially, but its conduct has extraterritorial effects. The ECtHR has progressively developed this pillar through the following leading cases: *Soering v the United Kingdom*, *Markovic v Italy*, *Rantsev v Cyprus and Russia*, *Al-Adsani v the United Kingdom*, *Jones and others v the United Kingdom* and *Nait-Liman v Switzerland.* In *Soering v the United Kingdom*, the UK was required to act territorially and had jurisdiction over a victim of a human rights abuse. In *Markovic v Italy* and *Rantsev v Cyprus and Russia*, the state was required to act territorially and had jurisdiction over a perpetrator of a human rights abuse. In *Al-Adsani v the United Kingdom*, *Jones and others v the United Kingdom* and *Nait-Liman v Switzerland*, the state had no jurisdiction over either the perpetrator or the victim of the human rights abuse. The analysis of these cases permits the development of a rule applicable to European states that should provide effective remedies within their territories with extraterritorial effects. This rule will read as follows: if a state has jurisdiction over either a perpetrator or a victim of the human rights abuse, the ECHR applies to the case. Instead, if, as it was in *Al-Adsani v the United Kingdom* and *Jones and others v the United Kingdom*, the state has no jurisdiction over either a victim or the perpetrator of a human rights abuse that occurred in a foreign land, the ECHR is not applicable, as there is no jurisdictional link between the state and the human rights violation.

The third pillar includes the cases when a state has no control over the foreign territory or persons. In these cases, states are still under a *best-effort* obligation to secure the respect for human rights abroad. Such an obligation depends on the state's ability to influence a foreign actor.

This chapter analysed how the duty to protect and the duty to fulfil fit within the extraterritorial framework described above.

The duty to protect applies when a state is acting territorially with extraterritorial effects. In the three hypothetical case studies, the procedural duty to protect requires the United Kingdom to provide effective legal remedies for the human rights victims Bodhi, Elsa and Naoki against the UK-incorporated holding company H, the subsidiaries of which are responsible for human rights abuses. Providing effective legal remedies against the holding company H is a territorial action, because such a company is incorporated in the United Kingdom. Therefore, under the ECHR, the United Kingdom should provide effective remedies to the victims, because it has jurisdiction over the alleged perpetrator of human rights abuses (H). As a result, the procedural duty to protect fits within the existing ECHR's second pillar: the obligations of states to act territorially with extraterritorial effects.

The duty to fulfil may apply either when a state is acting territorially or extraterritorially. The specific action to be taken by a state to comply with its duty to fulfil will be different in each individual case, because such a duty requires the state to do its utmost in a given situation to secure human rights. When the duty to fulfil requires the United Kingdom to influence the conduct of multinational companies headquartered within its territory, two policy areas are particularly relevant: trade and investment. The case studies would fit within the existing ECHR's third pillar: the obligation of states to influence the conduct of foreign actors, such as corporations.

This interpretation of the ECtHR's jurisprudence as applicable to the duties to protect and fulfil vis-à-vis the conduct of multinational enterprises is supported by the numerous decisions, Concluding Observations, and General Comments of human rights courts, committees and Treaty Bodies. Although different in their content, all of these decisions confirm that home states have positive obligations to ensure human rights against multinational enterprises acting transnationally.

5

An Agenda for Legal Reform

THIS BOOK HAS proposed empowering human rights victims to bring legal action before the ECtHR against European states for their failure to regulate the overseas activities of European multinational enterprises. Recently, several groups of human rights victims, which had suffered from abuses committed by multinational companies, have filed suits against corporate groups in European domestic courts. These lawsuits were often unsuccessful, as domestic company and tort laws are not designed to adequately address the highly complex corporate engineering of current multinational enterprises.[1] The state of the law is not satisfactory as it does not secure the rights of stakeholders adversely affected by European corporate groups.

Under the ECHR, states shall meet their positive obligation to secure, which includes the duties to protect and fulfil. According to the duty to protect, states must guarantee effective remedies for the victims of human rights abuses against European parent companies. According to the duty to fulfil, states should also do their utmost to prevent multinational enterprises from abusing human rights.[2]

[1] See eg Menno T Kamminga, 'Transnational Human Rights Litigation against Multinational Corporations Post-Kiobel', *What's Wrong with International Law? Liber Amicorum AHA Soons* (Brill/Nijhoff, 2015); Liesbeth Enneking, *Foreign Direct Liability and Beyond – Exploring the Role of Tort Law in Promoting International Corporate Social Responsibility and Accountability* (Eleven International Publishing, 2012); Liesbeth Enneking, 'The Future of Foreign Direct Liability? Exploring the International Relevance of the Dutch Shell Nigeria Case' (2014) 10 *Utrecht Law Review* 44; Richard Meeran, 'Tort Litigation against Multinational Corporations for Violation of Human Rights: An Overview of the Position Outside the United States' (2011) 3 *City University of Hong Kong Law Review* 1; Philipp Wesche and Miriam Saage-Maaß, 'Holding Companies Liable for Human Rights Abuses Related to Foreign Subsidiaries and Suppliers before German Civil Courts: Lessons from *Jabir and Others v KiK*' (2016) 16 *Human Rights Law Review* 370; Nicola Jägers and Marie-Jose van der Heijden, 'Corporate Human Rights Violations: The Feasibility of Civil Recourse in the Netherlands' (2008) 33(3) *Brooklyn Journal of International Law* 833.

[2] See Manfred Nowak, *U.N. Covenant on Civil and Political Rights: CCPR Commentary* (2nd edn, Engel 2005) 37–40; Pisillo Riccardo Mazzeschi, 'Responsabilité de l'état Pour Violation Des Obligations Positives Relatives Aux Droits de l'homme' in *Collected Courses of the Hague Academy of International Law* 333 (M Nijhoff 2008) 242–249 and 311–389; Ioannis Panoussis, 'L'obligation générale de protection des droits de l'homme dans la jurisprudence des organes internationaux' (2007) 70 *Revue trimestrielle des droits de l''homme* 427; Magdalena Sepúlveda Carmona, *The Nature of the Obligations under the International Covenant on Economic, Social, and Cultural Rights* (Intersentia 2003) 115–248; Eyal Benvenisti, 'Sovereigns as Trustees of Humanity: On the Accountability of States to Foreign Stakeholders' (2013) 107 *The American Journal of International Law* 295; Dimitris Xenos, *The Positive Obligations of the State under the European Convention of Human Rights* (Routledge 2011); Frédéric Sudre, 'Les "obligations positives" dans la jurisprudence européenne des droits de l'homme' (1995) 23 *Revue trimiestrelle des droits de l'homme* 363;

However, as set out in Chapters 1 and 2, the current state of the law neither provides effective remedies for the victims of human rights abuses, nor adequately prevents multinational companies from abusing human rights. Chapter 2 demonstrated, with respect to three hypothetical case studies, the real-world legal hurdles that overseas victims of human rights abuses encounter when they want to bring the European-based parent company controlling the foreign subsidiaries responsible for such abuses to justice. Victims Bodhi, Elsa and Naoki would have limited chances of succeeding in holding a European multinational enterprise liable for the human rights abuses perpetrated by its subsidiaries in Bangladesh, Ecuador or Nigeria under both international, European or domestic UK law. The United Kingdom was taken just as an example of a jurisdiction that has one of the most developed company and tort laws in Europe, but a similar analysis could apply to many other, if not all, European jurisdictions. Under the ECHR, the absence of effective remedies in the United Kingdom available to Bodhi, Elsa and Naoki against a holding company H constitutes a violation of the United Kingdom's duty to protect the victims of human rights abuses from private entities. Furthermore, under the ECHR, the failure of UK domestic law to prevent human rights abuses committed by British multinational enterprises is a breach of the duty to fulfil.

Against this background, this book argued that the victims of human rights abuses, whose claims are unsuccessful in domestic courts, should bring actions against states in the ECtHR. By holding states responsible for their failure to regulate the activities of multinational companies, the victims of human rights abuses would encourage European states to take a closer look at the role of multinational enterprises in their domestic and foreign policies and the effects which the overseas activities of such companies have on human rights. If the victims of human rights abuses, Bodhi, Elsa and Naoki, had attempted, unsuccessfully, to sue the holding company H in English courts and had exhausted all domestic remedies, they could file a complaint against the United Kingdom at the ECtHR. As set out in Chapters 3 and 4, they may argue that the United Kingdom is in breach of Article 1 of the ECHR, which sets out a positive obligation of states to secure the rights of individuals affected by the activities of private parties, including companies. Furthermore, it may be argued that the United Kingdom violates Article 13 in conjunction with Articles 3 and 8 as it pertains to the duty to protect the victims of workplace abuses, environmental degradation and militarised commerce, and Articles 3 and 8 as it pertains to the duty to fulfil the overall objective to stop companies from abusing human rights.

To comply with their ECHR obligations, states must reform the current state of the law. The open question would be how to reform the law. As explained

Colombine Madelaine, *La technique des obligations positives en droit de la convention européenne des droits de l'homme* (Dalloz 2014); AR Mowbray, *The Development of Positive Obligations under the European Convention on Human Rights by the European Court of Human Rights* (Hart Publishing 2004).

in Chapter 3, under the ECHR, states have a wide margin of appreciation in regulating the activities of multinational companies. The ECtHR has consistently ruled that it is not for the court to determine the regulations that states should adopt to meet their obligations. However, whatever rule the states decide to implement, they must, first, guarantee effective remedies for the victims of human rights abuses as required under the duty to protect, and, second, prevent companies from abusing human rights in compliance with the duty to fulfil.

Given that the ECtHR does not provide further guidance as to the exact laws and regulations that states could implement to meet their duties, this chapter proposes some avenues for legal reform. The proposals below clarify what states could, but fail to, do to meet their duties. It analyses how states could improve the conditions of human rights victims by changing domestic, EU and international law. Given that ultimately each state is the duty-bearer towards the victims of human rights abuses, it is for the state to change its laws in accordance with the ECHR. States could implement the legal reforms needed to comply with the ECHR requirements at the national, international or EU level. Furthermore, if the states parties to the Council of Europe would decide to introduce, together with non-European countries, some new legislation regulating the activities of multinational companies, they would also be bound to implement such international legislation in accordance with the ECHR.

Accordingly, this concluding chapter proposes an agenda for legal reform to be implemented by European States.

I. DUTY TO PROTECT

According to the duty to protect, states have to provide the victims of human rights with effective legal remedies against corporate groups. This means that states should hold multinational companies accountable on the basis of an effective standard of review or secondary norm.[3] The combination of international, EU and domestic laws determines the standard of review or secondary norm applicable to multinational companies. However, as set out in Chapter 2, the standard of review currently applicable to multinational corporations in Europe does not meet the requirements of the duty to protect. This is for the following reasons. First, there is no legally binding international framework to hold multinational companies accountable for human rights abuses.[4]

[3] See Nowak (n 2) 39–40; Mazzeschi (n 2) 311–89; Panoussis (n 2); Sepúlveda Carmona (n 2) 115–248; Eva Brems, 'Procedural Protection', in *Shaping Rights in the ECHR: The Role of the European Court of Human Rights in Determining the Scope of Human Rights* (Cambridge University Press, 2014).

[4] See Surya Deva, 'Human Rights Violations by Multinational Corporations and International Law: Where from Here?' (2003) 19 *Connecticut Journal of International Law* 1; Sarah Joseph, 'Taming the Leviathans: Multinational Enterprises and Human Rights' (1999) 46 *Netherlands International Law Review* 171; Peter Muchlinski, *Multinational Enterprises and the Law*, 2nd edn (Oxford University Press, 2007).

Second, EU rules regulating the conflict of laws do not take into account the objective to protect human rights (as, for example, they take into account the overall purpose to protect the environment), and, as a result, do not favour laws complying with the ECHR over laws violating human rights.[5] Third, the domestic laws of European states lack effective judicial remedies aimed at preventing corporate groups from evading their human rights obligations.[6]

This section proposes two main solutions for states to meet the duty to protect. First, states could establish new binding human rights obligations for businesses under either international, European or national law. Second, states could modify the standard of review or secondary norms currently applicable to multinational corporations in their domestic systems. This second solution would require states to change the rules regulating civil litigation against companies at both the EU and national level. Specifically, states could change the conflict-of-laws and liability regimes applicable to multinational enterprises.

A. New Binding Obligations

States could comply with the ECHR by imposing binding obligations on multinational enterprises. In order to provide stakeholders with effective remedies against companies and, therefore, be in compliance with the duty to protect, the laws establishing binding obligations for multinational enterprises should, as a minimum requirement, include the following elements. First, such laws should be applicable horizontally among private parties, including companies and individuals. Second, such laws should establish a court competent to receive individual

[5] See Alexandra Gatto, *Multinational Enterprises and Human Rights: Obligations under EU Law and International Law* (Edward Elgar, 2011); Daniel Augenstein, 'Study on the Legal Framework on Human Rights and the Environment Applicable to European Enterprises Operating Outside the European Union' (University of Edinburgh, 2010) http://ec.europa.eu/DocsRoom/documents/11865/attachments/1/translations/en/renditions/native, accessed 17 March 2019; Jan Wouters and Cedric Ryngaert, 'Litigation for Overseas Corporate Human Rights Abuse in the European Union: The Challenge of Jurisdiction' (2008) 40 *George Washington International Law Review* 939; Claire Bright, 'L'accès à la justice civile en cas de violations des droits de l'homme par des entreprises multinationales' (2013) http://cadmus.eui.eu/handle/1814/29602, accessed 15 April 2016; Antonio Gigante, 'La politica delle istituzioni comunitarie in materia di responsabilita sociale d'impresa: voluntary o mandatory approach?' (2008) IV *Diritto pubblico comparato ed europeo* 1991.

[6] See David Kershaw, *Company Law in Context: Text and Materials*, 2nd edn (Oxford University Press 2012) 30–78; Karen Vanderkerckhove, *Piercing the Corporate Veil* (Kluwer/Aspen, 2007) 66–76; Phillip I Blumberg, 'Limited Liability and Corporate Groups' (1985) 11 *The Journal of Corporate Law* 573; David W Leebron, 'Limited Liability, Tort Victims, and Creditors' (1991) 91 *Columbia Law Review* 1565; Gwynne Skinner, 'Rethinking Limited Liability of Parent Corporations for Foreign Subsidiaries' Violations of International Human Rights Law' (2015) 72 *Washington and Lee Law Review* 1769.

complaints when multinational enterprises abuse human rights.[7] States could establish such a law at the international, European or domestic level.

Two main issues are fundamental in terms of adopting laws that are binding on multinational enterprises. First, what would the content of such laws be. Second, what enforcement mechanism would ensure that such laws are implemented in practice. This section considers each of these issues in more detail.

(i) The Primary Rules: The Obligations

Looking at the possibility of adopting an international treaty, the Human Rights Council has already approved the resolution proposed by Ecuador and South Africa for the *Elaboration of an international legally binding instrument on transnational corporations and other business enterprises with respect to human rights*[8] (the 'UN treaty'). The proposal seems encouraging and, if adopted, could establish the liability framework necessary to meet the requirements of a state's duty to protect. However, the Human Rights Council has circulated a 'zero draft' of the prospective treaty, which does not provide for the accountability of corporations for human rights abuses. Instead, it establishes the binding obligations of both host and home states to ensure that corporations respect human rights.[9] In this sense, the treaty would be a traditional instrument of international law only obliging states to protect human rights. Multinational enterprises would be free from any obligation at the international level. It would then be for states to ensure that corporations respect human rights. There are numerous doubts as to whether this draft would be a make-up treaty designed to cover up the absence of an international liability framework for multinational enterprises. The stakeholders representing victims of human rights abuses are in fact proposing alternative drafts to introduce legally binding obligations for corporations.[10] At this stage, it is not clear how the negotiations will move forward.

Against this background, this chapter analyses the possibility that states would establish binding human rights obligations on multinational enterprises at the international or European level.

[7] See Joseph (n 4).

[8] HR Council, 'Elaboration of an International Legally Binding Instrument on Transnational Corporations and Other Business Enterprises with Respect to Human Rights' (2014) A/HRC/26/L.22/Rev.1. See David Bilchitz, 'The Necessity for a Business and Human Rights Treaty' (2016) 1 *BHRJ* 203.

[9] IGWG, Zero Draft Treaty Legally Binding Instrument to Regulate, in International Human Rights Law, the Acvitities of Transnational Corporations and other Business Enterprises 2018.

[10] See eg Global Campaign to Reclaim Peoples Sovereignty, Dismantle Corporate Power and Stop Impunity, Treaty on Transnational Corporations and their Supply Chans with Regard to Human Rights 2017, https://www.stopcorporateimpunity.org/wp-content/uploads/2017/10/Treaty_draft-EN.pdf.

The content of a business and human rights treaty could be based on existing CSR frameworks. The CSR guidelines, and specifically the UN Guiding Principles[11] and the OECD Guidelines,[12] are already an established source of responsibilities for multinational enterprises. UN Member States have already endorsed and accepted the UN Guiding Principles and the OECD Guidelines as leading CSR frameworks. Furthermore, CSR guidelines already provide for the definitions of the human rights abuses committed by multinational companies. There is no good reason to disregard the existing legal foundation that has already been built during past years, aimed at recognising the responsibility of multinational corporations for human rights abuses. The only significant drawback of the current CSR mechanisms is their voluntary nature.[13] Therefore, this book encourages states to change the soft-law status of the CSR frameworks in relation to binding obligations.

A few states have already pioneered certain legislative initiatives to sanction companies refusing to adopt CSR policies. These laws are increasingly transforming the nature of CSR mechanisms from voluntary to binding frameworks, as they sanction those companies that refrain from adopting socially responsible policies.

For instance, the EU adopted new Accounting Directives which came into effect from the financial year starting in 2017. These Accounting Directives set out a binding obligation for certain large companies or corporate groups to publish their CSR policies.[14] This is a comply-or-explain type of obligation, as

[11] See Radu Mares (ed) *The UN Guiding Principles on Business and Human Rights: Foundations and Implementation* (Martinus Nijhoff, 2011); Nicola Jägers, 'UN Guiding Principles on Business and Human Rights: Making Headway towards Real Corporate Accountability' (2011) 29 *Netherlands Quarterly of Human Rights* 159; Astrid Sanders, 'The Impact of the "Ruggie Framework" and the United Nations Guiding Principles on Business and Human Rights on Transnational Human Rights Litigation' (2014) 18 *LSE Law, Society and Economy Working Paper*; John Gerard Ruggie, 'Business and Human Rights: The Evolving International Agenda' (2007) 101 *The American Journal of International Law* 819; John Gerard Ruggie, 'The Construction of the UN "Protect, Respect and Remedy" Framework for Business and Human Rights: The True Confessions of a Principled Pragmatist' (2011) 2 *European Human Rights Law Review* 127.

[12] See Ashley L Santner, 'A Soft' Law Mechanism for Corporate Responsibility: How the Updated OECD Guidelines for Multinational Enterprises Promote Business for the Future' (2011) 43 *The George Washington International Law Review* 375; Leyla Davarnejad, 'In the Shadow of Soft Law: The Handling of Corporate Social Responsibility Disputes under the OECD Guidelines for Multinational Enterprises' (2011) *Journal of Dispute Resolution* 351; John Gerard Ruggie and Tamaryn Nelson, 'Human Rights and the OECD Guidelines for Multinational Enterprises: Normative Innovations and Implementation Challenges' (2015) 66 *Corporate Social Responsibility Initiative Working Paper*.

[13] See Radu Mares, 'The Effects of CSR for the Protection of Human Rights' (2003) 7 *Mediterranean Journal of Human Rights* 113; Deva (n 4); Surya Deva, 'Human Rights Standards and Multinational Corporations Dilemma between "Home" and "Rome"' (2003) 7 *Mediterranean Journal of Human Rights* 69; AJAJ Eijsbouts, *Corporate Responsibility, Beyond Voluntarism: Regulatory Options to Reinforce the Licence to Operate* (Maastricht University Press, 2011); Florian Wettstein, 'Normativity, Ethics, and the UN Guiding Principles on Business and Human Rights: A Critical Assessment' (2015) 14 *Journal of Human Rights* 162.

[14] Directive 2014/95 amending Directive 2013/34/EU as regards disclosure of non-financial and diversity information by certain large undertakings and groups (Text with EEA relevance) [2014] OJ L330.

companies may not adopt CSR policies if they '[p]rovide a clear and reasoned explanations for not doing so'.[15] At this stage, it is not yet clear how and under which circumstances states will sanction those companies that neither adopt appropriate CSR policies, nor provide an explanation for avoiding such policies. Furthermore, in 2013 the Accounting Directives introduced an obligation for large extractive and logging industries to publish the details of any payment made to any government worldwide. The Accounting Directives are encouraging as, although they do not sanction multinational companies committing human rights abuses, they force European companies to make their human rights records public. The goal is to keep the consumers and civil society informed concerning the CSR records of transnational companies and, by doing so, encourage European multinationals to respect human rights for fear of public uproar.[16]

A recent piece of UK legislation, the 2015 Modern Slavery Act, seems to follow the same trend by requiring companies to publish a yearly statement concerning the steps that they took or failed to take to ensure that no slavery or human trafficking occurred in their supply chain.[17] Although the 2015 Modern Slavery Act is not a groundbreaking piece of legislation, as it imposes a mere obligation on companies to publish a statement, it is interesting to note that it opens up a possibility for the Secretary of State to detail companies' duties as these pertain to slavery and human trafficking. Specifically, the Secretary of State '[m]ay issue guidance about the duties imposed on commercial organisations'.[18] Such guidance might define the steps that companies should take in order to avoid involvement in slavery and human rights trafficking.[19]

Canada undertook another interesting initiative as it pertains to the implementation of CSR policies. Starting from 2015, it declared that it would discontinue its support for Canadian companies that refuse to accept the good offices of the Canadian NCP or comply with CSR best practices. Withdrawing Canadian support entails that Canada could sanction those companies that are unwilling to participate in NCP proceedings. It effectively means that Canadian companies could no longer benefit from economic diplomacy, including for instance advocacy and financial support.[20] In the *Final Statement on*

[15] ibid art 19a, 29a.

[16] Directive 2013/34/EU of the European Parliament and of the Council on the annual financial statements, consolidated financial statements and related reports of certain types of undertakings, amending Directive 2006/43/EC of the European Parliament and of the Council and repealing Council Directives 78/660/EEC and 83/349/EEC [2013] OJ L182/19, ch 10, arts 41–48.

[17] Modern Slavery Act 2015 (c 30) ch 30, part 6, s. 54 Transparency in supply chains, etc.

[18] ibid 54(9).

[19] Marco Fasciglione, 'Corporate Human Rights Responsibility, States' Duty to Protect and UN GPS' National Action Plans: Some Thoughts after the UK NAP Update' (2016) 1 *European Papers* 621, 625–29.

[20] Foreign Affairs Trade and Development Canada Government of Canada, 'Canada's Enhanced Corporate Social Responsibility Strategy to Strengthen Canada's Extractive Sector Abroad', www.international.gc.ca/trade-agreements-accords-commerciaux/topics-domaines/other-autre/csr-strat-rse.aspx?lang=eng#4, accessed 10 June 2016.

the Request for Review regarding the Operations of China Gold International Resources Corp Ltd, at the Copper Polymetallic Mine at the Gyama Valley, Tibet Autonomous Region, the Canadian NCP decided that '[t]he Company's non-participation in the NCP process will be taken into consideration in any applications by the Company for enhanced advocacy support from the Trade Commissioner Service and/or Export Development Canada (EDC) financial services, should they be made'.[21] This decision provides an example as to what consequences companies could face when they disregard CSR codes of conduct. Although the potential sanction is soft, as it merely refers to the possibility that companies may lose the support of the government, it is the first time that enterprises face a sanction for their failure to participate in a CSR mechanism. Accordingly, states are increasingly recognising the OECD Guidelines and the non-judicial mechanisms of NCPs as a point of reference in establishing the framework that companies should follow. The OECD Guidelines are a fundamental source of CSR, as they incorporate the Guiding Principles and provide a non-judicial mechanism to assess the responsibility of multinational companies.[22]

The examples above are not sufficient to meet the requirements of the duty to protect, as they are not effective sanctioning mechanisms. However, these recent developments are encouraging, as they show that states are increasingly establishing some sort of sanctions for multinational companies that are unwilling to adopt CSR policies.

Therefore, the content of the human rights obligations included in a business and human rights treaty should come from the existing CSR frameworks, such as the Guiding Principles or the OECD Guidelines, because they are already a point of reference for both states and industries.

(ii) The Secondary Rules: The Enforcement Mechanisms

Even if states were willing to adopt a binding treaty on business and human rights, the most controversial issues would be related to the monitoring body and sanction mechanisms applicable to multinational companies. States could establish such a monitoring body and sanction mechanisms at the international, EU or domestic level. One could think of two possibilities as to how to monitor the activities of multinational enterprises and ensure that such companies are held accountable when they abuse human rights: the creation of a specialised monitoring body or the use of existing domestic courts.

[21] *Final Statement on the Request for Review regarding the Operations of China Gold International Resources Corp Ltd, at the Copper Polymetallic Mine at the Gyama Valley, Tibet Autonomous Region* (NCP Canada, 2015), Analysis and Considerations, www.international.gc.ca/trade-agreements-accords-commerciaux/ncp-pcn/statement-gyama-valley.aspx?lang=eng, accessed 17 March 2019.

[22] Santner (n 12); Davarnejad (n 12); Ruggie and Nelson (n 12).

(a) Specialised Monitoring Body

The first possibility is for states to opt for a specialised monitoring body competent to hear individual petitions from the victims of human rights abuses against multinational companies. Such a body could be established at the international, European or national level.

The monitoring body could be an international or regional court. This requires recognising multinational enterprises as subjects of international law with active and passive personality and, therefore, establishing an international cause of action applicable to multinational companies. This solution would be in line with the academic proposal put forward by Manfred Nowak, Julia Kozma and Martin Scheinin, who suggested setting up an international human rights court with worldwide jurisdiction. Such a court would have the competence to rule on any human rights violation committed by either states or private actors, including companies.[23] Although their proposal envisages a classic human rights court, an alternative could also be another type of tribunal competent to receive individual claims from victims whose human rights are abused by companies.[24]

It should be recalled that the zero draft treaty proposes to establish a treaty body on business and human rights. However, such a body would not have the power to monitor corporate behaviour. It would instead merely monitor the conduct of states and their obligations to ensure the accountability of corporations at the domestic level.[25] In this sense, such a monitoring body would not represent a secondary rule potentially applicable to corporations, but instead a secondary rule applicable only to states. There is also an additional problem with such a UN monitoring body: the zero draft does not include an individual complaint mechanism to hold states accountable. The lack of an individual complaint procedure would certainly compromise the efficiency of a business and human rights treaty, and it is, therefore, commendable that such a monitoring body would allow victims to effectively hold states to account when they fail to secure their rights against corporations.

Alternatively, states could set up a national or European authority assessing whether companies comply with human rights.

One could envisage a system of penalties, similar to the current enforcement regime of competition law, with an EU or domestic law establishing an authority that would assess whether multinational companies comply with human rights standards. The law could explicitly provide that a breach of human rights

[23] Julia Kozma, Manfred Nowak and Martin Scheinin, *A World Court of Human Rights: Consolidated Statute and Commentary* (Neuer Wissenschaftlicher Verlag, 2010); Manfred Nowak, 'The Need for a World Court of Human Rights' (2007) 7 *Human Rights Law Review* 251; Jenny Goldschmidt, 'International Human Rights Implementation: Strengthen Existing Mechanisms, Establish a World Court for Human Rights, or Both?', in *What's Wrong with International Law?: Liber Amicorum A.H.A. Soons* (Brill – Nijhoff 2015).

[24] See eg the proposal put forward by Eijsbouts (n 13) 53–54 for '[a] supranational forum … [with] global substantive liability norms … [s]uch as the WTO'.

[25] IGWG Zero Draft Treaty (n 9).

by the overseas subsidiaries of the European parent companies would result in legal responsibility for such enterprises. As a result, the parent companies would be sanctioned for the human rights abuses perpetrated by their foreign subsidiaries on the basis of binding obligations. Furthermore, such an enforcement mechanism could be established at either the domestic or EU level: for example, a Directorate General within the European Commission, similar to the Directorate General assessing the violation of competition law.[26] Such an authority would effectively monitor the extraterritorial activities of European companies and their supply chains. The monitoring and sanctioning mechanism would be independent of the liability of multinational corporations in the civil justice system.

(b) Domestic Courts

The second possibility would be for states to use their domestic legal systems as a tool to enforce the primary rule established at the international, EU or domestic level.

This option entails the horizontal application of human rights obligations in national courts.[27] The domestic courts would have extraterritorial jurisdiction over the human rights abuses committed by multinational corporations. One can find inspiration as to how an extraterritorial civil jurisdiction of domestic courts could work in the ATS, according to which: 'The district courts shall have original jurisdiction of any civil action by an alien for a tort only, committed in violation of the law of nations or a treaty of the United States.'[28]

Human rights litigators interpreted the ATS as a tool to apply customary international law to corporate groups outsourcing their production to developing countries.[29] In *Jesner v Arab Bank*,[30] a plurality of the US Supreme Court justices held that customary international law had no prescriptive authority over corporations and, therefore, the ATS is not applicable to extraterritorial

[26] 'European Commission – Competition', http://ec.europa.eu/competition/index_en.html, accessed 27 December 2016.

[27] See John H Knox, 'Horizontal Human Rights Law' [2008] 102 *The American Journal of International Law* 1; Raphael Thomas, 'The Problem of Horizontal Effect' (2000) 5 *European Human Rights Law Review* 493; Niels Beisinghoff, *Corporations and Human Rights: An Analysis of ATCA Litigation against Corporations* (Peter Lang, 2009) 76–78; Joseph (n 4).

[28] Alien's action for tort 1948 (US Code) s 1350.

[29] Tyler Giannini and Susan Farbstein, 'Corporate Accountability in Conflict Zones: How Kiobel Undermines the Nuremberg Legacy and Modern Human Rights' (2010) 52 *Harvard International Law Journal* 119; Tyler Giannini, Susan Farbstein and Anthony Clark Arend, 'The Alien Tort Statute and Corporate Liability' (2011) 160 *University of Pennsylvania Law Review* 99; Simon Baughen, 'Holding Corporations to Account: Crafting ATS Suits in the UK' (2013) 2 *British Journal of American Legal Studies* 533; Enneking, 'Future of Foreign Direct Liability' (n 1); David M Golove and Daniel J Hulsebosch, 'A Civilized Nation: The Early American Constitution, the Law of Nations, and the Pursuit of International Recognition', (2010) 85 *New York University Law Review* 932; Stewart Jay, 'The Status of the Law of Nations in Early American Law', (1989) 42 *Vanderbilt Law Review* 819; Dalia Palombo, 'The Law of Nations in the United States Constitution after the

corporate abuses. However, assuming that states would ratify an international treaty with binding human rights obligations for multinational enterprises, then litigators would be able to file complaints on the basis of such a treaty instead of customary international law. However, despite this nuance, two main issues, which litigators have already encountered in ATS cases, would be equally relevant and, therefore, should be taken into account while drafting a binding international treaty establishing the obligations of multinational companies.

First, an international treaty should oblige states to provide appropriate causes of action in their domestic systems to ensure that human rights victims could effectively file complaints against multinational enterprises. The absence of a cause of action was one of the main issues of ATS-based human rights litigation in the United States. In *Sosa v Alvarez*, the US Supreme Court had to consider whether the ATS provided for new causes of action against private individuals violating customary international law. It ruled that the ATS is only a jurisdictional act and it is for the common law to provide such causes of action in tort.[31] A similar problem would be equally relevant if, instead of applying customary international law, domestic courts would have to apply a human rights treaty. Therefore, states should ensure that domestic causes of action are available to victims of human rights abuses to file complaints against companies before national courts. Such causes of action could be either already existing tort law causes of action or newly established causes of action to file suits against multinational companies for human rights abuses.

Second, under such a human rights treaty, states should ensure judicial cooperation between foreign judicial systems. One of the main issues in *Kiobel v Royal Dutch Shell* was whether the ATS could be applicable extraterritorially and potentially harm the relationship between the United States and Nigeria where the human rights abuses occurred.[32] This was an important issue given the risk that Nigeria could interpret the ATS extraterritorial reach as an intrusion in its domestic justice. For the same reason, any international human rights treaty on the accountability of multinational companies should consider the sensitivities related to the purported intrusion into the jurisdiction of other state parties and address this issue by providing a mechanism for judicial cooperation

Cases Sosa v Alvarez and Kiobel v Royal Dutch Petroleum CO' (2014) 6 *Cuadernos de Derecho Transnacional* 397; Liesbeth Enneking, 'Crossing the Atlantic – The Political and Legal Feasibility of European Foreign Direct Liability Cases' (2008) 40 *The George Washington International Law Review* 903; Sarah Joseph, *Corporations and Transnational Human Rights Litigation* (Hart Publishing, 2004) 21–63; Michael Byers, 'English Courts and Serious Human Rights Violations Abroad: A Preliminary Assessment', in *Liability of multinational corporations under international law* (Kluwer, 2000) 209–305; Menno T Kamminga and Saman Zia-Zarifi (eds), *Liability of Multinational Corporations under International Law* (Kluwer, 2000) 241–305; Beth Stephens et al. *International Human Rights Litigation in US Courts* (Martinus Nijhoff, 2008) 309–333.

[30] *Jesner v Arab Bank, PLC* [2018] US Supreme Court 584.

[31] *Sosa v Alvarez*, [2004] US Supreme Court 542, 692, 724. See also Virginia Monken Gomez, 'The Sosa Standard: What Does it Mean for Future ATS Litigation?' (2006) 33 *Pepperdine Law Review* 469; Palombo (n 29); Baughen (n 29).

[32] *Kiobel v Royal Dutch Petroleum Co* [2013] US Supreme Court 133 SCt 1659.

between the courts of different countries.[33] Such rules on judicial cooperation must ensure that human rights victims do not find themselves without any effective remedy, because, either in the host state or home state, domestic courts are afraid to intrude in matters pertaining to foreign justice and, on these grounds, deny access to justice for such victims. These rules on judicial cooperation must ensure that, in any case involving multinational companies with subsidiaries incorporated in different countries, the domestic courts of any of these countries could assert jurisdiction over the case.

An example of an efficient judicial cooperation between various domestic agencies dealing with the enforcement of CSR norms are the NCPs. When a corporate group has a number of companies incorporated in different countries, NCPs from the home and host countries consult to resolve the specific instance and elect one leading NCP. The leading NCP then offers its good offices to address the specific instance.[34]

One can imagine a similar system for domestic courts dealing with human rights abuses committed by corporate groups with a number of companies incorporated in different countries. National courts could cooperate and decide which court has jurisdiction over the particular case. For instance, the zero draft of the UN Treaty dedicates Article 11[35] to judicial cooperation and sets up various ways in which national courts could cooperate in terms of exchanging evidence and information concerning transnational abuses committed by multinational enterprises. This would be a promising avenue for home and host states to ensure effective remedies at the national level.

B. Existing Domestic Laws*

Rather than establishing a new set of obligations for European multinational companies, states could use existing legal frameworks to hold European parent companies liable for the torts committed by their foreign subsidiaries. However, this necessitates two broad changes to current laws. First, there is a need to modify the current European conflict-of-laws rules, as they do not take into

[33] Olivier De Schutter, 'Le contrôle du respect des droits de l'homme par les sociétés transnationales: le rôle de l'état d'origine', in *Justice et mondialisation en droit du travail: du rôle du juge aux conflits alternatifs* (Dalloz, 2010); Olivier De Schutter, 'Extraterritorial Jurisdiction as a Tool for Improving Human Rights Accountability for Transnational Corporations' (Business and Human Rights Resource Centre, 2006) https://www.business-humanrights.org/en/pdf-extraterritorial-jurisdiction-as-a-tool-for-improving-the-humanrights-accountability-of-transnational-corporations.

[34] OECD, *OECD Guidelines for Multinational Enterprises, 2011 Edition* (OECD Publishing, 2011), Commentary on the Implementation Procedures of the OECD Guidelines for Multinational Enterprises 23–24, www.oecd-ilibrary.org/governance/oecd-guidelines-for-multinational-enterprises_9789264115415-en, accessed 22 April 2016.

[35] IGWG Zero Draft Treaty (n 9) art 11.

*This section is partly included in the Article Dalia Palombo, 'The Duty of Care of the Parent Company: A Comparison between French Law, UK Precedents and the Swiss Proposals' (2019) 4 *BHRJ* 265.

consideration the overriding imperative to protect human rights when establishing which law applies to an abuse.[36] Second, it is necessary to change the liability regime applicable to European parent companies with respect to the damage inflicted by their subsidiaries. Current rules providing for an almost universal application of the principle of limited liability of the parent company are inadequate, because they do not take into consideration the special case of involuntary tort victims.[37]

The zero draft of the UN Treaty does not establish the accountability of corporations for human rights abuses. However, it clarifies that states should apply their laws extraterritorially and cooperate at the international level to hold parent corporations accountable for transnational human rights abuses committed by their supply chains. If adopted, the Treaty would be helpful in terms of detailing how states should modify their conflict of laws, corporate and tort laws to ensure the accountability of multinational enterprises.[38] Furthermore, a recent French law[39] and two alternative Swiss legislative proposals[40] have proposed different avenues to hold French and Swiss parent corporations accountable for their extraterritorial human rights and environmental abuses. This section, therefore, considers whether the zero draft UN Treaty, the French law and the Swiss legislative proposals could be viable avenues for states to change the current state of the law.

This section proposes certain plausible amendments to the current conflict-of-laws rules and the limited-liability regime applicable to parent companies so that European states could comply with their duty to protect under the ECHR.

(i) Conflict of Laws

Conflict-of-laws rules regulate, among other things, the choice of law applicable to the torts committed by foreign subsidiaries of a European holding company.

[36] See Pietro Franzina, 'Il regolamento n 864/2007/CE sulla legge applicabile alle obbligazioni extracontrattuali ("Roma II")', (2008) 1 *Le nuove leggi civili commentate* 971; Bright (n 5); Alberto Mattei, 'Prospects for Industrial Relations: Overriding Mandatory Provisions in the Transnational Labour Market' in *Labour Markets, Industrial Relations and Human Resources Management: from Recession to Recovery* (Kluwer, 2012); Veerle Van Den Eeckhout, 'Corporate Human Rights Violations and Private International Law. The Hinge-Function and Conductivity of PIL in Implementing Human Rights in Civil Proceedings in Europe: a Facilitating Role for PIL or PIL as a Complicating Factor?' (2012) *Contemporary Readings in Law and Social Justice* 178.

[37] Henry Hansmann and Reinier Kraakman, 'Toward Unlimited Shareholder Liability for Corporate Torts' (1991) 100 *The Yale Law Journal* 1879; Vanderkerckhove (n 6); Beisinghoff (n 27) 13–41.

[38] IGWG Zero Draft Treaty (n 9).

[39] Loi 2017-399 du 27 mars 2017 relative au devoir de vigilance des sociétés mères et des entreprises donneuses d'ordre 2017 (JORF).

[40] '16.077 | CO. Droit de La Société Anonyme | Objet | Le Parlement Suisse' (15 June 2018) www.parlament.ch/fr/ratsbetrieb/suche-curia-vista/geschaeft?AffairId=20160077, accessed 29 July 2018; 'Responsible Business Initiative – The Initiative', http://konzern-initiative.ch/initiativtext/?lang=en, accessed 26 April 2018; RK-N, 'Eidgenössische Volksinitiative "Für verantwortungsvolle Unternehmen – zum Schutz von Mensch und Umwelt" Indirekter Gegenentwurf' 2018, www.parlament.ch/centers/documents/de/dok-gegenentwurf-mm-rk-n-2018-05-04.pdf.

The ECHR requires European states to regulate their conflict of laws in compliance with the duty to protect.

The Council of Europe Committee of Ministers has specifically addressed this issue in its Recommendation on the Guiding Principles. The Recommendation points out the obligation of European states to regulate their conflict of laws in compliance with the ECHR and take human rights into consideration. The Council of the EU, ie the political body expressing the opinions of the EU Member States' governments, endorsed the Recommendation in a declaration concerning the implementation of the Guiding Principles in Europe.[41] This is of particular importance, as the EU has an active role in regulating the choice of law that, as set out in Chapter 2, may result in the application of a low standard of review for European multinational companies.

The main problem of the current EU conflict-of-laws rules, as these pertain to bringing an action against a European holding company for the human rights abuses perpetrated by its overseas subsidiaries, is that the choice-of-law rules have no regard for human rights. Various factors may influence the prescribed choice of law, but none of them explicitly includes an imperative to protect human rights. The only factor that may be potentially interpreted as taking into consideration human rights law, as a matter affecting the choice of law, is the forum law exception. According to this exception, a judge may refuse to apply a law that is in conflict with domestic public policy or mandatory rules. However, the forum law exception is not detailed enough to provide legal remedies against multinational companies for the following reasons. First, the forum law exception is not mandatory: a domestic judge has discretion to determine when and if the exception is applicable. Judges have so far applied such an exception in very limited circumstances. Second, public policy and mandatory rules do not necessarily include human rights law. Third, even if a domestic court interprets public policy and mandatory rules as including human rights law, the characterisation problem is likely to limit the application of the forum law exception exclusively to the narrow question of human rights obligations and not to the liability framework applicable to multinational companies. As a result, the forum law exception may not apply to business and human rights cases.[42]

[41] Committee of Ministers, 'Recommendation of the Committee of Ministers to Member States on Human Rights and Business' (2016) CM/Rec(2016)3; General Secretariat of the Council, 'Council Conclusions on Business and Human Rights' (2016) 10254/16.

[42] See Regulation (EC) No 864/2007 of the European Parliament and of the Council of 11 July 2007 on the law applicable to non-contractual obligations (Rome II); Andrea Bonomi, 'The Role of Internationally Mandatory Rules in an European Private International Law System' [2007] *Revista de drept international privat si drept comparat* 159; Arif Yascha, 'Overriding Mandatory Provisions and Administrative Authorisations According to the Rome II Regulation' [2011] *European Legal Forum* 113; Angelika Fuchs, 'Art 26 Rome II', in *Rome II Regulation: Pocket Commentary* (Sellier, 2011); Angelika Fuchs, 'Art 16 Rome II', *Rome II Regulation: Pocket Commentary* (Sellier, 2011); Jan von Hein, 'Article 16 Overriding Mandatory Provisions', in *Rome Regulations: Commentary on the European Rules on the Conflict of Laws* (Kluwer/Aspen, 2011); Jan von Hein, 'Article 26 Public Policy of the Forum', in *Rome Regulations: Commentary on the European Rules on the Conflict of Laws*

The current state of conflict-of-laws rules is, therefore, unsatisfactory, as a European judge could apply foreign law even in the circumstances when the application of such a law does not permit the protection of human rights. The legislator should adjust the conflict-of-laws rules and ensure that no European judge applies any foreign law that is inconsistent with the ECHR. Applying this principle to the hypothetical case studies, a UK-incorporated holding company H should not be able to take advantage of different human rights standards available in the United Kingdom and in the overseas host states where its subsidiaries S are operating. H should not be shielded behind more flexible, foreign laws to avoid its obligations. The conflict-of-laws rules should prevent European judges from applying any law which does not entitle a tort victim to an effective legal remedy against the holding company H for the human rights abuses perpetrated by its subsidiaries S.

I propose the adoption of a choice-of-law rule that would be in compliance with the ECHR. Such a rule could be modelled on the principle established in Article 7(2) of the zero draft UN Treaty, according to which:

> At the request of victims, all matters of substance regarding human rights law relevant to claims before the competent court may be governed by the law of another Party where the involved person with business activities of a transnational character is domiciled. The competent court may request for mutual legal assistance as referred to under Article 11 of this Convention.[43]

If adopted as conflict-of-laws rule, Article 7 of the zero draft would entitle the claimant to the privilege of choosing the applicable law, because it recognises that victims are often at a disadvantage to sue a foreign investor under the laws of a state where a tortious act was committed. In its current form, however, Article 7 would just require states to implement an appropriate conflict-of-laws rule, instead of establishing a conflict-of-laws rule itself.

In any case, if states would adopt their own conflict-of-laws rule, this rule could be in principle similar to Article 7 of Rome II on environmental damages.[44] As explained in Chapter 2, according to Article 7 of Rome II, when a tortious act causes environmental damage, the claimant can choose to sue the respondent under either the place of injury law or '[t]he law of the country in which the event giving rise to the damage occurred'.[45] The idea is again to entitle victims of environmental torts to a benefit in consideration of their status as weaker parties. However, as explained in Chapter 2, it is unclear whether the '[t]he law of the country in which the event giving rise to the damage occurred'[46] would be

(Kluwer/Aspen, 2011); Jan von Hein, 'Article 7 Environmental Damage', in *Rome Regulations: Commentary on the European Rules on the Conflict of Laws* (Kluwer/Aspen, 2011).

[43] IGWG Zero Draft Treaty (n 9) art 7(2).

[44] Regulation (EC) No 864/2007 of the European Parliament and of the Council of 11 July 2007 on the law applicable to non-contractual obligations (Rome II), art 7.

[45] ibid.

[46] ibid.

the home state law in a case of corporate transnational tort. Instead, Article 7 of the zero draft clarifies that the choice would be between home and host state laws, leaving the victim with a choice of law which would balance its weak position in relation to a powerful multinational enterprise.

Two recent Swiss legislative proposals for the adoption of a due-diligence obligation on Swiss parent corporations also suggest an interesting solution. As it pertains to the choice-of-law analysis, both legislative proposals state that Swiss law would apply irrespective of any other law that may be applicable under private international law rules.[47] In the context of these legislative proposals, where Swiss law would arguably become the most advanced jurisdiction in terms of the transnational protection of human rights abused by corporations, such a rule makes sense and would certainly be of help to human rights victims.

However, the solution proposed by the zero draft UN Treaty is still preferable, because there may be situations in which host state laws would be more favourable to victims than home state laws. Leaving the choice of law to the claimant would therefore correctly balance the unfavourable position of victims which may be forced to file a complaint in a foreign country in order to seek redress against a multinational corporation.

(ii) Liability Regime

The procedural duty to protect requires states to provide effective legal remedies for the stakeholders affected by the activities of European multinational enterprises. Therefore, states must also provide the victims of human rights abuses with a cause of action in domestic courts against parent companies incorporated within their territory. States have a wide margin of appreciation in defining the cause of action applicable to a parent company. However, whatever ultimate mechanism the state opts for, the cause of action should be an effective instrument to prevent companies from abusing fundamental human rights, including through the wrongful acts of their foreign subsidiaries.[48] The zero draft of the UN Treaty addresses this issue. It establishes that states should hold parent corporations accountable for the conduct of their supply chain '[t]o the extent it exhibits a sufficiently close relation with its subsidiary or entity in its supply chain and where there is strong and direct connection between its conduct and

[47] RK-N (n 40); PARL INT, 'Commission des affaires juridiques du Conseil national' 16.077 (23 May 2018), www.parlament.ch/centers/documents/fr/bericht-rk-n-16-077-2018-05-18-f.pdf; 'Responsible Business Initiative–The Initiative' (n 40).

[48] See Sudre (n 2); Sergio Bartole, Pasquale De Sena and Vladimiro Zagrebelsky (eds), *Commentario breve alla Convenzione europea per la salvaguardia dei diritti dell'uomo e delle libertà fondamentali* (CEDAM, 2012) 303–11; Pieter van Dijk, Fried van Hoof, Arjen van Rijn and Leo Zwaak (eds), *Theory and Practice of the European Convention on Human Rights*, 5th edn (Intersentia, 2018) 725–50; Xenos (n 2) 57–172.

the wrong suffered by the victim',[49] or, alternatively, on the basis of a control or foreseeability test. To achieve these objectives, states could establish either a direct or indirect liability framework or a framework which would be based on a combination of both types of corporate liability.

(a) Indirect Liability

One potential option for a domestic lawmaker to provide the victims of human rights abuses with an effective cause of action against the holding companies of multinational groups is to establish a regime of indirect liability. A state could, for example, establish an exception allowing the corporate veil to be pierced for cases of human rights abuses. The exception would extend the liability of a subsidiary to its parent company, and, therefore, the parent and the subsidiary would be jointly liable. The broad purpose of such an exception would be to consider a holding company and its subsidiaries as a single corporate unit in cases of human rights abuses.[50] States would establish a standard of review for holding companies by disregarding the separate corporate legal personality of their subsidiaries. Such an indirect liability framework should be applicable any time a subsidiary and its holding company abuse human rights.

This indirect-liability regime would, therefore, be different from the currently available exceptions to the principle of limited liability which allow for the piercing of the corporate veil. As set out in Chapter 2, piercing the corporate veil is exceptional in the United Kingdom. The *evading existing legal obligation* exception is applicable when a parent company establishes a subsidiary for the purpose of evading a pre-existing legal obligation of the parent, whereas the *single economic unit* may be applicable, if ever, only when a subsidiary is a complete empty company, a shell, conducting no commercial activities.[51] As demonstrated in Chapter 2, these exceptions are insufficient to provide effective remedies for human rights victims of multinational companies. States should introduce a broader indirect liability framework that would, as a general principle, disregard the corporate veil of the subsidiary any time its shareholder is a company, rather than an individual, and the case relates to involuntary tort victims of human rights abuses.[52]

This proposal may sound too ambitious and, accordingly, unacceptable. However, it should be noted that disregarding the corporate veil as a general principle of regulating corporate groups has already been accepted in certain areas of law. For example, EU competition law provides a general indirect

[49] IGWG Zero Draft Treaty (n 9) art 6.

[50] See Kershaw (n 6) 46–77; Vanderkerckhove (n 6) 66–76; Enneking, *Foreign Direct Liability and Beyond* (n 1); Joseph (n 29) 129–43; Hansmann and Kraakman (n 37).

[51] See Kershaw (n 6) 46–77; Vanderkerckhove (n 6) 66–76.

[52] See Hansmann and Kraakman (n 37).

liability regime that would be suitable to regulate multinational enterprises abusing human rights. The European Commission and the CJEU have developed comprehensive antitrust case-law that takes the central role of multinational companies in the economy and their global reach into account.[53] Specifically, EU competition law has successfully addressed the liability and extraterritoriality problems by extending its competition laws to any company that is part of a European corporate group. According to the *economic entity* doctrine, subsidiaries and parent companies are considered one entity under the jurisdiction of the European Commission when at least one of the companies is located in the European Union and the parent and subsidiaries act as a single *economic entity*.[54] In the historical *ICI v Commission* case, the CJEU ruled:

> The fact that a subsidiary has separate legal personality is not sufficient to exclude the possibility of imputing its conduct to the parent company. … [I]n the circumstances the formal separation between these companies, resulting from their separate legal personality, cannot outweigh the unity of their conduct on the market for the purposes of applying the rules on competition.[55]

Accordingly, for the purpose of competition law, the European Commission may sanction a parent company incorporated within the EU when its foreign subsidiary violates antitrust law. The veil is pierced on the sole basis that the parent company and the subsidiary are part of the same corporate group acting as an *economic entity*.[56] This doctrine addresses the liability and extraterritorial issues. By applying the *economic entity* doctrine to multinational companies, a European parent company would be responsible for the abuses committed by its subsidiaries in developing countries.

It is clear that, for the purpose of an efficient enforcement of antitrust law, the European states and the Union were able to establish a sanctioning mechanism which efficiently addresses the current status of multinational companies as private actors in a globalised world. This jurisprudence proves that states can sanction both national and foreign corporations violating antitrust law. The states could meet their duty to protect by establishing a human rights standard of review applicable to multinational enterprises, largely replicating the approach taken by EU competition law. Applying the same principle to the three hypothetical case studies, the liability of the British holding company H would also extend to the activities of its foreign subsidiaries, once the veil is pierced under the *economic entity* doctrine.

[53] See Richard Whish and David Bailey, *Competition Law*, 7th edn (Oxford University Press, 2012) 92–99; Jennifer A Zerk, *Multinationals and Corporate Social Responsibility: Limitations and Opportunities in International Law* (Cambridge University Press, 2006) 104–13; A Kalintiri, 'Revisiting Parental Liability in EU Competition Law' (2018) 43 *European Law Review* 145.

[54] See C-48/69 *Imperial Chemical Industries Ltd. v Commission* ECLI:EU:C:1972:70; Whish and Bailey (n 53) 92–99.

[55] C-48/69 *Imperial Chemical Industries Ltd. v Commission* (n 54) paras 132–40.

[56] See Whish and Bailey (n 53) 92–99.

(b) Direct Liability

Another potential option for states to provide stakeholders with effective causes of action against the holding companies of multinational groups is to establish the direct liability of the parent company. In this case, the parent company is liable for its failure to effectively control the activities conducted by its subsidiaries, which resulted in the abuse of human rights. Importantly, under the direct liability framework, the liability of a holding company would not depend on the liability of its subsidiaries, because a direct liability framework entails a cause of action in tort against the parent company, independent of any cause of action available against its affiliates.[57] The aim of such a cause of action would be to ensure that a company cannot avoid its liability by diluting its participation in the subsidiary.

To meet the standards set out in the ECHR, such a direct duty of care of a parent company towards the individuals whose human rights are abused by the acts of its overseas subsidiaries should differ, however, from the parent company's duty of care established in the recent UK case-law analysed in Chapter 2.

The Supreme Court in *Lungowe v Vedanta*[58] delivered a promising ruling on jurisdiction that could potentially open up the litigation against UK parent companies for extraterritorial human rights abuses. However, whether or not a parent company owes a duty of care towards its subsidiary's neighbours is still a matter of case by case analysis. The key question seems to be whether the parent company and its subsidiary are in such a close relationship for the former to reasonably foresee the human rights abuses committed by the latter. This is a question of facts that would depend on the circumstances of each case as well as on judicial discretion. In *Chandler v Cape Plc*[59] and *Thompson v The Renwick Group Plc*,[60] two cases decided also on the merits, the UK Court of Appeal ruled that a parent company has a duty of care towards its subsidiaries' employees when it has superior knowledge and expertise about the activities conducted by the group. This requirement, which seemed rather flexible in *Chandler v Cape*, was tightened in *Thompson v The Renwick Group Plc*, where the Court of Appeal required the victim to prove superior knowledge and expertise of the parent. As a result, the outcomes of the cases are opposite: while the Court of Appeal decided *Chandler v Cape Plc* in the victims' favour, it held for the company in *Thompson v The Renwick Group Plc*. Furthermore, there are a number of jurisdictional cases including

[57] See Enneking, 'Future of Foreign Direct Liability?' (n 1); Joseph (n 29) 129–43; Enneking, 'Crossing the Atlantic' (n 29); Enneking, *Foreign Direct Liability and Beyond* (n 1); Kershaw (n 6) 146–55; Skinner (n 6).

[58] *Vedanta Resources PLC and another v Lungowe and others* [2019] UKSC 20.

[59] *Chandler v Cape Plc* [2012] (QB), X (appeal taken from Eng) EWCA Civ 525.

[60] *Thompson v The Renwick Group Plc* [2014] EWCA Civ 635.

Lungowe v Vedanta, Okpabi v Royal Dutch Shell Plc and *AAA & Others v Unilever PLC and Unilever Tea Kenya Limited* which assessed the arguability of the claims by analysing the relationship between parent company and subsidiary. However, while in *Lungowe v Vedanta*, the Supreme Court, Court of Appeal and High Court all ruled that the relationship between parent and subsidiary was arguably close enough for the parent to possibly owe a duty of care towards the tort victims damaged by its subsidiary,[61] in *Okpabi v Royal Dutch Shell Plc* and *AAA & Others v Unilever PLC and Unilever Tea Kenya Limited*, the High Court and Court of Appeal held that the parent company and its subsidiary were not in a sufficiently close relationship for the former to arguably owe a duty of care in respect of the activities of the group.[62] The difference between *Thompson v the Renwick Group Plc*, *Okpabi v Royal Dutch Shell Plc* and *AAA & Others v Unilever PLC and Unilever Tea Kenya Limited* on the one hand, and *Chandler v Cape Plc* and *Lungowe v Vedanta*, on the other, is fact-based. However, the dichotomy between these rulings is telling about how undetermined the criteria to establish a duty of care of a parent company for abuses committed by its subsidiaries are in UK case law.[63] Against this background, *Lungowe v Vedanta* opened the door for UK courts to asset jurisdiction over potentially any transnational tort committed by a subsidiary of a UK parent company. This could arguably change the rulings in *Okpabi v Royal Dutch Shell Plc* and *AAA & Others v Unilever PLC and Unilever Tea Kenya Limited*.

Different from this duty-of-care regime, which is limited in scope, the direct-liability framework, that this book advocates for, should include a holding company's duty of care towards any person affected by the activities of any subsidiary in the corporate group. Any time a holding company is the controlling shareholder of its subsidiary, it should owe a duty of care towards the stakeholders whose human rights are abused by such a subsidiary. These accountability goals could be achieved either through a significant development of UK jurisprudence on point or a legislative reform. For instance, assuming that the UK Supreme Court would clarify that a parent company is presumed to have superior knowledge and expertise about the activities conducted by its subsidiaries, the level of protection provided by UK law could meet the requirements of the duty to protect.

In addition, there are a number of legislative proposals in various jurisdictions to introduce a direct liability framework for parent companies by statute. France, so far, is the only jurisdiction where such proposals became law, but the

[61] *Lungowe & Ors v Vedanta Resources Plc & Anor* [2016] EWHC TCC 975; *Lungowe & Ors v Vedanta Resources Plc & Anor* [2017] 1528; *Vedanta Resources PLC and another v Lungowe and others* (n 58).

[62] *Okpabi & Ors v Royal Dutch Shell Plc & Anor* [2017] EWHC TCC 89; *Okpabi & Ors v Royal Dutch Shell Plc & Anor (Rev 1)* [2018] EWCA Civ 191; *AAA & Ors v Unilever Plc & Anor* [2018] EWCA Civ 1532; *AAA & Ors v Unilever Plc & Anor* [2017] EWHC 371 (QB).

[63] See Uglješa Grušić, 'Responsibility in Groups of Companies and the Future of International Human Rights and Environmental Litigation' (2015) 74 *CLJ* 30.

United Kingdom and Switzerland have also considered, or are considering, the introduction of similar laws.

First, as early as 2002, the UK Parliament analysed the proposal for a Corporate Responsibility Bill.[64] The bill specifically addressed the liability of British companies as it pertains to 'the preservation of the environment; ... public health and safety; ... the goal of sustainable development; ... employement; ... human rights; and ... consumer protection'.[65] According to Article 6 of the proposal:

> (1) A parent company of a corporate group shall be liable to pay compensation in respect of the classes of damage set out in subsections (1)(c)(i) to (iii) below where—
>
> (a) the manner in which the group's activities are organised managed or undertaken falls below the standards that can reasonably be expected of the group in all the circumstances of the given case; and
> (b) the manner in which the group's activities are organised managed or undertaken fails to ensure – (i) the health and safety of persons working in or affected by those activities; (ii) the protection of the environment; and
> (c) such a failure may be regarded as a cause of – (i) serious physical or mental injury to persons working in or affected by those activities; (ii) serious harm to the environment; or (iii) both.
>
> (2) For the purposes of this section it shall be immaterial whether the injury to persons or harm to the environment occurred within the United Kingdom.
>
> (3) It shall be the duty of a company to which subsection (1)(a) applies to ensure that – (a) any other entity which is under that company's operational control wherever registered or domiciled complies with sections 3, 4, 5, 7 and this section; and (b) any subsidiary undertaking of that company wherever located complies with sections 3, 4 and 5.[66]

Article 6 of the proposal was remarkable, because it specifically addressed the damages caused to any third party affected by the activities of the group, it applied to any entity under the holding company's control, even if it was incorporated outside the United Kingdom, and it specifically referred to extraterritorial harms and injuries. The reference to the '[s]tandards that can reasonably be expected of the group in the circumstances of the given case'[67] arguably refers to the negligence standard of the duty of care.[68] Accordingly, Article 6 could effectively hold parent companies accountable if they do not act as the reasonably prudent holding company should. This line could reconcile the current divergence between the standard of conduct and the standard of review applicable to multinational enterprises. It would essentially eliminate the alternative standard of review created by the combination of limited-liability and

[64] Corporate Responsibility Bill 2002 [129].
[65] ibid 2.
[66] ibid 6.
[67] ibid.
[68] SF Deakin, Angus Charles Johnston and BS Markesinis, *Markesinis and Deakin's Tort Law*, 7th edn (Clarendon Press, 2013) 99–153.

conflict-of-laws rules for all those cases when UK multinational enterprises damage the environment or the health and safety of involuntary tort victims. Although the Corporate Social Responsibility Bill did not pass, it triggered a serious dialogue in the UK parliament.[69] Most recently, in 2017, the UK Parliament called on the government to adopt a law establishing binding due-diligence obligations for UK parent companies.[70] Therefore, further developments in this area of law are expected.

Second, France has recently included two new articles L 225-102-4 ('Article 4') and L 225-102-5 ('Article 5') in its Commercial Code.[71]

Article 4 lays out the due-diligence obligation of parent companies, controlling a corporate group with at least 10,000 or 5,000 employees (depending on whether or not the affiliates are incorporated in France) to oversee the activities conducted by any subsidiaries, or supply chains under its direct or indirect control. The law defines the due-diligence obligation as a parent company's duty to set up a monitoring plan for its supply chain. Such a plan should identify, target and prevent any serious threat to human or environmental rights, health or security committed by any affiliate. Specifically, the parent company has to determine the risks arising in connection with the activities conducted in its supply chain, establish monitoring procedures that would regularly assess whether the enterprises in its supply chain comply with the law, lay out the actions that it will take to prevent any abuse of human rights, and institutionalise an internal mechanism for trade unions to signal any risk of abuse within the supply chain. The parent company must publish its monitoring plan and present it to its shareholders' general meeting.

The due-diligence obligation of Article 4 is the first ever duty established by a law of general application specifically requiring multinational enterprises to monitor the human rights abuses of their supply chains. This duty is a real breakthrough, as it applies not only when a parent company outsources its production through foreign subsidiaries, but also when such a holding company conducts its extraterritorial activities through companies with which it has an established commercial relationship. These include supply chains where any formal corporate control by participation in the capital or cross-management is absent. However, it should be noted that this due-diligence obligation of the parent company is not equal to a general duty to prevent human rights abuses

[69] See 'UK CSR Bill Spirit Lives on Despite Failure – Sustainability-Reports.Com', www.sustainability-reports.com/titel-378/, accessed 28 December 2016; 'UK: New Bill Would Inject Substance into Corporate Social Responsibility', www.amnesty.org.uk/press-releases/uk-new-bill-would-inject-substance-corporate-social-responsibility, accessed 28 December 2016; Peter Muchlinski, 'Implementing the New UN Corporate Human Rights Framework: Implications for Corporate Law, Governance, and Regulation' (2012) 22 *Business Ethics Quarterly* 145.

[70] Joint Commitee on Human Rights UK Parliament, '6th Report – Human Rights and Business 2017: Promoting Responsibility and Ensuring Accountability – Joint Committee on Human Rights – House of Commons' (2017) HL Paper 153, HC 443, https://publications.parliament.uk/pa/jt201617/jtselect/jtrights/443/44302.htm, accessed 21 January 2019.

[71] Loi 2017-399 du 27 mars 2017 relative au devoir de vigilance des sociétés mères et des entreprises donneuses d'ordre 2017–399.

committed within its supply chain. The obligation explicitly requires French holding companies to set up a monitoring plan. As a result, the French judiciary could interpret this law in a restrictive way and argue that, as long as a French parent company publishes a monitoring plan that correctly identifies the risks related to its supply chain, it should not be responsible for ensuring that its subsidiaries effectively implement such a plan. Furthermore, the application of the French due-diligence obligation is limited to severe threats to human or environmental rights, health or security. It is, therefore, unclear what abuses the French judiciary will consider severe enough to trigger the application of Article 4.

If a parent company violates its due-diligence obligation, it will then owe a duty of care towards the victims of human rights abuses perpetrated by its affiliates. Article 5 lays out the direct liability of the parent company for a breach of its duty of care towards the victims. On the one hand, under Article 5, the duty of care of parent companies is far-reaching as it establishes the extraterritorial responsibility of French multinational holding corporations for the conduct of any entity that is part of their supply chain. On the other hand, such a liability of parent companies is limited to those cases when (a) the holding corporation breaches its due-diligence obligation, ie it does not set up an effective monitoring plan, (b) because of such a breach, an affiliate in its supply chain was able to abuse health, security or human and environmental rights, and (c) such abuses resulted in damages. The parent company breaches its duty of care and is liable only if conditions (a), (b) and (c) are met. The open question is how French courts will interpret the relationship between these three elements and therefore the causality that a victim will have to prove to seek damages against the parent company.[72]

Therefore, although encouraging, only time and future French jurisprudence will confirm whether the recent amendments of the French commercial law have established a liability framework that is effectively able to hold multinational corporations to account.

A third example are two different proposals for a due-diligence obligation for parent companies that are likely to become law in Switzerland: a proposal for a constitutional referendum that would include corporate accountability as part of the Swiss constitution ('proposal'), and a watered-down

[72] See Xavier Delpech, 'Bientôt un devoir de vigilance à la charge des sociétés mères et des donneurs d'ordre' [2015] *Dalloz Actualité*; Renée-Claude Drouin, 'Le développement du contentieux à l'encontre des entreprises transnationales: quel rôle pour le devoir de vigilance?' [2016] *Droit social* 246; Pierre-Louis Périn, 'Devoir de vigilance et responsabilité illimitée: qui trop embrasse mal étreint' [2015] *Revue trimestrielle de droit commercial et de droit économique* 215; Stéphane Brabant and Elsa Savourey, 'A Closer Look at the Penalties Faced by Companies' [2017] *Revue internationale de la compliance et de l'éthique des affaires* 50; Nicolas Cuzacq, 'Le devoir de vigilance des sociétés mères et des donneurs d'ordre', *La RSE saisi par le droit: perspectives interne et internationale* (Pedone, 2015); Pauline Dufourq, 'Devoir de vigilance des multinationales : quelle évoluations ?' [2017] *Dalloz Actualité*.

counter-proposal for a due-diligence law ('counter-proposal'). The proposal is wider in its scope, human rights protection and corporate liability, but would require long-lasting proceedings to change the constitution, including a referendum, whereas the counter-proposal, although less ambitious in terms of the liability of parent companies, is currently the object of a legislative ping-pong between the two branches of the Swiss Parliament, which are in the process of amending it. The counter-proposal has limited the scope of the law only to the subsidiaries of multinational corporations with more than 500 employees and/or with a high business turnover. Furthermore, it applies only to those human rights or environmental abuses that cause bodily harms or damage to property.[73] Instead, the proposal extends to all supply chains and to all abuses of human rights and internationally recognised environmental standards.[74]

Both proposals set out, first, a duty to respect, and, second, a due-diligence obligation for parent companies. As to the duty to respect, parent companies must ensure the respect of human rights and environmental laws within their corporate group. As to the due-diligence obligation, parent companies have to monitor the activities of their affiliates world-wide in order to prevent human rights or environmental law abuses. In both proposals, the parent companies would be directly liable for the human rights and environmental abuses perpetrated by their foreign subsidiaries unless they demonstrate that they have complied with their due-diligence obligation. In this context, the due-diligence obligation becomes a tool to reverse the burden of proof. Swiss parent companies would have a duty to ensure the respect of human rights by their affiliates, and, in case of breach of such a duty, they would have an extraterritorial direct liability for any tort committed by their affiliates. However, if a Swiss company could demonstrate that it complied with its due-diligence obligation, and nevertheless its subsidiaries managed to abuse human or environmental rights, then it would no longer have direct responsibility.[75] This is an innovative approach requiring corporations, which should have the relevant information concerning their business activities, to defend themselves from nuisance lawsuits, while, at the same time, not overburning human rights victims with a high standard of proof that they are unlikely to meet.

The most significant difference between the two proposals lies in the liability clause. Whereas in both proposals this clause would allow companies to avoid liability if they have adequately complied with their due-diligence obligation, the counter-proposal also requires effective control of the parent company over

[73] RK-N (n 40); Commission des affaires juridiques du Conseil des Etats, '16.077 Droit de la société anonyme (projet 2)'; Commission des affaires juridiques du Conseil national (n 47).

[74] 'Responsible Business Initiative – The Initiative' (n 40).

[75] See Sandra Cossart, Jérôme Chaplier and Tiphaine Beau de Lomenie, 'The French Law on Duty of Care: A Historic Step Towards Making Globalization Work for All' (2017) 2 *Business and Human Rights Journal* 317.

the subsidiary and adds an additional possibility for Swiss companies to free themselves from liability if they are unable to influence the conduct of their subsidiaries. This addition could open a Pandora's box in Swiss courts. As it pertains to the notion of effective control, the Swiss National Council (the equivalent of the House of Commons) and Council of States (the equivalent of the House of Lords) Legal Commissions[76] clarify that it is not sufficient for parent companies to control a subsidiary on paper, but that such control must be effective in practice and that the burden to prove such control is on the victim. This essentially means that, even when a parent company would have a significant number of shares in a subsidiary, this would not necessarily entail effective control. The victim will still have to prove that such control exists in practice, because the parent company effectively oversees and intervenes in the subsidiary's activities. As it pertains to the notion of influence, it is unclear what level of influence the parent company must exercise over its subsidiary to be responsible for its conduct.

If the counter-proposal becomes law and Swiss courts were to interpret this clause narrowly, this could potentially undermine the accountability of parent companies when the abuse happens down in their chain of control. Essentially victims would have to prove the liability of subsidiaries and the effective control of parent companies on such subsidiaries, whereas parent companies would avoid liability if they prove that they have met their due-diligence obligations, or they do not exercise a sufficient level of influence over the activities conducted by their subsidiaries. Instead, if the proposal would pass, any level of control that parent companies exercise over subsidiaries or supply chains would be enough for the victims to hold them accountable. Furthermore, Swiss parent companies would have to demonstrate that they have adequately complied with their due-diligence obligations in order to avoid liability. However, regardless of which one of the Swiss proposals would be adopted, they represent the most advanced liability framework that would be applicable to corporations abusing human rights extraterritorially. They provide for the reversed burden of proof clause that would require parent companies to prove that they are not accountable for the human rights abuses committed by their subsidiaries. This would not result in uncontrolled corporate liability, because it would always be for the victims to prove that the subsidiary of a Swiss parent company did abuse human or environmental rights. The victim would be saved from the high burden to also prove the liability of the parent for the conduct of its subsidiaries.

Therefore, although it is difficult to assess in the abstract whether such recent laws and legislative proposals would provide victims with effective remedies meeting the ECHR's requirements, they clearly are a step forward in the right direction. Overall, the aim is to establish a direct liability framework that would

[76] Commission des affaires juridiques du Conseil national (n 47); Commission des affaires juridiques du Conseil des Etats (n 73).

effectively guarantee victims an avenue to sue for extraterritorial human rights abuses committed by multinational enterprises.

II. DUTY TO FULFIL

To meet their duty to fulfil, states should modify their policies towards multinational enterprises. The obligations under this duty go beyond guaranteeing effective judicial remedies against multinational companies. Given how exceptionally difficult and costly it is for the victims of human rights abuses to initiate litigation against a holding company incorporated in a foreign jurisdiction, multinational enterprises could simply opt to take the risk of any potential civil liability cost, rather than alter their commercial conduct in developing countries. For this reason, the duty to fulfil requires states to do their utmost to ensure that multinational enterprises respect human rights. The meaning of *best effort* entails a process to reach the ultimate result of ensuring respect for human rights.[77] As clarified by the Guiding Principles, States should establish a '[r]ange of permissible preventive and remedial measures'[78] to stop human rights abuses. The specific policies sufficient to meet the duty to fulfil depend on the facts of each particular case. The ECtHR has consistently ruled that states have a wide margin of appreciation in deciding how to comply with their duty to fulfil.[79] However, through a comparative analysis of other areas of law, it is possible to set out certain mechanisms that a country could put into place to meet its duty to fulfil. This section proposes some possible avenues for legal change that are likely to make a state compliant with its duty to fulfil. It takes into account multiple decisions of the Treaty Bodies, pointing at investment and trade policies as the main avenues to influence the conduct of multinational companies abroad,[80] and proposes some changes in the investment and trade policies of European states.

[77] See Mazzeschi (n 2) 242–49; Sepúlveda Carmona (n 2) 115–248; Benvenisti (n 2) 313–26.

[78] John Ruggie Gerard, 'Report of the Special Representative of the Secretary-General on the Issue of Human Rights and Transnational Corporations and Other Business Enterprises' (2011) 29 *Netherlands Quarterly of Human Rights* 224, 229.

[79] See Sudre (n 2); Bartole, De Sena and Zagrebelsky (n 48) 303–11; Dijk and Arai (n 48) 725–50; Xenos (n 2) 57–172.

[80] See CESCR, 'Concluding Observations on the Second Periodic Report of China, Including Hong Kong, China, and Macao, China' (2014) CO 2, para 12; CRC, 'General Comment No 16 (2013) on State Obligations Regarding the Impact of the Business Sector on Children's Rights' (2013) GC 16, para 46; CESCR, 'Consideration of Reports Submitted by States Parties under Articles 16 and 17 of the Covenant Concluding Observations of the Committee on Economic, Social and Cultural Rights Switzerland' (2010) CO 2–3, para 24; HR Council, 'Report of the Working Group on the Universal Periodic Review, Switzerland' (2012) 22/11, para 123.85; CRC, 'Consideration of Reports Submitted by States Parties under Article 44 of the Convention Concluding Observations: Republic of Korea' (2012) CO 3–4, paras 26–27; CESCR, 'Concluding Observations on the Fifth Periodic Report of Norway' (2013) CO 5, para 6; CESCR, 'Consideration of Reports Submitted by States Parties under Articles 16 and 17 of the Covenant Concluding Observations of the Committee on Economic, Social and Cultural Rights Germany' (2011) CO 5, para 10.

A. Bilateral Investment Treaties and Free Trade Agreements

BITs are international treaties between states that, generally, set out the minimum protection available to foreign investors. The purpose of BITs is to attract investors by guaranteeing them equal and fair treatment under foreign law.[81] A recent tendency is for countries to sign comprehensive FTAs that also include an investment chapter which serves essentially the same function as a BIT. An investment chapter of an FTA would guarantee the rights of foreign investors within the trade agreement.[82]

Investment law may affect the enjoyment of human rights in host states, because foreign investors may use it to avoid respecting human rights. This mainly becomes possible as a result of a wide interpretation of expropriation and fair and equitable treatment clauses typically included in BITs or investors' protection chapters of FTAs.[83] The original purpose of such clauses was to prevent states from depriving a foreign investor of ownership of its assets without fair compensation. However, some of these clauses are drafted so broadly that arbitration tribunals interpret them as a basis to prevent host states from applying any domestic regulations that could result in a loss of profit to a foreign investor. For these reasons, many scholars have criticised BITs.[84] The Treaty Bodies are equally increasingly concerned as to the negative externalities of investment law on human rights.[85] The debate regarding the legitimacy of BITs is outside

[81] See M Sornarajah, *The International Law on Foreign Investment*, 3rd edn (Cambridge University Press, 2010) 172–235; Rudolf Dolzer and Christoph Schreuer, *Principles of International Investment Law*, 2nd edn (Oxford University Press, 2012) 130–215.

[82] See Joshua Waleson, 'Corporate Social Responsibility in EU Comprehensive Free Trade Agreements: Towards Sustainable Trade and Investment' (2015) 42 *Legal Issues of Economic Integration* 143.

[83] See Burt Neuborne, 'A Plague on Both Their Houses: A Modest Proposal for Ending the Ecuadorean Rainforest Wars' (2013) 1 *Stanford Journal of Complex Litigation* 509; Chiara Giorgetti, 'Mass Tort Claims in International Investment Proceedings: What Are the Lessons from the Ecuador–Chevron Dispute?' (2013) 34 *University of Pennsylvania Journal of International Law* 787.

[84] See Sornarajah (n 81) 144–235; Fons Coomans and Rolf Künnemann (eds), *Cases and Concepts on Extraterritorial Obligations in the Area of Economic, Social and Cultural Rights* (Intersentia, 2012) 5–102; De Schutter, 'Le Contrôle Du Respect Des Droits de l'homme Par Les Sociétés Transnationales: Le Rôle de l'Etat d'origine' (n 33); De Schutter, 'Extraterritorial Jurisdiction as a Tool for Improving Human Rights Accountability for Transnational Corporations' (n 33); Joseph E Stiglitz, 'Multinational Corporations: Balancing Rights and Responsibilities' (2007) 101 *Proceedings of the ASIL Annual Meeting* 3; James Harrison, 'Human Rights Arguments in Amicus Curiae Submissions: Promoting Social Justice?', in *Human rights in international investment law and arbitration* (Oxford University Press 2009) 63–117; Patrick Dumberry and Gabrielle Dumas-Aubin, 'How to Impose Human Rights Obligations on Corporations under Investment Treaties?' (2011) 4 *Yearbook on International Investment Law and Policy* 569; Ryan Suda, 'The Effect of Bilateral Investment Treaties on Human Rights Enforcement and Realization', *Transnational Corporations and Human Rights* (Hart Publishing 2006).

[85] See CESCR, 'Concluding Observations on the Second Periodic Report of China, Including Hong Kong, China, and Macao, China' (n 80) para 12; CRC, 'General Comment No. 16 (2013)

the scope of this book. However, it is useful to note two main lines of critique advanced against BITs on the basis of which one could propose possible changes of the investment arbitration regime in order to comply with the duty to fulfil.

The basis for the first line of critique is that, through investment arbitration, BITs provide investors with international causes of action against the host state, but neither the host state, nor private persons, are granted an equal international cause of action against investors in connection with their activities in the host state.[86] This skewed balance of powers resulted from a long-lasting historical process that a number of scholars have analysed in terms of the emancipation of the investors' rights under BITs.[87] Traditionally, states were the only parties entitled to bring an action under BITs, with the general justification being that it is for the states to protect the interests of their investors. However, under this regime, investors felt that their rights were not adequately protected, because such protection depended on whether their home states were willing to file complaints against host states. To address this issue, BITs have increasingly included arbitration clauses entitling investors to file complaints directly against a host state for violations of the investment treaty. As a result of this change, '[c]laimants are permitted for convenience to enforce [through investment arbitration] what are in origin the rights of Party States'.[88] Some scholars have labelled this process the emancipation of an investor which is granted the rights to exercise their own diplomatic protection.[89] Other scholars disagree with the

on State Obligations Regarding the Impact of the Business Sector on Children's Rights' (n 80) para 46; CESCR, 'Consideration of Reports Submitted by States Parties under Articles 16 and 17 of the Covenant Concluding Observations of the Committee on Economic, Social and Cultural Rights Switzerland' (n 80) para 24; HR Council (n 80) para 123.85; CRC, 'Consideration of Reports Submitted by States Parties under Article 44 of the Convention Concluding Observations: Republic of Korea' (n 80) paras 26–27; CESCR, 'Concluding Observations on the Fifth Periodic Report of Norway' (n 80) para 6; CESCR, 'Consideration of Reports Submitted by States Parties under Articles 16 and 17 of the Covenant Concluding Observations of the Committee on Economic, Social and Cultural Rights Germany' (n 80) para 10.

86 See Sornarajah (n 81) 172–235; De Schutter, 'Le Contrôle Du Respect Des Droits de l'homme Par Les Sociétés Transnationales: Le Rôle de l'Etat d'origine' (n 33); Robin Broad, 'Corporate Bias in the World Bank Group's International Centre for Settlement of Investment Disputes: A Case Study of a Global Mining Corporation Suing El Salvador' (2015) 36 *University of Pennsylvania Journal of International Law* 851; Dolzer and Schreuer (n 81) 130–215; Giorgetti (n 83); Harrison (n 84) 82–117; Dumberry and Dumas-Aubin (n 84).

87 See Francesco Francioni, 'Access to Justice, Denial of Justice and International Investment Law' (2009) 20 *European Journal of International Law* 729; Mathias Forteau, 'La Contribution Au Développement Du Droit International Général de La Jurisprudence Arbitrale Relative Aux Investissements Etrangers' (2009) IV *Anuário Basileiro de Direito Internacional* 11; Annemarieke Vermeer-Künzli, 'As If: The Legal Fiction in Diplomatic Protection' (2007) 18 *The European Journal of International Law* 37; Matthew S Duchesne, 'The Continuous-Nationality-of-Claims Principle: Its Historical Development and Current Relevance to Investor-State Investment Disputes' (2004) 36 *The George Washington International Law Review* 783.

88 *Loewen v United States* [2003] ICSID ARB(AF)/98/3 [233].

89 See Francioni (n 87); Forteau (n 87); Vermeer-Künzli (n 87); Duchesne (n 87).

view that an investor is acting on behalf of the state and have argued that, under BITs, investors have their own procedural right to file complaints against states:

> This view of investor–State investment arbitration as a *reinforcement* of the traditional system of diplomatic protection seems erroneous. It is strange because it switches the role of the individual and the State in a kind of 'protection diplomatique inversée':[90] Not the State sues on behalf of the individual but the individual on behalf of the State.[91]

Whatever analytical approach is adopted, either the one recognising that investors have their own procedural rights or the one assuming that investors derive such rights from their home states, the net practical result of the change to the scope of their application is that BITs often grant investors causes of action against host states, which they can exercise independently of their home states. This results in investors becoming, as some scholars proposed, '[P]artial Subject[s] in Public International Law'.[92]

Importantly, an investor typically does not need to exhaust any domestic remedy in the host state before initiating an arbitration under a BIT alleging its breach and, accordingly, can de facto avoid litigation in domestic courts. Furthermore, arbitration clauses in BITs are usually skewed in favour of investors. They envisage either state-to-state arbitration or investor-to-state arbitration as a means of dispute resolution. However, although the clauses setting out state-to-state arbitration are usually reciprocal, the clauses setting out investor-to-state arbitration are not. Investors can file a complaint against states, but neither states nor stakeholders can commence proceedings against the investor in connection with its activities in the host state. Given this approach, stakeholders in a host state negatively affected by activities of foreign investors have no international cause of action against investors or states under BITs. Such stakeholders can neither commence an arbitration against an investor or a state, nor become a party to the arbitration proceedings initiated by an investor.[93] They may only attempt to influence the arbitral tribunal by filing an *amicus curiae* brief during a pending arbitration proceeding.[94] Although it is true that investors may be subject to various obligations towards the local community in

[90] Forteau (n 87) 38.

[91] Anne Peters, *Beyond Human Rights: The Legal Status of the Individual in International Law* (Cambridge University Press, 2016) 306.

[92] Rudolf Braun Tillmann, 'Globalization-Driven Innovation: The Investor as a Partial Subject in Public International Law – An Inquiry Into the Nature and Limits of Investor Rights' (2013) 4 *Jean Monnet Working Paper Series*.

[93] See Sornarajah (n 81) 172–235; De Schutter, 'Le Contrôle Du Respect Des Droits de l'homme Par Les Sociétés Transnationales: Le Rôle de l'Etat d'origine' (n 33); Broad (n 86); Dolzer and Schreuer (n 81) 130–215; Giorgetti (n 83).

[94] See Eugenia Levine, 'Amicus Curiae in International Investment Arbitration: The Implications of an Increase in Third-Party Participation' (2011) 29 *Berkeley Journal of International Law* 200; Harrison (n 84).

host states under national laws theoretically enforceable in domestic courts, as a practical matter, as demonstrated in Chapter 2, host countries are often unable or unwilling to enforce their domestic legislations against foreign investors. Even in those circumstances when the individuals whose human rights are abused by a foreign investor find justice in national courts, such decisions can be challenged by foreign investors under BITs and denied enforcement on that basis. As a result, the victims of human rights abuses are left with neither domestic, nor international remedies against foreign investors. This is not just a hypothetical scenario. In the case brought by local communities in Ecuador against Chevron alleging mass environmental degradation, the Supreme Court of Ecuador held Chevron responsible for damaging the Ecuadorian population.[95] However, to prevent the enforcement of this judgment, Chevron commenced arbitration proceedings against Ecuador under the Treaty Concerning the Encouragement and Reciprocal Protection of Investment.[96] The arbitration panel urged Ecuador to refrain from enforcing the Supreme Court's judgment.[97] As a result, the Ecuadorian victims of human rights abuses were effectively left with no means of redress against Chevron: on the one hand, an arbitration award effectively voided the Supreme Court's ruling; and, on the other hand, the arbitral tribunal had no jurisdiction to hear human rights claims against Chevron.[98]

The second line of critique typically points out that BITs include a list of investors' rights but set out no duties with which an investor should comply. BITs entitle investors to both substantive and procedural rights to file a complaint against a host state under an international treaty. Conversely, investors' obligations continue to be regulated solely under the domestic laws of host states. This situation raises a number of concerns among civil society, the international community and academia.[99]

A possible avenue to comply with the duty to fulfil would be for states to renegotiate BITs and FTAs in order to rebalance the relationship between investors, stakeholders and host states. First, states should ensure that investors are not the only ones entitled to an international cause of action against host states, while stakeholders affected by their activities are not entitled to file complaints

[95] *Maria Aguinda Salazar y otros v Chevron Corporation* [2012] Corte Nacional de Justicia (CNJ) Judicio No 174.

[96] Treaty Between the United States of America and the Republic of Ecuador Concerning the Encouragement and Reciprocal Protection of Investments 1993 (Treaty Doc No 103-15).

[97] *Chevron Corporation & Texaco Petroleum Company v The Republic of Ecuador* [2018] PCA 2009–23.

[98] See Neuborne (n 83); Giorgetti (n 83).

[99] See Sornarajah (n 81) 144–71; Coomans and Künnemann (n 84) 5–102; De Schutter, 'Le Contrôle Du Respect Des Droits de l'homme Par Les Sociétés Transnationales: Le Rôle de l'Etat d'origine' (n 33); De Schutter, 'Extraterritorial Jurisdiction as a Tool for Improving Human Rights Accountability for Transnational Corporations' (n 33); Stiglitz (n 84); Pierre-Marie Dupuy, Francesco Francioni and Ernst-Ulrich Petersmann (eds), *Human Rights in International Investment Law and Arbitration* (Oxford University Press 2009) 82–117; Suda (n 84).

in investment arbitration tribunals. Second, states should ensure that BITs and FTAs grant investors not only rights but also obligations to respect human rights when they conduct their industrial activities in host states.

To address these concerns, most recent BITs and FTAs are increasingly recognising the fundamental role of public policies within investment law. Several BITs and FTAs signed recently by the European Union include a chapter on sustainable development, which promotes CSR. For example, the EU–South Korean FTA establishes a stakeholders' platform open to civil society to discuss the negative externalities of foreign investment.[100] Although all of these new generation treaties set out the commitment of state parties to promote CSR and human rights, which is a major step forward, unfortunately none of these treaties ever mention that investors should also have obligations.[101] Essentially, these BITs establish primary conduct norms for states, but not for investors that do not have any obligations towards the stakeholders affected by their activities.

Exceptions to this general approach are two African regional trade agreements, the Common Market for Eastern and Southern Africa (COMESA)[102] and the Economic Community of West Africa (ECOWAS),[103] as well as the Ghana Model BIT,[104] which include human rights obligations for investors. According to these treaties, investors shall respect human rights both before and after starting commercial activities in host states. Furthermore, these treaties specifically detail the obligations of the investors towards local stakeholders.[105] Other similar examples are recent Brazilian BITs and the Indian BIT Model, which also include obligations for investors. Whereas the Brazilian BITs refer to the voluntary responsibility of investors,[106] the Indian BIT model is more explicit and specifically mentions human rights law as part of binding domestic Indian law that the investor must respect.[107] Also, the Brazilian BITs admit only

[100] Free Trade Agreement between the European Union and its Member States, of the one part, and the Republic of Korea, of the other part [2011] OJ L127, art 13.

[101] See Waleson (n 82).

[102] Investment Agreement for the COMESA Common Investment Area, 2007, art 13.

[103] Supplementary Act Adopting Community Rules on Investment and the Modalities for the Implementation with ECOWAS, A/SA.3/12/08 2008, art 14.

[104] Government of the Republic of Ghana, 'BIT Model', 2008, art 12.

[105] See Waleson (n 82).

[106] This book refers to the Malawi–Brazil BIT, art. 9, given that the treaty is available in English. However in 2015 Brazil signed similar BITs with a number of countries including Angola, Chile, Colombia, Mexico and Mozambique. Investment Cooperation and Facilitation Agreement between the Federative Republic of Brazil and the Republic of Malawi 2015.

[107] Government of the Republic of India, 'Model Text for the Indian Bilateral Investment Treaty', www.mygov.in/sites/default/files/master_image/Model%20Text%20for%20the%20Indian%20Bilateral%20Investment%20Treaty.pdf, arts 8–12; Azernoosh Bazrafkan, 'The (R)Evolution of Indian Model Bilateral Investment Treaty: Escaping Liability without Mitigating Risks' (2016) 7 *Jindal Global Law Review* 245; Grant Hanessian and Kabir Duggal, 'The Final 2015 Indian Model BIT: Is this the Change the World Wishes to See?' (2017) 32 *ICSID Review – Foreign Investment Law Journal* 216.

state-to-state arbitration and deny the investor any cause of action.[108] Instead, the Indian BIT model provides investors with causes of action against the host state subject to the exhaustion of domestic remedies.[109] Remarkably the Indian BIT model also refers to an obligation of the home state to ensure effective remedies against its investors when they act extraterritorially.[110]

Although it is impossible to assess with certainty whether or not these BITs are in compliance with the ECHR in the abstract, it is clear that, if adopted by European states, they would represent a significant step towards improving the human rights of foreign stakeholders affected by corporate activities. In this sense, adopting such BITs could be, on a case-by-case basis, a sufficient measure for states to meet their duty to fulfil.

B. Ethical Investment Policies

Besides BITs and FTAs, there are other trade and investment policies that could influence companies' behaviour towards stakeholders adversely affected by the overseas activities of multinational enterprises.

The term 'investment' includes not only direct participation in a company but also any form of credit, insurance or development aid that states provide for enterprises. States should consider the negative externalities that their investment and trade policies have on human rights.[111] There are various ways for a state to regulate and monitor such negative externalities. For instance, Daniel Augenstein proposes:

> [t]wo main … [m]easures [for the EU] to protect human rights and the environment against corporate abuse outside its territory: trade restrictions that prevent corporations from exporting or importing goods harmful to human rights and the environment (a); and conditions imposed upon preferential trade under free trade agreements and preference regimes that aim at ensuring human rights and environmental protection in third countries in which European corporations operate (b).[112]

Furthermore, he also suggests that '[t]he EU Member States could ensure that investments in European corporations through public pension funds and/or State-owned banks do not contribute to corporate abuses of human rights and the environment outside the European Union'.[113]

[108] Investment Cooperation and Facilitation Agreement between the Federative Republic of Brazil and the Republic of Malawi, art 13.

[109] Government of the Republic of India (n 107) art. 14.

[110] ibid art 13.

[111] Ruggie, 'Report of the Special Representative of the Secretary-General on the Issue of Human Rights and Transnational Corporations and Other Business Enterprises' (n 78) 232.

[112] Augenstein (n 5) para 108.

[113] ibid 160.

This section provides some examples of investment and trade policies that, by taking into account human rights, are likely to comply with the duty to fulfil under the ECHR.

One example could be adjusting the investment policies of public sovereign wealth funds so that they take into consideration the human rights record of the multinational companies in which they invest. Such funds have recently accumulated enormous wealth. For example, the Norwegian Government Pension Fund, a sovereign wealth fund that invests the surplus Norwegian oil proceeds, is one of the largest public investors in the world.[114] Typically, sovereign investment funds pursue a long-term investment strategy and dispose of enormous financial resources either coming from public contributions (eg pension contributions) or excessive revenues from trade in commodities (eg oil revenues). Historically, the investment strategy of such funds has been profit-driven. However, recently some sovereign funds have voiced their commitment to build-in other factors as part of their investment strategy.[115]

The Norwegian Government Pension Fund, for instance, adopted some ethical guidelines which a Council of Ethics applies to investments. According to such ethical guidelines:

> Section 3. Criteria for conduct-based observation and exclusion of companies
>
> Companies may be put under observation or be excluded if there is an unacceptable risk that the company contributes to or is responsible for:
>
> a) serious or systematic human rights violations, such as murder, torture, deprivation of liberty, forced labour and the worst forms of child labour
> b) serious violations of the rights of individuals in situations of war or conflict
> c) severe environmental damage
> d) acts or omissions that on an aggregate company level lead to unacceptable greenhouse gas emissions
> e) gross corruption
> f) other particularly serious violations of fundamental ethical norms.[116]

Although non-binding, the Norwegian Government Pension Fund is likely to follow the advice of its Council on Ethics and essentially exclude companies

[114] See David Reid, 'Norway Taps its Oil Fund for the First Time', *CNBC* (7 March 2016) www.cnbc.com/2016/03/07/norway-taps-its-oil-fund-for-the-first-time.html, accessed 30 December 2016.

[115] See Gro Nystuen, 'Disinvestment on the Basis of Corporate Contribution to Human Rights Violations: The Case of the Norwegian Government Pension Fund', in *Human Rights, Corporate Complicity and Disinvestment* (Cambridge University Press, 2011); Bruno Demeyere, 'Sovereign Wealth Funds and (Un)Ethical Investment: Using "Due Diligence" to Avoid Contributing to Human Rights Violations Committed by Companies in the Investment Portfolio', in *Human Rights, Corporate Complicity and Disinvestment* (Cambridge University Press, 2011).

[116] Council of Ethics for the Norwegian Government Pension Fund Global, 'Guidelines for the Observation and Exclusion from the Government Pension Fund Global', s3, https://www.regjeringen.no/globalassets/upload/fin/statens-pensjonsfond/formelt-grunnlag/guidelines-for-observation-and-exclusion-from-the-gpfg---17.2.2017.pdf, accessed 17 March 2019.

abusing human rights from its investment targets. This is a powerful disinvestment policy that states could use to, on the one hand, encourage those businesses that respect human rights with the possibility of receiving funding, and, on the other, sanction those enterprises that abuse human rights by simply not investing in their projects.[117]

Another interesting example is PKA, a Danish pension fund, the assets of which exceed €35 billion. In 2016, it announced that it would revise its investment policies to divest from those companies which generate more than 25 per cent of their revenues from coal and that do not have an appropriate plan to reduce such emissions. This change in investment policy was justified by increased economic risks related to investing in environmentally unsafe industries, but it would equally serve the purpose of environmental protection.[118]

Furthermore, a number of international financial institutions conduct human rights impact assessments prior to providing credits for a project. The World Bank, the European Bank for Reconstruction and Development and the European Investment Bank have already adopted such an approach.[119] These development banks are quasi-public institutions, providing financing to both public entities (eg states, regional governments, public institutions) and private corporate borrowers. The purpose of such financing is always aimed at promoting the development of the relevant state, rather than a pure profit-driven commercial activity. Recently, international development banks have started to include detailed CSR standards as a part of the covenants which a borrower seeking financing shall comply with.

States should draw inspiration from these initiatives and apply similar principles to the investments which sovereign wealth funds and national financial institutions make in companies abusing human rights. If sovereign wealth funds and financial institutions divest from companies responsible for human rights abuses, this would be a step towards compliance with the ECHR duty to fulfil.

However, it should be noted that the disinvestment policies described above often do not go far enough. For example, in the case of the Norwegian Government Pension Fund, the Council of Ethics focuses only on future projects and not on the human rights record of companies seeking investments. As a

[117] See Demeyere Bruno (n 115); Council of Ethics for the Norwegian Government Pension Fund Global, 'FAQ |' <http://etikkradet.no/en/faqs/> accessed 30 December 2016; Nystuen (n 115).

[118] 'Danish Pension Scheme Threatens to Blacklist Coal Companies', *Financial Times*, www.ft.com/content/861d652e-2971-11e6-8ba3-cdd781d02d89, accessed 30 December 2016; Damian Carrington and Caelainn Barr, 'Coal Crash: How Pension Funds Face Huge Risk from Climate Change', *The Guardian* (15 June 2015) www.theguardian.com/environment/2015/jun/15/coal-crash-how-pension-funds-face-huge-risk-from-climate-change, accessed 30 December 2016.

[119] World Bank, '2015 GRI Index', http://documents.worldbank.org/curated/en/523821467987823156/pdf/100004-WP-PUBLIC-Box393216B-World-Bank-GRI-Index-2015.pdf, accessed 17 March 2019; European Investment Bank, 'Environmental and Social Standards' www.eib.org/attachments/strategies/environmental_and_social_practices_handbook_en.pdf, accessed 17 March 2019; EBRD, 'Environmental and Social Sustainability Overview', www.ebrd.com/who-we-are/our-values/environmental-and-social-sustainability.html, accessed 17 March 2019.

result, as long as a company is not currently abusing human rights or is not expected to commit such abuses in the future, the Council of Ethics will allow the investment. This was the case of an investment in Total that the Council of Ethics allowed, despite admitting that in the past the company may have abused human rights.[120] Furthermore, as it pertains to international financial institutions, their assessments are also made on a project-to-project basis. Therefore, the interested bank will not consider the overall CSR that the company seeking financing has, but it would instead assess the impact of each particular project. As a result, such an impact assessment may have limited effects, because it does not take into consideration the broader picture of the human rights abuses committed by the companies it finances.[121]

Despite these limitations, the fact that there is an increasing demand for the banking and pension fund sector to conduct environmental and CSR impact assessments is an encouraging change that should not be limited to international institutions, but should also be extended to state-owned financial institutions, insurance and credit companies.[122] Given that the financing provided by such institutions is often more advantageous than the terms of financing available in a general market, such a change of financing policies can be another effective mechanism by which states can comply with their duty to fulfil.[123]

Another possibility would be for the EU to adopt trade policies that encourage host states and companies to respect human rights. These policies could also be adopted at the national level. However, given that the Treaty of Lisbon established the EU's exclusive competence over trade, as part of the EU common commercial policy, this paragraph takes into account trade policies at the EU level only.[124] Since the European Union is the biggest world market, it is, therefore, in an advantageous position to negotiate trade agreements with developing countries.[125] Mindful of its position, the EU included the so-called *human rights clauses*, providing favourable trading conditions to countries endorsing and promoting fundamental rights, in a number of trade agreements. With time,

[120] See Demeyere Bruno (n 115); The Advisory Council on Ethics for the Government Petroleum Fund, 'Recommendation of 14 November 2005' <https://www.regjeringen.no/en/dokumenter/Recommendation-of-14-November-2005/id419590/> accessed 30 December 2016; Nystuen (n 115).

[121] See World Bank (n 119); European Investment Bank (n 119); EBRD (n 119).

[122] For an analysis of the CSR impact assessment that private banks conduct on a voluntary basis, see Bert Scholtens, 'Corporate Social Responsibility in the International Banking Industry' (2009) 86 *Journal of Business Ethics* 159.

[123] See Demeyere Bruno (n 115); Andreas Follesdal, 'Human Rights Investment Filters: A Defence', in *Human rights, corporate complicity and disinvestment* (Cambridge University Press 2011).

[124] Consolidated versions of the Treaty on European Union and the Treaty on the Functioning of the European Union [2012] OJ C326; Marc Bungenberg, 'Going Global? The EU Common Commercial Policy After Lisbon' in 1 *European Yearbook of International Economic Law* (Springer, 2010).

[125] See Joanne Scott, 'Extraterritoriality and Territorial Extension in EU Law' (2014) 62 *American Journal of Comparative Law* 87; Cedric Ryngaert, 'Whither Territoriality? The European Union's Use of Territoriality to Set Norms with Universal Effects', in *What's Wrong with International Law? Liber Amicorum AHA Soons* (Brill/Nijhoff, 2015).

human rights clauses became increasingly more demanding, and they passed from requesting third countries to promote human rights in general terms to requiring them to comply with a list of specific human rights treaties. In addition, the EU has increasingly included *human rights clauses* as an essential element of trade agreements, meaning that, if not respected, the parties could avoid executing such agreements.[126] For instance, the EU adopted an innovative Generalised Scheme of Preferences Regulation (GSP+) that allows developing countries to apply for preferential trade treatment assuming they ratify a list of core human rights treaties. As part of the GSP+, the states benefiting from the preferential treatment have to periodically report their human rights situation to the European Commission and allow a monitoring process of their human rights record.[127]

The recent approach taken by the EU encourages developing countries to meet higher human rights standards by way of offering them economic preferences. However, these trading policies have not yet been tailored to ensure that multinational companies respect human rights and environmental standards in developing countries.[128] Accordingly, as a next step in the same direction, the EU could adopt a favourable trading policy under the condition that host states ensure multinational companies respect human rights in their domestic system. If the EU combines such a trading policy with an effective liability framework for European parent corporations in Europe, the final result could be that both the European parent companies and their foreign subsidiaries would be accountable for human rights abuses.

Therefore, influencing the conduct of multinational enterprises through trade and investment policies are specific examples of how states could move towards compliance with their duty to fulfil. The above examples are by no means comprehensive and any state could think about additional policies that could influence the conduct of multinational enterprises.

III. CONCLUSION

The victims of human rights abuses, such as Bodhi, Elsa and Naoki in the hypothetical case studies, may be able to successfully bring an action against European states for the extraterritorial human rights abuses committed by European corporate groups. European states violate both the duty to protect and the duty to fulfil when they fail to regulate the overseas activities of European corporate

[126] See Olufemi Amao, *Corporate Social Responsibility, Human Rights and the Law: Multinational Corporations in Developing Countries* (Routledge 2011) 227–48; Nicolas Hachez, '"Essential Elements" Clauses in EU Trade Agreements: Making Trade Work in a Way that Helps Human Rights?' [2015] 53 *Cuadernos Europeos de Deusto* 81.

[127] Regulation No 978/2012 of the European Parliament and the Council applying a Scheme of Generalised Tariff Preferences and repealing Council Regulation (EC) No 732/2008 [2012] OJ L303.

[128] Amao (n 126) 227–48.

groups. I have verified this general conclusion by reference to the United Kingdom and demonstrated that, in three hypothetical cases, the UK violates its duty to protect, because it does not provide the victims Bodhi, Elsa and Naoki with an effective remedy against the holding company H, which controls overseas subsidiaries S responsible for human rights abuses. The United Kingdom also violates the duty to fulfil, because its domestic and foreign policies do not take into consideration the stakeholders affected by British-based corporate groups.

The duty to protect requires states to entitle stakeholders to effective remedies against multinational enterprises abusing human rights. This includes setting up a liability framework that would enable human rights victims to seek damages against multinational companies. As a general principle, the law applicable to torts committed by multinational companies would be the law of the place of injury, irrespective of whether or not it complies with human rights. Furthermore, the existing combination of UK company and tort laws makes it highly unlikely for victims of human rights abuses to file a complaint against a UK holding company in connection with the wrongful actions of its foreign subsidiaries. Therefore, in the hypothetical cases, the United Kingdom violates its duty to protect, because its laws permit UK holding companies to avoid accountability for the extraterritorial human rights abuses committed by their subsidiaries. Against this background, this book proposed two alternative avenues for legal change. First, states could acknowledge that multinational companies are subject to international law, and are therefore bound by human rights. This solution entails recognising the horizontal application of human rights between private actors and establishing an enforcement mechanism when such rights are abused. Second, states could guarantee effective remedies for foreign stakeholders in domestic courts against multinational enterprises abusing human rights extraterritorially.

Whereas the duty to protect demands that states guarantee effective legal remedies for human rights victims that are able or willing to bring an action in court to protect their rights, the duty to fulfil requires states to prevent human rights abuses by private actors, and therefore to do their utmost to ensure that multinational enterprises respect human rights. The exact scope of the policies that would meet such a *best-effort* obligation will depend on each individual case. Different states may be able to adopt various policies to stop multinational companies from abusing human rights, and such policies may all comply with the ECHR duty to fulfil. This chapter purported to offer an outline of the policies that the United Kingdom could implement to meet its ECHR obligations. These include a broad range of measures starting from the UK rebalancing its existing BITs and FTAs to changing domestic, EU or international trading policies.

Bibliography

Addo MK and Grief N, 'Does Article 3 of the European Convention on Human Rights Enshrine Absolute Rights?' (1998) 9 *European Journal of International Law* 510.

Ago R, 'Second Report on State Responsibility, by Roberto Ago, Special Rapporteur – The Origin International Responsibility' (1970) II *Yearbook of the International Law Commission.*

Alston P (ed), *Non-State Actors and Human Rights* (Oxford University Press, 2005).

Alston P and Crawford J (eds), *The Future of UN Human Rights Treaty Monitoring* (Cambridge University Press, 2000).

Amao O, *Corporate Social Responsibility, Human Rights and the Law: Multinational Corporations in Developing Countries* (Routledge, 2011).

Andenæs MT and Wooldridge F, *European Comparative Company Law* (Cambridge University Press, 2009).

Andrianova S, Demetriades P and Xu C, 'Political Economy Origins of Financial Markets in Europe and Asia' (2011) 39 *World Development* 686.

Anghie A, *Imperialism, Sovereignty, and the Making of International Law* (Cambridge University Press, 2005).

Arendt H, *The Origins of Totalitarianism* (Mariner Books, 1973).

Antkowiak T, 'Rights, Resources, and Rhetoric: Indigenous Peoples and the Inter-American Court' (2013) 35 *University of Pennsylvania Journal of International Law* 113.

——, 'A Dark Side of Virtue: The Inter-American Court and Reparations for Indigenous Peoples' (2014) 25 *Duke Journal of Comparative and International Law* 1.

Arif Yascha, 'Overriding Mandatory Provisions and Administrative Authorisations According to the Rome II Regulation' [2011] *European Legal Forum* 113.

Augenstein D, 'Study on the Legal Framework on Human Rights and the Environment Applicable to European Enterprises Operating Outside the European Union' (University of Edinburgh, 2010) http://ec.europa.eu/DocsRoom/documents/11865/attachments/1/translations/en/renditions/native.

Bach I, 'Art 4 Rome II', in Hubner P (ed) *Rome II Regulation: Pocket Commentary* (Sellier, 2011).

——, 'Art 17 Rome II', in Hubner P (ed) *Rome II Regulation: Pocket Commentary* (Sellier, 2011).

Backer LC, 'Rights and Accountability in Development (Raid) V Das Air and Global Witness V Afrimex: Small Steps Toward an Autonomous Transnational Legal System for the Regulation of Multinational Corporations' (2009) 10 *Melbourne Journal of International Law* 258.

Bakan J, *The Corporation: The Pathological Pursuit of Profit and Power* (Free Press, 2004).

Barker SE (ed), *Social Contract: Essays by Locke, Hume, and Rousseau* (Oxford University Press, 1962).

Bartlett CA et al, *Transnational Management: Text and Cases*, 4 edn (McGraw-Hill/Irwin, 2003).

Bartole S, De Sena P and Zagrebelsky V (eds), *Commentario breve alla convenzione europea per la salvaguardia dei diritti dell'uomo e delle libertà fondamentali* (CEDAM, 2012).

Baughen S, 'Holding Corporations to Account: Crafting ATS Suits in the UK' (2013) 2 *British Journal of American Legal Studies* 533.

Bazrafkan, A, 'The (R)Evolution of Indian Model Bilateral Investment Treaty: Escaping Liability without Mitigating Risks' (2016) 7 *Jindal Global Law Review* 245.

Beckers A, *Enforcing Corporate Social Responsibility Codes: On Global Self-Regulation and National Private Law* (Hart Publishing, 2015).

Beisinghoff N, *Corporations and Human Rights: An Analysis of ATCA Litigation against Corporations* (Peter Lang, 2009).

Benvenisti E, 'Margin of Appreciation, Consensus and Universal Standards' (1999) 31 *International Law and Politics* 843.

——, 'Sovereigns as Trustees of Humanity: On the Accountability of States to Foreign Stakeholders' (2013) 107 *The American Journal of International Law* 295.

Besson S, 'The Extraterritoriality of the European Convention on Human Rights: Why Human Rights Depend on Jurisdiction and What Jurisdiction Amounts To' (2012) 25 *Leiden Journal of International Law* 857.

Betlem G, 'Transnational Litigation against Multinational Corporations before Dutch Civil Courts', In Kamminga MT and Zia-Zarifi S (ed), *Liability of Multinational Corporations under International Law* (Kluwer, 2000).

Bhavnani S, 'ECtHR Extends Application of Convention beyond Council of Europe Borders' [2011] 16 *EHRAC Bulletin* 1.

Bhuta N, 'The Frontiers of Extraterritoriality – Human Rights as Global Law', in Bhuta N (ed), *The Frontiers of Human Rights* (Oxford University Press, 2016).

Bianchi A, 'Immunity versus Human Rights: The Pinochet Case' (1999) 10 *European Journal of International Law* 237.

——, *International Law Theories: An Inquiry into Different Ways of Thinking* (Oxford University Press, 2017).

Bilchitz D, 'The Ruggie Framework: An Adequate Rubric for Corporate Human Rights Obligations?' (2010) 7 *SUR* 199.

——, 'The Necessity for a Business and Human Rights Treaty' (2016) 1 *BHRJ* 203.

Birmingham P, *Hannah Arendt and Human Rights: The Predicament of Common Responsibility* (Indiana University Press, 2006).

Blumberg PI, 'Limited Liability and Corporate Groups' (1985) 11 *Journal of Corporate Law* 573.

Bonomi A, 'The Role of Internationally Mandatory Rules in an European Private International Law System' [2007] *Revista de drept international privat si drept comparat* 159.

Borges C, 'Bilateral Agreements Brazilian Style – Conectas Human Rights' (2015) www.conectas.org/en/actions/business-and-human-rights/news/40181-bilateral-agreements-brazilian-style, accessed 29 December 2016.

Boyd DR, *The Environmental Rights Revolution: A Global Study of Constitutions, Human Rights, and the Environment* (University of British Columbia Press, 2012).

Boyle A, 'Human Rights or Environmental Rights – A Reassessment' (2007) 18 *Fordham Environmental Law Review* 471.

Brabant S and Savourey E, 'A Closer Look at the Penalties Faced by Companies' [2017] *Revue internationale de la compliance et de l'éthique des affaires* 5.

Brackman A, *The Other Nuremberg: The Untold Story of the Tokyo War Crimes Trials* (Harper Collins Publishers, 1988).

Braithwaite J, 'Neoliberalism or Regulatory Capitalism', in *Regulatory Capitalism: How It Works, Ideas for Making It Work Better* (Edward Elgar, 2008).

Braun TR, 'Globalization-Driven Innovation: The Investor as a Partial Subject in Public International Law – An Inquiry Into the Nature and Limits of Investor Rights' (2013) 4 *Jean Monnet Working Paper Series*.

Brems E, 'Procedural Protection', in Brems E and Gerards JH *Shaping Rights in the ECHR: The Role of the European Court of Human Rights in Determining the Scope of Human Rights* (Cambridge University Press, 2014).

Briggs A, *The Conflict of Laws*, 2 edn (Oxford University Press, 2008).

Bright C, 'L'accès à la justice civile en cas de violations des droits de l'homme par des entreprises multinationales' (2013) http://cadmus.eui.eu/handle/1814/29602, accessed 15 April 2016.

Broad R, 'Corporate Bias in the World Bank Group's International Centre for Settlement of Investment Disputes: A Case Study of a Global Mining Corporation Suing El Salvador' (2015) 36 *University of Pennsylvania Journal of International Law* 851.

Buckley C and others, *Towards Convergence in International Human Rights Law: Approaches of Regional and International Systems* (Brill/Nijhoff, 2017).

Bullimore T, 'Sins of the Father, Sins of the Son' (2012) 28 *Professional Negligence* 212.

Bungenberg M, 'Going Global? The EU Common Commercial Policy After Lisbon' in Herrmann C and Terhechte JP (eds), 1 *European Yearbook of International Economic Law* (Springer, 2010).

Burke J, 'Foreclosure of the Doctrine of Forum Non Conveniens under the Brussels I Regulation: Advantages and Disadvantage' (2008) 3 *European Legal Forum* 121.

Byers M, 'English Courts and Serious Human Rights Violations Abroad: A Preliminary Assessment', in Kamminga M and Zia-Zarifi S (ed), *Liability of Multinational Corporations under International Law* (Kluwer, 2000).

Cancado Trindade AA, 'Une ère d'avancées jurisprudentielles et institutionnelles : souvenirs de la Cour interaméricaine des droits de l'homme', in *Le particularisme interaméricain des droits de l'homme: En l'honneur du 40e anniversaire de la Convention américaine des droits de l'homme* (Editions A Pedone, 2009).

Cancado Trindade AA, 'The Merits of Coordination of International Courts on Human Rights' (2004) 2 *Journal of International Criminal Justice* 309.

Caplan LM, 'State Immunity, Human Rights, and Jus Cogens: A Critique of the Normative Hierarchy Theory' (2003) 97 *The American Journal of International Law* 741.

Carbonnier G, 'Corporate Responsibility and Humanitarian Action. What Relations between the Business and Humanitarian Worlds?' (2001) 83 *International Review of the Red Cross* 947.

Carozza PG, 'Human Dignity and Judicial Interpretation of Human Rights: A Reply' (2008) 19 *European Journal of International Law* 931.

——, 'Subsidiarity as a Structural Principle of International Human Rights Law' (2003) 97 *The American Journal of International Law* 38.

Cernic JL, *Human Rights Law and Business Corporate Responsibility for Fundamental Human Rights* (Europa Law Publishing, 2010).

Chng K, 'A Theoretical Perspective of the Public Policy Doctrine in the Conflict of Laws' (2018) 14 *Journal of Private International Law* 130.

Clapham A, *Human Rights Obligations of Non-State Actors* (Oxford University Press, 2006).

——, 'Extending International Criminal Law beyond the Individual to Corporations and Armed Opposition Groups' (2008) 6 *Journal of International Criminal Justice* 899.

Cohen-Jonathan G, 'Quelques considérations sur l'autorité des arrêts de la Cour européenne des droits de l'homme', in *Liber amicorum Marc-André Eissen* (Emile Bruylant, 1995).

Contreras-Garduño D and Rombouts S, 'Collective Reparations for Indigenous Communities before the Inter-American Court of Human Rights' (2011) 27 *Utrecht Journal of International and European Law* 4.

Coomans F, 'The Ogoni Case before the African Commission on Human and Peoples' Rights' (2003) 52 *ICLQ* 749.

Coomans F and Kamminga MT, 'Comparative Introductory Comments on the Extraterritorial Application of Human Rights Treaties', in Coomans F and Kamminga MT (ed), *Extraterritorial Application of Human Rights Treaties* (Intersentia, 2004).

Coomans F and Künnemann R (eds), *Cases and Concepts on Extraterritorial Obligations in the Area of Economic, Social and Cultural Rights* (Intersentia, 2012).

Cossart S, Chaplier J and Lomenie TBD, 'The French Law on Duty of Care: A Historic Step Towards Making Globalization Work for All' (2017) 2 *Business and Human Rights Journal* 317.

Cox J and Eisenberg M, *Business Organizations Cases and Materials*, 12th edn (Foundation Press, 2019).

Cuniberti G, 'Forum Non Conveniens and the Brussels Convention' (2005) 54 *ICLQ* 973.

Cuzacq N, 'Le devoir de vigilance des sociétés mères et des donneurs d'ordre', in Martin-Chenut K and De Quenaudon R (ed), *La RSE saisi par le droit: perspectives interne et internationale* (Pedone, 2015).

Damrosch L et al, *International Law, Cases and Materials*, 5th edn (West, 2009).

Dandurand Y, 'Strategies and Practical Measures to Strengthen the Capacity of Prosecution Services in Dealing with Transnational Organized Crime, Terrorism and Corruption' (2007) 47 *Crime, Law and Social Change* 225.

Danielsen D, 'Corporate Power and Global Order' in Anne Orford (ed), *International Law and its Others* (Cambridge University Press, 2006).

Davarnejad L, 'In the Shadow of Soft Law: The Handling of Corporate Social Responsibility Disputes under the OECD Guidelines for Multinational Enterprises' (2011) *Journal of Dispute Resolution* 351.

De Schutter O, 'The Accountability of Multinationals for Human Rights Violations in European Law' in Alston P (ed), *Non-State Actors and Human Rights* (Oxford University Press, 2005).

——, 'Reasonable Accommodations and Positive Obligations in the European Convention on Human Rights', in Lawson A and Gooding C (ed), *Disability Rights in Europe: From Theory to Practice* (Hart Publishing, 2005).

——, 'Extraterritorial Jurisdiction as a Tool for Improving Human Rights Accountability for Transnational Corporations' (Business and Human Rights Resource Centre, 2006).

——, 'Le contrôle du respect des droits de l'homme par les sociétés transnationales : le rôle de l'état d'origine', in Muir Watt H, Morea M, Rodière P (ed), *Justice et mondialisation en droit du travail: du rôle du juge aux conflits alternatifs* (Dalloz, 2010).

De Schutter O et al, 'Commentary to the Maastricht Principles on Extraterritorial Obligations of States in the Area of Economic, Social and Cultural Rights' (2012) 34 *Human Rights Quarterly* 1084.

De Vylder H, 'The Territorial Scope of the American Convention on Human Rights' (2014) 1 *Inter-American and European Human Rights Journal* 204.

Deakin SF, Johnston AC and Markesinis BS, *Markesinis and Deakin's Tort Law*, 7th edn (OUP, 2012).

Delpech X, 'Bientôt un devoir de vigilance à la charge des sociétés mères et des donneurs d'ordre' [2015] *Dalloz Actualité*.

Demeyere B, 'Sovereign Wealth Funds and (Un)Ethical Investment: Using "Due Diligence" to Avoid Contributing to Human Rights Violations Committed by Companies in the Investment Portfolio', in Nystuen G, Follesdal A, and Mestad O (ed), *Human Rights, Corporate Complicity and Disinvestment* (Cambridge University Press, 2011).

Deva S, 'Human Rights Standards and Multinational Corporations: Dilemma between "Home" and "Rome"' (2003) 7 *Mediterranean Journal of Human Rights* 69.

——, 'Human Rights Violations by Multinational Corporations and International Law: Where from Here?' (2003) 19 *Connecticut Journal of International Law* 1.

Dickinson A, *The Rome II Regulation: The Law Applicable to Non-Contractual Obligations* (Oxford University Press, 2008).

Dolzer R and Schreuer C, *Principles of International Investment Law*, 2nd edn (Oxford University Press, 2012).

Dörr O and Schmalenbach K (eds), *Vienna Convention on the Law of Treaties: A Commentary* (Springer, 2012).

Drouin, Renée-Claude, 'Le développement du contentieux à l'encontre des entreprises transnationales: Quel rôle pour le devoir de vigilance?' [2016] *Droit social* 246.

Duchesne MS, 'The Continuous-Nationality-of-Claims Principle: Its Historical Development and Current Relevance to Investor-State Investment Disputes' (2004) 36 *The George Washington International Law Review* 783.

Dufourq Pauline, 'Devoir de vigilance des multinationales : quelles évolutions ?' [2017] *Dalloz Actualité*.

Dumberry P and Dumas-Aubin G, 'How to Impose Human Rights Obligations on Corporations under Investment Treaties?' (2011) 4 *Yearbook on International Investment Law and Policy* 569.

Dunoff JL and Trachtman JP, *Ruling the World? Constitutionalism, International Law, and Global Governance* (Cambridge University Press, 2009).

Dupuy P-M, Francioni F and Petersmann E-U (eds), *Human Rights in International Investment Law and Arbitration* (Oxford University Press, 2009).

Duranti M, 'Curbing Labour's Totalitarian Temptation: European Human Rights Law and British Postwar Politics' (2012) 3 *Humanity: An International Journal of Human Rights, Humanitarianism, and Development* 361.

——, *The Conservative Human Rights Revolution: European Identity, Transnational Politics, and the Origins of the European Convention* (Oxford University Press, 2017).

Dworkin RM, 'The Model of Rules' (1967) 35 *University of Chicago Law Review* 14.

Dzehtsiarou K, 'European Consensus and the Evolutive Interpretation of the European Convention on Human Rights' (2011) 12 *German Law Journal* 1730.

Easterbrook F and Fischel DR, *The Economic Structure of Corporate Law* (Harvard University Press, 1996).

Eeckhout P, 'Opinion 2/13 on EU Accession to the ECHR and Judicial Dialogue: Autonomy or Autarky' (2015) 38 *Fordham International Law Journal* 955.

Eide A, 'Report on the Right to Adequate Food as a Human Right' (1987) E/CN.4/Sub.2/1987/23.

Eijsbouts AJAJ, *Corporate Responsibility, beyond Voluntarism: Regulatory Options to Reinforce the Licence to Operate* (Maastricht University Press, 2011).

Eisenberg MA, 'The Divergence of Standards of Conduct and Standards of Review in Corporate Law,' (1993) 62 *Fordham Law Review* 437.

Elver Hilal, 'Report of the Special Rapporteur on the Right to Food' (2015) UN Doc A/HRC/28/65.

Enneking L, 'Crossing the Atlantic – The Political and Legal Feasibility of European Foreign Direct Liability Cases' (2008) 40 *George Washington International Law Review* 903.

——, *Foreign Direct Liability and Beyond: Exploring the Role of Tort Law in Promoting International Corporate Social Responsibility and Accountability* (Eleven International Publishing, 2012).

——, 'The Future of Foreign Direct Liability? Exploring the International Relevance of the Dutch Shell Nigeria Case' (2014) 10 *Utrecht Law Review* 44.

Erdal U and Bakirci H, *Article 3 of the European Convention on Human Rights: A Practitioner's Handbook* (OMCT, 2006).

Esposito G and Carobolante A, 'Imporre o invitare? Le politiche di corporate social responsibility alla ricerca di un'identità europea' (2013) 8 *Ianus-Diritto e Finanza* 5.

Fabri HR, 'Human Rights and State Sovereignty: Have the Boundaries Been Significantly Redrawn?' in Philip Alston and Euan Macdonald (eds), *Human Rights, Intervention, and the Use of Force* (Oxford University Press, 2008).

Fasciglione M, 'Corporate Human Rights Responsibility, States' Duty to Protect and UN GPS' National Action Plans: Some Thoughts after the UK NAP Update' (2016) 1 *European Papers* 621.

Feldman D, 'The Human Rights Act 1998 and Constitutional Principles' (1999) 19 *Legal Studies* 165.

Fitzmaurice GG, 'The Foundations of the Authority of International Law and the Problem of Enforcement' (1956) 19 *MLR* 1.

Follesdal Andreas, 'Human Rights Investment Filters: A Defence', in Nystuen G, Follesdal A and Mestad O (ed) *Human Rights, Corporate Complicity and Disinvestment* (Cambridge University Press, 2011).

Forteau M, 'La contribution au développement du droit international général de la jurisprudence arbitrale relative aux investissements étrangers' (2009) IV *Anuário basileiro de direito internacional* 11.

Francioni F, 'Alternative Perspectives on International Responsibility for Human Rights Violations by Multinational Corporations', in Benedek W, De Feyter K and Marrella F (ed) *Economic Globalisation and Human Rights* (Cambridge University Press, 2007).

——, 'Access to Justice, Denial of Justice and International Investment Law' (2009) 20 *European Journal of International Law* 729.

Franzina P, 'Il regolamento n 864/2007/CE sulla legge applicabile alle obbligazioni extracontrattuali ("Roma II")', (2008) 31(5) *Le nuove leggi civili commentate* 971.

Fredman S, *Human Rights Transformed* (Oxford University Press, 2008).

French D and Stephens T, 'ILA Study Group on Due Diligence in International Law First Report' (International Law Association, 2014).

Friedman M, 'The Social Responsibility of Business Is to Increase its Profits' in Walther Ch Zimmerli, Markus Holzinger and Klaus Richter (eds), *Corporate Ethics and Corporate Governance* (Springer, 2007).

Friedmann W, *The Changing Structure of International Law* (Stevens & Sons, 1964).

Frishman O, 'Transnational Judicial Dialogue as an Organisational Field' (2013) 19 *European Law Journal* 739.

Fuchs A, 'Art 7 Rome II', in Hubner P (ed), *Rome II Regulation: Pocket Commentary* (Sellier, 2011).

——, 'Art 16 Rome II', in Hubner P (ed), *Rome II Regulation: Pocket Commentary* (Sellier, 2011).

——, 'Art 26 Rome II', in Hubner P (ed), *Rome II Regulation: Pocket Commentary* (Sellier, 2011).

Fura-Sandstrom E, 'Business and Human Rights: Who Cares?', in Caflisch L and Wildhaber L (ed), *Liber Amicorum Luzius Wildhaber: Human Rights – Strasbourg Views Droits de l'homme – Regards de Strasbourg* (Engel, Norbert, 2007).

Gamble A and Kelly G, 'The Politics of the Company', in Parkinson J, Kelly G and Gamble A (ed), *The Political Economy of the Company* (Hart Publishing, 2001).

Gatto A, *Multinational Enterprises and Human Rights: Obligations under EU Law and International Law* (Edward Elgar, 2011).

Giannini T and Farbstein S, 'Corporate Accountability in Conflict Zones: How Kiobel Undermines the Nuremberg Legacy and Modern Human Rights' (2010) 52 *Harvard International Law Journal* 119.

Giannini T, Farbstein S and Arend AC, 'The Alien Tort Statute and Corporate Liability' (2011) 160 *University of Pennsylvania Law Review*.

Gigante A, 'La politica delle istituzioni comunitarie in materia di responsabilitá sociale d'impresa: voluntary o mandatory approach?' (2008) IV *Diritto pubblico comparato ed europeo* 1991.

Gillman M and Eade T, 'The Development of the Corporation in England, with Emphasis on Limited Liability' (1995) 22 *International Journal of Social Economics* 20.

Giorgetti C, 'Mass Tort Claims in International Investment Proceedings: What Are the Lessons from the Ecuador – Chevron Dispute?' (2013) 34 *University of Pennsylvania Journal of International Law* 787.

Goldhaber MD, 'Corporate Human Rights Litigation in Non-US Courts: A Comparative Scorecard' (2013) 3 *University of California Irvine Law Review* 127.

Goldschmidt, J, 'International Human Rights Implementation: Strengthen Existing Mechanisms, Establish a World Court for Human Rights, or Both?', in Ryngaert C, Molenaar E and Nouwen S (ed) *What's Wrong with International Law? Liber Amicorum AHA Soons* (Brill/Nijhoff, 2015).

Golove DM and Hulsebosch DJ, 'A Civilized Nation: The Early American Constitution, the Law of Nations, and the Pursuit of International Recognition' (2010) 85 *New York University Law Review* 932.

Gomez VM, 'The Sosa Standard: What Does It Mean for Future ATS Litigation?' (2006) 33 *Pepperdine Law Review* 469.

Gondek M, *The Reach of Human Rights in a Globalising World: Extraterritorial Application of Human Rights Treaties* (Intersentia, 2009).

Gonza A, 'Integrating Business and Human Rights in the Inter-American Human Rights System' (2016) 1 *Business and Human Rights Journal* 357.

Gonzalez G, 'La responsabilité des états parties à la Convention européenne des droits de l'homme du fait de leurs actions extraterritoriales' [2007] *Annuaire de droit europeen* 755.

Goodwin-Gill Guy S, 'Obligations of Conduct and Result', in Alston P and Tomaševski K (ed), *The Right to Food*, Stichting Studie- en Informatiecentrum Mensenrechten (Martinus Nijhoff, 1984).

Grušić U, 'Responsibility in Groups of Companies and the Future of International Human Rights and Environmental Litigation' (2015) 74 *CLJ* 30.

Hachez I and Dumont H, 'Les obligations positives déduites du droit international des droits de l'homme, dans quelles limites ?', in Cartuyvels Y, Dumont H, Ost F, van de Kerchove M, Van Drooghenbroeck S (ed), *Les droits de l'homme, bouclier ou épée du droit pénal ?* (Publications des Facultés Universitaires Saint-Louis, 2007).

Hachez N, 'Essential Elements' Clauses in EU Trade Agreements: Making Trade Work in a Way That Helps Human Rights?' [2015] 53 *Cuadernos Europeos de Deusto* 81.

Hajiyev K, 'The Evolution of Positive Obligations under the European Convention on Human Rights – By the European Court of Human Rights', in Spielmann D, Tsirli M, Voyatzis P and Rozakis C (ed), *La Convention européenne des droits de l'homme, un instrument vivant: mélanges en l'honneur de Christos L Rozakis = The European convention on human rights, a living instrument: essays in honour of Christos L Rozakis* (Bruylant, 2011).

Hanessian G and Duggal K, 'The Final 2015 Indian Model BIT: Is this the Change the World Wishes to See?' (2017) 32 *ICSID Review – Foreign Investment Law Journal* 216.

Hansmann H and Kraakman R, 'Toward Unlimited Shareholder Liability for Corporate Torts' (1991) 100 *The Yale Law Journal* 1879.

Harris D et al, *Law of the European Convention on Human Rights*, 3rd edn (Oxford University Press, 2014).

Harrison, J, 'Human Rights Arguments in Amicus Curiae Submissions: Promoting Social Justice?', in Dupuy P, Petersmann E, Francioni F (ed) *Human Rights in International Investment Law and Arbitration* (Oxford University Press, 2009).

Hart HLA, *The Concept of Law*, 3rd edn (Oxford University Press, 2012).

Hartley TC, 'Choice-of-court Agreements, Lis Pendens, Human Rights and the Realities of International Business: Reflections on the Gasser Case', in Ancel B, Audit B, Ballarino T, Romano GP (ed), *Le droit international privé: esprit et méthodes: Mélanges en l'honneur de Paul Lagarde* (Dalloz-Sirey, 2005).

Hausmann R and Queirolo I, 'Introduzione', in Simons T, Hausmann R (ed), Regolamento Bruxelles I: Commento al Regolamento CE 44/2001 e alla Convenzione di Lugano (IPR-Verlag, 2012).

Henkin L, 'The Universality of the Concept of Human Rights' (1989) 506 *The Annals of the American Academy of Political and Social Science* 10.

——, *The Age of Rights* (Columbia University Press, 1990).

——, *Human Rights*, 2nd edn (Foundation Press, 2009).

Higgins R, *Problems and Process: International Law and How We Use It* (Clarendon Press, 1995).

Hoffmann F, 'Human Rights, the Self and the Other: Reflections on a Pragmatic Theory of Human Rights' in Anne Orford (ed), *International Law and its Others* (Cambridge University Press, 2009).

Hovell D 29 'The Authority of Universal Jurisdiction' (2018) *European Journal of International Law* 427.

International Law Commission, 'Draft Articles Responsibility of States for Internationally Wrongful Acts' (2001) II *Yearbook of the International Law Commission.*

Jägers N, *Corporate Human Rights Obligations: In Search of Accountability* (Intersentia, 2002).

——, 'UN Guiding Principles on Business and Human Rights: Making Headway towards Real Corporate Accountability' (2011) 29 *Netherlands Quarterly of Human Rights* 159.

Jägers N and Heijden M-J van der, 'Corporate Human Rights Violations: The Feasibility of Civil Recourse in the Netherlands' (2008) 33 *Brooklyn Journal of International Law* 833.

Jägers N, Jesse K and Verschuuren J, 'The Future of Corporate Liability for Extraterritorial Human Rights Abuses: The Dutch Case against Shell' (2013) 107 *The American Journal of International Law* 36.

Jay S, 'The Status of the Law of Nations in Early American Law' (1989) 42 *Vanderbilt Law Review* 819.

Joseph S, 'Taming the Leviathans: Multinational Enterprises and Human Rights' (1999) 46 *Netherlands International Law Review* 171.

——, *Corporations and Transnational Human Rights Litigation* (Hart Publishing, 2004).

Joseph S and Castan M, *The International Covenant on Civil and Political Rights: Cases, Materials, and Commentary*, 3rd edn (Oxford University Press, 2013).

Kairys D (ed), *The Politics of Law: A Progressive Critique*, 3rd edn (Basic Books, 1998).

Kaczmarek SC and Newman AL, 'The Long Arm of the Law: Extraterritoriality and the National Implementation of Foreign Bribery Legislation' (2011) 65 *International Organization* 745.

Kalintiri A, 'Revisiting Parental Liability in EU Competition Law' (2018) 43 *European Law Review* 145.
Kamminga MT, 'Holding Multinational Corporations Accountable for Human Rights Abuses: A Challenge for the EC', Alston P (ed), *The EU and Human Rights* (Oxford University Press, 1999).
——, 'Due Diligence Mania', in Westendrop I (ed), *The Women's Convention Turned 30: Achievements, Setbacks, and Prospects* (Intersentia, 2012).
——, 'Transnational Human Rights Litigation against Multinational Corporations Post-Kiobel', in Ryngaert C, Molenaar E and Nouwen S (ed), *What's Wrong with International Law? Liber Amicorum AHA Soons* (Brill/Nijhoff, 2015).
Kamminga MT and Zia-Zarifi S (eds), *Liability of Multinational Corporations under International Law* (Kluwer, 2000).
Karavias M, *Corporate Obligations under International Law* (Oxford University Press, 2013).
Keller H and Ulfstein G (eds), *UN Human Rights Treaty Bodies: Law and Legitimacy* (Cambridge University Press, 2012).
Kennedy D, 'The Critique of Rights in Critical Legal Studies' in Brown W and Halley J (ed), *Left Legalism/Left Critique* (Duke University Press, 2002).
Kelsen H, 'Collective and Individual Responsibility in International Law with Particular Regard to the Punishment of War Criminals' [1943] *California Law Review* 530.
Kershaw D, *Company Law in Context: Text and Materials*, 2nd edn (Oxford University Press, 2012).
Kingsbury B, Krisch N and Stewart RB, 'The Emergence of Global Administrative Law' (2005) 68 *Law and Contemporary Problems* 15.
Kissinger HA, 'The Pitfalls of Universal Jurisdiction' (2001) 80 *Foreign Affairs New York* 86.
Knight CJS, 'Owusu and Turner: The Shark in the Water?' (2007) 66 *CLJ* 288.
Knox JH, 'Horizontal Human Rights Law' [2008] 102 *The American Journal of International Law* 1.
Koh HH, 'Transnational Legal Process' (1996) 75 *Nebraska Law Review* 181.
——, 'Why Transnational Law Matters' (2005) 24 *Penn State International Law Review* 745.
Koskenniemi M, 'Solidarity Measures: State Responsibility as a New International Order?' (2002) 72 *British Yearbook of International Law* 337.
Kozma J, Nowak M and Scheinin M, *A World Court of Human Rights: Consolidated Statute and Commentary* (Neuer Wissenschaftlicher Verlag, 2010).
Kraakman R et al, *The Anatomy of Corporate Law: A Comparative and Functional Approach*, 2nd ed (Oxford University Press 2009).
Kreuzer K, 'La comunitarizzazione del diritto internazionale privato in materia di obbligazioni extracontrattuali ("Roma II")', in Picone P (ed), *Diritto internazionale privato e diritto comunitario* (CEDAM, 2004).
Kuipers J-J and Migliorini S, 'Qu'est-ce que sont les lois de police? Une querelle franco-allemande apres la communautarisation de la Convention de Rome' (2011) 19 *European Review of Private Law* 187.
Lagarde P (ed), 'Les Lois de Police Devant la Cour de Justice des Communautés Européennes', in Schulze R and Seif U (ed), *Richterrecht und Rechtsfortbildung in der Europäischen Rechtsgemeinschaft* (Mohr Siebeck, 2003).
Lang A and Wiener A, *Handbook on Global Constitutionalism* (Edward Elgar, 2017).
Lawson R, 'Life after Bankovic: On the Extraterritorial Application of the European Convention on Human Rights', in Coomans F and Kamminga MT (ed), *Extraterritorial Application of Human Rights Treaties* (Intersentia, 2004).
Lazowski A and Wessel RA, 'When Caveats Turn into Locks: Opinion 2/13 on Accession of the European Union to the ECHR' (2015) 16 *German Law Journal* 179.
Leebron DW, 'Limited Liability, Tort Victims, and Creditors' (1991) 91 *Columbia Law Review* 1565.
Letnar Cernic J, 'Corporate Responsibility for Human Rights: A Critical Analysis of the OECD Guidelines for Multinational Enterprises' (2008) 3 *Hanse Law Review* 1981.
——, *Human Rights Law and Business: Corporate Responsibility for Fundamental Human Rights* (Europa Law Publishing, 2010).

Letsas G 'The ECHR as a Living Instrument: Its Meaning and Legitimacy, in Føllesdal A, Peters B and Ulfstein G (ed), *Constituting Europe the European Court of Human Rights in a National European and Global Context* (Cambridge University Press, 2013).

Levan A, 'Legal Nature of Jus Congens in Contemporary International Law', in *Collected Courses of the Hague Academy of International Law* (Martinus Nijhoff, 1981).

Lever J, 'Why Procedure Is More Important than Substantive Law' (1999) 48 *ICLQ* 285.

Levine E, 'Amicus Curiae in International Investment Arbitration: The Implications of an Increase in Third-Party Participation' (2011) 29 *Berkeley Journal of International Law* 200.

Lock T, 'End of an Epic? The Draft Agreement on the EU's Accession to the ECHR' (2012) 31 *Yearbook of European Law* 162.

Londoño-Lázaro MC, Thoene U and Pereira-Villa C, 'The Inter-American Court of Human Rights and Multinational Enterprises: Towards Business and Human Rights in the Americas?' (2017) 16 *Law and Practice of International Courts and Tribunals* 437.

Loucaides L, 'Environmental Protection through the Jurisprudence of the European Convention on Human Rights' (2005) 75 *British Yearbook of International Law* 249.

——, *The European Convention on Human Rights: Collected Essays* (Martinus Nijhoff, 2007).

Macleod S, 'Reconciling Regulatory Approaches to Corporate Social Responsibility: The European Union, OECD and United Nations Compared' (2007) 13 *European Public Law* 671.

Madelaine C, *La technique des obligations positives en droit de la Convention européenne des droits de l'homme* (Dalloz, 2014).

Mares R, 'The Effects of CSR for the Protection of Human Rights' (2003) 7 *Mediterranean Journal of Human Rights* 113.

Mares R (ed), *The UN Guiding Principles on Business and Human Rights: Foundations and Implementation* (Martinus Nijhoff, 2011).

Marks S, 'Naming Global Administrative Law' (2005) 37 *New York University Journal of International Law and Politics* 995.

——, 'Human Rights in Disastrous Times' in Koskenniemi M and Crawford J (ed), *The Cambridge Companion to International Law* (Cambridge University Press, 2012).

Marrella F, 'Regolazione internazionale e responsabilità globale delle imprese transnazionali' (2009) 3 *Diritti umani e diritto internazionale* 229.

Mattei A, 'Prospects for Industrial Relations: Overriding Mandatory Provisions in the Transnational Labour Market' in Blanpain R, Bromwich W, Rymkevich O, Senatori I (ed), *Labour Markets, Industrial Relations and Human Resources Management: From Recession to Recovery* (Kluwer, 2012).

Mazzeschi PR, *Democracy Promotion Institutions, International Law and Politics* (Martinus Nijhoff, 2009).

Mazzuoli VDO and Ribeiro D, 'Indigenous Rights before the Inter-American Court of Human Rights: A Call for a Pro Individual Interpretation' (2015) 2 *The Transnational Human Rights Review* 32.

McCorquodale R, 'Waving not Drowning: Kiobel Outside the United States' (2013) 107 *The American Journal of International Law* 846.

McCorquodale R and Simons P, 'Responsibility Beyond Borders: State Responsibility for Extraterritorial Violations by Corporations of International Human Rights Law' (2007) 70 *MLR* 598.

McGregor L, 'State Immunity and Human Rights: Is there a Future after Germany v Italy?' [2013] 11 *Journal of International Criminal Justice* 125.

Meeran R, 'Tort Litigation against Multinational Corporations for Violation of Human Rights: An Overview of the Position Outside the United States' (2011) 3 *City University of Hong Kong Law Review* 1.

Melo M, 'Recent Advanced in the Justiciability of Indigenous Rights in the Inter-American System of Human Rights' (2006) 4 *SUR* 31.

Milanovic M, *Extraterritorial Application of Human Rights Treaties: Law, Principles, and Policy* (Oxford University Press, 2011).

——, 'Al-Skeini and Al-Jedda in Strasbourg' (2012) 23 *European Journal of International Law* 121.

Miltner B, 'Revisiting Extraterritoriality after Al-Skeini: The ECHR and its Lessons' (2012) 33 *Michigan Journal of International Law* 693.

Mokhtar A, 'Nullum Crimen, Nulla Poena Sine Lege: Aspects and Prospects' (2005) 26 *Statute Law Review* 41.

Möldner M, 'Responsibility of International Organizations – Introducing the ILC's DARIO' (2012) 16 *Max Planck Yearbook of United Nations Law Online* 281.

Mougeolle P, 'Sur la conformité constitutionnelle de la proposition de loi relative au devoir de vigilance des sociétés mères et des entreprises donneuses d'ordre. Responsabilité juridique des entreprises' [2017] *La revue des droits de l'homme.*

Mowbray A, 'A Study of the Principle of Fair Balance in the Jurisprudence of the European Court of Human Rights' (2010) 10 *Human Rights Law Review* 289.

——, *The Development of Positive Obligations under the European Convention on Human Rights by the European Court of Human Rights* (Hart Publishing, 2004).

Moyn S, *The Last Utopia: Human Rights in History* (Belknap Press of Harvard University Press, 2012).

Muchlinski P, *Multinational Enterprises and the Law*, 2nd edn (Oxford University Press, 2007).

——, 'Implementing the New UN Corporate Human Rights Framework: Implications for Corporate Law, Governance, and Regulation' (2012) 22 *Business Ethics Quarterly* 145.

Neuborne B, 'A Plague on Both Their Houses: A Modest Proposal for Ending the Ecuadorean Rainforest Wars' (2013) 1 *Stanford Journal of Complex Litigation* 509.

Nollkaemper A, 'Public International Law in Transnational Litigation Against Multinational Corporations: Prospects and Problems in the Courts in the Netherlands', in Kamminga MT and Zia-Zarifi S (ed), *Liability of Multinational Corporations under International Law* (Kluwer, 2000).

Nowak M, *UN Covenant on Civil and Political Rights: CCPR Commentary*, 2nd edn (Engel, 2005).

——, 'The Need for a World Court of Human Rights' (2007) 7 *Human Rights Law Review* 251.

Nystuen G, 'Disinvestment on the Basis of Corporate Contribution to Human Rights Violations: The Case of the Norwegian Government Pension Fund', in Nystuen G, Follesdal A, and Mestad O (ed), *Human Rights, Corporate Complicity and Disinvestment* (Cambridge University Press, 2011).

Nystuen G, Føllesdal A and Mestad O (eds), *Human Rights, Corporate Complicity and Disinvestment* (Cambridge University Press, 2011).

Olivares Alanís EC, 'Indigenous Peoples' Rights and the Extractive Industry: Jurisprudence from the Inter-American System of Human Rights, (2013) 5 *Goettingen Journal of International Law* 187.

Oliver C, 'The Attorney-General of the Government of Israel v Eichmann' (1962) 56 *The American Journal of International Law* 805.

Oliver D and Fedtke J, *Human Rights and the Private Sphere: A Comparative Study* (Routledge, 2007).

Paine T, *Rights of Man* (Dover Publications, 1999).

Palmer E, 'Protecting Socio-Economic Rights through the European Convention on Human Rights: Trends and Developments in the European Court of Human Rights' (2009) 2 *Erasmus Law Review* 397.

Palombo D, 'The Law of Nations in the United States Constitution after the Cases Sosa v Alvarez and Kiobel v Royal Dutch Petroleum CO' (2014) 6 *Cuadernos de derecho transnacional* 397.

——, 'The Duty of Care of the Parent Company: A Comparison between French Law, UK Precedents and the Swiss Proposals' (2019) *BHRJ*.

——, 'Chandler v Cape: An Alternative to Piercing the Corporate Veil Beyond Kiobel v Royal Dutch Shell' (2015) 4 *BJALS*, 453.

Panoussis I, 'L'Obligation générale de protection des droits de l'homme dans la jurisprudence des organes internationaux' (2007) 70 *Revue trimestrielle des droits de l'homme* 427.

Papantoniou A, 'Advisory Opinion on the Environment and Human Rights' (2018) 112 *The American Journal of International Law* 460.

Parkinson JE, *Corporate Power and Responsibility Issues in the Theory of Company Law* (Oxford University Press, 1995).
Pascale G, 'Extraterritorial Applicability of the African Charter on Human and Peoples' Rights' (2014) 8 *Diritti umani e diritto internazionale* 644.
Pasqualucci JM, 'The Evolution of International Indigenous Rights in the Inter-American Human Rights System' (2006) 6 *Human Rights Law Review* 281.
Peers S and others (eds), *The EU Charter of Fundamental Rights: A Commentary* (Beck/Hart Publishing, 2014).
Périn Pierre-Louis, 'Devoir de vigilance et responsabilité illimitée: Qui trop embrasse mal étreint' [2015] *Revue trimestrielle de droit commercial et de droit économique* 215.
Peters A, *Beyond Human Rights: The Legal Status of the Individual in International Law* (Cambridge University Press, 2016).
Petrin M, 'Assumption of Responsibility in Corporate Groups: Chandler v Cape Plc' (2013) 76 *MLR* 603.
Pitkanen M, 'Fair and Balanced Positive Obligations – Do They Exist?' [2012] *European Human Rights Law Review* 538.
Popovic D, *The Emergence of the European Human Rights Law: An Essay on Judicial Creativity* (Eleven International Publishing, 2011).
Puppinck Gregor, 'Status of the Recommendations of the Committee of Ministers in the Legal Field of the Council of Europe – Synthesis', European Centre for Law and Justice www.academia.edu/2083218/Status_of_the_recommendations_of_the_Committee_of_Ministers_in_the_legal_field_of_the_Council_of_Europe_Synthesis, accessed 9 December 2016.
Raam D and Abdurrahman E, 'Background Paper – Rana Plaza: Legal and Regulatory Responses' (Asser Institute, 2018), https://www.asser/nl/doingbusinessright/blog/background-paper-rana-plaza-and-regulatory-responses-by-raam-dutia-and-abdurrahman-erol.
Raisz A, 'Indigenous Communities before the Inter-American Court of Human Rights – New Century, New Era' (2008) 5 *Miskolc Journal of International Law* 35.
Rajagopal B, *International Law from Below: Development, Social Movements, and Third World Resistance* (Cambridge University Press, 2003).
Ratner SR, 'Corporations and Human Rights: A Theory of Legal Responsibility' (2001) 111 *The Yale Law Journal* 443.
Renner M, 'Article 9: Overriding Mandatory Provisions', in Calliess GP (ed), *Rome Regulations: Commentary on the European Rules on the Conflict of Laws* (Kluwer/Aspen, 2011).
Rivers J, 'The Presumption of Proportionality' (2014) 77 *MLR* 409.
Robinson PH, 'The Criminal–Civil Distinction and the Utility of Desert' (1996) 76 *Boston University Law Review* 201.
Rogerson P, *Collier's Conflict of Laws*, 4th edn (Cambridge University Press, 2013).
Rosemann N, 'Business Human Rights Obligations – The Norms of the Responsibility of Transnational Corporations and Other Business Enterprises with Regard to Human Rights' (2005) 23 *Nordic Journal of Human Rights* 47.
Roth K, 'The Case for Universal Jurisdiction' (2001) 80 *Foreign Affairs New York* 150.
Ruggie JG, 'Business and Human Rights: The Evolving International Agenda' (2007) 101 *The American Journal of International Law* 819.
——, 'Protect, Respect, and Remedy: The UN Framework for Business and Human Rights', in Baderin MA and Ssenyonjo M (ed), *International Human Rights Law* (Ashgate, 2010).
——, 'Report of the Special Representative of the Secretary-General on the Issue of Human Rights and Transnational Corporations and Other Business Enterprises' (2011) 29 *Netherlands Quarterly of Human Rights* 224.
——, 'The Construction of the UN "Protect, Respect and Remedy" Framework for Business and Human Rights: The True Confessions of a Principled Pragmatist' (2011) 2 *European Human Rights Law Review* 127.

Ruggie JG and Nelson T, 'Human Rights and the OECD Guidelines for Multinational Enterprises: Normative Innovations and Implementation Challenges' (2015) *Corporate Social Responsibility Initiative Working Paper* 66.

Russell D, 'Supplementing the European Convention on Human Rights: Legislating for Positive Obligations' (2010) 61 *Northern Ireland Legal Quarterly* 281.

Russo D, 'La promozione della responsabilitá sociale d'impresa nell'unione europea' (2011) XVI *Il diritto dell'unione europea* 477.

Ryngaert C, 'Clarifying the Extraterritorial Application of the European Convention on Human Rights' (2012) 28 *Merkourios: Utrecht Journal of International and European Law* 57.

——, 'Whither Territoriality? The European Union's Use of Territoriality to Set Norms with Universal Effects', in Ryngaert C, Molenaar EJ and Nouwen S (ed), *What's Wrong with International Law? Liber Amicorum AHA Soons* (Brill/Nijhoff, 2015).

Sanders A, 'The Impact of the "Ruggie Framework" and the United Nations Guiding Principles on Business and Human Rights on Transnational Human Rights Litigation' (2014) 18 *LSE Law, Society and Economy Working Papers*.

Sanger A, 'Crossing the Corporate Veil: The Duty of Care Owed by a Parent Company to the Employees of its Subsidiary' (2012) 71 *CLJ* 478.

Santner AL, 'Soft Law Mechanism for Corporate Responsibility: How the Updated OECD Guidelines for Multinational Enterprises Promote Business for the Future' (2011) 43 *George Washington International Law Review* 375.

Saranti V, 'International Justice and Protection of Indigenous Peoples – The Case-Law of the Inter-American Court of Human Rights' (2012) 9 *US-China Law Review* 427.

Schabas W, *The European Convention on Human Rights: A Commentary* (Oxford University Press, 2015).

Schrempf-Stirling J and Wettstein F, 'Beyond Guilty Verdicts: Human Rights Litigation and its Impact on Corporations' Human Rights Policies' [2015] *Journal of Business Ethics* 1.

Scholtens B, 'Corporate Social Responsibility in the International Banking Industry' (2009) 86 *Journal of Business Ethics* 159.

Scott J, 'Business and Human Rights at the UN: What Might Happen Next?' (2009) 31 *Human Rights Quarterly* 299.

Scott Joanne, 'Extraterritoriality and Territorial Extension in EU Law' (2014) 62 *The American Journal of Comparative Law* 87.

Sepúlveda Carmona M, *The Nature of the Obligations under the International Covenant on Economic, Social, and Cultural Rights* (Intersentia, 2003).

Sen A, 'Human Rights and the Limits of Law' (2006) 27 *Cardozo Law Review* 2913.

Shany Y, 'Taking Universality Seriously: A Functional Approach to Extraterritoriality in International Human Rights Law' (2013) 7 *The Law & Ethics of Human Rights* 47.

Sharpston M, 'International Sub-Contracting' (1975) 27 *Oxford Economic Papers* 94.

Shue H, *Basic Rights: Subsistence, Affluence, and US Foreign Policy*, 2nd edn (Princeton University Press, 1996).

Skinner G, 'Rethinking Limited Liability of Parent Corporations for Foreign Subsidiaries' Violations of International Human Rights Law' (2015) 72 *Washington and Lee Law Review* 1769.

Slaughter A-M, 'Judicial Globalization' (2000) 40 *Virginia Journal of International Law* 1103.

Soboka TB, 'Patching the "Legal Black Hole": The Extraterritorial Reach of States' Human Rights Duties in the African Human Rights System' (2011) 27 *South African Journal on Human Rights* 249.

Sornarajah M, *The International Law on Foreign Investment*, 3rd edn (Cambridge University Press, 2010).

South African Institute for Advanced Constitutional, Public, Human Rights and International Law, 'The State Duty to Protect, Corporate Obligations and Extra-Territorial Application in the African Regional Human Rights System' (2010).

Stapleston J, 'Duty of Care and Economic Loss: A Wider Agenda' (1991) *Law Quarterly Review* 249.

Steiner H, Alston P and Goodman R (ed), *International Human Rights in Context: Law, Politics, Morals*, 3rd edn (Oxford University Press, 2008).
Steinhardt RG, 'Corporate Responsibility and the International Law of Human Rights: The New Lex Mercatoria', in Alston P (ed), *Non-State Actors and Human Rights* (Oxford University Press, 2005).
Steinitz M and Gowder P, 'Transnational Litigation as a Prisoner's Dilemma' (2016) 94 *North Caroline Law Review* 751.
Stephens B et al, *International Human Rights Litigation in US Courts* (Martinus Nijhoff, 2008).
Stiglitz JE, 'Multinational Corporations: Balancing Rights and Responsibilities' (2007) 101 *Proceedings of the ASIL Annual Meeting* 3.
Suda R, 'The Effect of Bilateral Investment Treaties on Human Rights Enforcement and Realization', in De Schutter O *Transnational Corporations and Human Rights* (Hart Publishing, 2006).
Sudre F, 'Les "obligations positives" dans la jurisprudence européenne des droits de l'homme' (1995) 23 *Revue trimiestrelle des droits de l'homme* 363.
——, 'L'Article 3bis de la Convention européenne des droits de l'homme: Le droit à des conditions de détention conformes au respect de la dignité humaine', in *Libertés, justice, tolérance : Mélanges en hommage au Doyen Gérard Cohen-Jonathan*, vol 2 (Emile Bruylant, 2004).
Sullivan R, 'NGO Influence on the Human Rights Performance of Companies' (2006) 24 *Netherlands Quarterly of Human Rights* 405.
Symeonides SC, 'Rome II and Tort Conflicts: A Missed Opportunity' (2008) 56 *The American Journal of Comparative Law* 173.
Tavernier J, 'Compétence ratione loci: Extraterritorialité et recevabilité', in Dourneau-Josette P and Lambert Abdelgawad E (ed), *Quel filtrage des requêtes par la Cour européenne des droits de l'homme?* (Council of Europe, 2011).
Taylor G, 'Deconstructing the Law: The Politics of Law' (2015) 1 *Yale Law & Policy Review* 158.
Ten Wolde MH, De Maestri ME and Knot J-G, 'Articolo 60', *Regolamento Bruxelles I*: Commento al Regolamento CE 44/2001 e alla Convenzione di Lugano (IPR-Verlag, 2012).
Thomas R, 'The Problem of Horizontal Effect' (2000) 5 *European Human Rights Law Review* 493.
Touzé S, 'L'Approche communautaires de la responsabilité sociale des entreprises' (2009) 19 *Schweizerische Zeitschrift für internationales und europäischees Recht = Revue suisse de droit international et européen* 7.
Tulken F and Van Drooghenbroeck S, 'L'évolution des droits garantis et l'interprétation jurisprudentielle de la CEDH' (Collection Les Conférences Publiques du Pôle européen Jean Monnet, 2002).
Vagts DF, 'The Multinational Enterprise: A New Challenge for Transnational Law' (1970) 83 *Harvard Law Review* 739.
van Dam C, *European Tort Law*, 2nd edn (Oxford University Press, 2013).
Van Den Eeckhout V, 'Corporate Human Rights Violations and Private International Law. The Hinge-Function and Conductivity of PIL in Implementing Human Rights in Civil Proceedings in Europe: a Facilitating Role for PIL or PIL as a Complicating Factor' (2012) *Contemporary Readings in Law and Social Justice* 178.
van der Vyver JD, 'Prosecuting Offenses against the Law of Nations in the United States' (2006) 20 *Emory International Law Review* 473.
van der Wilt H, 'Corporate Criminal Responsibility for International Crimes: Exploring the Possibilities' (2013) 12 *Chinese Journal of International Law* 43.
Van Dijk P, Van Hoof F, Van Rijn A and Zwaak L (ed), *Theory and Practice of the European Convention on Human Rights*, 4th edn (Intersentia, 2006).
Van Hoof GJH, 'Legal Nature of Economic, Social and Cultural Rights: A Rebuttal of Some Traditional Views', in Alston P and Tomaševski K (ed), *The Right to Food* (Martinus Nijhoff 1984).
Vanderkerckhove K, *Piercing the Corporate Veil* (Kluwer/Aspen, 2007).

Vazquez CM, 'Direct vs Indirect Obligations of Corporations under International Law' (2005) 43 *Columbia Journal of Transnational Law* 927.

Velu J and Ergec R, *Convention européenne des droits de l'homme*, 2nd edn (Bruylant, 2014).

Vermeer-Künzli A, 'As If: The Legal Fiction in Diplomatic Protection' (2007) 18 *The European Journal of International Law* 37.

Vernon R, 'Economic Sovereignty at Bay' [1968] *Foreign Affairs* 110.

Viterbo A, 'L'Applicazione extraterritoriale del patto internazionale sui diritti economici sociali e culturali: I principi di Maastricht del 2011' (2012) 6 *Diritti umani e diritto internazionale* 210.

Voiculescu A, 'Human Rights and the Normative Ordering of Global Capitalism', in Voiculescu A and Yanacopulos H (ed), *The Business of Human Rights: An Evolving Agenda for Corporate Responsibility* (Zed Books, 2011).

von Bogdandy A and Venzke I, *In Whose Name? A Public Law Theory of International Adjudication* (Oxford University Press, 2014).

von Hein J, 'Article 4 General Rule', in Calliess GP (ed), *Rome Regulations: Commentary on the European Rules on the Conflict of Laws* (Kluwer/Aspen, 2011).

——, 'Article 7 Environmental Damage', in Calliess GP (ed), *Rome Regulations: Commentary on the European Rules on the Conflict of Laws* (Kluwer/Aspen, 2011).

——, 'Article 16 Overriding Mandatory Provisions', in Calliess GP (ed) *Rome Regulations: Commentary on the European Rules on the Conflict of Laws* (Kluwer/Aspen, 2011).

——, 'Article 17 Rules of Sagety and Conduct', in Calliess GP (ed), *Rome Regulations: Commentary on the European Rules on the Conflict of Laws* (Kluwer/Aspen, 2011).

——, 'Article 26 Public Policy of the Forum', in Calliess GP (ed), *Rome Regulations: Commentary on the European Rules on the Conflict of Laws* (Kluwer/Aspen, 2011).

Waldron J, 'Is Dignity the Foundation of Human Rights?' in Cruft R, Liao SM, Renzo M (ed) *Philosophical Foundations of Human Rights* (Oxford University Press, 2015).

Waleson J, 'Corporate Social Responsibility in EU Comprehensive Free Trade Agreements: Towards Sustainable Trade and Investment' (2015) 42 *Legal Issues of Economic Integration* 143.

Weber RH and Baisch R, 'Liability of Parent Companies for Human Rights Violations of Subsidiaries' [2016] *European Business Law Review* 669.

Weissbrodt D and Kruger M, 'Human Rights Responsibilities of Businesses as Non-State Actors' in Alston P (ed), *Non-State Actors and Human Rights* (Oxford University Press, 2005).

Wells C and Elias J, 'Catching the Conscience of the Kings: Corporate Players on the International Stage' in Alston P (ed), *Non-State Actors and Human Rights* (Oxford University Press, 2005).

Wesche P and Saage-Maaß M, 'Holding Companies Liable for Human Rights Abuses Related to Foreign Subsidiaries and Suppliers before German Civil Courts: Lessons from *Jabir and Others v KiK*' (2016) 16 *Human Rights Law Review* 370.

Wettstein F, 'Normativity, Ethics, and the UN Guiding Principles on Business and Human Rights: A Critical Assessment' (2015) 14 *Journal of Human Rights* 162.

Whish R and Bailey D, *Competition Law*, 7th edn (Oxford University Press, 2012).

Wouters J and Ryngaert C, 'Litigation for Overseas Corporate Human Rights Abuse in the European Union: The Challenge of Jurisdiction' (2008) 40 *George Washington International Law Review* 939

Xenos D, *The Positive Obligations of the State under the European Convention of Human Rights* (Routledge, 2011).

Yascha A, 'Overriding Mandatory Provisions and Administrative Authorisation According to the Rome II Regulation' [2011] *European Legal Forum*.

Zerk JA, *Multinationals and Corporate Social Responsibility: Limitations and Opportunities in International Law* (Cambridge University Press, 2006).

Index